The Journals of George M. Dawson: British Columbia, 1875-1878

One of nineteenth-century Canada's most distinguished scientists, George M. Dawson, began exploring and studying the virtually uncharted territory of British Columbia when he joined the Geological Survey of Canada in 1875. Though he was not the first geologist to visit the new province, he was the first to make systematic investigations over large areas, and his published reports on B.C's geology and natural resources were important aids to the region's economic development. In addition, in daily journals and in letters home to family members, he recorded much of what he experienced on his travels in the province.

The material brought together in these volumes was written by Dawson over the four years from his first field season in 1875 to the 1878 journey to the Queen Charlotte Islands that gave the world so many well-known and priceless photographic artifacts of the Haida culture. His journals from this time provide accurate, detailed and absorbing pictures. The entries roam, as the writer did, through the Chilcotin, Upper Fraser and South Central Interior areas, as well as over the Queen Charlottes, describing glaciation, landscape, wildlife, vegetation, Indian villages and pioneer settlements.

D1707567

Recollections of the Pioneers of British Columbia

The first volume is *The Reminiscences of Doctor John Sebastian Helmcken,* edited by Dorothy Blakey Smith. J.S. Helmcken was British Columbia's pioneer doctor, first Speaker in the legislature, and one of the negotiators of the colony's entry into Confederation.

The second volume is *A Pioneer Gentlewoman in British Columbia,* edited by Margaret A. Ormsby. The author of these recollections, Susan Allison, settled in the Similkameen Valley in the 1860s.

The third volume is *God's Galloping Girl,* edited by W.L. Morton. Monica Storrs's diaries describe her mission work on the Peace River frontier during the Depression.

The fourth volume is *Overland from Canada to British Columbia,* edited by Joanne Leduc. It contains the story of the Overlanders' trek from Ontario under the leadership of Thomas McMicking.

Letters from Windermere, edited by R. Cole Harris and Elizabeth Phillips, is the fifth volume in a series of editions of important documents of the colonial and early provincial history of British Columbia.

The Journals of George M. Dawson, edited by Douglas Cole and Bradley Lockner, were written between 1875 and 1878. They are published in two volumes.

The Journals of George M.Dawson: British Columbia,1875~1878

Volume I, 1875~1876

Edited by Douglas Cole and Bradley Lockner

University of British Columbia Press

Vancouver 1989

ISBN 0-7748-0276-6

Canadian Cataloguing in Publication Data
Dawson, George M., 1849-1901.
 The journals of George M. Dawson
 (Recollections of the pioneers of British Columbia)

 Includes bibliographical references and index.
 Contents: v.   1. 1875-1876—v.   2. 1877-1878
 ISBN 0-7748-0276-6 (v. 1).—ISBN 0-7748-0286-3 (v. 2)
 1. Dawson, George M., 1849-1901 – Diaries.   2. Geologists –
Canada – Diaries.   3. Geology – British Columbia.   4. Indians of
North America – British Columbia.   5. British Columbia –
Description and travel.   I. Cole, Douglas, 1938-   II. Lockner,
Bradley John, 1950-   III. Title.   IV. Series.
FC 3817.2.D39 1989   917.11′043   C88-091648-6 F1087.D39 1989

This book has been published with the help of a grant from the
Social Science Federation of Canada, using funds provided by the
Social Sciences and Humanities Research Council of Canada.

Contents

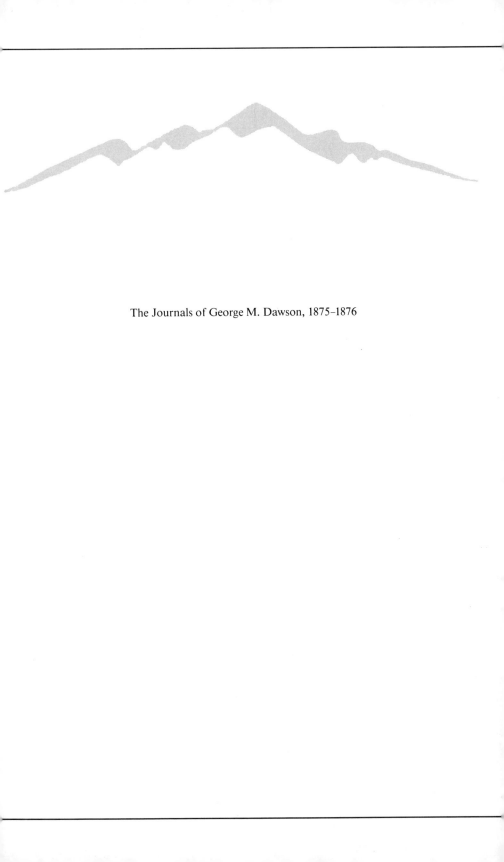

The Journals of George M. Dawson, 1875–1876

Introduction

George Mercer Dawson spent the first six years of his life in Nova Scotia, first in Pictou where he had been born on 1 August 1849, and then in the capital of Halifax. His grandfather, James Dawson, came to Nova Scotia from Banffshire, Scotland, in 1811. He built a thriving mercantile business in Pictou, but suffered severe financial reversals in the 1820's; heavily in debt, he re-established himself in a printing and book-selling firm.[1] His son, John William Dawson, the father of George Mercer, was born in Pictou in 1820 and attended Pictou Academy, a rigorous Presbyterian institution. William (he preferred this to John) developed an interest in geology at an early age and expanded his knowledge by exploring formations in the colony's Northumberland Strait region. He went abroad in 1840 to study at Edinburgh University, directing much of his attention toward geology under the tutelage of the great mineralogist Robert Jameson.[2] There he met and courted Margaret Mercer, the fourth daughter of an established Edinburgh family, before being forced by restricted family finances to return to Nova Scotia in 1841.[3] It was during this time that the eminent British geologist Charles Lyell, on a lecture tour of North

---

1. For more information about James Dawson, see his autobiographical "Recollections of the Life of James Dawson," ed. Marjory Whitelaw, *Dalhousie Review* 53 (1973): 501-19.

2. Charles F. O'Brien, *Sir William Dawson: A Life in Science and Religion* (Philadelphia: American Philosophical Society, 1971), 7-9.

3. Some of the correspondence between John William Dawson in Nova Scotia and Margaret Mercer in Edinburgh has been published in S. B. Frost, "A Transatlantic Wooing," *Dalhousie Review* 58 (1978): 458-70.

America, stopped in Nova Scotia and spent time exploring with Dawson. The two became immediate friends and Lyell greatly assisted in advancing the younger man's geological career. In 1846, Dawson revisited Edinburgh; a year later, in spite of opposition from the elder Mercers, he married Margaret.

After their marriage, William and Margaret Dawson returned to Nova Scotia where he went to work in his father's business, continuing his geological work on his own time, publishing articles in British and American scientific journals. A first son, James, was born in 1848 but died in July of the following year, less than a month before George's birth. Four other children would eventually be born into the Dawson household: Anna Lois, born in 1851; William Bell in 1854; Rankine in 1863; and Eva in 1864.

William Dawson's engagement to deliver a term's extramural lectures at Dalhousie College in 1849 led directly to Joseph Howe's offer that he become the province's first superintendent of education. Dawson was reluctant, worrying both about his qualifications for the position and about how the responsibilities would interfere with his geological papers and his field work into the pre-Carboniferous formations of southern Pictou County. But Howe insisted and Dawson, seeing how aspects of the task might complement his scientific research, capitulated. In his three years as superintendent, Dawson established a solid reputation as an educational administrator.

His geological studies, however, were hardly forgotten. Lyell revisited Nova Scotia in 1853 and the two friends geologized at the great fossil cliffs at South Joggins, discovering in that rich area an entirely new genus and the first reptilian animal recognized in a North American coal bed, as well as the first known Palaeozoic land shell. These discoveries, along with the 1855 publication of his *Acadian Geology*,[4] established Dawson's reputation as a geologist. At Lyell's suggestion, Dawson applied for the chair in natural history at Edinburgh, recently vacated by the death of Edward Forbes in 1854. Dawson lost the post, however, to "the candidate of the Biological party."[5]

"Then it was," Dawson later wrote, "that there occurred one of those coincidences, which impress us with the belief in a kind providence

---

4.   *Acadian Geology: An Account of the Geological Structure and Mineral Resources of Nova Scotia, and Portions of the Neighbouring Provinces of British America* (Edinburgh: Oliver and Boyd; London: Simpkin, Marshall, and Co., 1855).

5.   Rankine Dawson, ed., *Fifty Years of Scientific and Educational Work in Canada: Being Autobiographical Notes by Sir William Dawson* (London: Ballantyne, Hanson & Co., 1901), 91; Lyell to Dawson, 27 November 1854, cited in O'Brien, *Sir William Dawson*, 12. The successful candidate was Dr. G. J. Allman, a botanist. Dawson applied twice more for positions at Edinburgh, both without success.

overruling our affairs.''[6] Almost simultaneously with the news of the failure of his Edinburgh candidacy, Dawson received an unexpected and unsolicited offer of the principalship of McGill College. Behind the offer lay the influence of Sir Edmund Head, governor general of Canada, but previously governor of New Brunswick, where he had met Dawson and was impressed with his educational and scientific work. Already prepared for a career change, Dawson readily accepted the Montreal offer.

In the fall of 1855, George Dawson, just past his sixth birthday, moved with his family into "very imperfectly finished" quarters, "destitute of nearly every requisite of civilized life," on the McGill campus.[7] At McGill, young George Dawson enjoyed a setting that was both urban and pastoral. Although adjacent to the core of Montreal, the few college buildings occupied only a small fraction of the spacious Mount Royal grounds; the campus was still criss-crossed by streams and covered in open fields browsed by cattle. George tended his garden next to his father's and his younger brother William's; he collected butterflies and plants on the mountain behind the college house, helped his father in the museum, and indulged in the more usual pastimes of boys his age. Then, by the winter of 1858-59, while in his ninth year, he began to experience the effects of a spinal illness which would permanently affect his life.

The surviving record gives only brief glimpses of George's travail. He had not been well the previous winter, but by March 1859 he seemed better. Then during the next winter, he had become ill enough for an aunt to "feel very much indeed for your suffering." In the spring he was sent off to the sea at Pictou, with his grandfather warned to "keep a watching eye on George's *appearance*."[8]

George was suffering from Pott's disease, tuberculosis of the spine, a slow-working and increasingly painful disease that caused the affected vertebrae to soften and collapse and the spine to twist and curve. His father arranged to take the family to Maine's Cape Elizabeth and George to Boston for consultation with Dr. Buckminster Brown, a leading orthopedic specialist, himself a victim of Pott's disease.[9] The physician

6. Dawson, *Fifty Years*, 91.

7. Ibid., 99.

8. Agnes Stewart to G. M. Dawson, 20 January 1859; J. W. Dawson to James Dawson, 21 June 1859, Dawson Family Papers, (MG 1022) McGill University Archives. All subsequent citations to correspondence, unless otherwise noted, are from the Dawson Family Papers.

9. The Dawson Family Papers refer only to "Dr. Brown." Buckminister Brown (1819-91) sounds much the more likely, though he was still associated with his father, John Ball Brown (1784-1862), who had established the Boston Orthopedic Institution and gained a wide reputation for the treatment of wry-neck, club-foot, and spinal curvature.

gave advice, medicine, and a body truss to prevent further distortion of George's upper body. The treatment seemed to help; the boy's appetite improved and his deformity seemed to stabilize. "I think," his father reported, "George is decidedly the better for it."[10] Better, but not well. He survived the threat of paraplegia and a roughly 30 per cent chance of death, but the only treatment available was immobilization and a brace, with the hope that the body itself would check further progress of the disease. For several years he was a bedridden invalid suffering from headaches and pain in his back and limbs. He was always in danger of a recrudescence of the disease, in the spine, the lungs, or elsewhere. And just as serious, his growth had been stunted and his upper body permanently deformed. He would never attain more than the stature of a ten-year-old, and he would always carry the bulky torso of a hunchback.

Regular schooling for the debilitated youth was impossible. He received lessons in his Montreal home from his father and tutors. George proved an excellent student with mature and diversified intellectual interests; he was fascinated by nature, read voluminously, wrote poetry, and drew in pencil and watercolour, and even experimented with cheese-making. Gradually his health improved and, as he gained strength and stamina, his headaches decreased in frequency and severity. He was able to resume many normal activities, spending his summers with family and friends at the favoured St. Lawrence resorts of Little Metis, Tadoussac, and Murray Bay, where he fished and even hiked and boated.

In 1865 George had recovered enough to accompany his father and sister Anna on a visit to Britain. He stayed several weeks with relatives in North Berwick and Musselburgh near Edinburgh, spending most of the time fishing with his cousins. He was often tired, but he suffered no headaches. His aunt found him an obliging lad whose care caused her no trouble. "I only trust," she wrote his mother, "that he may return to you greatly benefited by the change, though I fear he will never be a strong boy."[11] Back in Montreal, his life continued to be dominated by naturalist interests. An aquarium, his plants, and his father's specimens filled the Montreal winters; fishing along the St. Lawrence occupied his summers.

In 1868, now nineteen, George enrolled in McGill classes; by the following summer, he had determined to follow his father's geological footsteps by taking the three-year programme in geology and mining offered by London's Royal School of Mines. Aside from an occasional headache and

10. J. W. Dawson to James Dawson, 25 July and 1 August 1859; Margaret Dawson to James Dawson, 11 August 1859.

11. G. M. Dawson, Journal, 1865; Marian Mercer Primrose to Margaret Dawson, 16 (?) August 1865.

leg pains at the onset of winter, he felt well. His parents must have been confident about his condition, for they allowed him to depart for Glasgow aboard the *Lake Erie*, a 930-ton sailing vessel that took the wind badly. The boat reached the Clyde after a cold, wet, and "not very pleasant voyage" that lasted over a month.[12] The crossing was so rough that George had not even learned much navigation, one of the principal reasons for the sail. The long voyage prevented him from more than just a brief stay with his many Scottish relatives before arriving in London on 13 October, just one day before his classes began.[13]

Benjamin Davies and John Bigsby, geological friends of his father, had arranged lodging for George at 20 Halsey Street in Chelsea. Davies judged Mrs. Guest, his landlady, as a "kind, motherly woman" and George found the place comfortable and pleasant, though a little distant from his classrooms and, at £20 a quarter, including board, frightfully expensive.[14]

He plunged immediately into his studies at the School of Mines. The institution, founded as an auxiliary of the Geological Survey and under the auspices of the survey's director, Sir Henry De la Beche, had enrolled its first students in 1841. The school and the survey's Museum of Practical Geology moved to separate premises on Jermyn Street, in St. James's, in 1851. The strength of the school was its faculty: headed by Director Sir Roderick Murchison, the great stratigrapher and director-general of the Geological Survey from 1855 to 1871, it included Sir Warrington W. Smyth in mining, Edward Frankland in chemistry, Sir Andrew C. Ramsay in geology, and, from 1854, T. H. Huxley in biology and palaeontology. The school's purpose was kept judiciously practical. "The aim to be kept always in view," recommended a parliamentary report of 1862, "should be to make the School as directly useful as possible to the great mining interests." Although never large—the teaching staff was normally seven and the number of matriculating students during Dawson's years averaged the same number—the St. James's premises soon proved too small. The metallurgical laboratory was in the backyard of a tailor's shop and Huxley's anatomical preparations had to be made in a dark closet about eight feet square. "It was not possible for me to teach in any genuine fashion," Huxley recalled; "I had no room in which practical instruction

12. G. M. Dawson to J. W. Dawson, 7 October 1869.

13. As a compliment to his father, the Royal School of Mines required no fees for George's attendance. See Minutes of Council, Royal School of Mines, 14 May 1870, Archives of the Imperial College of Science and Technology, London.

14. Davies to Peter Bell, 8 October 1869; G. M. Dawson to J. W. Dawson, 14 October 1869.

could be given."[15] Most of the classes and laboratories eventually moved to South Kensington, but only after Dawson's time.

The course of studies at the school provided Dawson with training in geology, mineralogy, palaeontology, chemistry, physics, and natural history, augmented by more practical exercises in mining, metallurgy, applied mathematics, and mechanical drawing. A field season was normal after the second year, and Dawson spent a part of his 1871 summer in pleasant work under J. Clifton Ward at Borrowdale, near Keswick, in the scenic Lake District.

Dawson earnestly applied himself to his studies, diverting himself with sightseeing only occasionally. His father's many London friends "received him with much kindness." Huxley, Ramsay, Robert Etheridge, and W. B. Carpenter had him to dinner, and Bigsby and Sir Charles Lyell were particularly generous in their hospitality. Ramsay reported that he found George clever, well-informed, and "remarkably agreeable." "I have rarely met any one of his age who converses so well, and yet withal is so modest."[16] Student friends came more slowly and George seems to have spent most of the free time during his first year either alone or walking with a Mr. Fisson, a French lodger at Mrs. Guest's. By his second year, however, fellow students James Huxley (son of Professor Huxley), T. J. Parker (son of comparative anatomist W. K. Parker), and Arthur G. Phillips (son of metallurgist J. A. Phillips) figure often in his journal and letters.

His father and mother visited at the end of his first year. In London they stayed at Halsey Street, then rented a cottage at Burntisland, across the firth from Edinburgh, where George geologized, fished, and practised his watercolour sketching. His father returned to Montreal pleased that George "had passed through his first year in health and with credit."[17]

George's results, while creditable, had not been distinguished. Mediocre marks in physics and mechanical drawing left him far below the best students. The second year, however, brought remarkable improvement. He won the Duke of Cornwall's Scholarship and, after scoring ninety-nine in geology and ninety-two in mineralogy, received the Director's (Murchison) Medal and Prize, and, on T. H. Huxley's recommendation, the Edward Forbes Medal and Prize of books for standing first in natural history and palaeontology. In his third and graduating year, Dawson, though

15. *Nature*, 26 June 1882, quoted in Theodore C. Chambers, *Register of the Associates and Old Students of the Royal College of Chemistry, the Royal School of Mines and the Royal College of Science; with Historical Introduction and Biographical Notes and Portraits of Past and Present Professors* (London: Hazel, Watson and Viney, 1896), xliii.

16. Dawson, *Fifty Years*, 156; Ramsay to J. W. Dawson, 18 March 1871.

17. Dawson, *Fifty Years*, 156.

professing to be "on the lookout for an excuse to waste time," allowed himself few distractions. "Laboratory / Lectures / Notes" are recorded day after day in his pocket journal.[18] The results were the highest awards of the school. He finished first in his class, graduating with honours, and repeated his success in the Forbes competition. George was made an Associate of the Royal School of Mines; now he had to look to his future.

Two things were clear. He intended to return to Canada, and he wanted to follow a geological career. Even were he asked to join the Geological Survey of Great Britain—and he did not anticipate that—he would not accept the offer. "Firstly, on the whole I would rather be in Canada. Secondly, the geology now left here is of so minute a character, & of such local interest."[19] Although he agreed to work his passage home with a temporary commission to report on some Nova Scotia ore deposits for a British investor, he had no intention of pursuing that side of his training. His interests were in geology, not in mining.

Doubtless George had his eye on the Geological Survey of Canada, which offered meaningful scientific work within an organization of reputation and importance. Headquartered in Montreal, a position there would keep him close to family and friends when not in the field. And the survey, with its responsibilites enormously expanded by the addition of Manitoba, the Northwest Territories, and British Columbia to the Dominion, needed men.

By the end of 1872, George's future was falling into place. The geological survey's director, A. R. C. Selwyn, wanted him to work in British Columbia; he required only ministerial approval before offering a position. Meanwhile, George had accepted an engagement to give a course of evening lectures in chemistry at Quebec City's Morrin College, a small Presbyterian affiliate of McGill. The formal offer of a survey appointment came just after he moved to Quebec City in January. Everything seemed settled when, scarcely two weeks later, the position of naturalist and geologist with the joint British and American survey of the international border across central North America suddenly fell open.

Dawson's own preference was clear. He wanted the permanency of the geological survey, especially because it meant working on the challenging geology of unsurveyed British Columbia. His father, however, while admitting the inferior interest of prairie geology, felt the boundary work to be much more advantageous to his son's future. As a direct governmental appointment at a higher salary, the boundary commission position would immediately raise George to a level above Robert Bell, Walter McOuat,

18. G. M. Dawson to Anna Dawson, 21 April 1872; Dawson, Journal, 1872.

19. G. M. Dawson to Anna Dawson, 5 May 1872.

and others on the geological survey staff. Moreover, if George did not take it, someone else would, thus securing rank above him.

George resisted, but his father was insistent. "Consider boundary decided," the senior Dawson wired. And so it was, even though the rejection of the British Columbia appointment threw George into "a chronic state of misery." "When I think of anybody else getting the appointment to go to survey that splendid country with splendid scenery, it puts me in the blues."[20] Fortunately, Dawson got both the eating and the cake: Selwyn kept British Columbia open until he finished his boundary work two years later.

Captain D. R. Cameron, the leader of the British side of the boundary survey team, already had his party in the field at Dufferin, Manitoba.[21] Dawson joined it in the spring, travelling by steamer from Collingwood, Ontario, to Duluth, Minnesota, then by rail to Moorhead on the Red River, and thence across the border and north by wagon and steamer. His first field summer took him 285 miles west of the Red River to Porcupine Creek, where he turned back with the survey on 5 October. The next year, in August 1874, he reached the Rocky Mountains, continuing to the west side of Waterton Lake. He arrived back in Dufferin on 11 October, following an overland march of 860 miles.[22]

With the close of field work in 1874, Dawson retired to Montreal where he worked up his notes for publication. His portion of the boundary commission report[23] and a summary article on the geology and glacial features of the Prairies[24] both elicited immediate scholarly attention and established Dawson's reputation as a scientist. Even before these notices arrived, Dawson had moved into the geological survey position he had so desired two years earlier. On 1 July 1875, he was appointed a geologist with the survey; one month later he arrived in British Columbia.

20. G. M. Dawson to Margaret Dawson, "Friday" [January 1873]; J. W. Dawson to G. M. Dawson, 28 January 1873; G. M. Dawson to Anna Dawson, 7 and 4 February 1873.

21. For a discussion of the boundary commission's organization and activities, see John E. Parson, *West of the 49th Parallel: Red River to the Rockies, 1872-1876* (New York: William Morrow, 1963).

22. A portion of Dawson's personal journals kept while on the boundary commission has been edited and annotated by A. R. Turner, as "Surveying the International Boundary: The Journal of George M. Dawson, 1873," *Saskatchewan History* 21 (1968): 1-23.

23. Dawson, *Report on the Geology and Resources of the Region in the Vicinity of the Forty-Ninth Parallel* (Montreal: Dawson Brothers, 1875). The letter of transmission is dated 19 July 1875.

24. Dawson, "On the Superficial Geology of the Central Region of North America," *Quarterly Journal of the Geological Society of London* 31 (1875): 603-23.

In sending Dawson to British Columbia, Selwyn was seeking to fulfil the Geological Survey of Canada's mandate of exploring in detail the geology of all Canadian regions.[25] Since its founding in 1842, under the brilliant leadership of its first director Sir William Logan, the survey had established a fine record for elucidation of the geology of central Canada and the Atlantic provinces. Selwyn, who succeeded Logan in 1869, faced the great challenge of directing the examination of the vast territories of the newly acquired Canadian West. The Northwest Territories had been scarcely surveyed, and only limited and scattered geological studies had been done in the area of Canada's Pacific province. Most of British Columbia remained untouched by scientific geological exploration. The only serious geological work in British Columbia prior to Dawson's first surveys was that of Selwyn himself, who had made preliminary reconnaissances across the province in 1871 and 1875, and of James Richardson, who spent five or six months every summer between 1871 and 1875 in British Columbia, largely concentrating on Vancouver Island coal deposits and the anthracite beds of the Queen Charlotte Islands.[26]

Starting in 1875, then, George Dawson faced the task of establishing the fundamental configurations of British Columbia geology. In contrast to the self-taught Richardson, Dawson had behind him a lifetime of geological study, beginning at his father's knee and continuing with formal schooling in current geological methods and conceptions. With the boundary commission experience to complement his professional training and native intellect, he was well-qualified to investigate the complexities of British Columbia's geology.

Covered in these volumes are Dawson's first four field seasons in British Columbia, from 1875 through 1878, as well as the winter of 1875-76, which he spent in Victoria.[27] The summers of 1875 and 1876 were devoted to exploration of the central interior west of the Fraser River, in association with the government's Canadian Pacific Railway Surveys. In 1877, Dawson turned his attention to the Thompson-Shuswap region and the Fraser, Similkameen, Okanagan, and Nicola valleys of the southern interior. In 1878 he shifted to the coast, examining northern Vancouver Island and the Queen Charlotte Islands.

25. The history of the Geological Survey of Canada is admirably documented in Morris Zaslow, *Reading the Rocks: The Story of the Geological Survey of Canada, 1842-1972* (Ottawa: Macmillan, 1975). See 105-14 for the beginnings of work in British Columbia, including the initial field work and contributions of G.M. Dawson.

26. For Selwyn and Richardson, see Zaslow, *Reading the Rocks*, 108-10.

27. Subsequent volumes will cover his British Columbia and Yukon seasons from 1879 through 1900.

In all of these expeditions, but most particularly in the 1875, 1876, and 1878 seasons, the lack of knowledge of even the basic topography of the Pacific province was a major problem. The topographical foundations that had supported geological study in the settled eastern provinces did not exist. Thus Dawson was required to act as topographical surveyor as well as perform his assigned geological work. As he was to write some twenty years later,

the want of proper maps of the province of British Columbia has in all previous instances been the great cause of delay in carrying on the geological exploration of the country, work which should previously have been done by surveyors and topographers having been thrown upon the geologist in addition to his own duties.[28]

This problem bedevilled the survey in all new areas of the Dominion and, though Dawson only reluctantly incorporated topographical surveying into his geological expeditions, he took it seriously. He not only made careful measurements of regions covered but also produced topographical sketches and took numerous photographs to illustrate topographical features.[29] Where necessary, Dawson corrected existing maps or made new ones. His own maps, though not without error, were models of detail and accuracy produced from painstaking field surveys.[30] As the first topographer in many areas, Dawson had to name many physical features. Many of these names remain officially in use, particularly in the Queen Charlotte Islands. Scudder Point, Dana and Selwyn inlets, and Rankine, Huxley, Ramsay, Murchison, and Lyell islands are only some of the many place names Dawson left there in honour of associates, mentors, and models. He also attempted to delineate broader topographical units such as mountain ranges, a complex endeavour in British Columbia's varied terrain.[31]

28. Dawson to Tom Kains, 28 May 1896, Records of the Geological Survey of Canada, RG 45, vol. 92, Director's Letterbooks, Public Archives of Canada (PAC), Ottawa.

29. The topographical measurements and sketches are located in Dawson's Field Notebooks, Records of the Geological Survey of Canada, RG 45, vols. 134-36, 292, PAC.

30. Many of Dawson's survey reports had maps appended. Some noteworthy examples are Dawson, *Geological Map of a Portion of British Columbia between the Fraser River and the Coast Range* (Ottawa: Geological Survey of Canada, 1877); and Dawson, *Map of the Queen Charlotte Islands to Illustrate Report* (Ottawa: Geological Survey of Canada, 1879).

Heavily influencing the early years of Dawson's British Columbia activity was the close association of the Geological Survey with the Canadian Pacific Railway Surveys. Throughout the 1870's the government's railway surveys, under the leadership of Sir Sandford Fleming and Marcus Smith, explored vast areas, weighing the advantages of a variety of possible railway routes through British Columbia. The Geological Survey of Canada took on the task of furnishing the railway with data on the province's mineral and natural resources. Consequently, the operations of the Geological Survey "often were directed into regions and along lines that were of particular value in planning and executing the great railway enterprise."[32] In 1875 and 1876, the railway survey teams fanned out across north-central British Columbia to survey possible lines. Dawson accompanied railway parties into these isolated reaches of the province, concerning himself with the feasibility of railway routes and with their agricultural and resource potential.[33]

This close association with the railway surveys explains in part Dawson's preoccupation with coal, that vital fuel of the steam age. He followed every report and rumour, often travelling well out of his way to locate and examine coal seams on the North Thompson or the Nicola rivers or on Vancouver Island. A flourishing coal-mining industry already existed at Nanaimo, and in October 1878 Dawson inspected the Douglas Mine, outlining the salient features of the deposit and the problems encountered in mining it. That same year he inspected the abandoned works of the Cowgitz Coal Mines on Skidegate Inlet on the Queen Charlotte Islands, criticizing the company for developing the site before knowing its potential.

31. See D. F. Pearson, "Approaches to Delimiting Landform Units in British Columbia," *Canoma* 8, no. 2 (December 1982): 2-3. For a brief summary of Dawson's topographical work in Western Canada, see Don W. Thomson, *Men and Meridians: The History of Surveying and Mapping in Canada*, volume 2, *1867 to 1917* (Ottawa: Information Canada, 1972), 290-92.

32. Zaslow, *Reading the Rocks*, 108.

33. See Dawson, "Note on the Economic Minerals, and Mines of British Columbia; Appendix R," in Sandford Fleming, *Report on Surveys and Preliminary Operations on the Canadian Pacific Railway up to January 1877* (Ottawa: MacLean, Roger & Co., 1877), 218-45; Dawson, "Note On Agriculture and Stock Raising, and Extent of Cultivable Land in British Columbia: Appendix S," in ibid., 246-53; Dawson, "Report on the Climate and Agricultural Value, General Geological Features and Minerals of Economic Importance of Part of the Northern Portion of British Columbia, and of the Peace River Country; Appendix 7," in Sandford Fleming, *Report and Documents in Reference to the Canadian Pacific Railway* (Ottawa: MacLean, Roger & Co., 1880), 107-31; and Dawson, "Memorandum on the Queen Charlotte Islands, British Columbia; Appendix 9," in ibid., 139-43.

Coal was not the only area of mining potential that interested Dawson, the railway surveys, and the government. The Survey's mandate, iterated again and again by Parliament and ministers, emphasized the practical role of the federal agency. Since the gold rush to the Fraser River in 1858, British Columbia had attracted miners. Smaller gold rushes to the Big Bend of the Columbia River, the Omineca region, and the Stikine River sustained the interest in gold. In the 1870's, placer mining still prevailed, though lode mining was becoming more important with the exhaustion of superficial deposits. Still, by the time Dawson began his British Columbia explorations in the mid-1870's, knowledge of the province's mining resources was sketchy.

One of Dawson's first endeavours was the preparation of an inventory and mining history of known British Columbia ore deposits. He sought out reliable sources to authenticate reported deposits, and he visited many sites himself. Dawson's inventory, the first edition of which was published in 1877,[34] was a systematic guide to the deposits and mines of British Columbia. A revised edition, issued in 1889,[35] included data gathered in the intervening years. The inventories gave interested parties a precise idea of a deposit's location, its historical productivity, and its current mining status.[36]

In those years when he was associated with the proposed railway, Dawson assessed the resource potential of the areas he visited. Of the Chilcotin River valley in 1875, for example, he remarked that the region "cannot be called in any Sence [*sic*] an agricultural country. For the most part it is too high for wheat raising, & even potatoes in indian gardens east of Alexis Creek were observed to be frost Killed."[37] In his published work Dawson paid special attention to species of harvestable trees. An article

---

34. Dawson, "General Note on the Mines and Minerals of Economic Value of British Columbia, with a List of Localities," in Geological Survey of Canada, *Report of Progress for 1876-77* (1878), 103-49, which was also published under Canadian Pacific Railway auspices, with minor changes, as Dawson, "Note on Economic Minerals and Mines of British Columbia," Appendix R to Sandford Fleming, *Report on Surveys and Preliminary Operations of the Canadian Pacific Railway up to January 1877* (Ottawa: MacLean, Rogers, 1877), 218-45.

35. Dawson, "The Mineral Wealth of British Columbia. With an Annotated List of Localities of Minerals of Economic Value," in Geological Survey of Canada, *Annual Report, 1887-88*, n.s., 3 (1889), Part II, Report R, 1-163.

36. A. H. Lang, "G. M. Dawson and the Economic Development of Western Canada," *Canadian Public Administration* 24 (1971): 248.

37. Dawson, Journal, 31 August 1875, G. M. Dawson Papers, McGill University, Department of Rare Books and Special Collections.

appended to his survey report for 1879[38] presented basic scientific data and detailed potential economic uses for many British Columbia trees. Dawson also recorded the climatic characteristics of an area and attached meteorological records to his Geological Survey reports.[39]

The relationship between the railway surveys and the Geological Survey did provide practical benefits. Particularly in his first British Columbia season, Dawson hoped "to get a small organized pack-train from the C.P. Ry., & also to draw supplies from their depots there now established."[40] This simplified his planning; he did not need to organize his own expedition or break new trails. Dawson also relied heavily upon the knowledge of railway survey employees, men such as Marcus Smith, H. J. Cambie, and Joseph Hunter, who were seasoned field workers familiar with the country.

Despite the emphasis upon practical natural resource exploitation, Dawson's most important work was in the field of scholarly geology. He was a brilliant field geologist with an exceptional ability to synthesize information.[41] "In a way that has never been equalled Dawson was able not only to make thorough and valid observations quickly, but also to extend such observations to distant vistas and to extrapolate and generalize fairly accurately beyond his range of vision."[42] In British Columbia he initially adopted Selwyn's 1871 eight-fold stratigraphic system, but after several field seasons he replaced that with his own scheme.[43] In the course of his 1877 field work, he realized that the stratigraphy of British Columbia could not be correlated with that of eastern North America. These Cordilleran beds were so different that their classification must emerge

38. Dawson, "Note on the Distribution of Some of the More Important Trees of British Columbia," in Geological Survey of Canada, *Report of Progress for 1879-80* (1881), Report B, 167-77.

39. See, for example, Dawson, "Appendix F. Meteorological Observations on the Coast of British Columbia—May 28 to October 17, 1878," in Geological Survey of Canada, *Report of Progress for 1878-79* (1879), 224-32.

40. G. M. Dawson to Margaret Dawson, 6 August 1875.

41. While Dawson made a significant breakthrough in 1877 in the stratigraphic mapping of the province, his post-1878 field seasons contributed greatly to his final conclusions. This area will be dealt with more fully in the introduction to Volume II.

42. Lang, "Dawson and Economic Development," 242.

43. See Selwyn, "Journal and Report," 54-66; and for Dawson's new system see his "Preliminary Report on the Physical and Geological Features of the Southern Portion of the Interior of British Columbia, 1877," in Geological Survey of Canada, *Report of Progress for 1877-78* (1879), Report B, 171-72.

from field evidence alone.[44] In the report of his 1877 travels, Dawson "displayed his ability to observe accurately and generalize with clarity and ingenuity. His originality made the report a milestone in the geological study of the province."[45] This, with his later field work, enabled him to evolve a fairly complete stratigraphy for the province.[46]

Nothing stimulated Dawson's curiosity more than glacial phenomena, and he expended a great deal of intellectual effort in hypotheses to explain the terraces, drift deposits, and glacial striations so conspicuously a part of the surficial geology of the province. The ice-age question was one of the great controversies of nineteenth-century science, and leading geologists—J. W. Dawson, Lyell, Buckland, Murchison, Dana, Agassiz, the Geikies, Ramsay—took an active part in the debate. Dawson's father stood firmly on the side of the drift-ice proponents: those who rejected the idea of great glaciers covering enormous land areas, preferring to explain both drift deposits and large boulders out of geological context (erratics) as the result of icebergs depositing their detritus in then submerged areas remote from their arctic origin.

In his forty-ninth parallel work, Dawson had had to account for the presence of boulders of Laurentian origin as far west as the margins of the Rocky Mountains. He accepted the existence of a glacier formed on the Laurentian Highlands east of Lake Winnipeg but felt it inconceivable that such a body of ice could push seven hundred miles westward over an upward slope of thirty-five hundred feet, or that the Cretaceous escarpment at the Red River would not have been destroyed by such an enormous force. Instead, along the diluvial lines of his father, he posited a continental submergence that allowed the Laurentian glacier to float westward where it dropped its erratics across the inundated plains.[47]

44. "It is by the slow and laborious processes of accumulation of many observations and the attempted coordination of these in every probable manner, alone, that the interrelation and foreign equivalency of the rock-formations of such a region as that of British Columbia can be ascertained" (Dawson, "Report on the Southern Portion," 166).

45. Zaslow, *Reading the Rocks*, 112.

46. This will be dealt with more completely in Part II. For his revised version, see Dawson, "Report on the Area of the Kamloops Map-Sheet," in Geological Survey of Canada, *Annual Report, 1894*, n.s., 7 (1896), Report B, 26.

47. Dawson, "Superficial Geology of Central Region," 619-23; and Dawson, "Erratics at High Levels in North-Western America—Barriers to a Great Ice Sheet," *Geological Magazine* n.s., 5 (1878): 210-12.

The prairies were one thing; British Columbia was quite another. "The glaciation of the rocks in the vicinity of Victoria, Vancouver Island, is so well marked," Dawson wrote, "and presents itself so immediately to any one arriving in the locality" that he could not ignore the evidence.[48] "There appears to be no escape from the conclusion that a glacier swept over the whole south-eastern peninsula of Vancouver Island"; indeed, the entire Strait of Georgia must have been filled with a great glacier considerably more than six hundred feet thick.[49]

His work in the interior during 1875 and 1876 also led Dawson to consider a glacial explanation for the striking terraces and abundant boulder clays of the region, though this coexisted with an alternative drift-ice hypothesis. He observed glacial striation at such heights—up to 3700 feet on an outlying peak of Tsi-tsutl Mountain south of the Dean River—and with such bearings as to preclude it being formed by glaciers moving from any mountain system. Although retaining his opposition to the theory of a polar ice-cap affecting North America, here were indications which "more nearly answer to the kind of traces which such an ice cap would be expected to leave than any thing I have elsewhere seen."[50] He thought it possible that a great glacier, formed in the mountains of northern British Columbia, may have become the point of radiation for ice flowing south through the interior plateau across the forty-ninth parallel and westward across the Coast Range.

More plausible—and perhaps more congenial—to Dawson than a great ice sheet was the alternative explanation of floating ice entering the central plateau by the low Rocky Mountain gap in the Peace River region and flowing southward to exit through the Fraser River valley and other openings. He discerned no deposits "like those elsewhere ascribed to such gigantic ice-sheets"; instead he found the entire area marbled with unmodified boulder clay which indicated to him deposition by water-borne ice. "It appears necessary to call in the action of water with floating ice to account for the formation of the Boulder-clay, with its rounded pebbles and irregularly distributed erratics." A depression of three thousand feet, he thought, would suffice to open a wide strait from the Arctic to the Pacific, though a submergence of over five thousand feet was required to

---

48. Evidence of glaciation had been noted earlier by, among others, Hilary Bauermann, "On the Geology of the South-Eastern Part of Vancouver Island," *Quarterly Journal of the Geological Society of London* 6 (1860): 198-202; and Robert Brown, "On the Supposed Absence of the Northern Drift from the Pacific Slope of the Rocky Mountains," *American Journal of Science and Arts*, 2nd ser., 50 (1870): 318-24.

49. Dawson, "On the Superficial Geology of British Columbia," *Quarterly Journal of the Geological Society of London* 34 (1878): 92, 95.

50. Ibid., 118.

explain the well-marked upper terraces of the interior.[51]

Dawson's 1877 explorations of the southern interior both confirmed and modified his views. At Iron Mountain, at the junction of the Nicola and Coldwater rivers, he found evidence of glaciation at the 5280 foot level. This and other evidence seemed "to render it not impossible" that a great confluent glacier, moved by its own mass and centred north of the fifty-fourth parallel, had covered the province's interior. He did not, however, abandon the hypothesis of an arctic current bringing polar ice through the Peace River gap. Such "would serve almost equally well" to account for the evidence of interior glaciation.[52] Only in 1879, as a result of his northern interior exploration, did Dawson abandon his arctic drift-ice hypothesis. The absence of drift material on the mountains and the narrow gaps, which would not have allowed sufficient flow, argued against it.[53]

With the abandonment of a diluvial explanation, he was free to work out the problems presented by striations, terraces, boulder clay, and white silts within the context of a glacial hypothesis. Dawson's final position postulated a huge ice mass, which he termed the Cordilleran Glacier, that had once extended nearly twelve hundred miles from below the forty-ninth parallel north into the Yukon basin. The glacier would have been two to three thousand feet thick over the higher plateau and over six thousand feet above the main river valleys. At length, the land subsided and the glacier retreated, leaving behind englacial lakes that formed high level terraces composed of material resembling boulder clay. Another cycle of glaciation, subsidence, and retreat was responsible for further deposition of boulder clays and terraces. A period of ensuing stability explained the laying down of the remarkable white silts.[54] During both periods of deglaciation, Dawson felt that the terrace and silt deposits were best explained by a land submergence significant enough to allow sea water to

51. Ibid., 119-20.

52. Dawson, "Report on the Southern Portion," 150-52.

53. Dawson, "Additional Observations on the Superficial Geology of British Columbia and Adjacent Regions," *Quarterly Journal of the Geological Society of London* 37 (1881): 283-84.

54. Dawson, "On the Later Physiographical Geology of the Rocky Mountain Region in Canada, with Special Reference to Changes in Elevation and to the History of the Glacial Period," *Proceedings and Transactions of the Royal Society of Canada* 8 (1890), sec. IV, 55-74. This is summarized in Dawson, "On the Glaciation of the Northern Part of the Cordillera, with an Attempt to Correlate the Events of the Glacial Period in the Cordillera and Great Plains," *American Geologist* 6 (1890): 153-62. See also H. W. Tipper, *Glacial Geomorphology and Pleistocene History of Central British Columbia*, Geological Survey of Canada Bulletin no. 196 (Ottawa: Information Canada, 1971), 72.

enter the interior through the Fraser and other valley openings. He was convinced that the terraces were former shorelines, not river banks, and that the silts were a single formation laid down by glacial meltwater in a deep, tranquil sea.

Later research has undermined some of Dawson's conclusions. His postulation of a great Cordilleran glacier has been confirmed, though uncertainty and disagreement remain about its timing. During at least one stage of Pleistocene glacial advance, a domed ice sheet covered most of British Columbia along roughly the area assigned to it by Dawson, and it reached approximately the height he allowed. He underestimated the complexity of movement of various portions of the ice, however, partly because he tended to judge from striations, often rare, and overlooked evidence from drumlins, eskers, meltwater channels, and erratics. He did not have, of course, the aerial photography or laboratory analysis which illuminate such traces.

If Dawson was fundamentally sound in his glacial conclusions, he was considerably weaker in his hypothesized process of deglaciation. Submergence may have occurred, but it was not major enough to allow oceanic inundation. The deposition of boulder clay and silt and the formation of terraces occurred under normal circumstances of glacial decay. Most terraces are composed of material deposited by meltwater streams which flowed along the ice edges (kame terraces) or are abandoned floodplains and banks (outwash terraces). The white silts were deposited, largely derived from meltwater erosion of till, in a large number of independent lakes created by retreating ice dams.

While Dawson's interpretation of British Columbia glacial history erred in detail and missed some of the complexities within it, he laid down its general lines with sufficient clarity and correctness to form the substance upon which later investigation could build. As the first to suggest a Cordilleran glacier on evidence quickly accepted, he "contributed more to the overall concept of a Cordilleran ice sheet in British Columbia than any other geologist."[55]

On the other hand, Dawson never accepted a continental glacier as an explanation for the Pleistocene history of the prairies, opposing it strenuously in his final statement on the subject.[56] He and his father were the last major figures to oppose the idea of an ice sheet covering the great plains. Despite his opposition to this aspect of North American glacial history, Dawson remains one of the most significant contributors to its theory. Indeed, the great sea of ice that radiated out from the Canadian

55. Tipper, *Glacial Geomorphology*, 72.

56. Dawson, "Later Physiographical Geology."

Shield area and covered the northern prairies and great lakes has retained the name Dawson first assigned to it—the Laurentide ice-sheet.[57]

Sir William Dawson's early and stubborn insistence upon a drift-ice explanation for eastern Canadian and prairie deposits raises the inevitable question whether the son felt obliged to hew his own opinions to fit those of the father. The hypothesis is tempting but unlikely. The younger Dawson was certainly influenced by his father's idea of submergence, but he seemed persuaded by his own examination of the geological evidence, not only from his 1873-74 boundary survey work, but also from his later prairie surveys in the 1880's. By then George's views concerning the existence of a Cordilleran glacier, even of a larger Laurentide glacier, were fully accepted by Sir William, one of the few major modifications he made to his views of the North American Pleistocene. The elder Dawson's 1893 *The Canadian Ice Age*[58] was a repetition of his earlier position on eastern and central North America placed into a continental context by large extracts from his son's publications.

While physical geology and glaciology were the areas in which George Dawson made his greatest scientific achievements, his ethnological work gives him a prominent place in the history of Canadian anthropology. Since part of the Geological Survey of Canada's mandate was to collect ethnological data, Dawson could indulge his ethnographic interests. The personal journals, with their extensive ethnographic notes, testify to Dawson's fascination with native life. His published ethnographies on the Haida, Kwakiutl, and Interior Salish discussing subjects as diverse as tribal subdivisions, mythology, and ethnobotany.[59] An article written in

57. Dawson used the term Cordilleran glacier as early as 1888. See Dawson, "Recent Observations on the Glaciation of British Columbia and Adjacent Regions," *Geological Magazine* 5 (1888): 349. In 1890, first in "Later Physiographical Geology," 56; and then in "On the Glaciation of the Northern Part of the Cordillera," 162, he suggested the adoption of the terms *Cordilleran glacier* and *Laurentide glacier*, a practice which has, with exception and qualification, been accepted. See Richard Foster Flint's discussion of the identification and nomenclature of glacial units in his "Growth of the North American Ice Sheet during the Wisconsin Age," *Bulletin of the Geological Society of America* 54 (1943): 328-33.

58. *The Canadian Ice Age: Being Notes on the Pleistocene Geology of Canada, with Especial Reference to the Life of the Period and its Climatal Conditions* (Montreal: William V. Dawson, 1893). Compare this to his earlier "The Post-Pliocene Geology of Canada," *Canadian Naturalist* n.s. 6 (1872): 19-42, 166-87, 241-58, 369-416.

59. See Dawson, "On the Haida Indians of the Queen Charlotte Islands," in Geological Survey of Canada, *Report of Progress for 1878-79* (1880), Report B, Appendix A; Dawson, "Notes and Observations on the Kwakiool People of the Northern Part of Vancouver Island and Adjacent Coasts," *Proceedings and Transactions of the Royal*

1887 on the native utilization of jade merged geology with ethnological concerns.[60] Dawson ventured into the realm of linguistics in his collaboration with W. F. Tolmie on a comparative vocabulary of northwest Indian languages.[61] His ethnographic writings have remained of enduring value and are the more remarkable because his work in this field was necessarily secondary to the major charge of the survey. An even more enduring contribution in this field are his photographs, especially those of Haida villages during his 1878 survey of the Queen Charlotte Islands. Without them, the remarkable reconstruction of nineteenth-century Haida villages done by George F. MacDonald would hardly have been possible.[62]

While his ethnographic publications were largely devoid of theorizing, Dawson did not entirely avoid it. He was well aware that his anthropological observations provoked larger questions. As he himself intimated:

> The collection and study of details like these concerning the habits, customs, and thought of a people semi-barbarous, and disappearing even before our eyes in the universal menstruum of civilization, may seem to be of little importance. They lead, however, into a wide and interesting region of speculation, embracing the question of the origin and interrelaton of the American aborigines, their wanderings, and the unwritten pages of their history.[63]

Sometimes Dawson moved into that speculative domain. He offered the view that the original inhabitants of western North America might have come from eastern Asia.[64] In the journals Dawson pondered the significance of similarities of words in Carrier and Chilcotin languages of central

Society of Canada 5 (1887), sec. II, 63-98; and Dawson, "Notes on the Shuswap People of British Columbia," *Proceedings and Transactions of the Royal Society of Canada* 9 (1891), sec. II, 3-44.

60. Dawson, "Note on the Occurrence of Jade in British Columbia, and Its Employment by the Natives, with Quotations and Extracts from a Paper by Prof. A. B. Meyer, on Nephrite and Analogous Minerals from Alaska," *Canadian Record of Science* 2 (1887): 364-78.

61. W. Fraser Tolmie and Dawson, *Comparative Vocabularies of the Indian Tribes of British Columbia, with a Map Illustrating Distribution* (Montreal: Dawson Brothers, 1884).

62. MacDonald, *Haida Monumental Art: Villages of the Queen Charlotte Islands* (Vancouver: University of British Columbia Press, 1983).

63. Dawson, "The Haidas," *Harper's New Monthly Magazine* 65 (1882): 407.

64. "It is therefore more than probable that people with their rude arts may from time to time have been borne to the western coast of America, and it is to Eastern Asia that we must look for the origin of it inhabitants" (ibid., 408).

British Columbia to those much farther afield, even to the Nuhauatlan language of the Aztecs.[65] In pursuing such theoretical questions, Dawson
turned to whatever literature was available, including the unreliable volumes of H. H. Bancroft, who at that time was writing extensively on the
native peoples of the Americas.[66] While intrigued by the scattered evidence of linguistic similarities, Dawson's own conclusions were usually
cautious.

Dawson's concerns also included the less erudite question of public policy toward the native people.[67] He wholeheartedly accepted the assumption that native survival was contingent upon their integration into
Euro-Canadian culture. While traditional social structures were breaking
down under the pressure of European-dominated forces, Dawson felt the
more durable institutions, such as the seemingly pernicious potlatch,
should be suppressed in order to hasten integration. According to
Dawson, a native "possesses qualities which fit him not unequally to bear
his part with the other races which enter into the composition of our people in the building up the future greatness of the Dominion."[68] If governments provided adequate conditions, native economic activities could be
integrated into the Canadian economy.

> The policy obviously best for the natives of British Columbia, is to aid
> them in following those paths which they have taken already; to assist
> the tribes of the interior to become successful stockraisers and farm-
> ers, by granting them suitable reserves and grazing privileges; to en-
> courage those on the coast in fishing and becoming seamen, instruct-
> ing them in improving modes of preserving their fish, and of preparing
> it for sale to others. If the sites of their villages and fishing stations are
> secure to them, they will require little more in the way of reserves.[69]

While Dawson was optimistic about the future of British Columbia's
native people, he was singularly unimpressed with their present state. By
the time of Dawson's observations, British Columbia's native people had
suffered from extended exposure to the destructive elements of
Euro-Canadian culture. Disease and alcohol had had a serious impact on

65. Dawson, Journals, 10 June 1876.

66. See Hubert Howe Bancroft, *The Native Races of the Pacific States of North America*, 5
     vols. (San Francisco: H. H. Bancroft, 1874-76).

67. See Dawson, "Sketches of the Past and Present Condition of the Indians of Canada,"
     Canadian Naturalist and Quarterly Journal of Science n.s., 9 (1881): 156-58.

68. Ibid., 159.

69. Ibid., 157.

the integrity of native society. Dawson saw numerous examples of the debilitating effects of the European culture on native people. Of the Songhees in the Victoria harbour area, Dawson noted in 1876 that "they are a most degraded lot, & are to be seen parading the streets in all their native ugliness & dirt at any time of day."[70] It was not merely the decadence caused by contact with the Euro-Canadians that determined his negative judgement. Physically, Dawson viewed the native people as inferior to Europeans. He found that "their physiognomy is very varied, & though occasionally a really fine, & often a pleasant-enough face, is to be met with, many are baboonish & repulsive."[71] Dawson exemplified that ironical position where an appreciation of native cultural achievement was juxtaposed with disdain for native people and their mode of life. His notion of European superiority was never relinquished.

Dawson, however, wanted to preserve a record of native life. He sought to preserve as much as possible of traditional cultures by collecting tangible portions for Canadian museums. In his own exploring Dawson found opportunities to collect artifacts. Dawson's first major collection, from the Queen Charlotte Islands, went to McGill University; his later collections were kept for the Geological Survey of Canada museum.[72] After 1880, Dawson became the major influence within the survey in building its ethnological and archaeological collections, attempting within the limits of annual appropriations to create representative collections of Canadian, especially Northwest Coast, ethnology. The survey's collection was "not large," he reported in 1889, but its importance lay chiefly "in British Columbia ethnological and Ontario archaeological specimens," distinctions for which he was at least partly responsible.[73]

Dawson brought back a large Kwakiutl collection from his 1885 Vancouver Island survey and, in addition to the material he himself collected, secured acquisitions from old Hudson's Bay men W. F. Tolmie and Alexander Mackenzie. In the later years of the nineteenth century, when the need to preserve was becoming increasingly urgent, Dawson was able to obtain collections from Franz Boas and C. F. Newcombe. Most anthropological items were acquired by purchase from the native people, but some were more easily obtained by theft. Dawson's 1877 late-night snatch-

---

70. Dawson to Rankine Dawson, 6 February 1876.

71. Dawson, Journal, 18 October 1877.

72. The Haida collection is now in the McCord Museum, McGill University; the others are in the Canadian Museum of Civilization, Ottawa.

73. Dawson in *Internationales Archiv für Ethnologie* 2 (1889): 231.

ing of skulls from a Lytton burial site[74] was a method consistent with the ethos of the time—it was acceptable so long as the action remained undetected by the Indians or the law.

One result of Dawson's ethnological interest was his service on the Committee on the North-western Tribes, established in 1884 at the first Canadian meeting of the British Association for the Advancement of Science. Initially under the direction of Horatio Hale and nominally chaired by Oxford's E. P. Tylor, the committee included Dawson and Sir Daniel Wilson, president of the University of Toronto and an authority on prehistory. The committee engaged Franz Boas for a series of field expeditions to British Columbia, and Dawson arranged funds so that most of the artifacts collected would be kept within Canada. Dawson later took effective direction of the committee and, in 1897, he chaired its successor, the British Association's Ethnological Survey of Canada.

A consequence of Dawson's anthropological involvement was his promotion of Ottawa's museum facilities. As survey director, he expanded the ethnological collections of the survey's museum by purchase; with the Royal Society of Canada, he sought new premises for it. Despite the improvement in display cases and holdings during his tenure, concern for the collection declined after his death. Only with the establishment of the Victoria Memorial Museum in 1911 did museum conditions return to those of the Dawson era.[75]

One final area of Dawson's scientific interest deserves mention. In the late nineteenth century, the Geological Survey's concerns also extended to natural history; with his life-long naturalist interests supplemented by training under Huxley at the Royal School of Mines, Dawson enthusiastically recorded floral and faunal data on his geological excursions. His notes on mammalian species were often not just bare lists but fuller records of species abundance and distribution.[76] Dawson's observations extended to marine life when, on the 1878 voyage to the Queen Charlotte

74. Dawson, Journal, 25 September 1877.

75. Douglas Cole, "The Origin of Canadian Anthropology, 1850-1910," *Journal of Canadian Studies* 8 (February 1973): 40-42; Cole, *Captured Heritage: The Scramble for Northwest Coast Artifacts* (Vancouver: Douglas & McIntyre, 1985), 76-80; Zaslow, *Reading the Rocks*, 266-69.

76. See, for example, Dawson, Journal, 30 August 1878 (verso), where he discusses the distribution of deer and bear in northern British Columbia.

Islands, he employed a dredge to gather bottom samples.[77] He was equally interested in flora. Where the native people utilized plants, Dawson seldom failed to comment on practices employed. He sent specimens for identification to botanists such as John Macoun in Ontario or George Engelmann at the Missouri Botanical Gardens in St. Louis.[78] In fact, many of the plant species recorded and identified by Macoun in his multi-volumed *Catalogue of Canadian Plants*[79] had been collected by Dawson.

Dawson's personality and temperament emerge only vaguely from the field letters and journals. He displayed an impressive stamina and tenacity in the field, especially for one of his physical stature. The difficulties of carrying on geological and topographical explorations in British Columbia were legion. Poor trails or even a complete lack of paths recurringly thwarted progress, inclement weather often hindered operations, and insects in vast quantities were an unavoidable source of irritation. Dawson certainly complained about bad trails, the nuisance of snags, difficult terrain, and swarms of mosquitoes, but at worst these only slowed his work. His handicap is never mentioned, any physical ailments rarely. Personal discomfort, an expected part of life on a geological expedition, was apparently worthy of little notice. Even after mammoth exertion of personnel and animals in overcoming obstacles on the trail, and long hours in the saddle, Dawson unfailingly carried out his scientific studies. Geological formations were examined thoroughly; where necessary, topographical measurements taken. Long after the rest of his party had retired, Dawson often worked into the night, completing notes and journal entries and taking astronomical observations.

In many ways he was happiest when in the field. In London he had accepted invitations grudgingly. "I wish you would not stir up these people to ask me out," he had written his mother, "as I hate going out, & dinner especially." In Victoria, he socialized with the Creases, the Duponts, the

---

77. See, for example, ibid., 15 June, 28 August 1878. The marine specimens collected by Dawson were analyzed and the results published in J. W. Whiteaves, "Appendix C. On Some Marine Invertebrata from the Queen Charlotte Islands," in Geological Survey of Canada, *Report of Progress for 1878-79* (1879), 190-205; and S. I. Smith, "Appendix D. Notes on Crustacea Collected by Dr. G. M. Dawson at Vancouver and the Queen Charlotte Islands," ibid., 206-18.

78. Dawson to George Engelmann, 26 January 1876, George Engelmann Papers, Missouri Botanical Gardens, St. Louis, asking Engelmann's assistance in identifying species of coniferous trees.

79. John Macoun, *Catalogue of Canadian Plants*, 6 vols. (Montreal: Dawson Brothers, 1883).

Bakers, and others among the city's first families, but insisted that "there are *very* few people here whom I care to know well." In Montreal in 1880, the first summer in five years not spent in the field, he found the city less congenial than the bush. "I cant [*sic*] say I find being here in the hot weather at all equal to being in the woods, not that I feel the heat, but the solitude is more oppressive because less natural. The people one meets are no more to you than so many nine-pins."[80]

His physical appearance undoubtedly affected his social relations. "Keenly sensitive as he was by nature," noted an aquaintance, "he felt his deformity deeply and abstained from going into that society which his mental gifts and graces fitted him to adorn."[81] In none of his letters, in none of his journals, is there a single allusion to his physical condition. While his family might enquire about his health, they went no further. His appearance must have been, from youth on, an unmentionable subject. Victorian society was not easy on the odd and the deformed, and his mother may in some measure have intensified the taboo. A letter from her sister suggests that she kept George out of the sight of her close friends, an attitude that, if true, would have deeply impressed itself upon the boy.[82] George's deep reserve, on the other hand, could merely have been characteristic of the male side of the Dawson family. Even George found Rankine, his youngest brother, a quiet companion. And George once wrote of how rare was any "flash of the inner man" in his father's conversation and how he, similarly reticent by nature, also "lived behind entrenchments and fortifications raised by myself as he must have done, finding expression chiefly as he did in written words, guardedly, & hazarding nothing in open speech."[83]

Even the written word brought forth little intimacy. His sister Anna found his letters a test of her loving patience. "You are so reserved that the little confidences I am wont to gather from your eyes & manner of saying things, are now quite unattainable, & I only hear the *news* of your outer life." She wished it were otherwise, that "we might have been even more to each other, but after all every one must do as his own nature dictates."[84]

80. G. M. Dawson to Margaret Dawson, 29 December 1870, 9 April 1876, 1 July 1880.

81. R. W. Shannon, "The Late Dr. Dawson," *The Commonwealth* (Ottawa) 1 (March 1901): 50.

82. Marian Mercer Primrose to Margaret Dawson, 9 August 1865.

83. Dawson to Margaret Dawson, 13 May 1878; a loose slip, titled (in another hand) "George and his father—*Pathetic*," Box 56, folder 10, Dawson Family Papers.

84. Anna Dawson to G. M. Dawson, October [n.d.], 1875.

Among acquaintances Dawson could assume a cheerful geniality, expressed in witty sallies, good-natured badinage, and a quick, wise smile. While respected and liked by most of his colleagues, he made few—perhaps no—intimate friends. He lived at the family home in Montreal and, after the 1881 removal of the survey to Ottawa, in rented rooms. He never married.[85]

His parents, siblings, and closest in-laws such as Anna's husband, Bernard Harrington, were the focus of Dawson's social life. The Dawsons were always a close family and George's childhood illness and consequent deformity probably increased his dependence upon its members. He was, nevertheless, expected to bear "the responsibilities as the eldest to show a good example to the younger children." Anna, his nearest sister, had been indispensable to him in his period of recovery. She spent many quiet hours with him, sketching and painting. She remained faithful in her support and encouragement. At one time she expected to remain single so that she could keep house for him; her decision to marry Harrington (whom she had earlier refused) would not, she pledged, keep her from always having a "snug little home" for her brother.[86] His move to Ottawa made that unnecessary.

Intellectually and professionally, Dawson's father was his strongest supporter. He took pride in the young man's success in his own scholarly field and exercised his influence to advance George, even in directions the son did not choose. The elder Dawson, convinced that the boundary survey appointment was superior to that with the geological survey, overrode his son's objections; using his influence in Ottawa, especially with his Nova Scotian friends Samuel Tilly and Joseph Howe, he secured the position for George. In 1876, without being able to learn George's own wishes, he moved mountains to gain his appointment as palaeontologist with the survey and, when unsuccessful (his Liberal contacts were thinner), threatened Selwyn with public controversy.[87] His father's later pressures that he seek positions in eastern North America, at the University of Virginia or Kingston's Royal Military College, were aimed not only at advancing his son's career but also at bringing him nearer to Montreal.

---

85. In the early 1880's he formed a very strong attachment to a woman. The feeling was not returned and the collapse of the relationship sent him into severe depression. This will be explored more fully in the introduction to Volume II.

86. Margaret Dawson to G. M. Dawson, 10 July 1865; Joyce C. Barkhouse, *George Dawson: The Little Giant* (Toronto: Clarke, Irwin & Co., 1974), 26; and Anna Dawson to G. M. Dawson, 26 November 1875.

87. J. W. Dawson to G. M. Dawson, 21 August 1876; printed sheet of testimonials; J. W. Dawson to Selwyn, 1 September 1876 (copy); G. M. Dawson to Margaret Dawson, 1 October 1876; G. M. Dawson to J. W. Dawson, 21 October 1876.

George's absence in distant field work was deeply felt both at the paternal and the collegial level. The palaeontology position, his father wrote, would be "*near to us*, and the help you could give me in difficult questions of fossils, while I in return could place all my knowledge and means at your disposal."[88] Their collaboration had begun years before; George's undistinguished marks in his first London year may have been owing in part to the evenings he devoted to his study of their collection of foraminifera—shelled microorganisms—from the St. Lawrence.[89] Letters between father and son tended to be more scientific and professional than familial and, while William tended to be preemptory in some matters, he was dependent upon his son in other ways. There is no reason to doubt the frank sincerity of his statement that "it would be very pleasant to me if you could be near enough to aid me and advise with me, and to confer on scientific matters."[90]

Dawson's mother also maintained a close relationship with George. During his adolescent recuperation, her concern for his health was constant. Later, when George left home, Margaret Dawson kept him informed of family plans and concerns and inquired after his welfare. A devout Christian, she constantly encouraged him to aspire to the faith she so strongly experienced. On George's receiving his honorary degree from Princeton in 1877, his mother offered sincere congratulations but insisted that George's life would not be full "until you have sought & obtained the *highest* degree—the one which *completes* our nature as well as sanctifies our powers & that you know is the *gift* of God through faith in our Substitute."[91] George's mother, however, was not nearly so persistent as his father in urging George to accept fully the faith of revealed Christianity.

Always a man of unwavering Presbyterian convictions, William Dawson never hesitated to advise his son about his spiritual path. The elder Dawson's Christianity permeated his own life and scholarship and he was most anxious that George nurture his religious beliefs. In the family home, Bible-reading and prayer were daily routine. Active participation in the Presbyterian church was another feature of Dawson family life. If George was away from the family for extended stretches of time, his father worried about his son's spiritual growth. When George was spending the winter of 1875-76 in Victoria, for example, his father wrote that he

88. J. W. Dawson to G. M. Dawson, 16 June 1876.

89. The results became his first scientific publication, "On Foraminifera from the Gulf and River St. Lawrence," *Canadian Naturalist* n.s. 5 (1870): 172-80.

90. J. W. Dawson to G. M. Dawson, 4 May 1876.

91. Margaret Dawson to G. M. Dawson, 28 July 1877.

would "be glad to know . . . what churches or other means of religious improvement there are in Victoria."[92] While George, as an adult, was never able openly to espouse the orthodox, evangelical Christianity of his father and mother, he was sensitive to and aware of religious questions and sought answers to the challenges provoked by his parents' beliefs. Even if he could not accept his father's worldview, he always held the elder Dawson in deep respect.

Unlike his parents and such siblings as Anna and William, George never experienced the certainty or comfort of Christianity. He attended church with fair regularity, but he was skeptical and his spiritual concepts remained much more tentative. In Dawson's view, "must there not be some fundamental Connecting unity of purpose & single idea, of which we can balance part against part but of which we Cannot integrate the whole, of which we are a part Concious & and which is God."[93] Dawson acknowledged that a creator, whom he termed God, was behind the universe, but he himself was alienated from that creative force. To Dawson:

> when alone I turn
> To where the lights of heaven burn
> My lips refuse to utter prayer.[94]

Given the upbringing provided by his family, he knew how he ought to think and believe, but he was unable to accept Christ or even believe in the Christian God.

Dawson was much more able to envision a spiritual realm, even a God, in the natural world. In the tranquil yet ever-changing reality of the physical universe, Dawson saw the orderly expression of divine creativity. His most moving poems are those extolling the majesty and peace of the wilderness and natural phenomena.[95]

92. J. W. Dawson to G. M. Dawson, 29 November 1875.

93. Dawson, untitled essay.

94. Dawson, untitled poem.

95. See, for example, Dawson, "The South Wind," "Skeena River," and "Indian Summer." Dawson's poetry was private and never meant for publication. The poems appear to have been the products of reflective moments, written purely for self-expression and seldom revised or polished. A few were published posthumously by J. B. Harrington in his obituary of Dawson, *McGill University Magazine* 1 (December 1901): 123-33, reprinted in *Transactions of the Royal Society of Canada* 8 (1902), sec. IV, 183-201.

Morris Zaslow judged that Dawson was "probably the best of the several poets in the Survey's history," but, like other survey men, his importance rests upon his scientific contributions. Upon those, too, Zaslow gives a judgement which cannot be improved. "The acid test of any geologist," he writes,

> is how well his work will stand up when it is re-examined later on the ground by a geologist equipped with new tools and informed by new scientific knowledge. Dawson meets this test better than any man of his generation. Those who have followed his paths and examined his notes and observations continually stand amazed at how rarely he reached an incorrect conclusion, how precise and acute were his powers of observation, literally overlooking nothing; also how much territory the little man covered in a single day, week or season. His powers of observation were matched by a keen intelligence; his generalizations showed the rare clarity, imagination, and originality of his mind. His ability to form sound and lasting general conclusions from a few reconnaissance observations and distant scannings was unique.[96]

EDITORIAL PROCEDURES

This edition of George Dawson's journals, family letters, and poetry reproduces in chronological order and with as few exceptions as possible his manuscripts as written in the field. The personal journals are reposited in the Rare Book and Special Collections Department of the McLennan Library, McGill University. They are small bound volumes written in pen and, when first read by the editors, were still stored in the metal trunk owned by Dawson. To fill one gap, during a period in which Dawson did not keep a personal diary, we have used a field notebook from the Geological Survey of Canada records (RG 45), which are in the Public Archives of Canada. The letters are part of the Dawson Family Papers (MG 1022) in the McGill University Archives. Most of the poetry is from the same collection, though some is drawn from the Dawson material in the Rare Book and Special Collections Department.

We have chosen to restrict the selection of letters to those written by Dawson to members of his family. A search of professional letters in various repositories led to the conclusion that these were too routine to be of

96. Zaslow, *Reading the Rocks*, 112.

great value. Many which might have been of greater interest, such as those written to A. R. C. Selwyn, for example, are no longer extant. Where we have found poetry that could reasonably be dated to the period, we have included it. Letters and poetry have been inserted into the journal entries at the most appropriate dates.

Dawson's manuscripts are reproduced as faithfully as print allows. This was our goal and, though some readers may find the seemingly capricious capitalization, his odd misspellings, or his occasionally incomplete punctuation irritating, we felt certain that most would adjust to it and prefer this to the editors making "silent corrections" or peppering the text with intrusive [*sic*]s. Capitalization, then, reflects Dawson's hand (though it must be realized that this is sometimes the editors' subjective decision). Abbreviations have been neither regularized nor spelled out. Errors, though sometimes commented upon in a note, are not corrected. We have shown words or groups of words which he added as afterthoughts or corrections and shown where he has crossed out words, even supplying the excisions where they remain legible. We have done this, however, only when they are a whole word or longer, not when it involved the writing over or crossing out of letters within a single word. Headings (place and date), salutations, closings (routinely "Your loving son" and similar endings), and his signature have been omitted from the letters. An editorial comment notes the recipient and the place and date of the letter.

Dawson usually kept his day-by-day journal entries on the right hand page, reserving the left page for thematic comments on such subjects as ethnology or geology. In the present edition, this left-page material is indicated by [verso] and [end verso] and placed as appropriately as possible.

Items are, as a general rule, annotated only at their first mention in the text. In the case of people, however, we have flagged second and subsequent mentions with an asterisk, indicating that the person has already been annotated but may be found in the biographical directory. This directory, which duplicates rather than supplements information in the textual annotations, is included for the convenience of the reader; it is not intended as a substitute for indexed entries.

The following editorial symbols have been used:

Blank space in manuscript	[blank]
Material cancelled in manuscript	⟨......⟩
Material inserted in manuscript	{......}
Illegible reading	[......]
Conjectural reading	[conjecture?]
Editorial comment	[comment]
Person in biographical directory	name*

ACKNOWLEDGEMENTS

In preparing these manuscripts for publication the editors have relied upon the expertise of a large number of people. Special thanks must be given to W. H. Mathews whose knowledge of British Columbia geology contributed enormously to our understanding of Dawson's geological comments. We are also indebted for their expert assistance to Nancy J. Turner and Robert Ogilvie for advice on botany and ethnobotany; Don E. McAllister for fish; Ralph Maud and Randy Bouchard for folklore; Susan Pyenson for J. W. Dawson; Ingrid Birker for palaeontology; Arnoud H. Stryd, John G. Foster, and Grant Keddie for archaeology; Dawson's grandniece, Mrs. Anne V. Byers, R. Garth Walker, and David Mattison for biography. Al and Irene Whitney, aboard *The Darwin Sound II*, were graciously helpful with the marine topography of Moresby Island. We owe a deep obligation to the staff of the McGill University Archives, especially Rob Michel, and of the Rare Books and Special Collections Department of the McLennan Library, McGill University. Specialized information was provided by the Kamloops Museum; the Vernon Museum and Archives; the Provincial Archives of British Columbia, especially the Map Division; and the Public Archives of Canada, especially its Federal Records Division and the National Photography Collection. Other institutions who assisted were the Missouri Botanical Garden; the Royal School of Mines; the Canadian Museum of Civilization Library; the McCord Museum, especially Conrad Graham; the College Archives of the Imperial College of Science and Technology, London; the New Westminster Public Library, and the Cariboo/Chilcotin Historical Society. A number of Simon Fraser University students assisted in the project, including Don Dale, Shannon Steele, Karen Sanger, Beth Rheumer, Michelle Le Grange, Stephen Gray, Diane Dupuis, Todd Owen, Sheliza Lalji, Fred Fuchs, Robin Anderson, and Rod Fowler. Barbara Barnett Lange, while with the Dean of Arts office at Simon Fraser University, was responsible for all of the textual keyboarding, and our indebtedness to her and to the Dean are enormous. Margaret Sharon of Simon Fraser's Computing Services provided continued assistance in various ways that eased the process of transforming the manuscript into an edited text.

Financial assistance came through the Simon Fraser University's Programs of Distinction, with additional university assistance from the President's Club, the Dean of Arts, the Publications Committee, and the Historical Records Institute. The Leon and Thea Koerner Foundation and the John S. Ewart Foundation also generously provided assistance.

Almost all of the manuscripts used here are the property of McGill University, whose generous allowance of permission for us to publish them made the endeavour possible.

Editorial preparation has been carried out as part of the continuing programme of the Historical Records Institute of Simon Fraser University.

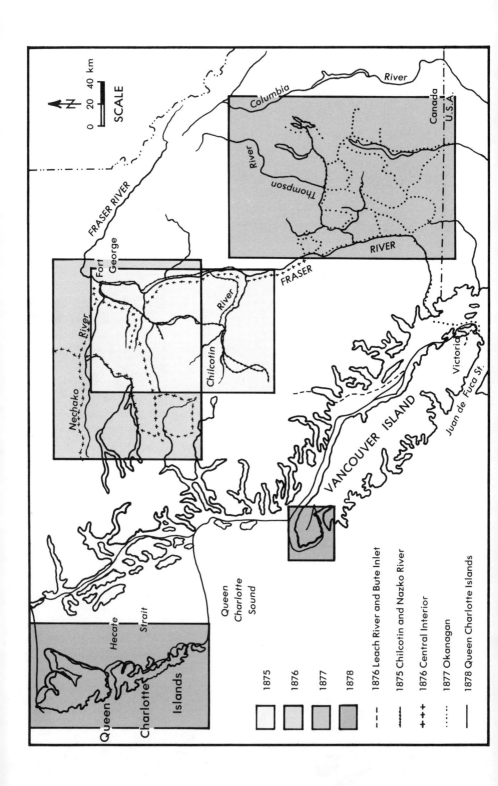

SCALE

0 20 40 km

Columbia River

Canada
U.S.A.

FRASER RIVER

River

Thompson River

FRASER RIVER

Fort George

Nechako River

Chilcotin River

VANCOUVER ISLAND

Victoria

Juan de Fuca St.

Queen Charlotte Sound

Queen Charlotte Islands

Hecate Strait

1875

1876

1877

1878

1876 Leach River and Bute Inlet

1875 Chilcotin and Nazko River

1876 Central Interior

1877 Okanagan

1878 Queen Charlotte Islands

Dawson's 1875 Route

10-12 AUGUST: Travelled by steamer to and from Nanaimo with James Richardson to survey Nanaimo area and meet with coal operators.

13 AUGUST: Travelled by the steamer *Enterprise* to New Westminster.

14-15 AUGUST: Travelled north by the river steamer *Royal City* to Yale.

15-18 AUGUST: Moved overland by coach to Boston Bar, Lytton, Ashcroft (Cornwall's),[1] and finally, Soda Creek.

19 AUGUST: Travelled by Fraser River steamer to Quesnel (Quesnelle).

20-22 AUGUST: Surveyed Quesnel area.

22 AUGUST: Back to Soda Creek by steamer.

23-24 AUGUST: Crossed Fraser and travelled by horse along west bank of river to Riske Creek.

25-27 AUGUST: Left Fraser and travelled overland to north side of Chilcotin River and Alexis Creek.

1. Current topographical names are given, with Dawson's most frequent usage in parentheses.

27-30 AUGUST: Crossed Chilcotin and moved along north bank of Chilanko River to the northeast end of Eagle Lake.

30 AUGUST-7 SEPTEMBER: Continued to southeast end of Cochin Lake, down the Homathko River, and along the east bank of Tatlayoko (Tallyoco) Lake to its southern end.

7-8 SEPTEMBER: Travelled back north along same route to Cochin Lake, and then northeast along new route to Patterson (Peterson) Lake.

8-11 SEPTEMBER: Travelled on to north shore of Tatla Lake.

11-15 SEPTEMBER: Travelled north at Chilanko Forks to Puntzi Lake, northeast to Chilcotin (Chinicut) Lake, and on to the Nazko River.

15-24 SEPTEMBER: Slowly followed the east bank of Nazko River to Marmot Lake.

24-29 SEPTEMBER: Travelled seven miles west on Kluskus Lakes Trail and then returned to route north along Nazko River to its junction with West Road (Blackwater) River.

29 SEPTEMBER-1 OCTOBER: Moved east down West Road River to Blackwater Canyon and Blackwater Depot.

1-11 OCTOBER: Held up at Blackwater Depot awaiting pack-train from Quesnel; travelled up West Road River for four miles, and then down valley for another ten miles on 8 October.

11-14 OCTOBER: Northeast to Punchaw Lake, ascending Mount Baldy Hughes (Ts-whuz Mountain) on route, and north to Prince (Fort) George.

14-18 OCTOBER: At Prince George, writing up notes and surveying the vicinity.

18-20 OCTOBER: Travelled from Prince George to Quesnel in boat and dugout canoe.

20–24 OCTOBER: Awaiting steamer at Quesnel.

24–25 OCTOBER: South by river steamer to Soda Creek.

25–28 OCTOBER: Travelled by stage to 100 Mile House (Bridge Creek), Clinton, Lytton, and Yale.

29 OCTOBER: By steamer to New Westminster and Victoria.

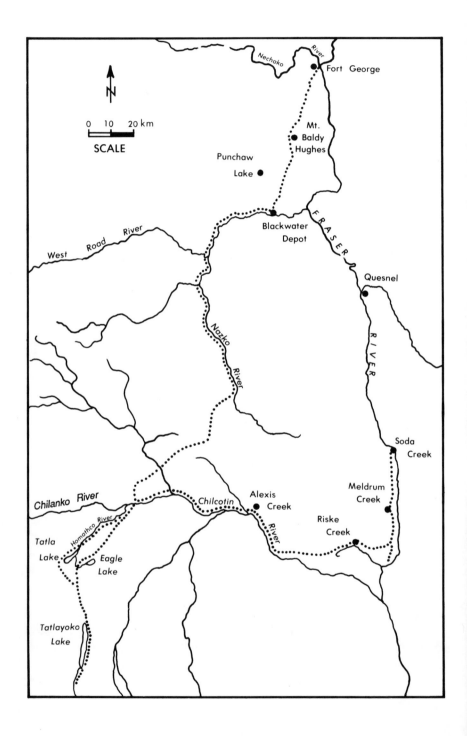

Dawson's 1876 Route

8-23 APRIL: Field trip to the Leech River and return.

1-16 MAY: Field trip to Bute Inlet. Left Victoria by steamer to Departure Bay, Stuart Island, and up Bute Inlet to Waddington Harbour. On return stopped at Marina Island, Drews Harbour, Ballenas Islands, Ganges and Victoria.

19-26 MAY: Travelled by steamer *Enterprise* to New Westminster. Continued on river steamer up the Fraser River to Yale, and then by stagecoach via the Cariboo Road to Lytton, Clinton, 150 Mile House and Soda Creek, where the journey then continued by steamer to Quesnel (Quesnelle).[1] Travelled with pack-train along the Telegraph Trail from Quesnel to Blackwater Bridge over the West Road (Blackwater) River. Then travelled west along the Bella Coola Trail following West Road River. Camped at Suscha Lake.

3-8 JUNE: Side trip north along the Euchiniko (Is-cul-taes-li) River to Klunchatistli Lake. Then along Taiuk Creek to Chutanli (Choo-tan-li) Lake. Turned southward towards Suscha Lake and then to the West Road River.

9-14 JUNE: Travelled up to Euchiniko Lakes, then to Kuyakuz Lake. Crossed West Road River to south bank at the mouth of Kluskus

---

1.   Current topographical names are given, with Dawson's most frequent usage in parentheses.

(Cluscus) Creek.

17 JUNE–2 JULY: Travelled west along West Road River and shore of Tsacha Lake, crossing river a third time, and moving west to Eliguk (Eliguck) Lake, to Gatcho (Gotcheo) Lake, and the Dean (Salmon) River to its junction with the Iltasyuko (Il-tas-you-co) River.

3–4 JULY: Returned north along the Iltasyuko as far as Sigutlat Lake.

7–12 JULY: Travelled down the Iltasyuko River to the crossing of the Dean River. Moved on to Tanya (Tany-a-bunkut) Lakes and then the Salmon House at the junction of the Tahyesco and Dean rivers. Then travelled back to Tanya Lakes.

13–23 JULY: Travelled south, parallel to the Tahyesco River, then along valley of the Tahyesco toward the Bella Coola River. Reaching height of land at the Bella Coola Valley, turned eastward across open country to the headwaters of Young (Cheddakulk) Creek, to the Tusulko (Too-cha-Koh) River and then down to the Dean River at Abuntlet Lake. Crossed Dean River, travelled northeastward around the east side of the Ilgachuz Range, and on to the West Road River.

24 JULY–6 AUGUST: Travelled west on Bella Coola Trail to Eliguk Lake, Gatcho Lake, Qualcho Lake, and on to a small lake east of Qualcho.

7–31 AUGUST: Moved northeast along the Entiako River from Gatcho Lake to Entiako (Eu-ta-ti-ta-chuck) Lake, then to the Nechako River. Travelled northeastward along the Nechako, cutting across country south of Fraser Lake to reach Telegraph Trail.

1–6 SEPTEMBER: Travelled north along the Telegraph Trail to Fort Fraser and camped for six days at the Fort.

7–20 SEPTEMBER: Across Fraser Lake, then via the Stellako River to François Lake. Moved along the north shore of François Lake to its western end, proceeding five miles up the Nadina (Nadinako) River. Returned along the south shore of François Lake to Fort Fraser.

21–23 SEPTEMBER: At Fort Fraser.

24–28 SEPTEMBER: Travelled to Sowchea (Sowchee) Bay on Stuart Lake, then canoed across Stuart Lake to Fort St. James. Excursion from Fort

St. James to Mount Pope, back to Sowchee, and then returned to Fort Fraser.

29 SEPTEMBER–1 OCTOBER: At Fort Fraser.

2–5 OCTOBER: Travelled down the Nechako River to Prince George.

6–9 OCTOBER: At Prince George.

10–20 OCTOBER: Travelled westward to the junction of the Chilako (Mud) and Nechako rivers. Then moved southward along the Chilako River towards the Blackwater Bridge, and on to Quesnel.

21 OCTOBER–11 NOVEMBER: Excursion to the Cariboo, then on to Kamloops, the Nicola Valley and back to Victoria.

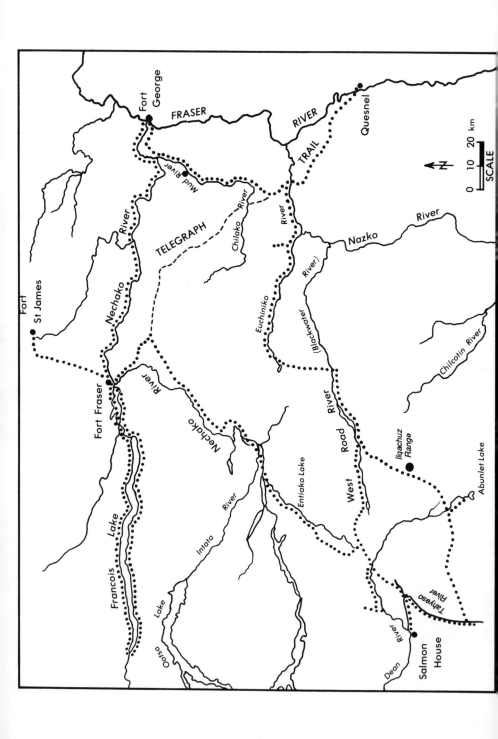

I

1875–1876

[Dawson left Montreal by train on 19 July 1875, for San Francisco, where he caught a boat northward. He arrived in Victoria on 4 August 1875. On the first page of the journal beginning 19 August 1875, Dawson mentions a "small blk note bk marked 1" which covers the period 19 July to 10 August 1875. This volume, however, is not reposited with either the personal diaries or the field notebooks and presumably has been lost.]

G. M. Dawson to Margaret Dawson,[1] *6 August 1875, Victoria*

Here I am at last at my first destination, staying at the St George's Hotel, a small house but a remarkably comfortable one, quiet & Clean, & with a very good table. There are larger hotels here, but I do not think quite equal to this one. Here I chanced to alight & I am very well pleased

---

1. Margaret Ann Young (Mercer) Dawson, (1830–1913), was the youngest of four daughters born to a prominent Edinburgh family. Over the strenuous objections of her parents, Margaret married J. W. Dawson on 19 March 1847 and left her native Scotland for life in British North America. Although possessing a retiring nature, Margaret Dawson fulfilled admirably the arduous role of university principal's wife and mother to five children. Deeply religious, Margaret sought to inculcate Christian values and instill a Christian faith in all her children. For an intimate picture of Margaret Dawson, see Clare Margaret Harrington, "Grandmother from Writings of Clare Margaret Harrington," edited and added to by Lois S. Winslow-Spragge, typescript, Dawson Family Papers, McGill University Archives, Montreal (MUA).

to remain for the few days before 'moving on'. I find Mr Richardson[2] here with full information about the best ways of doing things & getting about; which will save much trouble. I have also seen Mr Marcus Smith[3] of the Pacific Ry Surveys,[4] & he seems willing to do all he Can, & thinks the time of My arrival fortunate with regard to the position of his parties. Their pack trains are not at present very busy, & I think I may arrange to Start from here with one man who has been Cook for Mr Richardson,* & is highly recomended, & go right up the Frazer without other men, or trouble of carrying Supplies, nearly to Ft George.[5] There I hope to get a small organized pack-train from the C.P. Ry, & also to draw supplies from their depôts there now established. All this will simplify things very much. I am only Sorry that the delay arising from our Slow passage here from San Francisco prevented me from Starting this Morning. Not being able to get ready in time involves the loss of a week, as the boat to New Westminster, & Stages up the Frazer only connect on Fridays. The week will not be altogether lost, as I Can see all the maps &c. here, & also something of the Surroundings of this place, but it is a bother to be staying at a hotel with nothing particular or definite to do.

2. James Richardson (1810–83) was a geologist with the Geological Survey of Canada for some thirty-six years. Richardson came to North America early in life and farmed in Beauharnois County, Lower Canada, until he joined the geological survey in 1846 at the urging of Sir William Logan. Richardson's expeditions to British Columbia, conducted every season from 1871 to 1875, formed the basis of his pioneering work on British Columbia coal fields. See especially his "Report on the Coal Fields of Nanaimo, Comox, Cowichen, Burrard Inlet and Sooke, British Columbia," in Geological Survey of Canada, *Report of Progress for 1876–77* (1878), 160–92.

3. Marcus Smith (1815–1904) was the engineer-in-charge of the Canadian Pacific Railway Surveys (CPRS) in British Columbia. An outspoken champion of a Pine River-Bute Inlet route, Smith was often embroiled in conflict with those advocating other routes. Later in 1876, when he became chief engineer for the survey after Sandford Fleming left for England for two years, Smith continued to stir up controversy by his unrelenting advocacy of the Bute Inlet route. In spite of his strenuous efforts, however, the Canadian government eventually chose an alternate route through the Fraser Canyon to Burrard Inlet.

4. Dawson's reference is to the surveys of the Canadian Pacific Railway, headed by Sandford Fleming. During the 1870's, the government expended vast sums of money and energy choosing a British Columbia route and western terminus for the new railway. During the 1875 and 1876 seasons, Dawson travelled with various survey parties as they traversed north and central British Columbia, seeking alternatives for the railway. For documentation of the work during 1875–76, see Sandford Fleming, *Report on Surveys and Preliminary Operations on the Canadian Pacific Railway up to January 1877* (Ottawa: MacLean, Rogers & Co., 1877).

5. Now Prince George, at the confluence of the Fraser and Nechako rivers, Fort George was a North West Company fort built in 1807 and later taken over by the Hudson's Bay Company in the merger of 1821.

Mr Smith* received a letter lately from Mr Selwyn[6] from Ft McLeod,[7] which is on the head waters of the Peace & by travelled route I suppose about one hundred miles north of Ft George. If I remember rightly the letter was dated June 30. Mr. S. appeared well satisfied with his progress & said he hoped to get down Some time in September. In which hope however Mr Smith* Seems to think he will be disappointed.[8] Mrs Selwyn has no doubt received letters of Same date {long} before this. Victoria is a pretty little place with a population I suppose about twice that of Pictou N.S. but not built at all, in the style of that place, being much more diffuse, with Moderately wide streets generally well laid out & nearly at right angles. The buildings are chiefly of wood though with Some of brick, & a few very neat residences &c. & Some respectable churches & other public buildings. Most of the Streets have good plank-walks, & the Shops & houses are not high & of a rather miscellaneous style of Archticure. The former have very often a way of throwing out a projecting roof or veranda which is supported by light pillars or posts & stretches across the side walk. Business here appears to take its time, getting up not too early in the morning, & not absolutely rushing, or hurrying itself, but still going on. I am assured however that this is the dullest season of the year. The harbour is Small but well inclosed, & the outskirts of the town are very pretty & spread across several arms or narrow inlets running up in various directions. The country is all very dry at present, the roads dusty, & the grass generally brown or brownish, & the people do not expect much rain till September. There is little farming land in this {immediate} vicinity, but what there is is good, & there Are some very pretty gardens. The rock has a way of cropping up here there & everywhere, breaking up the surface generally. The woods seem to be very beautiful, & there are extensive areas in the vicinity of the town not thickly wooded but dotted with

6. Alfred Richard Cecil Selwyn (1824–1902) was director of the Geological Survey of Canada from 1869 to 1895, when Dawson assumed the position upon Selwyn's retirement. It was under Selwyn's direction that Dawson and his contemporaries began the immense task of surveying the western portion of British North America. See Morris Zaslow, *Reading the Rocks: The Story of the Geological Survey of Canada 1842–1972* (Toronto: Macmillan Company of Canada, with the Department of Energy, Mines and Resources and Information Canada, 1975), 105–22. Selwyn made several western expeditions, including this one in 1875, documented in his "Report on Exploration in British Columbia," in Geological Survey of Canada, *Report of Progress for 1875–76* (1877), 28–86. For biographical details, see H. M. Ami, "Sketch of the Life and Work of the Late Dr. A. R. C. Selwyn . . . ," *American Geologist* 31 (1903): 1–21.

7. Built under orders from Simon Fraser in 1805, on the west side of McLeod Lake, the fort was the first permanent post erected in British territory west of the Rocky Mountains.

8. Selwyn reached Fort George only in October, where Dawson met him on 16 October.

oaks & pines[9] & other trees, Singly or in small groves. The trees have an English way of growing, I hardly Know how else to explain it, but they seem to go in more for horizontal & gnarly branches.

The scenery visible from various points about here is Simply magnificent. Southward the broken Olympia Mts.[10] are in full view across the straits, with streaks & patches of Snow on their summits. Westward at a great distance Mt. Baker[11] rises like a great snowy dome & all around are islands, with pine clad or otherwise wooded hills, & the Sea.

I will perhaps be able to pick up some more points about the place before writing again, & if not this time I suppose I will have abundant opportunity to make myself acquainted with it afterwards.

I am writing to Anna[12] also by this mail & addressing to Métis.[13]

G. M. Dawson to Anna Dawson, 6 August 1875, Victoria

Your letter from Metis dated July 21 arrived today, & as a mail goes out from here tomorrow I sit down to report progress. I arrived here on Wednesday evening (day before yesterday) & have seen a little of the place, & hope to get off next week. The voyage from San Francisco was rather tedious, the distance being about 720 miles, & the steamer a very slow one. We had quite a number of passengers, making Cabin & steerage about ninety — but little freight. On leaving San Francisco we passes through the 'Golden Gate' at once out on the Pacific ocean — which though moderately pacific yet favoured us with a long unpleasant swell. This continued increasing & for the first two days we had quite a little tossing with some rather cold wind & overcast dull weather. All hands were at once prostrated with Sea sickness. At least I mean all the ladies, some gentlemen remaining ⟨....⟩ on deck. Personally I managed to Keep

9.   The "Oaks" were Garry oaks, *Quercus garryana* Dougl.; and the "pines" were probably a reference to evergreen trees generally.

10. The Olympic Mountains in Washington Territory.

11. Dawson has his directions confused since Mount Baker is on the mainland, east of Victoria.

12. Anna Lois (Dawson) Harrington (1851-1917), Dawson's oldest sister, was also his closest friend and confidant. Even after her marriage to Bernard Harrington in 1876, Anna continued to share an intimate and rich relationship with George. They corresponded regularly and George recurringly offered assistance to his sometimes beleaguered sister, who had nine children. Anna remained in Montreal for her entire adult life and eventually died of a lung tumour. See also Anna Harrington, "Early Life at McGill by a Professor's Wife—1867-1907," ed. Lois Winslow-Spragge, typescript, Dawson Family Papers, MUA.

13. At Métis Beach, ten kilometres from Mont-Joli, Quebec, on the St. Lawrence River where Dawson's parents built their summer home, "Birkenshaw," which still stands.

pretty well though with occasional unpleasant qualms. Our trip was quite a voyage of discovery, as neither the ship nor any of the officers had ever been to Vancouver before. The Pacific Mail Coy. to whose line the Salvador belongs have only just Commenced running Steamers here, having received the contract for carrying the Mails. Most of their vessels are on the Japan & Australian trades & {some} also run S. to Panama. The Captain a big burly, rough old goose, thinking discretion &c. — bore quite away from the coast, & after loosing sight of the country near Frisco. we never rightly saw it again till the day we reached Victoria. Times on board were not particularly lively as the passenger list was not a remarkably Select one. The food was very good, however, & what with reading a little, walking about the deck a great deal, & sleeping when these resources failed the time passed away. One morning I passed a great part of in the fruitless endeavour to fish up from the Surface of the briny Some peculiar Animals with which it was covered. The Animals were of the Jelly-fish nature, & looked like little 'portuguese men of war', having Some sort of floating body & a sort of hemispherical Crest rising up out of the water. In size they seemed to be from about 2 ½ to 3 inches long & downwards, & as I never could see them very plainly they may have been *velellas* instead of *porpitas*[14] for all I can tell. We Sailed through them for about two & a half days. That is to Say for that time you could seldom look overboard without seeing some of them. Often the water was quite dotted with them, & Sometimes we would come across large patches of them nearly in contact. The Captain expressed his belief that there must be 'fourteen million' of them. We Set to work to Catch them in a pail tied to a rope — I say we for Several of the passengers enlisted in the attempt — At one end of the rope was an ordinary wooden pail, at the other end a Small canvas bucket used for taking the temperature of the water. The experimenter used whichever of these he thought most hopeful, but we were going too fast, & I had now tow-net at hand, & even if I had had I do not think I could have used it. When we had quite Satisfied ourselves we could not do it we left the apparatus which was then Seized on by a hopeful foreigner — German I think — who within a few minutes Succeeded in loosing the whole affair overboard, & soon afterward the boy who washed up the deck cabins &c. was to be Seen anxiously enquiring in all directions for his bucket.

The Crew of the Steamer, I should tell you were chiefly chinese, even to the 'Bosun', & so also were the waiters. They appeared remarkably handy & neat, & extremely biddable, not grumbling, & seeming to find a pleasure

---

14. Could have been either the by-the-wind sailor, *Velella velella* (L.); or blue buttons, *Porpita linneana* Lesson.

was a sort of Chinese flavour reminding in a distant way of opium, about the dishes.

I shall not be able to write to William[15] this time, & fact I Suppose it will barely be worth while writing again to any English or Scotch address. If you write please let him Know I am 'all right'. Also let me hear from him when you Can. I think it likely that where I am going on the Frazer River, I will be in contact with Surveying parties, & they have some sort of Mail communication weekly or fortnightly. However it takes a long time to get letters brought round even this far, as you may judge from the date of receipt of your own.

I am writing to Mother also by this Mail & addressing to Montreal, supposing that she will have got back there from Detroit before this arrives.

G.M. Dawson to John William Dawson,[16] 9 August 1875, Victoria

15. William Bell Dawson (1854-1944), Dawson's brother, also became a prominent scientist, even though overshadowed for many years by George and his father. William graduated from McGill University in 1874 with his Bachelor of Arts, obtained a bachelor's degree in applied science the year after, then went to Paris to attend the prestigious Ecole des Ponts et Chaussées. Following a three-year course, William returned to Canada and, after he unsuccessfully applied for several positions, went into private engineering practice. In 1882, he joined the Dominion Bridge Company as an engineer and stayed until 1884 when he took a position as assistant engineer for the Canadian Pacific Railway Company. William spent ten years with the firm designing bridges for the many new lines being constructed. He took up, in 1884, what he considered his main professional undertaking: director of the Dominion Survey of Tides and Currents. For thirty years, until his retirement in 1924, he recorded and mapped tides and currents in the harbours and on the major steamship routes of the Canadian coasts. Upon retiring, he spent much energy writing articles and tracts proving the harmony of science with religion, a task not unlike that earlier done by his father. William married Florence Jane Mary Elliott (1864?-1945) and the couple had three sons and a daughter. See William Bell Dawson's obituary in the *Montreal Gazette*, 22 May 1944.

16. Dawson's father, Sir John William Dawson (1820-99) was one of the most prominent figures in nineteenth-century Canadian intellectual and scientific life. After studies at Edinburgh University in the 1840's, Sir William was appointed Nova Scotia's first superintendent of education by Joseph Howe. Serving for three years, he resigned in 1853 when seeking a position at Edinburgh University. Though unsuccessful in that pursuit, Sir William was unexpectedly offered the principalship of McGill in 1855. For some forty years, until his retirement in 1893, Sir William held the principal's position at McGill; under his leadership that institution emerged as a reputable centre for teaching and research. He was made a K.C.M.G. in 1884. Sir William was always active in a wide variety of intellectual activities. He published the standard text on the geology of the Maritime Provinces in 1855, wrote countless other articles on geological and palaeontological topics, and produced several volumes exploring the relationship between religion and science. Throughout his career, Sir William was in the centre of intellectual controversy. A staunch theological conservative, he was embroiled in bitter debate by his denunciation of Darwin's evolutionary theories, and long after most of his geological contemporaries had abandoned the "floating ice" theory of glaciation, Sir William unswervingly held onto the concept. For further discussion of Sir William's scientific and intellectual work, see Charles F. O'Brien, *Sir William Dawson: A Life in*

I have arranged to start tomorrow morning for Nanaimo with the intention of spending Wednesday there, & going over the ground with Mr Richardson*. I thought it worth while to do so that I might pick up the thread of his work there with him on the spot to explain. On Friday Morning I start for the Frazer R. Going by steamer to Yale & thence Northward by Stage to Soda Creek. There I hope to find a small pack train of the C.P.Ry. with which I Shall go westward to the Cascade Mts,[17] & then North Eastward to the Junction of the Frazer & Blackwater Rivers. Thence if time serves on to Ft George — Making use all the way of the Ry. depôts & Camps; & I hope covering a considerable stretch of ground tranverse to the general run of the formations, which would be at other times a difficult country to penetrate. There are rumours of drift lignite[18] in one part of the region — whatever that may amount to — & I hear of one richly fossiliferous Creek — whatever that may turn out to be.

I hope the editing of the remainder of that report[19] has not been a cause of much trouble to you. I have often reproached myself for leaving it to occupy a part of your Summer holiday.

I could not get a Remington gun of the Kind wanted either in San Francisco or here, & so finally have bought an English breech-loader which though costing considerably more is a better arm.

When you get back to Montreal finally, I should be much obliged if Sometime when you see Mr Grant[20] you would ask him to make my salary payable here ⟨at the⟩ to the end of September, that I may be able to Get some money when I come down   This in Case I do not get time to write to him myself

Science and Religion (Philadelphia: American Philosophical Society, 1971); A. B. McKillop, *A Disciplined Intelligence: Critical Inquiry and Canadian Thought in the Victorian Era* (Montreal: McGill-Queen's University Press, 1979), esp. 93-134; and Carl Berger, *Science, God, and Nature in Victorian Canada* (Toronto: University of Toronto Press, 1983), 38-65. Sir William's autobiography was edited by Rankine Dawson and published as the rather insipid volume, *Fifty Years of Work in Canada: Scientific and Educational,* ed. Rankine Dawson (London: Ballantyne, Hanson & Co., 1901). Additional biographical data is found in the fine summary by Henry M. Ami, "Sir John William Dawson: A Brief Biographical Sketch," *American Geologist* 26 (1900): 1-48, which also includes a bibliography of Sir John William Dawson's writings.

17. Dawson recurringly refers to the Coast Mountains as the "Cascades."

18. A brown, low-grade coal.

19. Probably Dawson's report on his boundary commission findings, later published as G. M. Dawson, *Report on the Geology and Resources of the Region in the Vicinity of the Forty-Ninth Parallel . . .* (Montreal: Dawson Brothers, 1875).

20. G. R. Grant, a clerk with the Geological Survey of Canada.

[The small journal in which Dawson begins his 1875 entries for British Columbia covers the period from 10 August to 18 August 1875; it also contains a miscellany of rough geological notes, expense lists, and sketches that have been omitted in the present edition.]

Tuesday Aug 10. 1875.

Left Victoria at 7 a.m. with Mr Richardson* for Nanaimo Arrived at wharf Just in time to Catch steamer which left a few minutes before her time. Followed the features of the Coast by the maps & Mr Rs verbal description of the rocks. The scenery really very fine in passing up through the archepeligo,[21] though the air somewhat too smokey to let it be seen to advantage. Steamer calls at a number of little places by the way. Shores always bold & water deep & running up among the mountains in fjords & deep bays. The shores everywhere but where very rocky, covered with tall straight pines, & in some places with groves of *Arbutus Menziesii*[22] conspicuous from its bright bark. The height of the pine trees being underestimated causes that of the cliffs & mountains to be also under-rated. The rocks of the coal formation are in places much disturbed, & thrown into a number of rather sharp anticlinals & synclinals[23] parallel to the general line of the coast of the island. The rocks about the same with regard to texture as those of the true Carboniferous but with much conglomerate[24] in thick beds. Mr R's subsequent exploration shows that his divisions as at first made are not so constant as he had thought, but that like the coal itself the Other beds are thicker & thinner, Sandstones Sometimes replaced by conglomerates &c. In [blank] bay Mr R. believes he has found Anthracite in connection with crystalline micaceous & dioritic rocks[25] underlying the Coal series. The Seam seen not workable however. on arriving at Nanaimo went up to a hotel & had supper, but found the arrangements so uncomfortable that came back to the Steamer for a bed.

---

21. Gulf Islands.

22. The madrona or arbutus, *Arbutus menziesii* Pursh. The thin, smooth bark peels in papery flakes and strips revealing a yellowish-green surface which soon reddens.

23. "Anticlinals" are strata folded convexly; "synclinals" are strata folded concavely.

24. A sedimentary rock which is composed of a significant amount of rounded pebbles and boulders.

25. The "micaceous" rocks contain the mineral mica; "dioritic" rocks are plutonic, igneous rocks cooled and hardened deep within the earth's crust.

Aug. 11. Breakfast in town & then went up to see the Vancouver Coy's mine[26] near here. Saw Mr Bates[27] & Mr Brydon,[28] the latter Showing us about the surface workings. Mr McKay[29] has come out to test the property of the Coy. with the diamond drill & now waits arrival of machinery. Mr Brydon* explained the Character of the seam. It appears that in following the bed its dip[30] increases, becomes vertical, — almost overturned. This part worked out by stoping[31] like a vein, but workings now carried on along the strike chiefly. Faults have occurred & in Some cases are reversed. [*Illus.*] The character of the measures[32] above & below the main seam are so unconstant & yet similar that can hardly judge which way the throw[33] on coming to the fault. Can only judge by the character of the break of the coal bed, or by the fact that the conglomerates above & below are more or less calcareous or ferrofirous.[34] Engines old & have been in use 20 years; Cars brought up the slope by wire rope wound on simple drums. Average output per man 2 ½ tons. Small streaks of shale seam apt

26. The Vancouver Coal Mining and Land Company's main colliery, the Old Douglas Mine, was located on the Douglas Seam, near the centre of Nanaimo. Incorporated in 1862 with the purchase of Hudson's Bay Company lands, the company was a joint stock company controlled by British interests. See Daniel Thomas Gallacher, "Men, Money, Machines: Studies Comparing Colliery Operations and Factors of Production in British Columbia's Coal Industry to 1891," (Ph.D. diss., University of British Columbia, 1979), 84-133.

27. Mark Bate (1837-1927) was manager of the Vancouver Coal Mining and Land Company operations in Nanaimo from 1869 to 1884. He was also elected Nanaimo's first mayor in 1875. For a more extended discussion of Bate and other Nanaimo colliery proprietors, see Daniel T. Gallacher, "Early Coal Personalities: Some Neglected British Columbians," *British Columbia Historical News* 12, no. 2 (February 1979): 5-8.

28. John Bryden (1831-1915) was mines manager for the Vancouver Coal Mining and Land Company. Bryden disagreed with Mark Bate's lenient labour policies and management practices and later left the company to work for his father-in-law, Robert Dunsmuir. Rising to the position of managing partner in the Dunsmuir organization, Bryden became one of the wealthiest men in British Columbia.

29. The Vancouver Coal Company brought McKay out to search for fresh seams with the aid of a diamond drill manufactured by Beaumont and Appleby. The process and progress is described in the *Victoria Daily British Colonist*, 16 October 1875, and in *Guide to the Province of British Columbia for 1877-8* (Victoria: T. N. Hibben, 1877), 99-100.

30. The angle by which a stratum or bed deviates from the horizontal. That angle is measured in a plane perpendicular to the strike, which describes the general trend or run of the beds.

31. A method of extracting ore from a vertical or steeply dipping vein by driving tunnels along the strike of a vein and extracting the ore from above and below the tunnel.

32. Probably used here as a synonym for "beds" of strata.

33. The measure of vertical displacement between the upthrown and downthrown sides of a fault.

34. "Calcareous" or containing calcium; "ferrofirous" or ferriferous, iron-bearing.

to appear in the coal. Saw two tree trunks in the office obtained in shale above a seam of irregular thickness. They may have been of pine but are curiously ribbed. Interesting as showing exactly how much coal a tree trunk will make. one measured where largest 12 by 3 ½ inches the other 14 x 3 inches. & originally more than 12 feet found. [*Illus.*]

Afternoon walked to Departure Bay (3 m) through the woods. Weather very close & warm. Saw the Dumps & wharf but did not go up to the mine.[35] Saw Mr Dunsmuir[36] & Egerton[37] proprietors & managers. Arrangements for shipping the coal imperfect. Men employed chiefly Chinese. Indians coal trimming[38] in the vessels hold at $2.50 Maude[39] Came in about 6 P.m. & after shipping some coal, & the blocks representing the thickness of the Seam returned to Nanaimo. Went down with her. Slept on board.

Aug 12. Steamer left at 7 am for Victoria & Arriving about 5.30 P.m. Saw Mr Sargison of Barnards express[40] & got from him a letter asking his agents up the Fraser to assist my by giving Credit, or cashing small checks. Mr Marcus Smith* who had been on the steamer to Nanaimo & returned

35. The Wellington Colliery of Dunsmuir, Diggle Limited, discovered in 1869 by Robert Dunsmuir, was in full production by 1875. For a discussion of the mine's early history see Gallacher, "Men, Money, Machines," 169–81.

36. Robert Dunsmuir (1825–89), British Columbia's most famous and controversial mine owner, came to Vancouver Island in 1851 under contract as a miner for the Hudson's Bay Company. In 1869 he discovered coal at Wellington, near Nanaimo, and by 1871 had a mine operating. Dunsmuir's operations grew rapidly until their production exceeded that of the older Vancouver Coal Mining and Land Company. Dunsmuir was a ruthless manager and his mines were continually plagued with labour unrest. See "Dunsmuir, Robert," *Dictionary of Canadian Biography*, 11: 290–94; and Paul M. Koroscil, "Robert Dunsmuir: A Portrait of a Western Capitalist," in *Canadian Frontier: Annual Number Three 1978*, ed. Gordon Stewart and Brian Antonson (New Westminster: Antonson Publishing, 1978), 15–20.

37. Captain F. W. Egerton was one of several naval officers who provided capital for Robert Dunsmuir's Wellington mines. As soon as the enterprise was established, Dunsmuir bought out the officers.

38. Storing coal so as to distribute the weight properly in the ship's hold.

39. Owned by J. S. Spratt and probably commanded by Captain Peter Holmes. See below, 20 December 1875.

40. George A. Sargison, accountant and partner, of F. J. Barnard & Company, founded by Francis Jones Barnard (1829–89). Born at Quebec City, Barnard travelled to the Fraser River goldfields, then, in 1861, established a mail service from Yale to Victoria, which became, after extending to the Cariboo, the British Columbia and Victoria Express Company and soon the major carrier of the mainland colony. In 1872, two of his drivers, Stephen Tingley and James Hamilton became partners in the F. J. Barnard & Company; in 1880, the British Columbia Express Company was incorporated with his son Frank and brother-in-law George Sargison. He served in the Legislative Council of British Columbia from 1867 to 1870 and as a member of Parliament for Yale from 1879 to 1887. See "Barnard, Francis," *Dictionary of Canadian Biography* 11: 50–51.

this evening gave me a letter to his Surveyors &c. to put me through. Mr Robsoson[41] also gave me a Circular letter to depôt men &c. & has telegraphed to have 3 pack animals & 2 riding horses at Soda Creek on my arrival. Got papers from Montreal but no letters.

Nanaimo has probably from 800 to 1000 inhabitants, miners, & tradesmen supplying them. Built on a Sloping hillside & straggling along to a considerable length. Saloons & billiard tables abundant, no good hotel accomodation. 'Streets' now extremely dusty, & weather much hotter than in Victoria from its more confined situation. Little arable land in the vicinity, though the whole country clothed with fine timber. A Mechanics institute, a couple of churches & a daily paper,[42] but not so much as a side walk in any part of the town. A stone bonded warehouse now in course of erection, being the first stone building of any pretension in the place. Close by a curious old wooden tower,[43] which constituted part of the defence of a Hudson's Bay pallisade. Chinamen abundant as everywhere along the coast. Washing & shop-Keeping, & doing surface work about the mines, or sometimes employed by the miners below as assistants.

Glaciation[44] northward among the Coal bearing series not Seen from

41. John Robson (1824–92) played a prominent role in the life of nineteenth-century British Columbia. From 1875 to 1879 he served as paymaster and purveyor to the CPRS. He founded *The British Columbian* newspaper in 1861, served in the provincial legislature and ministry, and in 1889 became premier.

42. The *Nanaimo Free Press*, founded by George Norris in 1874.

43. Dawson's reference is to the Bastion, erected by the Hudson's Bay Company in 1853 as a defence against possible Indian violence. For a brief description of the structure, see T. D. Sale, "The Last Original Bastion," in *Nanaimo Retrospective: The First Century*, ed. E. Blanche Norcross (Nanaimo: Nanaimo Historical Society, 1979), 22–25.

44. Dawson's theory of southern Vancouver Island glaciation is summarized in his statement that "there appears to be no escape from the conclusion that a glacier swept over the whole south-eastern peninsula of Vancouver Island at some time during the Glacial period; and on consideration of the physical features of the country it becomes apparent that the entire Straight of Georgia between the island and the mainland must have been filled with a great glacier" (George M. Dawson, "On the Superficial Geology of British Columbia," *Quarterly Journal of the Geological Society of London* 34 [1878]: 95). The glacial history of Victoria and southern Vancouver Island is documented in several studies. Comprehensive but dated coverage is provided in C. H. Clapp, *Geology of the Victoria and Saanich Map-areas, Vancouver Island, B.C.*, Geological Survey of Canada Memoir no. 36 (Ottawa: Government Printing Bureau, 1913), 107–21; and C. H. Clapp, *Sooke and Duncan Map-areas, Vancouver Island*, Geological Survey of Canada Memoir no. 96 (Ottawa: Government Printing Bureau, 1917), 339–55. Recent studies include W. H. Mathews, J. G. Fyles, and H. W. Nasmith, "Postglacial Crustal Movements in Southwestern British Columbia and Adjacent Washington State," *Canadian Journal of Earth Sciences* 7 (1970): 690–702; and John J. Clague, *Late Quaternary Geology and Geochronology of British Columbia: Part 2, Summary and Discussion of Radiocarbon-Dated Quaternary History*, Geological Survey of Canada

the Soft character of rocks. Coast near Victoria very heavily glaciated. Nothing more striking than the fact that the glaciation has evidently only partially succeeded in destroying previously existing irregularities of surface. Also the very determinate direction of grooving, & its evident production by *glacier* ice, which has in some places undercut vertical faces of rock. The Southward Side of all the hummocks comparatively, or quite, unaffected.

Friday Aug 13. Left at 8 am, with Reeves,[45] who is to act as Cook, for New Westminster in Steamer "Enterprise" Arrived in New Westminster about 4.30 P.m. Route lies for some distance northward as if to Nanaimo, thence westward through a narrow passage [blank] with high rocky shores.[46] Scenery very fine. Rocks of Islands Seen on either hand, conglomerates & Sandstones of Coal bearing series. Many islands S. & W. of Victoria show remains (sometimes extensive) of a terrace of Alluvial deposits answering to that along the Coast of V.I. near Beacon Hill & elsewhere. Even from a distance stratification is sometimes apparent. It is perhaps the Same terrace on which New Westminster is built (Get height) The latter where shown in cuttings on the Streets &c. appears to be formed of materials exactly like the Vancouver Island terraces.[47] Sands & argillaceous sands,[48] pale yellowish, often hard, containing many pebbles & Small boulders of all sorts of rocks. None of these evidently glaciated, but rather with the appearance of water worn pebbles. Also large boulders on the Surface. Both large & Small fragments of the whitish granite seen in drift[49] on V.I. here also represented

Paper no. 80–35 (Ottawa: Supply and Services Canada, 1981).

45. Nothing more can be found on Reeves, but see below, Dawson to Margaret Dawson, 5 September 1875.

46. Dawson again confused directions; he meant eastward through Active Pass, between Galiano and Mayne islands.

47. Dawson seems to be using the term "terrace" in a very broad sense as gently rolling land, underlain by unconsolidated material, now undercut by wave action. Beacon Hill Park, with a rolling, not flat, surface probably would not now be called a terrace, nor would New Westminster. The best example of an island northwest (not south and west) of Victoria, is James Island, underlain by well-bedded proglacial sand alluvial sediments exposed in a conspicuous sea cliff at its south end. This sand, mantled by glacial deposits with boulders, and by wave-washed beach deposits, has its equivalent in both the Victoria area and New Westminster. See J. J. Clague, "Quadra Sand and Its Relation to the Late Wisconsin Glaciation of Southwest British Columbia," *Canadian Journal of Earth Sciences* 13 (1976): 803–15. Thus, if Dawson was referring to the deposits beneath his "terrace," his comments were correct.

48. Largely composed of, or containing, clay-sized particles or clay minerals.

49. Unconsolidated sediment of glacial derivation.

Much low delta land about mouth of Frazer, with Shoal water off it. Foliage along the river borders very beautiful, spruce, Cedar, & poplar[50] of fine growth. Now 4 or 5 salmon tinning establishments[51] on the river. At present at work on second run of Salmon. chinese seem to do most of the labour. Told that 4 runs of salmon up this stream. The first of the best fish, the last of miserable lean creatures with hooked Jaws[52] in fact resembling spent fish.

Saturday Aug 14.

B. 9 a.m. 30.00.[53]

Left at 8 A.m. on Steamer 'Royal City' for Yale. The low Alluvial land seen near New Westminster extends some distance up the river but I am told does not contain much farming land. The prairie portions are liable to flood, & therefore unsuitable for raising grain, & the clearing of the wooded portions, covered with Such heavy pine &c. — can hardly yet be attempted. The valley narrows in about the Catholic Mission,[54] & above this point there is only a narrow belt of flat land between the river & the mountains, & even this in many places disappears. It would however be very difficult to get anything like a continuous section by following the river, as only points here & there, of rock, come out to the edge of the water, & the flat wooded land is nearly impenetrable. The chance for observation would probably be greater in following the road. The woods are not exclusively of pine, large areas of the lower ground being covered with poplar. These trees in many places have preserved a great uniformity in growth, ⟨ending⟩ fringing the river like a gigantic hedge. Mosquitoes still a little troublesome, & have been very bad this summer, on account of the overflow of so much land. Said that people even obliged to leave their farms or "ranches" for a time. The river is yet very high, & has been higher this year than ever Known before. Said to have been much Snow in

---

50. The "spruce" was the Sitka spruce, *Picea sitchensis* (Bong.) Carr.; "Cedar" the western red cedar, *Thuja plicata* Donn; and "poplar" black cottonwood, *Populus trichocarpa* Torr. & Gray.

51. By that time several canneries existed at the mouth of the Fraser River as the canning industry was emerging as a major commercial enterprise. For a discussion of the industry's early development, see Duncan A. Stacey, *Sockeye and Tinplate: Technological Change in the Fraser River Canning Industry 1871-1912*, British Columbia Provincial Museum Heritage Record no. 15 (Victoria, 1982).

52. Actually, there are many runs of salmon, *Oncorhynchus* spp., up the Fraser River below Hope. While all Pacific salmon develop hooked jaws at maturity, they are most hooked in the chum salmon, *Oncorhynchus keta* (Walbaum).

53. Dawson is perhaps noting a barometer of 30 inches.

54. Saint Mary's Mission near the present location of Mission, on the north bank of the river, was founded by the Oblate Father Leon Forquet in 1861.

the mountains, which was thawed suddenly by the hot weather occurring comparatively late in the season.

Tied up at Hope, for the night at 9.30 P.M.

Aug 15. Arrived at Yale early. breakfasted, & then finding that on account of the amount of express matter & passengers an extra was going out at once, decided to go on it, & thus have more time on the road. Left Yale 9.40. Arrive at Boston Bar 2.30 dinner. leave 3.30. Arrive at Lytton 9.15.

Yale is the head of Steamboat navigation & the river here somewhat suddenly changes its character, becoming at once a Cañon with rocky cliffs walling the river on either Side, & the stream becoming tumultuous & very rapid.

The Frazer below Yale has the appearance of having flowed formerly at a lower level, the land no doubt being higher. It now flows over the gravel deposits filling the bed cut in the rock below & is not materially increasing or deepening its valley, comparatively Seldom touching the Solid rock. What denudation is accomplished is upon the gravel banks & alluvial flats now bounding it. The river where it cuts through the mts. as a Cañon has probably at one time been full of falls, but has now attained a uniform grade. It is still so rapid however as to wear away, no doubt, its rocky bed to some extent.[55]

For some distance above Yale there are many Indian fish curing establishments, & in fact in following up the river they appear wherever Suitable localities for catching salmon occur. The Indians, or "Siwashes" as they are called in Chinook,[56] are now collected on the banks buisily engaged in laying up their winter stores. The Salmon is caught in a sort of scoop net,[57] the fisherman holding this in the water in a nearly vertical position, or moving it too & fro till a Salmon is found. The positions

---

55. Regrettably there is no comprehensive geomorphologic study of the Fraser River between Hope and Yale. Within this section the bedrock surface extends well below river level, a result of glaciers or a scour by the river at an earlier stage. At the end of the last glaciation the valley was partly filled with outwash gravels, which have subsequently been excavated by the river. Land movements, up and down, proposed by Dawson to account for the relationships are neither required nor precluded.

56. The Chinook Jargon was a trade language widely utilized among northwest coast Indians. For a discussion of the origin, characteristics, and use of Chinook Jargon, see Edward Harper Thomas, *Chinook: A History and Dictionary of the Northwest Coast Trade Jargon . . .*, 2d ed. (Portland: Binfords & Mort, 1970), 1–34. In the present edition, Thomas's dictionary has been utilized as a source for translating Chinook Jargon used by Dawson.

57. For an illustration of such a Fraser River dip net, see Hilary Stewart, *Indian Fishing: Early Methods on the Northwest Coast* (Vancouver: J. J. Douglas, 1977), 91. A more general discussion of Indian use of salmon in southern British Columbia is found in Fred Braches, "The Salmon and the Interior Salish of the Southern Plateau of British Columbia," *Midden* 13, no. 4 (October 1981): 3–7.

chosen are the eddies behind rocky points in the rapids, & the indian usually sits on a little platform built out from the rocks, or a structure of poles partly suspended from the higher parts of the bank.

The fish are cured without Salt or Smoking, being split & Strung up on sticks simply. For the purpose of drying them a scaffold of poles is made, into which to prevent the direct action of the Sun green boughs are woven Under these the fish hang in long rows. When dry they are stored in *Caches* in trees, & many of these may be seen in the pines along the road, sometimes high up the rocky banks of the hills. A framework of poles supports a little box like erection, perhaps 6 to 10 feet long & not quite So wide, at a considerable height above the ground. To prevent squirrels or other Small animals getting at the Store. A piece of tin is fixed round the trunk below, spreading downward & outward.[58]

The road up the Frazer to Lytton[59] has been made against great natural difficulties. It is sometimes near the water's edge, & sometimes about 800 feet above it. Going up to Get past "bluffs" & round their fronts by Side cuttings in the cliffs. Road also obliged to follow in & out all the notches made by streams in the Sides of the valley, to preserve its height, & road consequently not only very hilly but very tortuous. Scenery wonderfully fine, & the drive quite enjoyable. Creeping up long hills, & then rattling down again, & swinging round the curves with the river always on the left far below. Game of all sorts apparently very scarce, & woods though often thick nearly lifeless. have seen neither grouse nor rabbit all day

The country is evidently a very dry one, & I am assured that rain Seldom or never falls in summer. There are a few small "ranches" on this part of the road. Wherever the ground offers a level surface or even one not too steeply inclined for ploughing. It has been taken advantage of. There are a few whites & {a good} many indians living in this way.

Gold washing is now abandoned except as an occasional occupation by the indians, & by a few chinese.[60] Many places show still where the

58. Recent literature records practices similar to those observed by Dawson. See Donald Hector Mitchell, "Esilao — A Pit House Village in the Fraser Canyon, British Columbia," (Master's thesis, University of British Columbia, 1963), 32.

59. This was the most arduous stretch of the Cariboo Road constructed under the direction of Governor James Douglas in the early 1860's. The route was an important communications link between the British Columbia coast and the rapidly developing Cariboo gold fields in the Barkerville region.

60. Selwyn noted, in 1871, that "nearly all the Indians of the Fraser above Yale have now become gold-washers. They return to the same point on the river year after year, at the season of lowest water, to wash the sands, and, it is asserted, can almost always earn for a day's labour from one to two dollars' worth of gold. Besides the Indians there are quite a number of Chinese who make a living in the same way" (Alfred R. C. Selwyn, "Journal and Report of Preliminary Explorations in British Columbia," in Geological

Ground has been turned over & ransacked years back. It is noticable that these workings are superficial. That is to say when a high bank of drift[61] occurs at the Side of the river its upper layers only have as a rule been worked over to a depth of perhaps ten feet. The working also seems to have paid best near the up-current ends of terraces — thus — [*Illus.*]

The superficial character would either tend to show that the terraces are not yet exhausted, or rather that the workable gold deposits are sinchronous with some particular stage of depression of the country & that a comparatively deep one.

The drift wherever seen is not of the Character of moraine matter,[62] but Consists of sandy material with rounded pebbles & boulders, which so far as I have observed Show no sign of glaciation. The whole deposit is also almost always more or less roughly stratified, & generally in distinct relation to the Course of the Stream when running at a higher level in the valley. At Certain points the rounded river Gravel is interstratified or mixed with a quantity of angular material from the cliffs above, but this does not appear to be glaciated.

The Crystalline rocks of Selwyns Series VII.[63] met with immediately on leaving Yale appear much to resemble the white 'granitic' boulders found so abundantly westward, & on Vancouver Island.

See Selwins* description[64] for lithological character. In going north-ward toward Anderson R. their metamorphism Seems to increase — they almost loose their bedded structure, & are traversed by many Segregation Veins & dykes[65] which would be an interesting Study. Anderson R. group Seen first at Anderson R. (See Selwyns* description)[66] They run on

Survey of Canada, *Report of Progress for 1871–72* [1872], 56).

61. The "drift" visible in this part of the Fraser Canyon is mostly outwash, carried by stream action from a somewhat distant glacier-front at the end of the last (Wisconsin) glaciation. It corresponds only to the "Capilano" and "Fort Langley" sediments of the Fraser Lowland. See J. E. Armstrong, *Post-Vashon Wisconsin Glaciation, Fraser Lowland, British Columbia*, Geological Survey of Canada Bulletin no. 322 (Ottawa: Supply and Services Canada, 1981), 2–8.

62. An accumulation of material which has been transported or deposited by ice.

63. See Selwyn, "Journal and Report," 63–64, for his "Cascade Crystalline Series," made up of highly crystallic gneisses, granites, and diarites, typically developed in this loca-tion. Selwyn's eight-fold classification, largely as a result of Dawson's 1875–77 work, was almost totally abandoned.

64. Ibid.

65. A fissure in stratum filled with deposited matter.

66. Selwyn, "Journal and Report," 62–63.

beyond Butcher's Flat[67] nearly to the locality where the Jackass Mt Conglomerate said in Report to begin.[68] The formation is very distinctive where typically developed. It is said to be calcareous, is cool grey on weathered banks, & is intersected by innumerable jointage planes in all directions, causing it to break up into long *chip-like* fragments, resembling partly decayed wood. Shales greatly predominate, though Sandstones & dykes of intrusive[69] also exist.

Aug 16. Leave Lytton 6 A.m. & arrive at Cornwall's[70] 8 P.m. having stayed several hours of the afternoon at the next Station South. Weather extremely warm & dry. Thermom at 4.30 Pm in shade 92°

The appearance of the country changes much today. On leaving Lytton the woods are much thinner & become more so till toward evening they ⟨only form⟩ are only dotted over the hills. The country also becomes even drier than before & a new flora appears. *Artemisia Lynosiris*, *Stephanomeria*, *Cactus*[71] & other Such forms Come in & sparsely cover the dry hillsides. At the Same time the ⟨Jackdaw⟩ Magpie, Blue Jay, & Clarks Crow?[72] seen. The Mountains are however lower & more rounded & there is more flat land, which wherever irrigated appears extremely fertile, & bears large Crops. The rattlesnake[73] Abundant in this district.

Rocks according to Mr Selwyn of the 'volcanic' series[74] extend from the Jackass Mt Conglomerates to 4 or 5 miles above Spences Bridge. They are much shattered & full of Joints, & one can scarcely make Anything of

67. According to Selwyn, this locality was some "thirty-one and a half miles from Yale" (ibid., 22) up the Fraser River.

68. Ibid., 60.

69. An igneous rock body that has forced its way in a molten state into surrounding country rock.

70. Or Ashcroft Manor, a celebrated stopping place on the Cariboo Road constructed by two brothers, Clement Francis and Henry Pennant Cornwall, who settled in the area in 1862. Active entrepeneurs, the Cornwalls also ran an extensive ranch, sawmill, and grist mill. See L. Johanne Stemo, "Estate at Ashcroft," *The Beaver* 294 (Autumn 1963): 50–54; and Patrick A. Dunae, *Gentlemen Emigrants: From British Public Schools to the Canadian Frontier* (Vancouver: Douglas & McIntyre, 1981), 44–47.

71. "*Artemisia*" was sagebrush or wormwood, *Artemisia* spp.; "*Lynosiris*" probably the rabbitbrush, *Chrysothamnus nauseosus* (Pall.) Britt.; "*Stephanomeria*" the narrow-leaved stephanomeria, *Stephanomeria tenufolia* (Torr.); and "*Cactus*" the brittle prickly-pear cactus, *Opuntia fragilis* (Nutt.) Haw., or many-spined prickly-pear, *Opuntia polyacantha* Haw.

72. The "Magpie" was the black-billed magpie, *Pica pica* (L.); the "Blue Jay" Steller's jay, *Cyanocitta stelleri* (Gmelin); and "Clarks Crow" Clark's nutcracker, *Nucifraga columbiana* (Wilson).

73. The northern Pacific rattlesnake, *Crotalus viridis oreganus* (Holbrook).

74. Selwyn, "Journal and Report," 56–57.

them in passing along rapidly. A band of reddish weathering rock Appears frequently. At Nicomen[75] the rock is a porphyry[76] or dioritic porphyry. At this place there is a fine fall, the water coming down over the cliffs to the East from an immense height.

These rocks next succeeded by those of Mr Selwyns* *Lower* Cache Creek Series.[77] These Are, peculiar in the bright tints of brown & reddish, which hillsides composed of their rubbly fragments assume. Some exposures have a peculiar "whitewashed" aspect. Finding the Stage was to lie over at the Station 9 miles beyond spences bridge, to let the heat of the day pass, got off about 8 miles from the Bridge & walked on, examining the rocks. (For descript See Selwyn*)[78] The limestone[79] very thick but could see only very obscure traces of fossils. Bluish in colour internally, hard, traversed by {small} white veins of Compact Calcite[80] in many places. Also in some places by evident dykes, dioritic & epidotic?[81] Interstratified with the limestone beds which appear to me to be *volcanic ash*　　In some places these form compact rock with Some fragments more than an inch in length; but often rather more shaly & apparently Graduating into the limestone. Fragments then smaller & often only whitish lumps which might be taken for badly developed crystals. See specimens.

The limestone &c. from the fossils bound in it (See report)[82] may very well represent my Carboniferous limestone of the rocky mts.[83] Its general aspect is very similar, though more altered. The great Contemporaneous

75. The Nicoamen River which enters the Thompson River between Spences Bridge and Lytton.

76. An igneous rock containing numerous phenocrysts, or large crystals, surrounded by a finer matrix.

77. Selwyn, "Journal and Report," 61–62.

78. Ibid., 61.

79. The limestones are nearly all late Paleozoic in age. Up until a few years ago these would have been called Cache Creek, but in the past decade, with the development of plate tectonics, the term Cache Creek has become restricted to those limestones with a distinctive fossil fauna which accumulated on only one of several plate fragments later attached to the western margin of North America.

80. A common rock-forming mineral that is the principal constituent of limestone.

81. Epidotes, a group of rock-forming silicate minerals found in metamorphic rocks.

82. According to Selwyn, "the fossils from this locality, ten miles above Spence's Bridge, consist principally of the comminuted remains of several species of *Brachiopoda* in a greyish limestone" (Selwyn, "Journal and Report," 61).

83. See Dawson, *Geology and Resources*, 69–77.

trap[84] of my Section may have a similar origin to the ash beds here. It would appear however if this is the case, that the limestone is either here not so pure, or that part of Group C, or the overlying groups have been included in the foldings & also Classed as Lower Cache Creek.

The drift, on entering the Thomson valley changes its character considerably, becoming much more earthy. The benches not so entirely composed of Shingle.[85]

Aug 17. Leave Cornwalls 5 A.m. & come on to Clinton remain there during the heat of the day till 3.30 Then on again to 70 m. house where have supper Leave again at 8.30 ⟨& Stop at [blank] for the night.⟩

The Lower Cache Creek Group continues on the road to 4 or 5 miles past Clinton, where According to Selwyn overlaid by the Volcanic Series.[86] Change of formation accompanied by rapid rise, the volcanic rocks forming a plateau[87] of about 4000? feet altitude. They are exposed in the Chasm mentioned in the report.[88] Many beds shown of different texture & colour & some red bands. The whole horizontal, & thus differing much from any rocks yet seen. The Character of the country also changes on leaving clinton, & from the brow of the escarpment goes by the name of the *Green* ⟨*Woods*⟩ {*timber*}. It is pretty thickly wooded with pine, & underbrush, with many Grassy glades & has a general green appearance quite different from the brown country previously passed over. The Coniferous trees seem to belong to three species. One Pinus Contorta apparently. One the So Called pitch pine with reddish bark, 3 a large spruce like the black spruce.[89] The Sage & accompanying plants disappear, & other plants are seen, A {red} *Castillea Spirea* apparently *betulifolia* &c. *galium boreale*, the common *Epilobium*[90]

---

84. An old term for fine-grained, igneous rocks like basalt that form structures such as dykes.

85. Material of gravel or pebble grade accumulated on beaches.

86. Selwyn, "Journal and Report," 61.

87. Fraser Plateau.

88. According to Selwyn, "twelve miles above Clinton, a chasm has been excavated . . . from 200 to 300 feet deep, and about half a mile wide, which stretches for five or six miles to the southward" (Selwyn, "Journal and Report," 58).

89. "Pinus Contorta" was the lodgepole pine, *Pinus contorta* var. *latifolia* Engelm. ex S. Wats.; "pitch pine" the ponderosa pine, *Pinus ponderosa* Laws.; and "black spruce" probably the black spruce, *Picea mariana* (Mill.) B.S.P.

90. "Sage" was sagebrush, *Artemisia* spp.; "*Castillea*" was the Indian paintbrush, *Castilleja* spp.; "*Spirea betulifolia*" the birch-leaved spiraea, *Spiraea betulifolia* Pall.; "*galium boreale*" northern bedstraw, *Galium boreale* L.; and "common *Epilobium*" fireweed, *Epilobium angustifolium* L.

The drift boulders on the plateau appear to be chiefly of the volcanic rocks, & are Generally rounded, sometimes very well, but occasionally Somewhat angular. No great quantity of Cascade ⟨rocks⟩ Crystalline rocks, & probably none at all (?) though a few occur which cannot be distinguished with present Knowledge & opportunities of observation.

Elevation of the volcanic plateau Said to be too Great for growth of Crops, but where stopped for Supper a large Cattle ranch where butter said to be the best on the road is made.

Aug 18 Drove on all last night over very rough roads, on which there had been heavy rain. The Storm had prostrated trees some of which lay across the road. The Telegraph poles were also down in Some places & the wire hanging inconveniently across the road. The whole telegraph line on the road from Yale upwards is in a wretched condition. It only Keeps working because of the extreme dryness of the climate, & is often out of order. A party is now supposed to be executing repairs. At 3.30 A.m. got to Bridge Creek[91] cold & tired. Got a fire in the stove, then some breakfast, & started on again. At this place leave the "green timber" closes & we pass into a region of alternating prairie like country & patches of wood. The prairie generally in connection with Vallies, — the whole surface hilly without being mountainous. This country stretches nearly to Deep Creek[92] 14 miles from Soda Cr. It much resembles in general appearance the foot hills of the Rocky Mts, but is drier, as the Sage frequently covers large areas of hillside in the prairie regions. Saw some good grain crops here & there & many fine hay meadows. In addition to the general resemblance to the Foot Hill Country, some of the same plants there abundant recur & the aspect of the vegetation is similar. *Geranium Fremonti* is abundant. {*Solidago Castilleia* &c. luxurient.} Saw one specimen of the white Variety. *Lonicera involucrata*[93] Seen. Near Soda Creek a considerable altitude is again attained & the woods are now much like those of West Fork on the Kootanie Pass. *Pinus contorta* most abundant. The prairie & woodland country seems to occupy depressions in the general surface of the Plateau. Lac La Hache a fine Sheet of water about 12 miles long. There are many more or less Saline lakes with white efflorescent matter surrounding them. Many of these occupy curious basin-like hollows hard

---

91. 100 Mile House.

92. Hawks Creek.

93. "*Geranium Fremonti*" was the sticky geranium, *Geranium viscosissimum* F. & M.; "*Solidago*" was goldenrod, *Solidago* spp.; and "*Lonicera involucrata*" the black twinberry or twinflower honeysuckle, *Lonicera involucrata* (Rich.) Banks ex Spreng.

to account for.[94]

No rock exposures till between Deep & Soda Creeks where a few occur but small & could not examine them. The hill down to Soda Creek is about 3 miles long by the road & is steep & Sandy. At the Mill[95] a considerable exposure of the underlying rock seems to occur, & Soda Creek here falls ⟨by a⟩ as a fine cascade to the Frazer. Banks along the road near the Same place show the ⟨constitution⟩ structure of the terraces. A great thickness of fine stratified Sand, with occasional layers of gravel. Found Mr Glassey[96] Agent of C.P.R.S. at Soda Creek & learned that he had made all arrangements for my journey in compliance with Mr Robsons* telegram. ⟨but he⟩ Had 3 pack animals & 2 riding horses ready but only one indian & no guide. Man who could act as guide to the trail asked 80 dollars a month which Mr Glassey* considered too much altogether. The trail begins on the opposite side of the river to Soda Cr. & I must either go over in the morning at daylight when the steamer is ready to Start up the river, or wait till she returns on Sunday. Can get no other indian worth anything here & it appears useless to go over partly equipped, — with no time to make any arrangements. Mr Glassey* is going away in the morning to Quesnelle,[97] or the animals might be Crossed & perhaps another indian hunted up tomorrow & stuff &c. crossed in a canoe. On the whole thought best to put off departure for 4 days, & meanwhile go up with Steamer to Quesnelle to see about Getting another indian & if possible another horse from the Depot there. Will have a day or two at Quesnelle which may spend profitably. There appears ⟨to be⟩ not to be anything worth much attention near here (Soda Cr) Leave Reeves & the Indian already obtained at the hotel till my return. Are then to have everything ready for Crossing.

[The larger journal for 1875, entitled "1875 — No. II," continues through the winter of 1875-76 until 9 May 1876. Some loose notes, Indian vocabulary lists, newspaper clippings, and rough sketches have not been included.]

August 19. 1875. Leave Soda Creek in Steamer for Quesnelle Mouth with the intention of seeing what I can there during the delay unavoidable in

94. The "hollows" could be explained by differential scour or differential deposition by glaciers.

95. The "Mill" was a flour mill promoted by W. H. Woodcock and established by John R. Adams in 1867. See F. W. Laing, "Early Flour-mills in British Columbia: Part II—The Upper Country," *British Columbia Historical Quarterly* 5 (1941): 204-7.

96. John Glassey, then deputy purveyor for the CPRS, later operated a hotel in Ashcroft.

97. Quesnel, also referred to by Dawson as Quesnelle Mouth.

getting party prepared for trip westward. Had come on board Steamer the night before. Steamer started about daybreak. ⟨The⟩ Steamed up against a strong Current all day & arrived at Quesnelle about 6 P.m. The total distance is only about 60 miles, but the current very strong. Scenery pretty, but not remarkable, there being no Mountains of any size in sight. Day very warm & towards night fall a few drops of rain fall. Evening took a stroll down to the ferry on the Quesnelle with Dr Jones[98] who had been fellow passenger from Victoria. Ferry a swinging one operated by the force of the current of the river.

The river valley at Soda Creek & upward to Quesnelle has not the character of that Seen elsewhere on the Stage road from Yale. The 'bluffs' are in general Some distance from the stream, leaving a stretch of flat land on one or both sides of the river. This in some places has been occupied for farming, & I am told crops mature much earlier than in some of the more Southern, but higher, regions passed through on the Stage road.

There has been much washing for gold Carried on formerly on the bars & lower 'benches' of this part of the Frazer, but is now abandoned with the exception of perhaps a few claims held by Chinese

Terraces[99] are very well formed & distinct at many places. At Alexandria there are four distinct levels counting that which is now about 20 feet above the river & forms the flat land along it. Alexandria So called, is opposite the old H.B. Fort Alexander,[100] now abandoned. The whole place wears a deserted aspect. Quesnel is a little village of one row of houses facing a street which runs along the river. Like many of these mining towns it sprung up almost in a single year, but has ever since been going to decay.

The Drift[101] does not differ materially from that described already on other parts of the Frazer. It does not show signs of glacial action, but

98. Probably Dr. Thomas Joseph Jones, a well-known Victoria dentist. Jones later became involved in a number of mining claims in the Stump Lake region south of Kamloops.

99. The terraces, a major factor in Dawson's account of the historical geology of British Columbia, are a product of intermittent downcutting and valley widening by the Fraser River.

100. The fort Dawson saw was one built by the Hudson's Bay Company in 1836 on the west side of the Fraser River. Earlier, from 1800 to 1805, the North West Company had constructed Fort Alexandria about twenty-one miles above Soda Creek, on the east side of the river. When the North West Company and the Hudson's Bay Company amalgamated in 1821, the post was superseded by a new fort some miles to the north named Fort Alexander. That second fort was later abandoned when the last fort was built in 1836. Until the building of the Cariboo Road, Fort Alexander was the transfer point where goods coming north by the brigades were put on boats for transport to more northerly posts. However, the fort was rendered obsolete by the direct link furnished by the road.

101. The analogue of the "drift" situation between Hope and Yale.

consists of Sand & gravel beds, generally well stratified, though often false bedded.[102] These have apparently at one time filled the valley to the level of the highest terrace, & have since, during the recession of the water, been gradually cut away & formed into Steps.

At the Great Bend, Say 30 m. above Soda Cr. Lignite bearing rocks appear on the edge of the river. They are overlaid by about 100 feet of the stratified Sands & gravels of the drift. Either two or three Seams of lignite are seen, the doubt arising from the possible bending of no. 2 So as to make it appear twice. The seams separated by some feet of well Stratified Sands or soft Sandstones, & clays; & Crop out near the water level. The upper seam appears to be about 2 ft 6 inches thick, the next a little thicker, & the thickness of the lower is not well shown. They All appear to be well defined & clearly bounded seams. & dip S. Westward at a low angle — say 12°. They are Said to have been on fire at one time, & to appear on both banks of the stream when the water is low. At present only Seen on the East bank.

About a mile higher up on the West bank a cliff occurs which is apparently formed of volcanic rocks, including conglomerate or breccia;[103] but perhaps include some Sedimentary beds as well. They dip South westward at a high angle, & are traversed by dykes. One of these stands out Separate from the cliff.

A Short distance further on where the Steamer stopped for wood, observed the drift a few feet above the water line to be filled with large & small fragments of lignite, more or less rusty & decomposed, & breaking up into horizontal laminae.

About forty miles above Soda Creek a seam of lignite Several feet thick appears in the river bank on the East side, & is associated with rocks similar to those before described, but with a layer of large Spheroidal boulders. Dip Eastward at a moderate angle.

17 miles from Quesnel high massive hills apparently of trap border the river for some distance on the West Side.

8. miles from Quesnel on the East bank. The cliff composed of drift material, but a mass of older rocks, — no doubt of series associated with lignites — suddenly come up & form the cliff for a short distance. The are remarkable for their pea green colour, the material being probably Clay, but hard enough to form pebbles. Brown Stones resembling ironstone concretions[104] occur in some abundance & strew the shore below. These

---

102. Bedding affected by currents, usually erratic and with frequent changes in direction.

103. Sedimentary rocks composed of angular fragments of older rocks cemented together.

104. A rounded or irregular mass of certain constituents of sediments (such as iron) which concentrate in specific parts of the rock, often accumulating around a nucleus.

resisting the action of the weather have enabled some parts of the clay to Stand up while the rest has been washed away, giving the whole bank an extraordinary pinnacled appearance.

⅓ mile further up the stream, brownish & grey arenaceous clays[105] occur on both sides of the river. They are overlaid by drift, & dip North Eastward at Say 20°

Next appear heavy earthy conglomerates apparently of the Same formation.

About 7 miles from Quesnele Compact greenish clay like that already described, is brought in contact with conglomerates by a {nearly vertical} fault. The Conglomerates being to the north, & so hard as to form a vertical cliff to the waters edge without talus.[106] At least 30 feet of the conglomerates seen They are false bedded, but not very roughly So, & the component pebbles are small.

5 miles from Quesnele pale greenish & brownish beds appear, dip. N.N.W. at low angles.

4 ¾ m. from Quesnelle. Similar beds with conglomerates, dip E.S.E. 10° to 12°.

Next a gentle Synclinal of greyish & pale yellowish Sands & clays with thin Carbonaceous bands. axis about East & West.

About 1. mile below Quesnelle A rock appears in the Centre of the river. It is dark coloured, hard, much jointed, & probably trappean. The river bank is here very high on the E. side, composed of drift of the ordinary Character, but Showing here & there large lumps of lignite.

Bar at Noon 28.20 Temp. of water of Frazer 64°

If the volcanic & lignite bearing rocks conformable[107] & belong to Same series, seems little doubt that the rocks of this Series underlie the whole river valley from Soda Cr. to Quesnel, also that lignites are found in the Series throughout. If any difference of age between volcanic & lignite-bearing they must then be here folded together. The strike of the rocks is generally transverse to the river.

Aug 20. Morning walked northward up the East side of the Frazer, examining the sections in the bank. Afternoon examined the bank opposite the town & finding a plant & insect bed, spent the remainder of the afternoon & evening till dark working at it.

Sections appear in the bank for about a mile above here, & almost everywhere show more or less lignite. The beds appear to dip in Some places pretty steeply, but it is not clear how much of this may be due to

105. Rocks that have been derived from or contain sand.

106. Or scree, which is heaps of coarse debris at the foot of cliffs and steep slopes.

107. A sequence of beds or rock layers representing an unbroken period of deposition.

William and Margaret Dawson
with George (holding cane),
Anna, and William Bell Dawson,
on the steps of the Arts Building,
McGill College, 1865.

G.M. Dawson,
taken in Edinburgh.

2 July 1876.
Upper fall, Iltasyuko River
GSC 132-CI (PA 51037)

22 July 1876.
Northeast peaks of
Ilgachuz Range.
GSC 136-CI (PA 37548)

25 July 1876.
Gatcho Lake and Culla Culla House
with Dawson's camp.

GSC138-CI (PA52370)

28 September 1876.
(in Journal as 29th).
Fort Fraser and Fraser Lake.
GSC145-CI (PA51053)

5 October 1876.
Gravel bank,
Nechako River below
mouth of Chilako.
GSC149-CI (PA51049)

6 October 1876.
Junction Fraser and
Nechako rivers at
Fort George.

GSC150-CI (PA51048)

[6] October 1876.
Terraces, Blackwater
River near Depot.

GSC152-CI (PA51046)

16 June 1876.
Summit of Cascade Range
on Hope-Similkameen Trail
GSC-165-CI (PA 51040)

13.

1 July 1877.
Bluffs of white silt, lone
end of Okanagan Lake.
GSC 175-CI (PA 51066)

14 October 1877.
Tufaceous bluff with dykes
traversing, Nicola River.
GSC 202-CI (PA 51080)

[20] October 1877.
Typical fan Indian
reserve, Kamloops.
GSC 205-CI (PA 51082)

18 July 1878.
Skedan Indian village.
GSC250-C2(PA38148)

4 July 1878.
Grassy patch beneath
which hotspring rises
on Hotspring Island.
GSC235-C2(PA51103)

[24] August 1878.
Pillar Rock.
GSC27-C2 (PA51118)

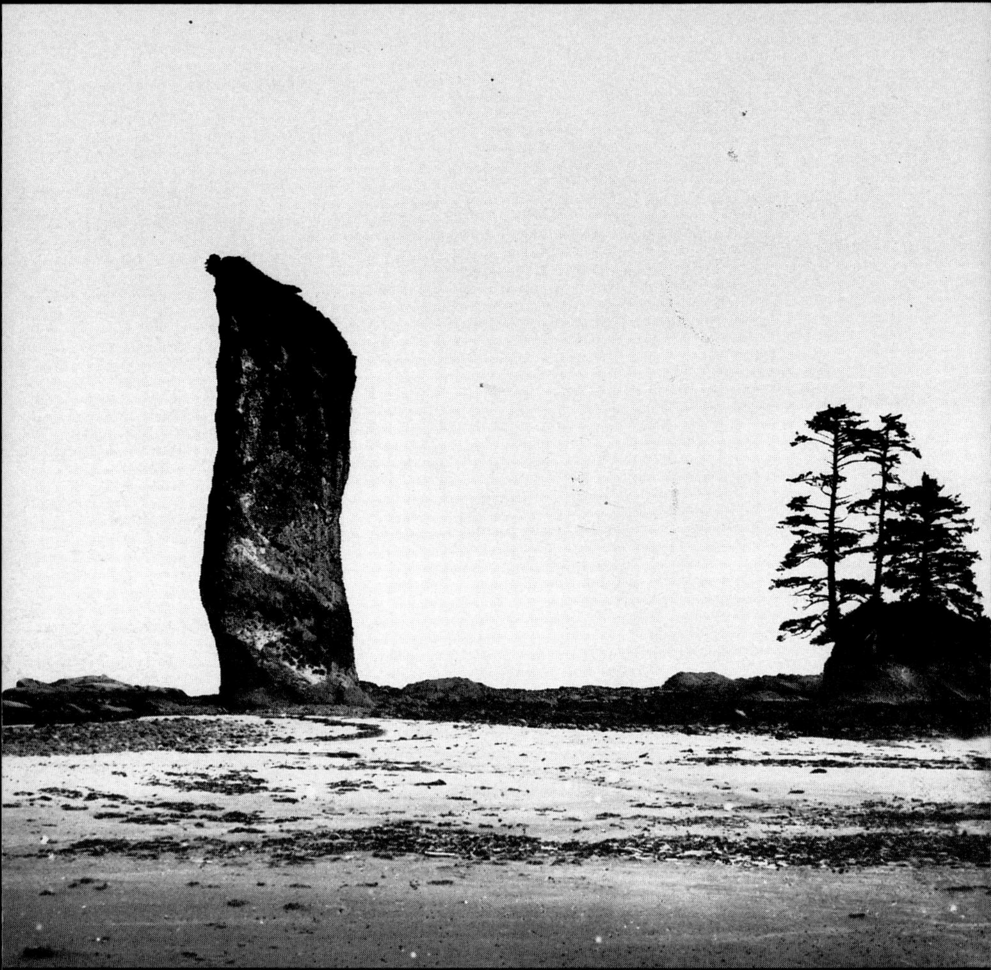

30 August 1878.
Port Simpson village
and church.

GSC269-C2 (PA44333)

Slips. The bank giving best Section Shows About 25 feet of beds, nearly or quite horizontal. Beds chiefly of greyish Sandy Clay, but with more or less lignite throughout. The lignite forms two or three pretty persistent zones, which vary but slightly in thickness, but include more or less Shale & carbonaceous clay throughout. In one place measured 5 feet of lignite moderately pure, but with some Shale partings[108] The whole bank however contains scattered flattened masses of lignite which have evidently been individual trees drifted to their present positions. There are also in some places layers of nodular ironstone & ferruginous sandstones of Small thickness. The indefinite character of the section renders it north worth while attempting Measurement. Amber[109] in large & small drops is abundant in the lignite & Carbonaceous Clays.

The beds immediately opposite the town are Somewhat different in character from those above described, being more uniformly bedded, & of finer material. Found fossil leaves in one layer which *exceedingly* fine, & shows alternations of greenish & whitish material about 1/16 inch in diameter. In looking for leaves found the wing of a dipterous insect[110] in position, & much resembling those of a common house fly, but Smaller.

This remarkably fine layer overlies a thin carbonaceous clay or impure lignite, about 1 inch. Various Seed-like bodies as well as leaves, & among them one pretty common which exactly resembles the winged seed of a birch.

Day very warm.

Aug. 21. Saturday Crossed the Quesnel river to examine sections there. Returned about 1 P.m. to the bank, & after Calling about half an hour attracted the ferry mans attention & got back. Devoted the afternoon & evening to Collecting insects & plants in beds opposite the hotel, & got quite a number of fragmentary Specimens.

Visited the red bluff about half a mile below the Quesnel Mouth on the E. bank of the Frazer. It stands over 100 feet in height above the water, & is coloured bright red & yellowish red, from top to base. It has been altered by the combustion of lignite, & the beds where a portion of them remain unchanged seem to be built up much like the section described yesterday. Lignits & carbonaceous clays being intercalated[111] throughout, without ever attaining great thickness of pure lignite. The cliff has been undermined by the stream & has fallen from time to time forming mounds

---

108. Thin layers of shale separating two parts of a coal seam.

109. A fossil resin from coniferous trees.

110. Or two-winged fly, one of a large and varied order of holometabolous insects, including the common housefly, gnats, and mosquitoes, of the order *diptera*.

111. Specific strata inserted among others.

of broken material & rubble which conceal the base. I am told that smoke was seen issuing near the water level about ten years ago, but a large fall taking place covered the bank up So deeply as to put it out. The ⟨cliff⟩ lignite bearing rocks have stood up as a little hill or mound, at this place, at the time of deposition of the drift, & the combustion Seems to have taken place from within outwards, or from the centre toward the Sides, as there is an edge of Strata unchanged intervening between the drift & the baked rocks. The combustion has probably been stayed by the wet state *of the rocks near the surface Roughly thus.* [*Illus.*]

The strata now present all the varieties of altered rock described in my report of ⟨by⟩ Lignite formation on Boundary Line.[112] Large ironstone balls, in Some cases more than three feet in diamteter occur in one part of the Section, their Centres appear to have been radially, crystalline Carbonate of iron, but are now Changed into oxide by the heat; & where exposed are breaking up into long splinters which give out a ringing Sound when struck, & look when lying loose like heaps of nails.

Amber occurs very abundantly in the unaltered parts of the Section.

Looked very carefully for fossil plants, but almost unsuccessfully. Many impressions but all obscure or like roots or branches, & could not find any leaf beds. The State of the material Singularly favourable for the collection of plants if only a good locality could be found. It would appear that most of the clays have been 'root clays' as the cylindrical or flattened impressions in a large proportion of cases ⟨runs⟩ run more or less across the planes of stratification. They may of course have been drift branches, but the appearance more that of roots. Made a small collection of the rocks arising from combustion.

The beds above described *appear* to be underlaid by earthy conglomerates & Sandstones (see section when passing in steamer.)

Next examined a Section in the S. bank of the Quesnel Just above the ferry. Have here a bank exactly resembling that described yesterday. Shows about three pretty persistent lignite zones, but flattened Masses throughout, & perhaps 1/8 of the entire bank composed of lignite.

This bank is being rapidly washed away, as is the whole of the South Side of the Quesnele at this place. The North Side at the Same time gradually advancing, & the Mouth of the river thus gradually passing further south.

The insects obtained today include probably 2 diptera one much like a

112. G. M. Dawson, *Tertiary Lignite Formation, in the Vicinity of the Forty-Ninth Parallel* (Montreal: Dawson Brothers, 1874).

gnat or mosquito. 1 Coleoptera.[113] & perhaps one or two other forms in a fragmentary state.

Day warm but pleasant, somewhat overcast.

The general resemblance between this lignite bearing formation & the Lignite Tertiary of the plains is very striking, though it may of course only be a resemblance due to Similarity of Conditions of deposit, & like absence of Metamorphism. The resemblance holds even to the colour of the beds, including the remarkable greenish tint elsewhere mentioned. The only real difference is in the fact that the lignites are much more clearly of *drift* material, than those of the plains. Even those which are there almost certainly of that character. Also the occurrence of earthy conglomerates, which likewise depends on more disturbed waters of deposition.

The fossil plants so far as I can recollect do not correspond closely. but it must be remembered that these vary much even in contiguous localities; & that these from this place are from a single thin layer.

Drift. The pebbles & boulders in the drift & banks of the Frazer & Quesnele are of rather mixed aspect, but show a great many which exactly resemble those of the *Quartzite*[114] *drift* of the plains. They include however more greenish & blackish Slaty or compact rocks. Also fragments of conglomerates apparently Serpentinic or epidotic, & also many varieties of volcanic rocks, amygdaloids, diorites,[115] porphyries &c.

G. M. Dawson to John William Dawson*, 21 August 1875, Quesnel

I now date as you will observe from Quesnel, where I have rather unexpectedly come. On arriving at Soda Creek I found Mr Glassey* the Agent of the C.P.R.S. had made arrangements to let me get off at once, but had not succeeded in obtaining a second indian, & was also minus one horse ⟨which⟩ of the complement. The trail begins on the side of the Frazer opposite Soda Creek, & the Crossing of the animals Can only be effected by the steamer which plies between Soda Cr & Quesnel. Now as we arrived at Soda Cr. on Wednesday night after dark, & the steamer started next morning at daylight it was either necessary to Cross on Thursday morning or wait till the return of the boat on Sunday evening. Thinking the loss of four days less important than the arrangements of the start being properly

---

113. Order *Coleoptera* or beetles, with front wings converted into sheaths for back wings.

114. A hard, white metamorphic rock formed from quartz arenite which is sandstone containing very little except quartz grains and cementing material.

115. Amygdaloids: a general name for volcanic rocks that contain numerous gas cavities filled with secondary minerals; diorites: a granular igneous rock consisting essentially of plagioclase feldspar and hornblende.

perfected, I decided on the latter course, & as Soda Cr. did not seem to offer much of interest, Came up here on the steamer, & shall return with her tomorrow. This place is about 60 miles north of Soda Cr. & in coming here I had a chance of seeing Sections of the lignite bearing rocks in the river banks, & also those exposed about here. The lignite here though occurring in quantity is not in thick seams, & is mixed with Shale &c. as though it had been drifted together, & had not grown on the spot.

The general aspect of the lignite bearing rocks is very much like that of the Lignite Tertiary of the plains, but the resemblance may of course be ⟨of⟩ only one of similarity of conditions of deposit. I think you examined specimens of plants Collected here Some years ago by Mr Richardson*.[116] I have only been able to find one thin plant-bearing bed, which contains *a few* leaves[117] in very good preservation. I found in the Same bed however, which is exceedingly fine grained, the remains of a dipterous insect not unlike a common fly but Smaller. I worked away at the bed all this afternoon, & in addition to a good many leaves, more or less perfect, have got fragments of at least two dipterous insects, one coleopterous & perhaps one or two others.[118] These will be interesting, but I cannot find a trace of a Mollusc, which would be more satisfactory as a test of age.

In journeying up the Frazer by the Stage I have got a glimpse of most of the formations which Mr Selwyn* has provisionally designated in his first report, & in going westward to the Cascades I Shall Cut across them again on another line if they are continuous Northward & Southward, as most things Seem to be here.

Please excuse this Short note & believe me your affectionate Son

Aug 22. Sunday. Morning made a slight examination of the neighbourhood of the insect bed, & measured the Section of which it is a part. Started about 3 P.m. in steamer to return to Soda Creek. Mr Glassey* has

---

116. See J. W. Dawson, "Appendix I. To Mr. Richardson's Report: Note on the Fossil Plants from British Columbia, Collected by Mr. James Richardson in 1872," in Geological Survey of Canada, *Report of Progress for 1872-73* (1873), 66-71.

117. Dawson subsequently sent the fossil plants collected here, and some others later acquired on the Blackwater River, to his father for analysis. J. W. Dawson's conclusions were presented in the printed report of Dawson's 1875 field season. See George M. Dawson, "Report on Explorations in British Columbia," in Geological Survey of Canada, *Report of Progress for 1875-76* (1877), 259-60.

118. Dawson indicated in his published report that the fossil insects found in bed number seven were sent to S. H. Scudder for examination (Dawson, "Report on Explorations," 259). Scudder's results were published as an appendix to the Dawson report. See Samuel H. Scudder, "Appendix to Mr. George M. Dawson's Report: The Insects of the Tertiary Beds at Quesnel," in Geological Survey of Canada, *Report of Progress for 1875-76* (1877), 266-80.

got me a second indian, who goes down with us, & is brother to the one already engaged. Train expected not having come in cannot get another horse. Found horses & traps ready on the bank at Soda Creek, got all on board the steamer & crossed them to the West bank. Left the two indians in charge, promising to return with Reeves early on Monday Morning. Paid hotel bill & did other little matters of business. Mr Dunlevy[119] showed me Samples of Quartz, Said to be Auriferous & argentiferous[120] from a vein near Cariboo. Left the Samples with Mr D. (proprietor of the hotel) intending to get them on return journey.

Section including Insect bed at Quesnel. (The bank at this place is traversed by two faults. The lowest beds seen are furthest up the river — North — The measured section begins at the lowest seen, measures thence to the top of the bank, then crosses the fault & takes the next bed in ascending order, disregarding those below it which have fefore been measured, but which must appear in a diagram showing the structure. The Section not only shows the association of the insect bed, but Serves as an example of the numerous small faults with which this formation is traversed.)

1	Greyish clay	4 – 0
2	*Yellowish Clay	2 – 6
3	Coarse gravel & Sand	– 6
	(Rusty irregular layer) say	
4	Coarse grey Sand with occasional flattened masses of lignite near the top	6 in to 1 ft
5	Grey Sandy Clay	2 – 0
6	+ Grey Sandy Clay with pebbles	1 – 6
7	Coarse yellowish grey Sandy clay	4 – 0

Fault. Downthrow to S. of 3 ft 6 in measured at right angles to bed.

8	Yellowish grey Sandy clay full of joints &c pretty distinctly bedded but in thick layers	13 – 0
9	Carb. Clay or impure lignite	0 – 2
10	Plant & insect bed, very finely laminated fine greyish & greenish grey clay	0 – 8 ½

119. Peter Curran Dunlevey (1834-1904) was an American who had participated in the early Cariboo gold finds. Later, he successfully operated a stopping house at Beaver Lake and the Colonial Hotel at Soda Creek. See Edith Beeson, *Dunlevey from the Diaries of Alex P. McInnes* (Lillooet, B.C.: Lillooet Publishers, 1971).

120. "Auriferous" or containing gold; and "argentiferous," containing silver.

11 Yellowish clay	0 – 2 ½
12 Grey clay — distinctly bedded.	2 – 0
13 Ferrug. Sandstone, nodular &	
irregular about	1 – 0

Fault reversed with a downthrow of about 6 ft. to the South.

14 Rather thin bedded fine Grey	
Sandy clays	11 – 9
15 Grey Sand	1 – 0
16 Sands & Sandy clays,whitish,	
regularly bedded	20 – 0

Dip of the beds 285° ⟨ 22° The bank being Somewhat oblique to the direction of dip.
Diagram of the Section. [*Illus.*]

G. M. Dawson to Margaret Dawson*, 22 August 1875, Quesnel

I take the opportunity of writing a few lines while waiting for the starting of the boat for Soda Cr. I hope to get all my material put across the river there this evening, & tomorrow morning steer westward. My party for the present will consist of Self, Reeves (Cook brought up from Victoria) & two indians. 3 pack horses, & two riding horses. I may not have another chance to write perhaps for some weeks, so that you need not wonder why if no letters arrive.

Mr Selwyn* has been indirectly heard of here lately, & it seems that his Canvas boat was upset on the Parsnip R — a tributary of the Peace — Mr S. was not in the boat himself at the time, (according to report) but some saddles were lost, & his cook nearly drowned There would probably be no difficulty in replacing the Saddles, & it is very likely that the whole thing has been exagerated.

The weather here for some time back has been very warm, but it always cools down at night, & next month heat will probably be a desideratum.

This Quesnel is a poor little place, & has already seen its best days. It was built up almost in a Summer at the time of the Cariboo gold excitement, & has ever Since been retrograding. There are two or three good enough farms in the neighbourhood, but I really cannot see what the people here live on, if not on each other. A stage arrives every week from Barkerville the Centre of Cariboo, & the steamer comes up once a week from Soda Cr. With the exception of an occasional teamsters train this constitutes the entire ⟨....⟩ {business} of the place.

I have not written to William* for some time, please make my excuses to him when you write, if he has not returned by the time this reaches. I have been traveling away so fast that I have not let home letters time to Catch up, & cannot now hope to receive any till I get round to Blackwater,[121] which may be in three weeks. Of William* I have not heard for an age.

I dont Know whether I told you that I have already come across three McGill M.Ds in this country. I daresay there are many more to be discovered.

I left a little bill at James'[122] for making two tin discs for the micrometer telescope. If he sends it in Father* will pay for me, & Keep the receipt as it is chargable to the survey.

With love to Yourself & all at home

Aug 23   Breakfast at 4 A.m. & then Crossed the Frazer in a Canoe Mr Glassey* accompanying us. Got horses packed & saddled & start made about 6 A.m. Had only gone part of the way up the steep Sloping trail which zig zags to the top of the high bench, when one of the horses missed its footing & went rolling & crashing down the bank among Sapling spruces. Found the animal however, after all not much hurt, though when brought to the top of the bank & load readjusted not able to stand under its pack, one leg being lame. While this trouble in progress heavy rain came on, & we were soon nearly wet through. Decided to pack ⟨of⟩ one of the riding animals & let the lame beast go light, but at all hazards to make at least a part of a day's journey. Got away finally at 8 a.m. & walked on through the wet till about 3.30. Weather improved considerably in the afternoon & before reaching Meldrums flat — about 20 miles from Soda Creek — we were nearly dry again, though very tired & hungry. Got Camp arranged, fire going, & some supper cooked & retired early. Mr Meldrum[123] paid us a visit, & got from him some useful information about the trail. He has a fine ranch & many Cattle in excellent condition, but complains like all the farmers here of the low prices produce now brings & the high wages. The trail passed over today pretty rough in places, & very few places where water Can be obtained. The road follows the benches which border the Frazer R & is obliged to descend the steep banks of transverse gullies, & at times to pass from one bench to the next. The water drains away rapidly through the porous drift material, Causing at this season of little rainfall the Scarcity of water mentioned.

---

121. Blackwater Depot, on the West Road or Blackwater River.

122. The Montreal tinsmith and metalworking firm of W. James & Sons.

123. Thomas Meldrum (1828–89) pre-empted land at Williams Lake in 1862 but sold out to Pinchbeck and Lyne in 1870 when he pre-empted land on what is now called Meldrum Creek.

Aug 24. Start away from Camp at Meldrums Flat 6.35 A.m. & travel all day along the higher benches of the Frazer, the Surface of which is generally more or less rolling either from irregularity of formation, or Subsequent denudation. A fine park like country with belts of timber alternating with large open patches of prairie, covered with luxuriant grass The trees forming the woods, which are rather open, are chiefly Abies Douglasi (not attaining a great height) & Pinus contorta, usually small & often slender & growing in thick clumps. Populus tremuloides, various willows, roses, & Sheperdia Canadensis form the undergrowth. Solidagoes & Asters of several species abound, Castilya (probably the same sp. as that got near waterton Lake, but representing only the red variety) occurs. Also Spirea betulifolia, now nearly past flowering, Gentiana acuta, or a species very like it, a delicate Astragalus, Galium boreale, past flowering.[124]

In the meadows in addition appear Geranium Fremonti, a white Heuchera, in Some places geum trifolium,[125] &c. Stopped half way where Some water occurs, & had lunch. Camped on Riskies Creek,[126] at the upper end of his farm, making during the latter part of the journey a rapid descent from the bench. Interviewed Mr Riskie, who is at present ill, & got from him much information about the trail. Also got him to promise to send down a sample of his wheat for the Exhibition[127] Should it prove sufficiently good. The approximate altitude of his farm is 2400 feet. He says though other places in the neighbourhood troubled occasionally with frost, that he has never suffered at all in that way. His crops are raised by the help of irrigation, water being tapped off at some distance up the

124. "Abies Douglasi" was the douglas-fir, *Pseudotsuga menziesii* var. *glauca* (Beissn.) Franco; "Populus tremuloides" the trembling aspen, *Populus tremuloides* Michx.; "willows" *Salix* spp.; "roses" roses, *Rosa* spp.; and "Sheperdia Canadensis" soapberry or soopolallie, *Shepherdia canadensis* (L.) Nutt. "Asters" were asters, *Aster* spp.; and "Castilya" Indian paintbrush, *Castilleja* spp. though not Dawson's, *Castilya pallida* (Waterton Lake species), the modern pallid paintbrush, *Castilleja sulphurea* Rydb., which is only found in southeastern British Columbia. "Gentiana acuta" was the northern gentian, *Gentianella amarella* (L.) Börner ssp. *acuta* (Michx.) Gillett and "Astragalus" milk vetch or locoweed, *Astragalus* spp.

125. "White Heuchera" was alumroot, *Heuchera* spp.; and "geum trifolium" purple avens, *Geum triflorum* Pursh.

126. Riske Creek. L. W. Riske took up land on the creek that bears his name, in 1859, and established what was called the Cotton Ranch. In the 1890's, Riske was involved with mining claims in the Vernon area.

127. The United States Centennial Exposition in Philadelphia was a major international event in which thirty-five nations participated. Opened on 10 May 1876 to celebrate one hundred years of American independence, the Philadelphia exposition consisted of 167 buildings on a 236-acre site. The contribution made by the Geological Survey of Canada was sizeable, with over sixty-thousand pounds of specimens shipped in 107 boxes and barrels. The collection, meant to be a representative sample of the geological and mineral resources of Canada, won several awards at the exposition.

Creek & lead away in distributing ditches. These lower benches & vallies seem drier than the high level plateau, for in coming down to them Artemisias (A frigida? & A Canadensis)[128] increase in abundance. Linosyris appears, also here & there A Stunted Cactus

Aug 25. Left Camp 6.20 A.m. & travelled on till 1.50 P.m. when arrived at place described by Mr Riskie as camping ground, & where also many poles cut for tents & other signs of former occupation. The country passed over is chiefly open & of the nature of prairie land, clothed with fine grass (bunch grass)[129] Saw several large herds of cattle in the morning, running about almost wild. All this plateau region, both that passed over from Soda Cr. to ⟨this⟩ Riskies, & that of today; splendid grazing & stock raising Country, though probably too high for successful Culture of most Crops. The resemblance of the rolling Surface of the plateau to the country of the Foot hills on Lat. 49° remarkable, & extends also to the flora, which as already remarked almost the same. Seems to be about the same stage at Same time of year, & it would appear that the foot hill country must enjoy a climate not dissimilar.

On crossing the point of high land between the vallies of the Frazer & Chilacotin, a magnificent view appears Across the bench or plateau in the foreground, & at a great depth below, the valley of the Chilacotin, across it a continuation of the Same plateau, rising slightly from the river, & partly prairie, partly wooded land. Then a bounding range of hills with gentle slopes, & wooded to the Summit, & through the lower parts of these the Serried & snow-clad peaks of the distant Cascades to the south-west, glittering in the sun.

Where evening Camp made within about a hundred yards of the precipitous edge of the great Chilacotin valley. The rim of the valley at both sides formed of basalt, & Scoreaceous[130] trap, with some {distinct} horizontal lines, & in many places largely columnar. The cliffs Show in some places more probably than 200 feet of these rocks, & are extremely ruinous, & show evidince of the yearly fall of great masses to add to the talus below.

The small stream by which we are camped falls suddenly over the edge, & passes down into a great amphitheatrical hollow in the edge of the valley.

128. "A frigida" was the pasture wormwood, *Artemisia frigida* Willd.; and "A Canadensis" the northern field wormwood, *Artemisia campestris* L. ssp. *borealis* (Pall.) Hall & Clem.

129. Bunchgrass, *Agropyron spicatum* (Pursh) Scribn. & Smith.

130. Scoriaceous, or porous.

In the valley of Riskies Cr, Several terrace levels[131] very distinct, & besides those with broad trees, the steep grass covered bank sloping down from the level of the highest bench on the S. side of the brook, Shows in favourable conditions of light, at least 8 (eight) perfectly horizontal marks, or small ridges. These would Seem certainly to mark different stages in elevation, & to show that it was not Sudden, as by breaking of a barrier. Also that in favourable circumstances may expect to find benches at almost any elevation.

Aug 26. Started 6.40 A.m. Passed for Some time through openly wooded Country with P. contorta, & A. Douglasi. Trail running along top of N Bank of Chilacotin. Then made descent into Valley, & travelled the rest of the way along lower benches, Sometimes lightly wooded, sometimes prairie like. The Valley bottom partakes of character of that of Riskies Creek, & shows the Same plants.

Arrived in Camp 2 P.m. Wrote out notes, Collected a few plants &c.

In descending into the valley passed over curious region of rock-strewn hummocky mounds, which at this place projects from the north bank. Probably moraine mounds, or at least remarkably like them.[132]

Aug 27. Morning Cold, & a sharp frost in the night. Leave Camp 6.40 A.m. & after travelling some miles find the genuine Alexis' Creek, & that we had camped Short of the proper place. Pass Several indian gardens with potatoes, carrots, & turnips; the former now all Killed down with the frost. Stop for lunch at a place where remarkable section of volcanic breccias (See notes)[133] Camp near a large band of indians. They are Alexis,[134] & his men, & say they are now going down to the Frazer to work. On Alexis' Creek there are a number of log Shanties erected, which belong to them. Day has been clouding up since noon, now rain setting

---

131. Dawson incorporated these observations of terraces in valleys into his theory of a general subsidence of the Interior Plateau. Later researchers, however, have questioned his ideas, asserting that it is not necessary "to postulate a great subsidence such as Dawson suggested in order to explain the glacial features observed. The terraced character of many valleys he considered were the result of wave action during the subsidence of the landmass. However these terraces may be kame terraces formed by lateral streams flowing along the sides of a glacier during the thinning and decay of the ice" (John E. Armstrong and Howard W. Tipper, "Glaciation in North Central British Columbia," *American Journal of Science* 246 [1948]: 307).

132. The "hummocky mounds" are possibly the product of an ancient landslide, a known occurrence at this locality.

133. See G. M. Dawson, Field Notebooks, RG 45, vol. 134, no. 2790, 7–8v, Public Archives of Canada, Ottawa (PAC).

134. Alexis was an important chief among the Chilcotins who controlled the area of the plateau between Alexandria and Puntzi Lake. He cooperated with authorities, though not without arousing suspicion, during the course of the 1864 Chilcotin "uprising."

steadily in. Had a crowd of the indians round the Camp till & during supper. They had caught today the first Salmon of the season which they presented to us. Gave them some tobacco & pork. After supper presented them with the remainder of the grouse stew, & a cup of tea all round &c. Being good Catholics, & this Friday they would not touch the grouse, but took it away to Keep till the morning, when it might be legitimately eaten. Fine grazing land in the valley bottom this morning, now ⟨more⟩ narrower & more Cañon like.

Aug 28.

Morning very wet, & has been raining steadily all night. Showed signs of improvement about 9 A.m. & Barometer rising, decided to move on a short days journey to the crossing of the Chilacotin R. Got packed up & off at 10.30, & got to camping place on S. bank of R at 3 P.m. The indians hanging round the camp from daybreak till we left camp, & prying into everything. Brought us another small Salmon, & a trout, for both of which they received exchange.

Valley of the Chilacotin where seen today pretty wide, but the bottom land swampy, & insead of being a grassy prairie as usual, covered with willows & other bushes. The stream itself is not large, & at the ford Scarcely comes up to the stirrup. Water dark coloured but clear Current rapid, & bottom stony.

Camped in a fine meadow with grass 3 feet high in places, & abundance of vetches[135] in the hollows.

Aug 29. Start 7.30 A.m. & travel on till 2.25 P.m. The trail following the N. bank of the Chilanco, which is struck by the trail immediately after leaving the crossing of the Chilcotin. For about 13 miles the character of the valley is forbidding, the trail passing for the most part over flats of gravel & sand, covered with a more or less dense growth of *Pinus contorta*, the ground beneath the trees being often nearly bare, or covered with bearberry[136] &c. The latter part of the way the valley is more open & has somewhat extensive grassy bottoms. The grass however not very thick. Camped at spot where trail crosses the Chilanco to go S.W.estward. Spot designated as Depôt camp, & also as Jenning's[137] Camp No 1. Two well built wooden shanties, now deserted, mark the site of the depôt. Passed two pretty little lakes by the way today. The Chilanco R. at first a large Swift flowing *brook* now much smaller, & forming long weedy lagoons with Shorter stretches of swift water between. Many ducks but have no

---

135. Possibly American vetch, *Vicia americana* Muhl., or bird vetch, *Vicia cracca* L.

136. Bearberry or kinnikinnick, *Arctostaphylos uva-ursi* (L.) Spreng.

137. W. T. Jennings was in charge of one of the divisions of the railway surveys.

dog.

Sketched the view looking up the stream. Pressed a few plants, wrote up notes &c.

⟨*Aug. 30*. Steady & heavy rain during the night, but ceased about daylight. Morning Calm & over cast. Left Camp 8.5 a.m. & travelled through thick woods & brush.⟩

Aug 30. Leave Camp 7.20 & travel on till 4 P.m. reaching the N.E. end of Eagle Lake   Day wet Since noon & still raining. Saw many ducks in pools this morning. one flock of geese, & a spruce partridge,[138] the latter Shot. Loon Lake[139] a pretty little sheet of clear-water, & true to its name inhabited by loons.[140] Eagle Lake a fine body of water. Clear & blue, with mountanous banks, & tonight a gentle sound of surf beating on the shore. Trail today very bad, & horses tired on arriving at Camp. All very tired & hungry & glad to get something to eat & turn in. Crossed & recrossed the located line of the CP Ry several times today. Clear line cut through the woods & chaining marked by posts. Seems an act of great faith to locate a Railway through this wild country.

Aug 31. Steady & heavy rain during the night, but Ceasing about dawn. Morning Calm & overcast with great Swathes of mist rolling up on the mountains. Left Camp 8.5 A.m. & travelled on through woods & brush loaded with moisture, which more wetting even than rain as shaken off. Crossed the outlet of the lake 11.40 a.m.

Passed White Water L.[141] & camped at S.E. end of Cochin L, where site of indian village marked on map really only a camp, & now abandoned. A newly made indian grave on the crest of a little knoll logs piled in square form on the ground, & a pole standing up with an old tin pan spiked upon it, & bearing a red rag for a flag. Found Cached in the bushes several fish traps[142] which had been used in the lake. Made of long round wooden withes or rods, neatly Smoothed down & bound together. Cylindrical, with a conical entrance at one end after the fashion of a rat trap.

The country of much the Same character. Soil gravely or sandy. Timber *A. Douglasi*, & *P. Contorta*, with aspen[143] &c. but more thickly & uniformly tree-clad than before.

---

138. The "geese" were Canada geese, *Branta canadensis moffiti* Aldrich; spruce partridge" was probably the spruce grouse, *Canachites canadensis franklinii* (Douglas).

139. Pyper Lake.

140. Probably the common loon, *Gavia immer* Brünnich.

141. Lunch Lake.

142. For an illustration of similar traps, see Stewart, *Indian Fishing*, 113.

143. Trembling aspen, *P. tremuloides*.

Saw a humming bird today, unable to tell exactly what species, but no doubt *Trochilis Colubris*[144] (no)

Eleagnus Argentea growing abundantly near the Camp tonight. *Ranunculus cymballaria* occurs wherever a suspicion of saline matter in the Soil all through this country, & the *Crotallaria*[145] is common.

The western edge of the basaltic region probably lies near the Junction of the Chilcotin & Chilanco, or a few miles East of that place, in going westward from it toward the Cascades the character of the country altogether changes, & instead of the uniform plateau, have rounded or irregular hills.

The watershed between the Frazer & Homathco, lies between Eagle & Cochin Lakes, & is not a feature of any importance, being easily crossed. Remarkable that small stream like the Homathco should rise E. of the Cascades & flow through them, though of course the same thing on a greater scale with the Frazer

The rolled appearance of much of the Moraine matter, referred to in notes,[146] cannot be accounted for on the supposition of water action Subsequent to formation of mounds, as to be Sufficient to wear these hard rocks, it must have been more than sufficient to obliterate the moraines. It would therefore appear possible or probable that the glaciers ploughed their way through previously rounded material, which they heaped up, with some of an angular character, immediately derived from the cliffs overlooking them. It would seem then possible that the terraces of the vallies are of origin antecedent to this glaciation, while the glaciation observed at the summit of the basaltic plateau, & overlaid by gravels which apparently belong to the terraces, may be of yet earlier date?[147]

The *Chilcotin* valley, including the basaltic plateau overlooking it, & all the better parts of the neighbouring Country, though in many places

---

144. Could have been either the rufous hummingbird, *Selasphorus rufus* (Gmelin), or calliope hummingbird, *Stellula calliope* (Gould).

145. "*Eleagnus Argentea*" was the silverberry, *Elaeagnus commutata* Bernh.; and "*Ranunculus cymballaria*" the shore buttercup, *Ranunculus cymbalaria* Pursh. "*Crotallaria*" was probably a plant in the Fabaceae (Leguminosae) family, since *Crotallaria alba*, a synonym for *Baptisia alba* (L.) Br., the plant referred to by Dawson, does not occur in western Canada.

146. See G. M. Dawson, Field Notebooks, RG 45, vol. 134, no. 2790, 11v, PAC.

147. Glaciers certainly can pick up stones already rounded by river action, but the glacier itself, or streams flowing on and from the glacier can also round homogeneous and unfractured stones. Water sorting, rather than rounding, might be the criterion Dawson should have looked for. Also, as a glacier or ice front retreats, its till deposits are commonly covered by its gravel outwash. However, till further upstream can be laid down at a still later stage, and it in turn can be covered with more outwash. None of the terraces (meltwater channels and deltas?) are known to precede glaciation.

excellently adapted for grazing & Cattle raising Cannot be called in any Sence An agricultural country. For the most part it is too high for wheat raising, & even the potatoes in indian gardens east of Alexis Creek were observed to be frost Killed. Some spots may of course be found, where, (as at Riskie's) wheat & all other Crops can be Grown

Sept 1. 1875. Left Camp 6 A.m. & travelled on to Cambies[148] Camp 17.[149] arriving at the Blaze 4.30 P.m. after a very long & fatiguing day. Found an indian Camp on the Trail near the N. end of Tallyoco L.[150] but the men all away. The women came out, but as they could speak but little Chinook, could not learn much from them, beyond the fact that the Camp of white men was *Si-yah* or far away. one hideous old hag Among them, & all ugly enough. The trail very bad along the E. side of the lake ascending & descending Constantly, & Crossing deep & muddy ravines & brook channels. the mountain sides thickly wooded. A *Douglisi* now preponderating. The lake seems to occupy nearly all the flat bottom of the valley, & is long & river-like; but leaves a sloping bank on the E. side along which a good line may be run for the Ry. Views of the lake, & snow-clad mountains towering above it magnificent. Did not actually go down to Cambie's* Camp, finding Horetzky[151] Camped on the branch trail about half way, & learning that the descent still about 600 feet & the road very bad, decided to remain for the night & let the animals come up, the packs now being a long way behind. Hearty supper, talk, & turn in.

A large glacier with moraine lines running down it visible in mountains at S.W. end of lake

Sept 2. Came down the hill to Mr Cambie's* Camp early, but found him already gone out on the line. Selected place for Camp near his, & got the things packed down, & Camp arranged. Wrote up notes. Changed paper of plants in press, & in the afternoon walked northward a short distance on the location line, which runs just past the tent door. Saw no rock in place. Saw mr C & party in the evening, & talked matters over with him.

---

148. Henry John Cambie (1836–1928) was born in Ireland in 1836; he came to North America in 1852 and to British Columbia in 1874. Cambie was in charge of the CPRS in British Columbia from 1876 to 1879 and superintended the Canadian Pacific Railway's construction in the province from 1880 to 1883, then became engineer-in-charge of its Western Division. He died in Vancouver, age 91, in 1928.

149. On the southeast side of Tatlayoko Lake.

150. Tatlayoko Lake.

151. Charles George Horetzky (1839–1900) was a photographer with the railway surveys. Though a competent photographer who took many invaluable photographs of British Columbia topography, Horetzky was extremely difficult to work with and fought constantly with his associates. See also Andrew Birrell, "Fortunes of a Misfit: Charles Horetzky," *Alberta Historical Review* 19 (1971): 9–25.

Sept 3. Breakfasted with Camby* 5.30 A.m. & started at 7 to ride back to the fossil Creek,[152] about 3 ½ miles from here, with the purpose of ascending it & getting a section. Took both the indians along. one to take care of the horses, the other to come with me up the Creek & carry specimens &c. Got back to Camp at 2 P.m. after a fatiguing scramble, most of the way wading in the water of the brook or climbing over or between tangled masses of logs in its bed. Attained a point about 1000 feet above the trail, & though unable to measure the Section, formed a good idea of its general character & collected some interesting fossils &c.

The most abundant form appears to be an *exogyra*[153] in which case the formation is probably Cretaceous, or at least Mesozoic. It almost undoubtedly represents Selwyn's Jackass Mt. Conglomerate Series &c.[154] & I think probably also the Coal bearing rocks of Vancouver Isd. (This on the supposition of its Cretaceous age being born out).

Sept 4. Cambie* moving Camp about 3 miles S. Westward along the lake shore to Keep up with his work, decided to go with him to Same place. Horses had strayed far, & before they had been brought into Camp, packed, & the new place reached, nearly 2 P.m. Afternoon walked back to the glacier stream[155] & up it to Some rock exposures, which examined. Day Showery.

Sept 5. (Sunday) Morning opened with heavy rain which continued till about noon. Afternoon clearing but raw & cold. Evening fine. Wrote letters to go on to Soda Cr. by Mail Carrier tomorrow. Read &c. Mr C. read prayers shortly after dark to such of the men as chose to attend.

G. M. Dawson to Margaret Dawson, 5 September 1875, Tatlayoko Lake

I fancy the family now all home again from Metis, & settled down again to Montreal life, but doing so, & writing is an act of faith when I have not heard from anyone for so long. Today being a wet day & a Sunday, & a Mail carrier going to Soda Creek from Mr Cambie's* Camp tomorrow, I am trying to make up arrears of correspondence. I think I told you before of the composition of my Small party. Of the two Indians, or *Siwashes* as they are called here there is not much to Say. They are of the semicivilized

---

152. It is still called Fossil Creek.

153. A Cretaceous oyster or clam-like fossil of the class Pelecypod.

154. One of Selwyn's eight series of 1871. "They consist of hard, close-grained and thick-hedded, greenish sandstones of quartzites, green and black shales, and, above these, massive thick-bedded pebble conglomerates, dipping generally at low angles in various directions" (Selwyn, "Journal and Report," 60).

155. Probably Cheshi Creek.

Kind & from Lilloet on the Frazer R.[156] One named Tommy & the other
Known as Jimmy; which names are no ⟨good⟩ doubt as good as any
others for the purpose of designating their respective owners. They are
brothers, & Jimmy, being the elder, seems to consider that Tommy should
do the hardest work. They both speak & understand English to a limited
extent, so that my Knowledge of Chinook does not advance so fast as it
otherwise might. Like most Indians their Capacity for food is about
double that of white men, & their Capacity for work about one half. Who
can wonder that under these Circumstances the Indian races should go to
the wall in the "struggle for existence". However of the indians in general
it may be said that they Can eat many things which white Men cannot. For
example, the woods all through this part of the country consist largely of a
small species of pine which I believe to be *P. Contorta*; & almost everywhere the natives have peeled great slabs of bark off the trees to get at the
soft Cambium layer beneath. In spring this is scraped off & eaten.[157]
Instance no 2. Two little Indian children are now squatting Close to the
fire just outside my tent — A boy & a girl I believe — Clothed inexpen-
sively but *not* neatly in dirt, & a few rags of skin & cloth — & sharing
between them [....] about a piece of bacon rind of about the consistency of
shoe leather; but with evident Satisfaction. The indians about here belong
to the Chilacotin bands, & are Known as *Stoneys*[158] (not to be confounded
with the Stoneys of the plains) & are many of them so barbarous as not to
understand the Chinook Jargon. They are good Catholics however — I see
the children have little brass medals strung round their necks — do not eat
meat on Fridays, & some of them even Cross themselves & say a grace
before Sitting down to a cup of tea. It was on the Homathco R. which
flows out of this lake, & not many miles from here, that Waddingtons
party were massacred by the Indians in 1864.[159] They were engaged in cutting out a trail for pack trains, which was destined to reach from Bute
Inlet to the Frazer R, but were attacked one night, the tent ropes Cut

156. They would be Lillooet (Interior Salish) Indians.

157. The cambium of the lodgepole pine, *P. contorta*, was an extremely popular food item
    with all interior Indians in British Columbia. See Nancy J. Turner, *Food Plants of
    British Columbia Indians, part II, Interior Peoples*, British Columbia Provincial
    Museum Handbook no. 36 (Victoria, 1978), 58.

158. A reference to those Chilcotin Indians who did not move eastward from their traditional
    grounds to reserves. These Indians, less influenced by Europeans than their reserve rela-
    tives, were known as Stone Chilcotin or Stonies.

159. Alfred Penderell Waddington (1801–72), a prominent Victoria merchant, was involved
    in a project to construct a short route to the Cariboo gold fields. After the attack, the
    project was abandoned. For a discussion of this incident see Edward Sleigh Hewlett,
    "The Chilcotin Uprising of 1864," *BC Studies*, no. 19 (1973): 50–72.

Suddenly, & before they could get out, or make any effectuall resistance all but two or three were Killed. Volunteers were through this country scattered about all the succeding Summer, looking after the guilty parties. The indians hardly dared to come down to the lakes to fish, & were afraid to fire off a gun in the woods, starvation at last reduced them, & I believe they gave up the most Culpable; & these were shortly afterwards tried & hung at Quesnelle.

— All this by way of a digression, as I was describing the *Materiel* of my party. The third component — *Reeves*, is quite a character. Picked up & engaged by Mr Richardson* in Victoria. He acts as cook, but is very useful generally, & a good hand at getting up in the morning & Calling the Camp, which Saves me the trouble. He is a sofisticated Cockney of I suppose about 50 years old, &, as I have little by little learned, Kept a Cook shop or Eating-house in London, but Suffering from rheumatic Gout, took the advice of his ⟨sister⟩ physician & voyaged abroad to see his sister who is married & lives in Vancouver Island. Finding it arduous to have nothing to do, he engaged as cook Successively on various surveying parties & is as he says "seeing the country" with the intention of returning to England in a year or two. He is a most loquacious individual, full of all sorts of yarns & stories, & with many queer ideas. He devotes himself to cookery however, even under the Most adverse Circumstances, & makes better Camp fare than I have Seen before, So that it is to be hoped I may grow fat. Thanks to Your, & Anna's* Care all travelling arrangements turn out excellently. I shall not be able to write to Anna* this time, but please tell her it shall be next opportunity. I have done very little in the way of sketching yet, though plenty of subjects present themselves, for So much time & energy are expended on travelling, that what with giving some attention to the geology, not much of either remains for anything else. Now that you are home again I hope you will make up your mind not to worry about domestic Management So much as last winter, & especially I think you should Make it a rule to go out for a walk every day, even if there is no absolute out door business to be done.

I want to write a few lines to William* & So must reserve a little time for that purpose, & pull up here.

Love to Eva,[160] & to yourself from your affectionate Son

---

160. Eva Dawson (b. 1864), Dawson's youngest sister, attended Montreal High School, graduating in 1877. She subsequently married Hope T. Atkin and moved to England where they resided permanently. Eva eventually had three children: two daughters, Silvia and Grace, and a son, Dawson, who was killed in the First World War.

G. M. Dawson to John William Dawson*, 5 September 1875, S.E. Side Tatlayoko Lake

A mail carrier is going out from here tomorrow, & I take the opportunity of writing home. I have got so far on my journey, & am now camped near Mr Cambie's* Surveying party, waiting to get a Couple of extra horses, & hoping to get off again day after tomorrow or thereabouts. I have pushed through to here rather fast, not Knowing how far Mr Cambie* might get if time was lost on the way. From here I return nearly on the same track for three days, & then strike N.N.E. for Blackwater. So far I have not met with anything of great geological interest by the way, the country being where one would most wish to see something of the rocks, thickly timbered. Here in the Eastern range of the Cascade Mountains, surrounded on all sides by snowy peaks, — some in this immediate vicinity standing 6'000 feet above the lake — there is no want of rock exposures; but the features are on So grand a scale that one can do but little. One of my chief objects in coming here was to visit a locality where fossils were reported to occur in great abundance. It is about 6 miles from this Camp, & I spent part of a day there. The fossils are nearly all of one Kind, & look like *Gyrodes*.[161] Evidently mesozoic & perhaps probably Cretaceous. They are very numerous, but in an exceedingly hard bluish sandstone or quartzite. On one or two pieces fallen from the cliffs I saw impressions of roots or branches of trees, but not ⟨recognizable⟩ identifiable. There is a magnificent Section in the Mountains on this side of the lake of Several thousand feet of Conformable strata, to which the fossil-bearing beds belong, but a measurement of it would require at least a weeks mountain climbing which I cannot now afford. The beds are probably the representations of those Called the Jackass Mt Series by Mr Selwyn*, & may eventually connect it with the Coal producing rocks of Vancouver Island.

In coming in here from Soda Creek, we have had frost nearly every Clear night, but often quite warm weather in the middle of the day. The last few days have been broken & showery, but I hope we have now about the last of it.

The scenery about here is very fine. This lake is about sixteen miles long, & filled with clear blue water evidently very deep. It runs westward right into the heart of the Cascades, & then discharges its waters by the Homathco R, into Bute Inlet. It is Curious that not only the Frazer but so many smaller streams should rise *East* of the Cascades, & flow quite

---

161. An important genera of gastropod mollusc fossils (marine snails) most commonly of Cretaceous age.

through them to the Pacific. In full view at the S. end of the lake, up among the mountains is a real glacier with moraine lines distinctly visible on it, & close by the camp a large brook enters the lake which from its milky & turbid appearance must also originate from a glacier up among the Mountains to the South East. Glacial striation appears in this valley, but exactly following its general direction. I also observed glacial scratching near the Mouth of the Chilacotin R about 3500 feet above the sea level on top of the basaltic plateau

I see in a Toronto Globe brought in by the Mail Carrier yesterday, among other items, the announcement of the discovery of Coal in the vicinity of Ft Francis Rainy R. You will remember Russell[162] sending me Samples from there last winter which were analysed & Mentioned in my report.[163] I wonder whether anything more definite has come to light on the question.

I hope to hear so many things when I get up to my letters at Blackwater about what has been going on, including Metis your visit to Detroit &c. &c. Please let me know from time to time how the Pictou iron business[164] proceeds. I hope you will not have any more trouble about it, at any rate, & if there is anything further I can do in it please let me Know.

I hope I shall be able to connect with Mr Selwyn* when he passes through on his way back, & I shall Certainly make an effort to do so if I can learn anything definite as to date.

With love to all at home

Sept 6. Started at 7 A.m. & rode down by the trail to the S End of the lake, examining the rocks &c. & to see where Mr Horetzky* might be, & when I might count on getting his horses back, to go on to Blackwater. Found him across the stream at the foot of the Lake.[165] Having crossed his stuff on a raft, & the horses by a shallow bar on which they scarcely need to swim at all. Time of return of horses appears uncertain, & Mr H. in a particular hurry. Mr Camby* Kindly offers to let me have the only spare horse he has, his own riding one, to make up my complement.

---

162. Alexander Lord Russell (1842-1922), from Port Arthur, Ontario, had held the principal surveying position on the British North American Boundary Commission. Russell should not be confused with Alexander Lindsay Russell, who was assistant surveyor general with the federal government.

163. The "coal" was mentioned on 139 and analyzed on 172-73 in Dawson, *Geology and Resources*.

164. In 1872, Dawson had carried out several surveys of mining regions in Nova Scotia. As late as 1877, he had still not received full remuneration for the professional services rendered in surveying iron deposits at Pictou.

165. Homathko River.

Decide to accept the offer & start tomorrow morning, though still one horse short. Find I cannot do much more here without plenty time, & anxious to get northward while season lasts.

Sept 7. Waiting for the new horse to be brought in, & did not get off till 8.30. Travelled on till 5 P.m. & then only reached a small Stream[166] not far north of the end of the lake. Trail very difficult, & devious.

Day undecided & threatening. Fine cloud effects on the Mountains, & just at sunset a beautiful burst of Crimson light on the snowy mountain tops of the south end of the lake.

viburnum opulus {pauciflorum}[167] grows abundantly in one place on the trail passed over today. Bunch grass comes to the N.E. end of the lake.

(Journey So far back on former track.)

Sept 8. Left Camp 6 A.m. riding ahead of the packs to examine rock exposures. overcast & showery. Back on the old trail to Cochin L. then round the north end of it & by another trail northward to Peterson L.[168] Had some difficulty in finding the beginning of the new trail, & obliged to make a long day, not meeting water for camping till arrival at old Depot at Peterson L. Camp 4 P.m. Horses all very tired & some quite sore already. Heavy fall of rain about 3.30. wetting everything. Horse rolled on his saddle on arriving at Camp, breaking among other things in the saddle bags my only thermometer. Evening clearing.

Sept 9 Left Camp 7 A.m. & travelled on till 1 P.m. Camping early on the N Shore of Tatla L. to let the horses have a rest. Some of them weak & backs very sore. Wrote up notes &c.

Observed *Cactus* growing sparingly at W. end Tatla L.

Tatla L. lies opposite the gap in the mts through which the W. branch of the Homathco[169] now flows S westward, & evidently a part of the same valley. Peterson L. lies in the same hollow & is probably only separated from Tatla by moraine matter.

Evident that last flow of ice *from* the Cascades Eastward, & no doubt westward also, though it *may* be a question whether at some former period ice flowed from the Central table-land *through* the passes of the Cascades.[170] one ice stream must have come from the W. Homathco

---

166. Probably Lincoln Creek.

167. If Dawson meant *"viburnum opulus"* he could have been referring to high-bush cranberry, *Viburnum opulus* var. *americanum* Ait.; and if "viburnum pauciflorum" the squashberry, *Viburnum edule* (Michx.) Raf.

168. Patterson Lake.

169. Mosley Creek.

170. It is now thought that at the glacier climax, ice flowed southwesterly from the interior through the Coast Mountains. However, at a later stage ice could have moved from the

hollow & flowed nearly in the direction of Tatla L. Another from the E. Homathco.[171] Must I think have flowed down Tatlayaco L & the valley including Cochin, Whitewater, & Eagle Lakes. Probably uniting. with the Tatla L. stream near Loon L. if not before. Some of this ice may have passed over into the Chilequoite Lake[172] valley, but I do not think there is any low gap.

Sept 10. Left Camp 7.15 & travelled on along N. Shore Tatla L. Many prairie chickens.[173] Struck 3 on the wing but owing to light charges, got one only. Lost about an hour looking for trail, having missed it, & supposing that should cross the Tatla L. Creek sooner than turned out correct. Got the right trail at last, & came back to former Camp at Crossing of the Chilanco.

Sketched Tatla L. & Cascades while packs arranging in the morning.

A magnificent day. Almost cloudless, & warm.

Tatla L. valley rather seems to become narrower & more abrupt eastward as though the stream forming it had flowed to the west. Some traces of moraine matter near the eastern end, but fragments water worn.

The indians of all this district seem to bury their dead,[174] & then place over the spot a pile of logs, with a covering of bark &c. Above the whole a pole set up with some rags, in some cases a tin pan or hat, & in one instance a musket observed. Many such graves along N side Tatla L.

Observed in Some places basin like hollows in the ground, quite Symetrical, & apparently the traces of underground winter houses of the indians. {(or fish caches)}[175]

---

high country southwest of Tatla Lake out toward the dwindling ice of the interior plateau. See H. W. Tipper, *Glacial Geomorphology and Pleistocene History of Central British Columbia*, Geological Survey of Canada Bulletin no. 196 (Ottawa: Information Canada, 1971), 84–86, and Map 1291A. Tipper's mapping indicates that ice indeed flowed from the Tatlayoko Valley easterly through a gap to Choelquoit Lake.

171. The main branch of the Homathko River.

172. Choelquoit Lake.

173. Sharp-tailed grouse, *Pedioecetes phasianellus columbianus* (Ord).

174. Before the middle of the nineteenth century, cremation was practised by the Chilcotin Indians, with the ashes buried under brush or a pile of stones. Later, probably under the influence of missionaries, the Indians began to bury their dead. A low fence of logs or a small house was placed around the grave for protection. See Livingston Farrand, "The Chilcotin," *British Association for the Advancement of Science, Report 1898* (London, 1899), 647–48; Barbara A. Leitch, *A Concise Dictionary of Indian Tribes of North America* (Algonac, Michigan: Reference Publications, 1979), 100; and Robert B. Lane, "Chilcotin," in *Handbook of North American Indians* vol. 6, *Subarctic*, ed. June Helm (Washington, D.C.: Smithsonian Institution, 1981), 405.

175. The winter houses of the Chilcotin Indians were semi-subterranean consisting of a large pit about four feet deep with several posts supporting a superstructure. These were

Sept 11. Start 7 a.m. & travel on till 1 P.m. Camping near the lower end of Puntzie L. where the trail leaves it for Chinicut L.[176] Afternoon fishing. The lake full of Small fish which appear to be a species of White-fish.[177] They are about to spawn & may be seen springing from the surface of the water in all directions. Came this morning on a small camp of indians near the lakeshore. Paterfamilias clad lightly in a hat, & rather short shirt.

Some of the horses very sore, & Tommy laid up with a sore leg. Intend to remain here all day tomorrow to rest & recruit.

Shot 2 ducks & a prairie hen *en route.*

Sept 12 Sunday did not Shift Camp. Rode back to examine rock exposures about 2 m. S.E. on the trail. Made sketch of lake, finished one of Tatlyoca L, effected some repairs. Collected a few shells &c.

Day fine & very hot in the sun

Sept 13. From Puntzie L. Camp about 20 m. in a general N Easterly direction. {Leave Camp 8.10. Camp 4.30 loosing about 20 minutes} Did not intend to make quite such a long day, especially as start late on account of Tommy being unable to assist in the packing; but found no water for a long way.

Shot 5 spruce partridges today & could have had more if thought any use. After Killing the first two an indian attracted by the reports, appeared, with his old flint lock in his hand. An old man & rather bent, probably out looking for a deer. Followed us Some miles to Chizicut L. crossing, where found his Camp, & Several squaws & children. They are now catching great numbers of whitefish? like those seen in Puntzie L, & are engaged drying them in the Sun. Fish strung in long lines on poles, & smokes Kept up below, probably to prevent the flies settling on them. A little boy from the Camp followed us to our Camp about 12 m., gave him some supper, & he evidently intends to stay all night, having ⟨fasten⟩ picketed out his horse.

---

located close together and not far from a lakeshore, so there was easy access to fishing. The use of these pit-houses may have been adopted from the neighbouring Shuswap Indians. Dried fish was stored in pits or caches, which were usually in the area around the winter pit-houses of the fishing sites. Cache pits were also found in the interior of the pit-houses. See Farrand, "The Chilcotin," 646; Lane, "Chilcotin," 402, 406; and Roscoe Wilmeth, "Historic Chilcotin Archaeology at Anahim Lake, British Columbia," in *Aboriginal Man and Environments of the Plateau of Northwest America,* ed. Arnoud H. Stryd and Rachel A. Smith (Calgary: University of Calgary Archaeological Association, 1971), 57.

176. Chilcotin Lake.

177. Possibly the pygmy whitefish, *Prosopium coulteri* (Eigenmann & Eigenmann), a small-sized species found in the region.

The poplars, willows, dwarf birches,[178] & other undershrubs & herbs are now rapidly changing colour.

Would be inclined to represent the relations of the uneven & moundy Sandy & Clayey deposits, charged with boulders & pebbles, to the benches, much as below. [*Illus.*] Seems that these upland deposits, whether formed by glaciers or floating ice, Stand in place of the *boulder clay* of other regions[179]

Sept 14 Delayed in starting as yesterday, but made a moderately good days Journey. Travelling from 7.50 to 3.40 with the loss of about ½ hour. The country undulating & broken, with some very fine displays of Moraine mounds. Pinus Contorta woods, with great areas of windfall & *brulé.* Camped at Camp 13 of C.P.R.S. left by them Aug 8. Fine spring of cold water.

Evidence of moraines seen today appears conclusive that country partially submerged at time of deposit, & rising gradually above water as ice receded. Suspected simultaneous action of iced water already in vicinity of Eagle & Tatla Lakes. The moraines seen today show some well rounded stones, with many not much rounded, or nearly angular, but observed none glaciated. The semicircular ridges[180] are evidently Glacier work, but are *flat topped like terraces*, but differ from terraces by being seperated from one another by deep narrow valleys, now often occupied by lakes or swamps, & flat bottomed. The top of the later formed moraine mounds *are also lower than the Earlier*, & less subsequently modified. In a rough diagramatic way thus. [*Illus.*]

These moraines evidence great extension of ice from Cascades, & probably belong to the same series as those of the lower parts of {the} Tatla Eagle & Loon L. valley.

I have now little doubt, that basin of Puntzie L. also formerly occupied by tongue of glacier ice coming over via the Chilanco valley. Abrup mounds 30 or 40 feet high ner the shore of the lower end, which can

178. Dwarf or scrub birch, *Betula glandulosa* Michx.

179. The deposits described are almost certainly a local variation of till. Dawson was still heavily influenced by the so-called "iceberg theory" of glaciation. For a summary of the development of Dawson's theory of Cordilleran glaciation, see Tipper, *Glacial Geomorphology*, 71–72.

180. The "semicircular ridges" are not confirmed by analysis of air photos. What appears, instead, is a gently rolling surface cut by a series of meandering channels supplied for a time, at the end of the last glaciation, by rivers from, and diverted by the melting ice, but now occupied only by swamps, lakes, or minor streams. Dawson seems to use the term "moraine" for any glacial deposit, regardless of its topographic form.

scarcely have had other origin. (See sketch for part of one of these)[181]

Sept 15. Horses finding poor feed showed tendency to stray away, & required attention several times in the night. Morning two gone, & only recovered some miles back on the trail after considerable detention. Did not get away till 8.20, & then unfortunately took a wrong trail, following nearly parallel with the location line, & finally disappearing. Lost nearly two hours hunting for trail, & by the rolling down a bank of one of the pack animals. 6 m. to [Jun?] falls Camp of Jennings*, wher a pretty little Cascade coming down over sep like ledge of basalt. N.E. of Camp 15 (C.P.R.S.) on the opposite bank of the river a fine cascade. The Nazco rapidly increasing in size. Came only about 13 miles, though 8 hr 40 m altogether on the road. Trail very bad & rocky, just before coming to Camp Reeves fell saddle & all from the horse going up a steep hill, & had a narrow escape, though getting off unhurt. My Saddle-bags however Kicked away from their fastnings in the struggle. Camped Somewhere near Jenning's Camp 15. Very warm in the Sun today, though frost last night.

Sept 16. Start 7.30 & travel on down the valley. Trail much improved, valley somewhat opened out with small meadows, & ponds. Day very warm & cloudless. Camped near picket 3788 & almost opposite a very prominent bluff. Passed a camp of indian women who said their husbands had all gone beaver[182] hunting & left them no Muck-a-muck.[183] Many ducks & geese, & much old beaver work, most of the lakes in the valley being probably thus Caused. Gathered a number of *sphaeriums*[184] in the river bed near camp, & found a fragment of *Unio* like *U. rectus*.[185]

Heard shots this evening, & also sound of distant chopping. These no doubt proceed from Mr Jennings* Camp which must be near.

Sept 17. Found men at work on the line soon after leaving Camp, & Mr Jenning's* Camp about 4 miles on. Camped. Examined rocks in hillside near Camp. Reading, writing up notes &c. Find no mail here for me. It is probably at Blackwater. The Clisbaco R enters the valley of the Nazco about 2 miles below this point. The stream of the former is almost as large as the latter, but the valley rises much more rapidly as followed upward.

Sept 18. Started out with one of Mr Jenning's* indians named 'Charley' & walked down to the Clisbaco & then several miles up the valley to see rock

---

181. The sketch is in Dawson's field notebook, RG 45, vol. 134, no. 2790, 28, PAC.

182. American beaver, *Castor canadensis sagittatus* Benson.

183. Chinook Jargon for "food."

184. One of the fingernail clams, *Sphaerium* spp.

185. Freshwater mussels of the superfamily Unionacea. The only species found in central British Columbia were the western-river pearl mussel, *Margaritifera falcata* (Gould), and the western floater, *Anodonta kennerlyi* Lea.

exposures there. No trail up the Clisbaco, & so consequently a scramble through woods all the way. Afternoon made search for fossils in rocks behind Camp. Collected 3 species of Juniper.[186] Charlie told us a story in broken Chinook, this evening, about the cliff on the Chelacotan R mentioned in notes of Aug. 27.[187] Says long ago, three generations at least, bad siwashes from the *Salt Chuck*[188] Came there, & camped on top of the bluff. Thence they used to watch the Chelacotan indians & shoot them as they passed along the valley, with arrows, & no one Knew how it was done. At last a Chelacotan Siwash passing saw a fire on the bluff, & went & told the others, who sent a man up, who while the bad indians were asleep found out how many there were. Then the other indians surrounded the bluff, & while they sent a clootchman[189] to walk along in the valley below, thus attracting the attention of the Marauders; Came up behind them & made a sudden onslaught, killing them all, except one indian, supposed to be the medicine man who flew away in the air from the edge of the bluff "All same wind *Klattawa*,[190] all same chicken." This at least is what the *oleman wa-wa*.[191]

Sept 19. Sunday. About Camp at writing odd jobs &c.

Sept 20. Morning walked up the river about two miles to Collect *unios* &c. Noticed drift lignite in the river bed. Afternoon rode about four miles back, to cliff beyond Cinderella Mt.[192] to see if lignite formation capping the cliffs. Found only weathered basalt.

Sept 21. Moved Camp with Mr Jennings'* party about six miles down the river. Walked down with gun observing rocks &c. day warm. but strong wind from S. Three of the horses still very sore, & two weak also. Tommie still ill & able to do next to nothing. Hardly in condition to move on, though feel that wasting time to stay here much longer.

Sept 22. Rode out with Mr Mckay* at 8.50, & returned at 4.30 after having made a reconnaissance some 7 ½ miles down the Quesnelle trail, & ridden altogether about 24 miles. Day showery, after a night of heavy rain. The valley from below the Clisbacko R. opens out considerably, &

---

186. The common juniper, *Juniperus communis* L., Rocky Mountain juniper, *Juniperus scopulorum* Sarg., and creeping juniper, *Juniperus horizontalis* Moench.

187. See G. M. Dawson, Field Notebooks, RG 45, vol. 134, no. 2790, 78v, PAC.

188. "*Chuck*" is Chinook Jargon for water, hence "Salt Chuck" means sea.

189. Or "Klootchman." In the Chinook Jargon, "a woman, a wife."

190. A Chinook Jargon term meaning "to flee, to travel."

191. Chinook Jargon for "the old man says."

192. Unidentifiable.

shows a good deal of meadow land at a somewhat higher level above the river, & which is probably not often flooded.

Sept 23. Walked down the West side of the valley examining some rock exposures, but found nothing of particular interest

Sept 24. Started from Camp about 7.15 & rode Northward with Mr Jennings* to the beginning of the trail to Cluscus Lake.[193] There separated & went on on the Cluscus trail with Jimmy. till 11.40. Then turned & got back to camp about 4 P.m. having got out on the Cluscus trail between 7 & 8 miles. The trail from Quesnelle to the South end of the long lake,[194] thence up the Nazco to & round the N end of the lake; & from there westward to Cluscus L; is the main trail, & has evidently been considerably used. Little or no trail exists N of this down the Nazco toward the Blackwater. Killed five grouse by the way.

Sept 25. Near camp all day. Tried washing gravel of river for gold, but without success. Tried fishing also unsuccessfully, the river being to shallow about here.

Tommy still quite useless, & the three pack animals very sore. The places skinned in packing have for the most part festered, & are now discharging matter. The brown horse especially very weak. The packs & ⟨trail⟩ mail now since some days expected from Quesnelle have not yet turned up, & till they do Mr Jenning's* can hardly spare a man & ⟨horses⟩ animals to take my stuff through to Blackwater. Delay very provoking as now nothing much remains to do here

The foliage {here} is now just about the stage at which it was last october during my trip through Turtle Mt.,[195] Showing the earlier onset of winter here.

Sept 26. Sunday. Morning engaged collating the Chilacotin vocabularies obtained by Mr Jenning's* & Myself from the Indian Charlie. Considerable difficulty in getting the right answers from him when here, & great trouble in spelling some of those obtained, from their nasal & gutteral sound.

Afternoon climbed the hillside to the West, & followed up the bank of a small creek N. westward; then descended into the valley bottom & followed the brook back to the river. Found a curious rocky gorge, with

193. Kluskus Lake.

194. Probably Marmot Lake.

195. The "trip" was part of the explorations undertaken by Dawson as geologist/naturalist to the British North American Boundary Commission. Turtle Mountain (lat. 49°N and long. 100°15′W) "is a broken, hilly, wooded region, with an area of perhaps about twenty miles square, and slopes gradually upward from the plain around it, above which it is elevated, at its highest points, about 500 feet" (Dawson, *Geology and Resources*, 223).

much calcareous deposit, & a waterfall of about 30 feet in height. Many deer tracks though mostly of some age.

Sept 27. {All packed up & ready to start with Mr Jennings* to ride through light to Mr Bell's[196] Camp; but found Mr White[197] unable to walk from axe cut of last night & Mr J. therefore obliged to stay to run the level.} Collected specimens of P. contorta, & an Abies which seems to be very near the ordinary black spruce but agrees exactly with the discription of A. Englemanni[198] & is probably that species. It has been abundant from about Eagle Lake on the route travelled to here, but also occurs further East. It forms dense woods of large trees in wet or clayey hollows of the plateau about here, & also fringes streams & swamps.

Revisited the ravine mentioned yesterday. The calcareous sinter[199] cliffs are honeycombed with openings, many of which are the moulds of Sticks & logs formerly imbedded. These are now inhabited by some Small animals, probably a species of marmot.[200] They have dragged a great quantity of sticks, leaves, &c to the Mouths of their holes. Set fire to one of the largest of these, & the smoke soon began to ooze out of the holes in various parts of the cliff. Caught a momentary glimpse of one of the animals, but most probably escaped by holes above.

Mr Marcus Smith*, & the long expected train from Quesnelle arrived this P.m. Got all arrangements made for start tomorrow, Mr Jennings* furnishing mules to take me to Blackwater Depôt, & sending out Some of his spare stuff At the same time. Leave the three sick horses, & two of the apparejoes,[201] getting receipt for them. My mail said to be at Blackwater.

Sept. 28. Up early making preparations for start, but did not get away till about Noon. Got letters from Mr Smith* to Depôt man at Blackwater &

196. H. P. Bell, one of the engineers-in-charge with the CPRS.

197. T. H. White, a transitman with the CPRS.

198. Dawson was probably correct in identifying the "Abies" as "A. Englemanni," the modern Engelmann spruce, *Picea engelmannii* Parry. The "ordinary black spruce" referred to was the black spruce, *P. mariana*.

199. Calcium deposited by hot or cold mineral springs.

200. Hoary marmots, *Marmota caligata* (Eschscholtz).

201. According to Daniel Gordon, who travelled with Dawson later in 1879, "the *aparacho*, or pack-saddle, which is made of strips of wood, leather and padding, as carefully as an ordinary riding-saddle, is first secured by a broad, firm girth, which is bound or 'sinched,' as tightly as two men can pull, each pressing his knee or foot against the animal's side to gain increased leverage, a blinder having been previously placed across the mule's eyes, to prevent all movement on his part, as this temporary sightlessness secures perfect stillness. Then the packers pile up the load, which has been already arranged in two large bundles" (Daniel M. Gordon, *Mountain and Prairie; A Journey from Victoria to Winnipeg, via Peace River Pass* [London: Sampson Low, Marston, Searle, & Rivington, 1880], 130).

to Mr Bell*.

Party has now added one of Mr Jenning's* packers (Joe) & an indian aide & guide brought from the Blackwater by Mr Smith*, & called Fanny. Made about ten miles down the Nazco & camped at the last grass for a long distance. Tried fishing but unsuccessfully.

Sept 29. Start 7.30 A.m. & travel on towards the Blackwater. Trail poor & in some places needing a good deal of cutting out. Mule overturned & mired in getting up the river bank at one of the fords, but no serious consequences. Travelled on till 3.40 P.m. when camped about 2 miles E. of the Mouth of the Nazco on the N. side of the Blackwater R. Fishing very successful tonight the stream being full of fine trout & white-fish.

Camp situated near one of last season's CP.R.S. Camps, on the Blackwater line.

Sept 30. Leave Camp 7.50 Travel on old Survey trail till Noon, eastward & northward nearly parallel to the Blackwater. Then travel southward on branch trail to Mr Bells* Camp 20 in Blackwater Cañon. An indian family camped at the branch trail, cleaner, better looking & apparently more comfortable; than any yet seen. Their winter houses are near Cluscus L. {Blueberries[202] observed today for the first time. In some abundance}

Spent the remainder of the afternoon examining the rocks of the Cañon, & in the evening dined with Mr B. & party. Got map information &c. from him, also a pack horse & apparejo which he does not need.

The rocks of the canon probably represent the Lower Cache Creek Series though no limestones like the typical ones, appear, nor are the flinty slates of that group well represented. The igneous dykes parallel to the stratification resemble those seen in the L.C.C.[203] on the waggon road.

The rocks of the Canon, with a few exceptions, are not such as to offer great resistance to blasting or rock work. most of the slates would be pretty easy to bore, & the shattered state of the rock would cause it to break into small pieces on blasting.

Oct. 1. Left Camp 8 A.m. & travelled on without stopping till about 4 P.m.; reaching Blackwater Depôt. Find the pack train now due for Ft George, & with which Mr Smith* had arranged that I should travel, not yet on hand. Appearance of break up in the weather. Barometer falling, wind rising. Clouds collecting all day. geese flying South. Find a large mail waiting here, though no dates later than Aug 20. from Montreal. Nothing yet heard from Mr Selwyn*

Oct. 2. Drizzling rain & occasional showers of sleet all day. overcast, windy, & cold. Examined the river banks near the depôt, but did not go

202. Blueberries, *Vaccinium* spp.

203. Lower Cache Creek rocks. See 16 August 1875.

far on account of the weather. Mail Carrier arrived from Quesnelle, having left this morning & ridden through. No mail for me.

Pack train for Ft George had not left this morning, is waiting for goods & may not leave for some days to come, which is very provoking. Pack train arrived here with oats. Part of the animals returning to Quesnelle & part going on to Mr Bell*. Mr Fisher (Bell's purveyor)[204] also arrived on business connected with the train.

Oct. 3. Sunday. Snow on the ground about 2 inches deep, & still falling a little. Writing home, reading & Keeping warm

G. M. Dawson to Anna Dawson*, 3 October 1875, Blackwater Depot, Blackwater River

'Snow, snow beautiful Snow' at last; after a term of the most splendid cloudless weather, Frost nearly every night & oppressively hot in the Sun in the middle of the day. On Friday as we travelled along to this place the signs of bad weather began to appear. The barometer fell, light clouds began to gather & thicken. Geese flying from the far north passed overhead, & towards evening the wind went round from W. to N. & became squally. All yesterday it drizzled & occasionally a half melted snow flake Came down, & last night the snow Came in earnest & was this morning about 2 inches deep, Soft, & clammy. Today it is melting away as fast as it Can & the weather Shows signs of clearing up again, & I have no doubt that when this petulant outburst is fairly over, we Shall have the indian Summer for a week or two

I am now here waiting the arrival of a pack train from Quesnelle for Ft George, Mr Smith* proposing that I should accompany it there & back the three pack animals I have had, having got So sore under the mismanagement of the indian packer, that they are for the present useless. The pack train may not get here for some days yet, but if the weather becomes settled I can occupy the time profitably in the neighbourhood.

I found quite a mail waiting my arrival here, the latest date being I think Aug. 23. Thanks for your letters & enclosures from William* &c. I have not yet received a copy of my report,[205] but may yet get it before leaving here, & if not then on my return. The pack train goes to Ft George in 4 days & will not probably remain there more than a day or two. From here to Quesnelle is three days by pack train, though one can ride through

204. Andrew Fisher, deputy purveyor to the CPRS.

205. Dawson was referring to the report on his work as geologist/botanist to the British North American Boundary Commission, published as Dawson, *Geology and Resources.*

light in a day, the distance being only about 45 miles. At Quesnelle of course one is on the regular travelled line of the Frazer & within less than a week of Victoria.

Nothing yet from Mr Selwyn*, though I expect daily to hear of or see him. It is just possible that he may go out to the Coast by Lake François, of which {route} Mr Smith* has written particulars to meet him at Ft George. In which Case I should not see him.[206]

I think it is your turn for a letter, but for the life of me cannot remember to whom I wrote last. As there is nothing particular to write about however it cannot make much odds.

Since leaving the Cascade Mts. there has been very little fine or remarkable scenery. The general surface of the country is a more or less regular plateau with hills & ranges of hills rising above it here & there, & river & stream Valleys cutting down into it. Some of the river vallies are very large & deep, but generally not rocky. There are occasional meadows, swamps, & hillsides with good grass, & in Some places open woods of large Douglas pines[207] with grass growing beneath them. As a rule however the country is pretty thickly wooded with Scrub pine,[208] Sometimes of fair growth & standing, often prostrate, often burnt, often burnt & prostrate with young scrub pines coming up in dense thickets &c. &c. Through & over & among all these varieties of country, the little paths they Call trails here, wind & twist seeking for lines of least resistance, or following the ⟨path⟩ track by which the first indian originally scrambled across the country. I think I once used the Simile before, but really the country much resembles a gigantic game of spillicans,[209] & I believe if one was to go to Ft George & begin shaking the pile, sticks would be Seen moving down at New Westminster on the Frazer!

There is Something very pleasant however in these autumn woods, now that the aspens are turning yellow among the spruces & pines. There are no maples however or other trees which take really beautiful tints.

I am progressing pretty rapidly in my knowledge of Chinook, & can now understand pretty well & Speak a little. It is very easy to learn of course there being no grammar at all & a few words going a long way, especially when the range of subjects usually forming topics of conversation

---

206. Selwyn did not return to the coast by that route but accompanied Dawson down the Fraser to Victoria in October.

207. Douglas-fir, *P. menziesii.*

208. Lodgepole pine, *P. contorta.*

209. Spillikin or spellican is a game played with a heap of slips or small rods of wood, bone, or the like, the object being to pull off each by means of a hook without disturbing the rest.

conversation is limited.

I am writing a few words to Father*, & May have time for another letter before leaving here. If not it will not now be long before I get back to more regular postal communications.

With love to yourself & all

Oct. 4. Walked down the river about 3 miles examining the rocks. Afternoon washing gravel from bank & hard-pan from below the bridge, but without finding colour in either. Day cold & raw with snow still remaining on the shady Sides of hills & in the woods where thick. Th cañon below the bridge though not So large as to be very grand — very picturesque.

Oct 5. Had arranged with Mr Sterrett[210] in charge of Depôt here to start early & ride up Bell's Trail about 14 miles, thence follow Indian trail to Mth. of Blackwater where indian houses. Stay there all night & get Indian to guide us back again up the valley of the Blackwater. Morning very threatening overcast & foggy. Did not start till 10 A.m. rode out to place where Indian trail begins, at an Indian graveyard, & there found some Indians camped, who told us that no Indians now at Mth. of Blackwater. Tried to induce one of them to go as guide, but they had no horses & would not. Engaged a lad to come back with me to Camp, who Knows the trail, & may also be useful in tending horses &c. now that the other men sent off. Started back at 2.15 & got in to Camp Just before dark, with heavy rain coming on.

The Indians were rather Surprised to see us come into their Camp. Engaged in curing fish &c. & have considerable quantity of trout, white fish, & suckers[211] strung up in process of drying. Also several beavers lately Killed, the flesh spread out flat with the tail still attached & hung over sticks near the fire — Smoky, brown, oily, & repulsive looking. Camp consisted of one very old man, very sick, & as they said "All same as tired all over" probably rheumatic. The day raw & chilly & the old fellow coiled up under a rabbit skin[212] blanket beside a little fire, hardly took any notice of us. His long grey hair standing up in shocks on his head. Half thought they had brought him here to be near the grave yard when he died. one lame man besides, & a young lad. Two young Klutchmen & 3 old squaws

210. R. Starratt was CPRS purveyor at Blackwater Depot.

211. The "trout" were probably rainbow trout, *Salmo gairdneri* Richardson, or the Dolly Varden, *Salvelinus malma* (Walbaum); "white fish" probably mountain whitefish, *Prosopium williamsoni* (Girard); and "suckers" the largescale sucker, *Catostomus macrocheilus* Girard, white sucker, *Catostomus commersoni* (Lacépède), or longnose sucker, *Catostomus catostomus* (Forster).

212. Skin of the snowshoe or varying hare, *Lepus americanus* Erxleben.

wizened & black.

The young women evidently thought themselves very attractive & put on airs accordingly. Arranged with the young lad to come back with us after a considerable amount of wa-wa[213] had been got through among the Indians in their own language. He put on his moccesins, wrapped a little old dirty Rob-Roy Shawl[214] — which seems to be quite the thing here — round his shoulders & started off. Keeping up with the horses all the way back to the Depôt. Some of the women tatooed,[215] as is the case in nearly every lot of Indians seen. The Colour employed blue, & the device usually adopted (in whole or in part) like this. [*Illus.*]

Oct 6. Raining heavily all night, & has continued overcast, foggy, & raining with slight intermission all day. Walked up the river about 1 ½ m. examining the rocks. Shot 3 prairie chickens.

Oct 7. Writing. sketching &c. Afternoon walked up the river about 4 miles examining the rocks, & got into a mass of windfall & brulé very unpleasant to travel through. The river banks have suffered very extensive alteration from land slips, which in some cases have extended from the top of the highest terrace, or summit of the plateau, to the water level.

The expressman from Peace R. passed the Depôt today, & some indians with two packs of furs from Stony Cr Camped here tonight. Nothing yet of the train either too or from Ft. George. Day fine & weather apparently about to improve.

Oct 8. Rode down the valley about ten miles with Mr Sterritt*, following an Indian trail which runs to the mouth of the Blackwater. Trail in some places very faint, but becoming better beaten eastward. The river valley becoming thickly timbered, it leaves it about two miles below the bridge & follows along the edge of the high land. Back to Camp 5.30 Macavoy's[216] arrived today & goes out tomorrow morning for Quesnelle. Wrote M.

213. Chinook Jargon for "conversation, speech."

214. The Rob Roy tartan of red and black checks.

215. Tatooing was very common in both sexes among the interior Indians, but facial tatooing was more prevalent among women than men. See James A. Teit, "Tatooing and Face and Body Painting of the Thompson Indians, British Columbia," in Smithsonian Institution, *Fifty-Fourth Annual Report of the Bureau of American Ethnology (1927-28)*, ed. Franz Boas (Washington: Government Printing Bureau, 1930), 404-5.

216. Probably Thomas McVoy, on the payroll with the CPRS train from Fort George in fiscal year 1876-77.

G. M. Dawson to Margaret Dawson*, 8 October 1875, Blackwater Depot

You will see by the date that I am Still here, waiting for the arrival of the pack-train for Ft. George. It will probably now be here early next week. There is nothing particular to add to what I wrote a few days ago, but as a pack train returning to Quesnelle leaves tomorrow I cannot resist the temptation of penning a few lines. The last mentioned 'train' left Ft George on Monday, Oct 4, & at that time Mr Selwyn* had not arrived, so that my chances of meeting him there are good. The season is now so far advanced that I hardly think it likely he will attempt going out by François Lake, but will come down by the Frazer & Wagon road to New Westminster. After the snow reported in my last, & Some days of rain, the weather has now taken a turn for the better, & is mild & even balmy with a Constantly clearing sky.

I have been riding out today from ten to half past five, & feel now rather inclined to turn in for the night, especially as from contact with Snags my nether Garments have suffered considerable injury which must be repaired before tomorrow. The result of the ride was nothing in particular. I had hoped that an indian trail of which I had heard would follow down the Blackwater R. toward the Frazer, & let me see any rocks that may be exposed. However, as it turned out, the trail soon left the Valley & took to the high land above it, altogether away from the river, & through thick woods & windfall. So fter getting on about ten miles we turned & came back.

I have pretty well exhausted the places of interest in this vicinity now, & so shall not be sorry to see that pack train as soon as it may appear.

I have found a *few* fossil plants in beds belonging to the lignite series, & think tomorrow of making search for some more, though I am not very hopeful of success.

I had intended to write to William*, but think I must put it off till next time. When he settles where he will be for the winter please let me have his address. I have just bought a Mink[217] skin from a wretched looking old indian who came prowling about, & now I have got it I dont' Know what to do with it. They do not trap many minks here, but a good many beavers, which animals, with fish, seem to constitute their staple foot. At an Indian Camp the other day I saw the flesh of several beavers, stripped off the Carcase in a sheet, & hung up in the smoke of the fire (tail attached) to dry. It looked oily & not inviting. Please ask Eva* to write & tell me if she

217. American mink, *Mustela vison energumenos* (Bangs).

is going to [Mrs?] Lay's[218] or not.

Oct 9. Morning variously occupied. Afternoon walked up the river about 2 ½ m. to look for fossils in the lignite formation beds, with poor Success however. Day fine & quite hot, & no frost now for some nights.

Oct 10. Sunday. Mail man arrived from Quesnelle with letters &c. & with him the Cargador Prefecto[219] & an Indian packer, turned back (having left here yesterday) by a letter from Mr Glassey* telling him to go with me to Ft. George.[220] Freight for McLeans[221] train not yet arrived at Quesnelle. Day fine & warm. Packing up fossils &c. & cutting everything down as much as possible to economise transport.

Oct 11. Up early, got all packed, provisions drawn from Depôt &c. & started by 8.35. Have now besides Reeves, the mexican packer Perfecto & one Indian. The two last sent back by Mr Glassey*. Discharged the Indian lad who has been working round camp for the last few days. Camped near the Indian Graveyard beside a rather large lake Called by the Indians *Pun-chaw*. Lake full of fish which the Indians are now catching in nets & drying for winter use. Tried fishing from a raft which the Indians have, as well as a bark Canoe for setting their nets; but with poor success. Fish jumping all about but only hooked one, which escaped.

Got Some of the Indians round the fire & completed the Blackwater vocabulary.

This lake is covered with a green scum, & is said to be always so characterized. The material as far as I can remember exactly resembles the *Aphamisomenon* found on the Lake of the Woods. Colour pale dull green. ⟨Form variable⟩ The minute threads are arranged in tufts or fassicles, rather irregular in form & size, but resembling {fine} chopped hay, or more frequenty Shuttle shaped, & grouped together So as to resemble a grain of oats with the husks attached & partly open. (See specimens). The Indians Call it *ta-tsa* [*Illus.*][222]

Oct 12. Up early & ready to Start, but horses had gone back on the trail

---

218. Presumably Mrs. Eleanor Lay, principal of Saybrook Hall, a Montreal finishing school for young ladies.

219. The name of the cargador, or packer, was Perfecto.

220. The letter told him that, with the train headed to Fort George delayed, he should take the required horses from the one coming from the fort, as well as "Perfecto the Spaniard" for their care. See John Glassey to G. M. Dawson, 6 October 1875, Dawson Family Papers, MUA.

221. There were three McLeans employed by the CPRS; this is probably Alexander McLean, a North Thompson packer.

222. This "green scum" was probably a filamentous blue-green alga such as *Oscillatoria*.

toward Blackwater, & did not get away till 11 a.m. Morning fine, but Soon Clouded over with upper current of air from the West. Several showers fell. Cleared about 11. Clouded gradually again. Heavy local shower with Some hail at 2 P.m. Evening partly Clouded nearly Calm. Camp at 4.10 near a nice little brook, & got dried by a large fire

Oct 13. Start 8 A.m. & after travelling along the N. trail till 9.30 turned off to ascend a prominent mountain which the trail passes to the East. Perfecto acting as guide, he having been on the top previously. Got up most of way on horseback, & had a magnificent view of all the surrounding country. Got bearings on many lakes hills &c. Followed along the crest of the ridge which runs northward from the mountain, & finally got back to the trail. Expected to have about 7 miles to go to camp, but the indian had mistaken the directions & gone 10 m. further. Got to camp about 4 P.m. Found some Indians just arrived from Ft. George, & learned from them that a party resembling Mr Selwyn's* had arrived

Indians Call the Mt. *Tsǎ-whus*.[223]

Oct 14. Left camp 7.50 A.m. Arrived at Depôt C.P.R.S. at Noon & at Ft George Proper at the Junction of the Frazer & Stewart[224] at 12.45. Near the trail on todays Journey two dead Indians, of whom the bones now only remain. They have only lately been partly buried, but have been dead some months. No one Knows how they died, & the Indians about here seem not to know who the are.

The Depôt is situated on the abrupt terrace edge of the higher level, from which a descent is made to the lower level flat, a triangular area at the junction of the two rivers. The upper level is gravelly & clayey, but the lower Seems to be fine fertile soil, & though mostly covered with small trees shows fine meadows.

The Fort a tumbled down looking place like Hudson Bay Posts generally, & surrounded by a number of shanties belonging to Indians, who are now nearly all absent hunting at the various Small lakes & Creeks over the Country. They will not return here again till about Christmas, & then disposing of their furs & having a Short holiday, start out again for the rest of the winter.

---

223. This is Tsa-whus mountain or the present Mount Baldy Hughes, described by Dawson as "an isolated basaltic outlyer, rising about 800 feet above the higher parts of the surrounding hilly plateau," with an approximate elevation of 3240 feet. On its summit Dawson found indistinct glacial striation and, a few feet from its hightest point, "a slightly overhanging surface of basalt was observed to be distinctly shaped and polished by ice" (Dawson, "On the Superficial Geology," 101). This became an important piece of evidence for his developing theory of a great confluent interior glacier.

224. Nechako River.

Find camped here Mr McLennan[225] & the remainder of Mr Selwyn's*
party. Mr S. himself with Mr Webster[226] having Started at Noon on
Monday down the Chilaccoh R[227] trail with the hope of meeting me or Mr.
Bell*, having been misinformed here as to our movements.

The waters of the Frazer & Stewart mingle here opposite the fort, the
former being turbid & whitish, the latter clear. The opposite bank of the
Frazer is high & steep, while a wide stretch of gravel bars & islands marks
the junction of the rivers.

Oct 15. Hourly expecting Mr Selwyns* return, & as in case of his arrival
he would probably wish to start at once to Catch Sundays boat from
Quesnelle; cannot go far from camp. Writing up notes, reading &c.

Oct.16. Morning about Camp. Afternoon walked some miles up the
Stewart R or (Nechaco) Shortly after return to camp about 5 P.m. Mr
Selwyn* & Mr Webster* appeared, having Gone through to Blackwater
Depôt by the Chillaco R & then hearing of my whereabouts returned by
Mr Bell's* straight trail.

Oct 17. Sunday. Reading &c. Afternoon washed out some Sand & Gravel
in the bars of the river above the Fort & got a Good many Colours of
gold. Weather gradually clouding up Since morning & about dark rain
commenced to fall & now falling heavily.

Oct 18. Leave Ft. George at 8.20 with Mr Selwyn* & party in boat &
dugout Canoe, for Quesnelle. Morning cold & foggy but soon clearing.
None of party know the river, ⟨&⟩ but have directions for running
through the two Cañons (Ft George & Cottonwood) which are the only
dangerous places.

Got through the Ft George Canon Safely today. The river is swift &
runs between rocky walls, with a couple of rocky islands in the middle.
The stream generally is rapid & riffles frequent, & often requiring Some
judgement in the steersman to pass them Safely. Rain commenced in the
afternoon, & continued to fall during the evening while we Camped on the
W. bank.

Oct 19. Leave Camp 7.55 & proceed down stream, but against a very
strong South wind. Stop for lunch 11.50 a.m. at Indian Village at Mouth

---

225. John McClennan was the foreman with Selwyn's survey party. In 1872, McClennan had
been in charge of the CPRS post in Kamloops. McClennan's brother Roderick was also
a surveyor with the railway surveys.

226. Arthur W. Webster was a topographer with the Geological Survey of Canada who was
employed from 1868 to 1882 and then briefly in 1902.

227. Chilako River.

of Blackwater R.[228] Start again 1.20 P.m. the wind now very violent & continued noise of trees Crashing down in the woods. Had a rough time Coming down a heavy rapid above the mouth of the Blackwater, the wind very strong & squally & raising a heavy short sea. — air full of flying spray, & while coasting along a cliff a large tree blown over above & only prevented by some smaller trees from coming down on top of us in the Canoe. Camp 4.35 on the E. bank.

Oct 20. Start 7.50 A.m. in steady rain which began at daylight. Camp just above the Cottonwood Canon which ran through the first thing this morning, & not found very rough, though the cliffs at the sides of the river are more abrupt, & the valley more Cañon like than the Ft George Cañon. Found a large party of Chinamen 'prospecting' just below the Cañon. Distance from Canon to Quesnelle said to be 18 m. but seems to be considerably less, as we arrived at Quesnelle at 10.55 A.m. Find all letters for me have been sent on to Blackwater Depôt, & must wait till they Come back from there. Got dinner at the hotel, & camped in Mr Robertsons[229] Garden.

Oct 21. Packing fossils & arranging Camp equipage &c. All not necessary to be left here in charge of the C.P.R.S. Walked down to Quesnelle R. & showed Mr Selwyn* the plant & insect bed found here last summer.

Oct. 22. At Quesnelle

Oct. 23   " "

Oct. 24. Morning went with Mr Selwyn* to see exposures of lignite about a mile up the Quesnelle R. Took photographs of the Quesnelle Bridge. Sarted about 1 P.m. in Steamer for Soda Creek, reaching the latter place after dark.

Oct. 25. Left Soda Creek in Stage before dawn, & reached Bridge Creek long after dark. Had an upset on the way, but without much damage.

In going Southward *Artemisia* first appears in any quantity not far from Soda Creek, near Deep Cr. *Lynosiris* a few miles S. of *Bates'*.[230]

Oct. 26. To Clinton, arriving in good time.

---

228. Probably the Carrier village "Nasietcah" (A. G. Morice, "Are the Carrier Sociology and Mythology Indigenous or Exotic?," *Proceedings and Transactions of the Royal Society of Canada* 10 [1892], sec. II, pl. II, opp. 109).

229. Duncan Robertson, a blacksmith at Quesnel.

230. Aschal S. Bates owned a farm here. According to John Macoun, who passed through in 1875, "Mr. Bates is very enterprising, and has erected a steam saw and grist-mill, with all the modern appliances, and does first-class work for the settlers in the neighbourhood" (John Macoun, "Report of Professor Macoun, Botanist to the Expedition," in Geological Survey of Canada, *Report of Progress for 1875–76* [1877], 124).

Pinus Ponderosa[231] first observed near the Chasm not far from the southern edge of the "Green timber"

Oct. 27. Wednesday. To Lytton, a long day

Oct. 28. Lytton to Yale, arriving just at dark The roads here very bad & showing evidence of long continued rain

Oct. 29. Started early on Str. Royal City & arrived at New Westminster before dark. Day overcast, with masses of mist among the mountains. The higher peaks heavily covered with fresh fallen snow.

Saw plants of a fine *Rhododendron*[232] at Hope in Gardens. It is found only in one place in the mountains about 20 miles from Hope & is said to be hard to transplant.

Saw Mr W. Fisher[233] about collecting specimens of produce &c. for the Exhibition.

Oct. 30.

Left at 8 A.m. & arrived in Victoria about 3 P.m. Stopping at Driard House[234]

Oct. 31. Victoria. Dined with Dr Helmkin[235]

Novr 1   "

*   " 2   "*

231. Ponderosa pine, *P. ponderosa*.

232. Probably the white rhododendron, *Rhododendron albiflorum* Hook., which was much more widespread in British Columbia than Dawson suspected but was, as he correctly noted, difficult to transplant.

233. William Fisher was a prominent New Westminster businessman who operated a dry goods, provisions, and wine store in partnership with Henry Holbrook.

234. The Driard House Hotel, at Broad and View streets, was the former St. George's Hotel, purchased and renamed in 1872 by the French-born Sosthenes Driard, who had come to British Columbia with the gold rush of 1858. Reputedly the finest hotel north of San Francisco, the building was improved by Driard, who added thirty-four rooms to it. It was replaced by a new building in 1892. Upon Driard's death in 1873, it was purchased by the owners of the Colonist Hotel and again enlarged. The hotel was a favourite with CPRS engineers.

235. Dr. John Sebastian Helmcken (1824–1920) was one of Victoria's best-known residents. Helmcken arrived in the settlement in March 1850 and served as medical officer and later surgeon to the Hudson's Bay Company. Actively involved in politics, he was speaker of the Vancouver Island Assembly in the colonial period and, in 1870, was one of three delegates sent to Ottawa to negotiate British Columbia's entry into Confederation. Subsequently, Helmcken devoted himself to private medical practice and was instrumental in founding Victoria's hospital system. For a narrative of Helmcken's life, see *The Reminiscences of Doctor John Sebastian Helmcken*, ed. Dorothy Blakey Smith (Vancouver: University of British Columbia Press, 1975).

G. M. Dawson to Anna Dawson*, 2 November 1875, Victoria

I Sit down at last to write a few lines in answer to a whole budget of letters, some received before leaving Blackwater. Your "important letter" was one of the latter, but I hope you will not think me neglectful in not answering it Sooner, as I have kept up with the mail on the way down. When you ask me what I think about it I really do not Know what to say, but that as I feel Sure from what you write that you are perfectly satisfied with your choice, I cannot be otherwise than of the same Mind. I am really very glad that Harrington[236] is the favoured, though why you should suppose that I ⟨had⟩ {must have} Suspected It, I cannot tell, especially when you took such pains to impress me with the attractions & Solitary position of Mr —— at Metis. Earnestly, I wish you all happiness & prosperity, but paper talking is at best unsatisfactory. Please continue to make me your confidante in your plans.

I arrive here only three days ago by Steamer from New Westminster, having met Mr Selwyn* at Fort George, & travelled all down the Frazer R with him. He sails from here for Montreal on the 10th. & meanwhile has business to occupy him, connected with the getting together of a collection for the Exhibition at Philadelphia next summer I have no very definite plans yet for my winter, but think it likely that I may have some weeks work at this exhibition Matter after Mr S. leaves.

Mr Walkem[237] the Premier of this province travelled part of the way with us on the Stage. His younger brother[238] is boarding at this hotel at Present & is an old McGill Medical student, & brother to the Mary W—— of whom I used constantly to hear when you were at Mrs Simpsons in the

236. Bernard James Harrington (1848–1907), who married Anna Dawson in 1876, was born at St. Andrews, Lower Canada, and educated at McGill and Yale universities. Harrington was appointed lecturer in mining and chemistry at McGill University in 1871 and was on staff for thirty-six years. From 1872 to 1879 he also served with the Geological Survey of Canada. Along with a large number of scientific articles, Harrington wrote a biography of William Logan, the founder of the Geological Survey of Canada, *The Life of Sir William E. Logan* (Montreal: Dawson Brothers, 1883).

237. George Anthony Walkem (1834–1908) was premier of British Columbia from 1874 to 1876 and again from 1878 until 1882. After legal training at McGill University, Walkem came to British Columbia in 1862, was called to the bar in 1864, and served in the colonial Legislative Council of British Columbia from 1864 to 1870. Upon leaving politics in 1882, Walkem was appointed a judge of the British Columbia Supreme Court.

238. William Wymond Walkem (1850–1919) was a Queen's Univeristy medical graduate who came to the province in 1875. Walkem moved to Nanaimo where he established a general practice and was medical officer for the East Wellington Company. He subsequently became coroner and in 1894 was elected a member of the provincial legislature. See W. Wymond Walkem, *Stories of Early British Columbia* (Vancouver: News-Advertiser, 1914).

old days.[239] So things turn up. I missed seeing a gentleman in N. Westminster who Said he knew my Grandfather[240] & Father* & was very anxious to know me, but I daresay I shall have an opportunity of giving him the pleasure in future. as I think it speaks well for the family when a man who has known your father & grandfather wants to Know you.

We were out today in the less genteel parts of this city looking for Indian or chinese Curiosities, but without meeting with any very great success. The Chinamen are most peculiar people for importing their customs into foreign countries wholesale. You can walk into their shops here & see Shelves full of Joss papers Joss-sticks,[241] Chop-sticks, chinese shoes &c. &c. & always on the stove a teapot "biling up," while on a neighbouring table half a dozen of their Small cups lie in a pan of water ready for extraction & use.

Camp bed-time at this season is about 7.30 & as it is now Somehow got to be past 11 o.C. I must postpone other letters till the Morning when I may Get a few Minutes

Novr 3 Victoria
    " *4* Spent afternoon & evening at Mrs Creas'[242]
Novr 5. Called on Dr Powell[243] & saw Correspondence referring to

---

239. Mary E. W. Walkem, whose sisters Philippa and Ellen also attended the school; the "Ladies' School" of Mrs. Lucy Simpson, at 108 Mansfield Street, in Montreal.

240. James Dawson (1789–1862), see introduction.

241. Paper sticks of fragrant tinder mixed with clay, as incense.

242. Sarah Crease (Lindley), 1826–1922, was the wife of Sir Henry Pering Pellew Crease, a prominent Victoria judge. On Dawson's visits to Victoria, he spent much time socializing with Mrs. Crease and her family. Crease (1823–1905) came to British Columbia in 1858 and was joined by his wife and children in 1860. After being called to the bar in 1859, he became attorney general of British Columbia, a position he held from 1861 to 1866. In 1870 he was made a puisne judge. Crease played an important role in British Columbia's entry into Confederation, drafting the Terms of Union in 1870 and opening debate on the subject of Confederation. See Susan Allison, *A Pioneer Gentlewoman in British Columbia: The Recollections of Susan Allison*, ed. Margaret A. Ormsby (Vancouver: University of British Columbia Press, 1976), 143–44.

243. Dr. Israel Wood Powell (1836–1915) was active in many facets of Victoria life. After graduation from McGill University in 1860, Powell came to Victoria in 1862, established a busy medical practice, and became heavily involved in politics. From 1863, he sat in the Vancouver Island House of Assembly until he lost his seat when the colony amalgamated with British Columbia. In 1872, he was appointed superintendent of Indian affairs by the Canadian government. He later profited handsomely from real estate investments in Vancouver during the 1880's. See B. A. McKelvie, "Lieutenant Israel Wood Powell, M.D., C.M.," *British Columbia Historical Quarterly* 9 (1947): 33–54.

Exhibition matters. Went with Mr S. to See Cowley's[244] collections of Shells Sea-weeds &c. Very heavy rain all day.

Novr 6. Interviewing Drs Carroll[245] & Powell* on exhibition matters, & looking up things for exhibition. Afternoon looking for fruit &, Called at Mrs Creas'*. Evening dined at Mrs Creas'.

Novr 7. Sunday Reading. Afternoon walked out beyond Beacon Hill with Mr Wheeler,[246] Evening talking to Mr Jennings*, Making out list for exhibition &c.

Novr 8. Afternoon drove round with Dr Carroll* collecting specimens of fruit. News of the loss of the Pacific[247] off Cape Flattery received & causing great agitation in town, many Victorians being on board, besides a large number of miners from Cassiar.

G. M. Dawson to John William Dawson, 8 November 1875, Victoria*

I have now been here more than a week, but there has been so much racing & chasing about, that since Sending the telegram announcing my arrival; I have not done more in the way of writing, than pen a brief note to Anna*.

I can hardly tell yet much about winter arrangements, though Victoria will in any Case be head quarters. Mr Selwyn* hope to leave for Montreal next Wednesday, & meanwhile is trying to make arrangements for the representation of this province in the Centennial Exhibition. With the exception of Mr Richardson's* mineralogical Collections, the thing has

244. John Joseph Cowley (1830–1909), a native of England, came to British Columbia in the 1860's and participated in the gold rush to the Stikine River in 1862. A naturalist and collector, Cowley spent many years in Victoria.

245. Robert William Weir Carrall (sometimes spelled Carroll), (1837–79) was a McGill M.D. who served in the American Civil War before coming to British Columbia in 1865. Carrall was an influential figure in British Columbia politics, a member of the Legislative Council in the 1860's and, along with J. S. Helmcken, one of the delegates who negotiated British Columbia's entry into Confederation. In 1871, Carrall was appointed to the Canadian Senate and remained in that position until his death. See "Carrall, Robert William Weir," *Dictionary of Canadian Biography*, 10: 138–40.

246. Perhaps W. Wheeler, a Victoria labourer.

247. The *Pacific*, an old wooden sidewheel steamer owned by Goodall, Nelson & Perkins Company, had sailed from Victoria en route to San Francisco on the morning of 4 November 1875, with about three hundred passengers on board. Around nine o'clock that evening, off Cape Flattery, the *Pacific* collided with the *Orpheus*, an American vessel, and quickly sank. The ship's quartermaster and one passenger, H. F. Jelly, were the only survivors of the tragedy. A coroner's jury in Victoria later pointed to the deteriorated condition of the ship, the shortage of lifeboats, the ineptness of captain and crew, and the failure of the *Orpheus* to remain on the scene as factors contributing to the immense loss of life. See the *Victoria Daily British Colonist*, 24 November 1875.

much fallen through, from the incapacity of the Secretary in Montreal (Perrault)[248] & jealousy between partisans of the Dominion & local governments here. If things can be Arranged, I may probably have a week or ten days work getting Collections together, which will not exactly be lost time, as the weather is almost too wet at present for outdoor work. As soon as I can get away I intend to go for a few days with the C.P.R.S. parties now engaged locating a line between here & Nanaimo, which line by the way, is a perfect farce, passing over very difficult country, & running parallel all the way to the coast & Gulf of Georgia, which is a splendid water way all the year round. I do not think the line will ever be built, but the carrying on of an expensive Survey on it is hardly in conformity with Mr McKenzie's idea of "Utilizing the magnificent water stretches &c."[249]

I had a letter from Capt. Anderson[250] the other day, written before he had received copies of our Report, in which he says that he had represented to Lord Derby[251] that it is desirable to publish a complete account of the work of the N.A.B.C. at a cost of £800, & thinks there will be money enough to embody all my Report in the general one. I am on the point of writing to him to Say that if this intention is carried out I shall furnish revised copy of plant list, & perhaps also other errata. Rowe,[252] he says is still very Shaky. I see the prospect of another Boundary Commission to settle a line between B.C. & Alaska is good, & if not undertaken immediately must be within a few years. I should of course like very much to go into that country, & do not see why geological & Natural history work should not be carried on partly in connection with the Can. Geol. Survey.

248. Joseph Xavier Perrault (1836–1905) was secretary-treasurer to the Canadian Commission for the Philadelphia Centennial Exposition.

249. Dawson's fears about Canadian Prime Minister Alexander Mackenzie's advocacy of the so-called Esquimalt and Nanaimo line were not born out by immediate federal support for the railway's construction. Even though Mackenzie had introduced a bill in Parliament earlier in 1875 to allow construction of the line, the bill was defeated in the Senate. The railway was only opened in 1886 when the Nanaimo coal magnate Robert Dunsmuir built the line.

250. Samuel Anderson (1839–81) served as chief astronomer to the British North American Boundary Commission. See John E. Parsons, *West on the 49th Parallel: Red River to the Rockies 1872–1876* (New York: William Morrow and Co., 1963), 19–20.

251. Edward Henry Stanley, fifteenth Earl of Derby (1826–93), was at that time secretary of state for foreign affairs in the Disraeli government, having taken office in February 1874. It was under the auspices of the Foreign Office that the British North American Boundary Commission had operated.

252. Valentine Francis Rowe (1841–1920), an officer with the Royal Engineers, had joined the boundary commission as an assistant astronomer in the spring of 1873 to take charge of a special survey of the Lake of the Woods. See ibid., 54.

There is some excitement here at present about the Murder of a Catholic priest by an Indian chief on the West Coast of the Island, near Barclay Sound.[253] It seems to have been in Some way connected with the plague of small pox which is at present Causing many deaths there. As yet we have only heard one side of the Story, but a steamer has been Sent round to enquire into the matter & if possible arrest the offender.

With regard to the Thermometer &c. Sent out by William*, I think the would come safely enough by post is Strongly packed. The rate of postage is not very high now I think. However I hope you will Keep a postage bill against me, as I shall likely require to Send out for books &c. from time to time. I have to acknowledge Copies of our Report, Natures, Leasure Hour with your portrait,[254] Various newspapers, & many letters, Including a large budget concerning my Report. At all these I have glanced & hope to go over them more Carefully Soon

Novr 9. Went with Mr Selwyn* to meet Dr Carroll* & Mr Armstrong[255] at govt. buildings to make arrangements for Exhibition. Afternoon, made some calls about fruit, but without getting anything more. Evening dined at Mrs Creas'

Novr. 10. Mr S & Webster* left in tender for Str. Salvador at 2 P.m. Afterwards walked round to Beacon Hill where races[256] going on. Evening reading.

Novr 11, 12, 13. Engaged chiefly making enquiries & arranging about articles for Exhibition with Dr Carroll*.

Novr. 14. Sunday. Wet & bleak all day. Reading writing &c. First few flakes of snow seen today. Steamers Los Angeles & Dakota arrive from San Francisco, & bring news that Crew of Ship orpheus, which it appears was the vessel in collision with the Pacific, landed at Barclay Sound.

---

253. Dawson is referring to an incident that took place at Hesquiat on 28 October 1875, when the Hesquiat chief, Matlahaw, shot the Catholic priest Father A. J. Brabant. Wounded in the hand and right shoulder, Brabant lived to resume his work on the west coast of Vancouver Island in March 1876 after recuperating in Victoria. See Barry M. Gough, *Gunboat Frontier: British Maritime Authority and Northwest Coast Indians, 1846–90* (Vancouver: University of British Columbia Press, 1984), 174–75; for Brabant's narrative of the affair see Chas. Moser, *Reminiscences of the West Coast of Vancouver Island* (Victoria: Acme Press, 1926), 42–47.

254. *Nature* was a popular British weekly scientific magazine first published in 1869, and *Leisure Hour* another British journal published in London since 1852.

255. Probably William J. Armstrong (1826–1915), who was then minister of agriculture in the provincial government. Armstrong was an early New Westminster settler and merchant who represented that community for many years in the provincial assembly.

256. Horse races were held at a course in Beacon Hill Park.

G. M. Dawson to Anna Dawson*, 14 November 1875, Victoria

{I have not written to W. for Some time. Please tell him I will answer soon. If this family gets much more scattered one will have time for nothing else but writing.}

Many thanks for your last long letter received a day or two ago, & first to answer your question as to the proper times for mailing letters — The mail steamers Sail from San Fran. on the 10th 20 & 30 of Each month, & the newspapers are kept back for them. Letters generally come overland arriving once or twice a week. The time of transit overland or by steamer is about the Same.

I had stored up quite a lot of information about our journey down the Frazer & waggon road to this place, but not having had opportunity to write it on first arrival here, have almost forgotten it all. From Ft George to Quesnelle, a distance of about 80 miles, we came down the river in a Canoe & boat; the same which Mr Selwyn* had with him on his long trip. The stream is very ⟨rapid⟩ {swift}, & full of little riffles or small rapids which generally require to be run with Some Care. There are also two 'Cañons' so called, with larger rapids in them, but these did not turn out so formidable as we had thought, the water being low. The voyage occupied 2 days & a half, & it blew a Gale all one day dead ahead. It must have been a remarkably heavy gale, for during its height we Could hear & see trees Crashing down in the woods in all directions. on one occasion we tried to cross the stream but drifted down into the wrong Channel of a rapid, where the current was very boisterous & the waves were all turned backward & their tops blowing off with the wind. Just as we got the Canoe out of this into dead water at the foot of the cliff, a great pine almost directly above our heads blew over, but was fortunately prevented from coming down on us by Some smaller trees which did not give way. We had to wait Several days at Quesnelle, which is a dismal place, for the Steamer; when our afternoons steaming brought us to Soda Creek. Here we got the stage, & after four long days staging — from before dawn till long after dark, — arrived at Yale. The only noteworthy Circumstance in this part of the journey was an upset which we were unlucky enough to meet with. This took place by the driver getting off the road & onto the sloping side of a bank. Mr S & I were Sitting on the box, & as it was extremely dark I cant' tell you exactly what attitudes we assumed in falling, though if I may be allowed to judge by the appearance of my hat, I Should be of the opinion that I fell at least partly on my head. The other passengers were tightly buttoned up inside, & as soon as they could make an orifice they emerged hurridly, one by one. Last Came Mr Walkem* the premier of this Great Province, much crushed & speechless. He declares that all the rest fell on him, & then scrambled on top of him to get out. Fortunately the driver kept the reins, & the horses stood Still till they were detached. Such are the pleasures of travel in this country. No bad accident has ever happened to the stage on the Frazer R. road which almost Seems miraculous when one sees how the drivers come Skimming down the long hills cut in the sides of the cliffs & mountains, & sometimes actually overhanging the river below.

Oct. 15.[257]

Here I stopped last night, & now take a few moments to add a line or two.

First as to the question on which you ask advice in your last, *viz* the house. Now I do not know how at this distance you can expect me to give a rational opinion on the subject, So much seems to depend on circumstances, & especially on your own opinion & wishes. I am afraid to give any opinion in Case it ⟨might⟩ {may} influence you where your own judgement Must be so much better. At the same time it does Seem to me that so large a house, & one especially with such large rooms *might* prove rather a burden than otherwise, & would be uncomfortably large for two people to inhabit.

I dont' Know how it is but when I sit down to write my thoughts never flow freely enough, & I cannot think of any quantity of nice things to Say as you do. I dont' think I am reserved as you say, but only unfortunate in not being able to catch the right idea at the right time.

Please tell Father* that I have answered Capt. Featherstonehaugh's question as to height of W. Butte.[258] Also that I hope to write soon. Also congratulate O'Hara[259] for me on his success, & tell Rankine[260] that If Mr

---

257. Read 15 November.

258. Captain Albany Featherstonhaugh, who had been assistant astronomer on the boundary commission, wrote to J. W. Dawson to clarify an apparent discrepancy in the altitude measurements of Western Butte in Montana Territory, made by George Dawson while on the boundary commission, and those made by Americans at Fort Benton. Dawson's measurements can be found in his *Geology and Resources*, 123.

259. Dan O'Hara, a boyhood friend who dropped out of McGill and now qualified as a notary. See Anna Dawson to G. M. Dawson, "October" 1875, Dawson Family Papers, MUA.

260. Dawson's youngest brother Rankine (1863–1913) graduated from McGill Medical School in 1882. After spending time as a medical officer for the Canadian Pacific Railway in Manitoba, he left for further training in London. For four years Rankine acted as surgeon on liners of the P & O Company before settling in London. In 1896, he married Gloranna Coats and they had one child, Margaret Rita. Always prone to depression and instability, Rankine uprooted his family and moved back to Montreal. Never achieving a permanency there, they subsequently returned to London where Gloranna left Rankine. Depressed, estranged from his family, and separated from his Montreal relatives, Rankine died in a London nursing home. For a sympathetic

Selwyn* gives him a Cartridge, I hope he will keep it, till I write & tell him what I want done.

The proof photo received some time since was nearly black from action of light. It seems good however what can be seen of it, & I long to have a decent Copy.

G. M. Dawson to Margaret Dawson*, 14 November 1875, Victoria

In answer to my many letters from home I Must write from time to time, even though I can find no particularly interesting topics. Mr Selwyn* left here on Wednesday last, & you will no doubt see him before long & learn many little items which Sift through my memory before they can be written. I Sent with him a few little articles which I picked up at a chinese shop here, & which I thought might perchance be interesting. 1 Two small lead caddies, each containing 1/6 of a pound, of tea; Supposed to be of very Superior quality, or peculiar in some way, & costing at the rate of $3.000 per pound. 2 A bundle each of two kinds of Joss papers. These are burned as Sacrifises to the dead. The square papers represent silver money, the peculiar shaped ones Clothes. 3. Three very common paper fans, only remarkable on account of the peculiarity of the figures painted on them. 4 two bulbs imported direct from China, & supposed to be the roots of Some amazingly beautiful flower. Warranted to grow in the house in pots. Please do whatever you see fit with all these things. I was much tempted to buy a Chinese & English dictionary printed in Canton by some learned Chinese Scholar, but it was in six Volumes at a dollar each, & no particular way that I could see of looking up the words. — so I abandoned it. I have Some insence sticks, & chop-sticks which I will take a Chance of Sending over soon in a box of specimens.

The loss of the Pacific is still the universal topic here. The news has Just arrived that the crew of the ship which Came into collision with her, have been found at Barclay Sound, having landed there from their boats. This settles the question as to the immediate Cause of the disaster, & shows that the steamer did not fall to pieces from meer rottenness as was at first supposed. It also now Seems certain that from the Pacific there are only two Survivors. One of these is the Quartermaster of the ship, the other A Man called Jelly, a Canadian from Sarnia, who was returning home after having worked all Summer with Mr Jennings*.[261] Steamers are out along the

---

portrayal of Rankine, see Lois Winslow-Spragge, "Rankine Dawson—1863–1913," Dawson Family Papers, MUA.

261. See 8 November 1875. Jelly had been axeman on R Division of the CPRS during the summer of 1875.

the Coast picking up bodies, which have been blown back on the coast by Strong South Westerly winds. one Came ashore yesterday within a mile of this place, & the Shore is strewn with wreckage. Many of the Passengers were miners on their way South from Cassiar to spend their summer's earnings. Five men from Mr Cambie's* Party, Some returning to Canada others going on to New Zealand, were among the lost. Mr Selwyn* though at first intending to go with the Pacific afterwards fortunately decided not to do So.

I am still living at the Driard Hotel not having been able to get other Suitable quarters, though I have already made pretty extensive enquiry. Most lodging houses &c. are full, but I think I will by & by be able to get rooms Somewhere, & make arrangements for meals at Some restaurant; which is the most Comfortable way.

The climate here is very mild as compared with Montreal. We have seen a few flakes of snow today for the first time, & many of the trees still hold a portion of their leaves, & autumn flowers are still blooming in the Gardens. To make up for all this it is horribly wet & windy, & almost continually overcast & dull. I dont think I have once Seen realy dry plankwalks since My arrival here, now two weeks ago. It has rained *more* or *less every* day, & generally more. The streets are fordable only at the Crossings. I must be excused for longing for a little Clear Cold Canadian weather

Novr 15. Snowing all morning. Met Dr Carroll* & made arrangements for various exhibits. Evening tested some specimens of ore, reading.
Novr 16. Heavy Snow & storm. Engaged with exhibition matters. passed evening at Walkem's*.
Novr 17. Exhibition business. Called on Mr Armstrong. Evening at Mr Duponts,[262] getting back to hotel quite late.
Novr 18. Exhibition business. Interview with Dr Powell* & Jelly*. P.m. Engaged making tracing of Tatlayaco L. country in C.P.R.S. offices. Wrote Mr Selwyn* giving account of work. Evening revising plant list in report.[263]
Novr 19. Packing & moving from Driard House to Mrs Bowmans.[264]

262. Probably Charles Thomas Dupont (1837–1923) who was the collector of inland revenue in Victoria. Dupont, like many other British Columbians, was actively involved in the development and promotion of mining schemes.

263. Presumably, "List of Plants Collected During the Summers of 1873–74 . . .," published as Appendix A of the *Geology and Resources*, 69–77.

264. Mrs. Sarah A. Bowman (d. 1900) kept a boarding house on Yates Street in Victoria. Her husband William Gile Bowman (d. 1903) owned a livery stable at Broad and View streets.

Novr. 20. Called on Dr Carroll*. Working at tracing in C.P.R.S. offices.
Novr 21. Sunday Reading &c. rain during the night has cleared nearly all
the snow away. The ground having been covered for about a week.

Gold discovered on Frazer 1858. Negroes in Calafornia much perse-
cuted & talk of passage of law excluding them from the state. Combined &
chartered Ship to Come to Vancouver Isd. & form a settlement.[265] Capt
[blank] of the ship on arriving at Victoria heard of discovery of gold on
the Frazer, & purchased the specimen brought down — a small one —
Added a quantity of gold dust already in his posession, & put the whole in
a bottle. on return to San Francisco took measures to spread reports of
discovery in every way, to produce a rush. Posted placards &c. stating that
gold could be seen on board the ship, & showed the bottle specimens.
Great furore arose, all Sorts of people packed up for Victoria, sold property & cleared out. Landed property in S.F. greatly declined. Ship after
ship sailed for Victoria Crowded. Discovery early in spring, & by midsum-
mer estimated that 10,000 people camped on site of Victoria, where had
been formerly only one or 2 hundred & a H.B. Post. Dismay of H.B. Coy.
Miners congregated at Victoria & could not get over to Frazer. Hundreds
of skiffs being built along the shore. In Aug. reaction set in & most
returned to S.F. without getting further than Victoria. Many got up the
Frazer too late, while others got good pay.[266]
Novr 22. Working at tracing in C.P.R. office. Called on Mr Armstrong*
on business connected with ehxibition. Wrote home M.P.[267]

G. M. Dawson to John William Dawson*, 22 November 1875, Victoria

I had intended leaving here to spend a few days at Burrard's Inlet,
tomorrow, but have decided to wait & give the Snow a *chance* of getting
out of the woods, till next Friday. I want to see what can be done in the
way of getting Samples of timber there, & specimens of foliage &c. to
properly identify the trees. Also *en route* to arrange some matters

265. The group of black settlers Dawson mentions set sail from San Francisco on 20 April
     1858 in the *Commodore*, commanded by Captain Jeremiah Nagle. The group arrived in
     Victoria on 25 April 1858. For a discussion of the circumstances of the black migration
     and subsequent settlement in the Victoria region, see Crawford Kilian, *Go Do Some
     Great Thing: The Black Pioneers of British Columbia* (Vancouver: Douglas & McIntyre,
     1978).

266. Gold was first discovered during the summer of 1857 on the Thompson River. Reports
     of the find drew more miners who made their way down river to the Fraser where they
     found substantial quantities of gold. News reached California in the spring of 1858 and
     the rush began. See Margaret A. Ormsby, *British Columbia: A History* (Toronto:
     Macmillan of Canada, 1958), 138–82.

267. Mamma and Papa.

connected with specimens for the exhibition at New Westminster Getting a few things for the exhibition takes a *great deal* of time, & I want to get it over as it breaks up the day so much that I can hardly attend to anything else. At Burrards Inlet I may however get a chance of seeing Something of the Coals or lignites there.

I had hoped to write at some length, but must defer doing so till next time. In writing to Capt. Anderson*, I promised to send a corrected list of plants, in case he may want to reprint my report or any part of it. I have looked over the printed list for errata, & will send a Memorandum of these this mail or next. Perhaps Anna* might insert Hooker's[268] names & corrections in the margin of a copy of the list, & put up the whole addressed to Capt A. Foreign Office. I dont' suppose there is the Slightest hurry in the matter, & it will do quite as well after Xmas as before. I only wish I had time & opportunity to work up the shells thoroughly & get them published.

In Scudders[269] note enclosed to me you will have noticed that he had not at the time of writing received his extra copies of Entomological Notes.[270] I left instructions with the Herald people, & they have no doubt been attended to before this. I wrote to Scudder* a few days ago telling him of my little Collection of flies from the Tertiary here, in hopes that he would like to examine them.[271] I spoke to Selwyn* on the Subject before he left, & he seemed quite willing that Scudder* Should have the examination of them if he would undertake it.

---

268. Joseph Dalton Hooker (1817–1911) was one of the foremost botanists of the nineteenth century. Author of numerous papers and monographs, Hooker was director of the Royal Botanic Gardens, Kew, from 1865 to 1885. He made several noteworthy field expeditions, including a visit to western North America in 1871 with his friend, Asa Gray. Though publishing in a wide range of fields, Hooker's enduring interest was in taxonomy and plant geography. See *Dictionary of Scientific Biography*, s.v. "Hooker, Joseph Dalton."

269. Samuel Hubbard Scudder (1837–1911) was one of the great figures in American entomology. Scudder was especially interested in fossil insects and carried out extensive, pioneering work in the field. In his working lifetime Scudder produced some 791 scientific articles and several large treatises. See *Dictionary of American Biography*, s.v. "Scudder, Samuel Hubbard."

270. Presumably Dawson is referring to "Notice of the Butterflies and Orthoptera, Collected by Mr. George M. Dawson, as Naturalist of the B.N.A. Boundary Commission," by Samuel H. Scudder, published as Appendix D of the *Geology and Resources*, 341–45.

271. Scudder's results were published as "Insects of the Tertiary." He later supplemented that report with his "Additions to the Insect-fauna of the Tertiary Beds at Quesnel, British Columbia," in Geological Survey of Canada, *Report of Progress for 1876–77* (1878), 457–64.

With regard to the Grasshopper Circulars,[272] of which you Say some More have been returned from the N.W. If Rankine* would take the trouble of going to my Secretary drawer he will find the whole bundle. He Can easily Select those from Manitoba & N. of the Line, — I think they are all in one bunch — If you think ⟨the⟩ with the additional ones lately received there are enough to be of interest, please bundle them up & send them by mail, & I will take an early opportunity of Abstracting them, & Send the abstract to the Naturalist.[273] I hardly think it would be worth while going into the region S. of the Line, which has already been pretty fully discussed & for some parts of which My information is slim.

Novr. 23. Saw Dr Carroll* & Called on a number of people about exhibits. Working some time at map in C.P.R. offices. Walked round by Beacon Hill & mouth of harbour. Evening reading Sky clear with hard frost tonight.

Novr 24 Finished map at C.P.R. offices. Saw a number of specimens from W. Homathco which Mr Tieddiemann[274] had brought away. Beside granites &c. the rocks like those bearing fossils on Tatlayoco L. seem to be represented. Mr T. is confident of existence of Tin on Homathco, though I did not see the specimens.

Novr 25. on business connected with Exhibition. Writing home &c. Posted corrected plant list to J.W.D. & photos. of Indians to Selwyn*. Specimens of Hops &c. received from Anderson[275] at Saanich.

Went on board steamer Enterprise, which starts at 7 a.m. for New Westminster.

Novr 26. Sailed at 7 a.m. for New Westminster. Air cold & clear though

272. The "Circulars" were a set of questions sent by Dawson to various people in the prairie region, asking about locust conditions in the summer of 1875. The returned information formed the basis of Dawson's article, "Notes on the Appearance and Migrations of the Locust in Manitoba and the North-West Territories — Summer of 1875," *Canadian Naturalist and Quarterly Journal of Science*, n.s., 8 (1878): 207-26.

273. The magazine *Canadian Naturalist and Quarterly Journal of Science*, founded by Elkanah Billings.

274. Herman Otto Tiedemann (1821-91) was employed in 1875 as a topographer for the CPRS. Tiedemann was also known as a civil engineer and, among other accomplishments, designed British Columbia's first legislative buildings, the so-called "Birdcages."

275. Alexander Caulfield Anderson (1814-84) came to the northwest coast during 1832 in service with the Hudson's Bay Company. Anderson retired from the company in 1854 then moved to Vancouver Island in 1858 to become collector of customs and postmaster at Victoria. Later, Anderson served on the Indian Land Commission from 1876 to 1878 and acted as dominion inspector of fisheries from 1876. Anderson was a competent writer who authored numerous essays and pamphlets. See Anderson, Alexander Caulfield," *Dictionary of Canadian Biography*, 11: 16-18.

sky overcast. Islands snow-clad & a splendid view of the distant Mountains of the Cascade Range in the vicinity of Burrards Inlet & How's Sound. Captain afraid that the Frazer R. frozen, but found it all clear. Arrived At Westminster about 3 P.m. Find about 6 inches of wet snow on the ground, & good sleighing. Called on Fisher* & arranged about exhibits.

27. Started by stage for Burrards Inlet at 9 A.m. Stage an open three seated Sleigh, with a pair of horses. Occupants besides Self & driver, two Chinamen & a Klootchman. Sky lowering & heavy with occasionally a few flakes of snow. Woods full of snow & every branch & twig heavy with soft flakes. After leaving New Westminster a few miles get beyond area denuded for firewood or by fires, & enter the primaeval Woods. Country between Frazer R. & Burrard's Inlet undulating or even hilly, but not high. Soil yellowish, Sandy & gravelly, though open probably pretty rich, though the great size & thickness of trees renders clearing well nigh impossible. Arrive at Max's[276] about 11. A sort of tavern with a few outbuildings. Here embarked on a diminutive ferry steamer, & soon got across to Moodyville the Site of Moody & Nelsons Mill,[277] on the N. side Water perfectly Calm, sky cloudy, & the woods & hills Soft, pearly grey.

"The Mill" is of course the Centre & *raison d'etre* of the village which is a straggling little place. The houses perched on the front of a steep bank, & forming a broken line along it. Here as everywhere in this country a very mixed assemblage of people. While Europeans or at least Whites fill the responsible posts, Indians (Squa'mich) Chinamen, Negroes & Mulattoes & half breeds & Mongrels of every pedigree abound. Many of the lumber men originally from the lower Provinces.

The mill on a large scale & well appointed. A pair of large Circular saws, & a large gang saw, besides a small circular saw with long traversing table for cutting up the large planks, & others for cutting boards into lengths &c. Two planing machines, Mill driven by steam, but water power formerly used & still available, often employed to drive planers when other machinery Standing. The logs are very large & fine, & run up to about 60 inches. Sizes larger than these are not brought to the mill, or are first split by dynamite, as it is not practicable to have circular Saws much larger

---

276. Also called "Maxie's" and so named after Maximillien Michaud who operated a hostelry at New Brighton.

277. Even though the first mill on the north shore of Burrard Inlet was built by T. W. Graham & Company in 1862, Sewell Prescott Moody, who bought the sawmill in 1865, most influenced the economic development of the early community. See F. W. Howay, "Early Shipping in Burrard Inlet 1863–1870," *British Columbia Historical Quarterly* 1 (1937): 4–8, 12–14. Partially burned in 1873 and rebuilt the following year, the Moodyville sawmill operated until 1901 when it closed permanently. For a brief discussion of the social development of Moodyville, see F. W. Howay, "Early Settlement on Burrard Inlet," *British Columbia Historical Quarterly* (1937): 109–14.

than those in use, the plates being apt to "buckle".

A log hauled up out of the boom into the mill, is first rolled by means of hooks & chains & friction gearing overhead, onto a travelling cradle. There arranged in position & wedged up, & then run through the saws. Outer slab taken off & rejected, then two or three planks, Log then turned on the flattened Side & again run through & perhaps turned yet again after a few boards have been taken off, So as to manage to get the greatest possible quantity of clean lumber from the outside. Log advanced after each cut by a pair of screws worked each by a man, distance regulated by character of log & sort of lumber required.

"Mary Ann Wilson" Capt. Stoddart[278] loading at wharf. went on board with Mr N.[279] in the evening & spent an hour or two.

Novr 28. Heavy snow during the night & all day, increasing that already on the Ground to over 12 inches.

Service in the reading room — a very creditable institution kept up by the men — by a Mr Derrick[280] Methodist. Attendance rather Scanty. Reading & talking. Snow succeeded by rain about dark.

29. Heavy cold rain all night, & till about 2 P.m. turning the Snow to slush but scarcely removing Any of it. Mill not working. Witnessed the method of Killing fish by Dynamite. Cartridge fitted with fuse & after being fired thrown off wharf. Explosion dull heavy sound, but not much commotion of water, immediately followed by the appearance of *thousands* of herring[281] & other Small fish jumping above the surface. Not in the immediate vicinity of the discharge but in a circle Surrounding it, & as if trying to escape from it. In a few minutes hundreds of dead fish begin slowly to rise to the Surface & can be secured from a boat.

See man Called Trim,[282] a fisherman. Tells me that *verillia*[283] found in

---

278. The *Mary Ann Wilson* was a British barque. Captain Stoddart is unidentifiable.

279. Probably Hugh Nelson (1830–93), who was vice-president and manager of the Moodyville Saw Mill Company, owned by the firm Moody, Dietz and Nelson. Nelson was also an active politician, having served in the British Columbia Legislative Assembly before Confederation, in the House of Commons from 1871 to 1874, and in the Senate from 1879 until 1887. He was appointed British Columbia's lieutenant-governor, serving from 1887 to 1892.

280. Thomas Derrick (d. 1880) came to British Columbia under Methodist auspices in 1868 to work in the Cariboo, at Barkerville. In 1871 he left for Nanaimo where he spent three years before taking up the work at Moodyville. In deteriorating health, he died in California while en route to eastern Canada.

281. Pacific herring, *Clupea harengus pallasi* Valenciennes.

282. Henry Trim resided on Howe Sound.

283. An obsolete name for hydroids of the phylum coelenterata, animals which attach themselves to the sea bottom.

great abundance only in English Bay Burrard Inlet, but also seen occasionally in suitable localities in Hows Sound & elsewhere: Effects muddy bottom & the "bulb" firmly rooted in the mud. In fishing for Dog fish[284] a long line with smaller lines depending from it, Set out. Dog fish when hooked in trying to escape twists the lines round the *Verillia*, which is thus pulled up. Found in from ten to forty fathoms, & perhaps deeper.

Tells me also of existence of beautiful trumpet shaped sponges on How's Sound, & of a branching hydrozoon?[285] like porcelain in texture, near the N. end of Texada Island.

Told that three Kinds of bears found in the vicinity of the Inlet. Common black, cinnamon, & black with a white spot on the breast. Latter Said to be as large & fierce as the Cinnamon. Grisly not in this part of the Cascades though said to come to the Coast further north. Puma not found here, though common South of the Frazer & on Vancouver Island. Black-tailed deer very abundant. Mountain Goat common on the hills, but only in very Severe weather Known to come down on the flats. Said to try to Keep just at the Snow-line, & this in summer in the highest & most inaccessible parts of the range.[286]

30 Rain & slush.

31[287] Rain & slush. "Blasting for fish" with Capt Stoddart

Decr 1. Morning warm & though still much Snow looked more promising. Soon began to rain however & continued with little intermission all day. Took the ferry steamer & Crossed to the Hastings Mill.[288] Saw Capt Raymur[289] the manager & inspected the mill, which is not much different

284. Spiny dogfish, *Squalus acanthias* L.

285. The "trumpet shaped sponges" were possibly a vase sponge, *Scypha* spp.; and the "branching hydrozoon" possibly one of the wine-glass hydroids, *Campanularia* spp.

286. The "three Kinds of bears" were all probably the American black bear, *Ursus americanus altifrontalis* (Elliot), as colour variations, from jet black through brown to white, occur in different locations. The "Grisly" or grizzly bear, *Ursus arctos horribilis* Ord, does indeed inhabit the heads of most north coastal inlets. The "Puma" or the cougar, *Felis concolor* Kerr was, however, found on southern coastal localities such as Burrard Inlet. "Black-tailed deer," the coast or Columbian blacktail deer, *Odocoileus hemionus columbianus* (Richardson) were in fact numerous; and the "Mountain Goat," mountain goat, *Oreamnos americanus* (Blainville), does come down to sea level in severe weather.

287. Presumably this is a continuation of the 30 November entry.

288. Also known as Stamp's Mill, after Captain Edward Stamp who started construction of the sawmill in 1865. The first sawmill on Burrard Inlet's south shore, it began operating in 1867 and soon attained, as Dawson noted, a reputation for production of ships' spars. See Howay, "Early Shipping," 8–12, 14–15.

289. Captain James Arnold Raymur (1823–82) was born in Halifax, Nova Scotia, and spent several years on vessels in the West Indian trade before coming to British Columbia in 1864. Initially employed by Anderson & Company of Alberni, Raymur later took over

from Moody & Nelsons*, but not quite so well appointed & having a poorer engine. Houses & offices forming a little village clustered about. Ships spars made more a specialty here & many exported. About half a mile from the mill is the village of Granville or "Gas town"[290] as it is more popularly Called. Taverns & saloons not allowed about the mills, are concentrated here for the convenience of the hands.

Sandstone occurs all along the shore here, & in False Creek lignite in thin Seams exists. The sandstone seen by me Soft, greenish, coarse, & micaceous with impressions of sticks & traces of carbon. Weather prevented any ⟨full⟩ examination of the Coast.

A boaring several hundred feet deep formerly made at Granville.

Visited Indians near Moody's mill (Squamish) & bought a goat wool blanket, with yarn &c. & specimen of diatomaceous earth[291] used in twisting the strand. Wool said to be rolled into yarn on the bare Knee with the hand & aid of this earth. Balled up. Frame used in weaving a simple square of four sticks, & the process of weaving might better be called plaiting.[292]

Told that the Indian women not infrequently Commit Suicide[293] by hanging, or choking by a cord, on Slight occasion & often very determined. Also that though Indians on this coast do not take scalps they are superstitious about letting Anyone get a fragment, however Small of their hair. Thinking apparently that its posession gives ⟨the one⟩ a supernatural

management of the Hastings mill and stayed in that capacity throughout the 1870's.

290. The colloquial name "Gas town" developed when John Deighton, commonly known as "Gassy Jack," opened a hotel near the Hastings mill in 1867. Howay notes that even after the settlement was officially named Granville in 1870, "the old name persisted in local use and even succeeded, as late as 1877, in finding its way to a place on the Admiralty Charts" (Howay, "Early Settlement," 108). Granville or "Gastown" was later to form the core around which the future city of Vancouver developed.

291. Or tripole earth which is siliceous sediment made up more or less entirely of the 'skeletal' remains of the microscopic plants called diatoms. It is exceedingly fine-grained, incoherent, and highly absorbent. According to Dawson, "the tripole earth is used to prevent the wool slipping while it is being made into yarn by rubbing between the hand & naked Knee" (George M. Dawson, "Memorandum of Particulars for Official Catalogue of Canadian Commission. International Exhibition at Philadelphia . . .," Dawson Family Papers, MUA).

292. For details of traditional weaving techniques used by the Squamish (Salish) Indians, see Paula Gustafson, *Salish Weaving* (Vancouver: Douglas & McIntyre; Seattle: University of Washington Press, 1980), 87–102.

293. It is possible that the suicides were related to unwanted pregnancy. Because chastity and demure behaviour were prized assets for a girl, an illegitimate child brought shame upon not only the child but also the family of its mother. Most informants state that, aboriginally, both a child and its mother would have been killed. See Homer G. Barnett, *The Coast Salish of British Columbia* (Eugene, Oregon: University of Oregon Press, 1955), 180–81.

power over the looser.[294]

Evening on board the Mary Ann Wilson.

Decr 2. A steady downpour of rain all day. Again gave up intention of going to the logging camp.

Decr 3. Decided to return to New Westminster today & so obliged to make visit to logging camp. Weather fortunately finer. Started at 8 a.m. with Mr Nelson* on the tug "Jerk"[295] & got to camp about 9.20. "Camp" rather a permanent affair. A large stable erected for the oxen & Mules, & houses for the men. These on the bank above the shore. Lumbering roads radiating back into the woods in all directions for Several miles. Roads well made, & wide, bankes often cut through & ravines bridged to get greater uniformity of grade. Cross pieces imbedded in the road at intervals, & notched in the centre. oxen tackled to log, which rests on the Cross pieces, man going before with brush & smearing them with dog-fish oil to make the logs run easily. Trees when felled ⟨cut in⟩ first deprived of bark by chopping. Then sawn up into lengths by hand saw.

Truly magnificent woods. Chiefly of Douglas fir, but also gigantic cedars, & undergrowth of vine maple[296] &c. Lichens & moss hanging yards long from the lower branches, & the long straight Clean trunks of the Douglas firs stretching up fifty or a hundred feet without a branch The age of the larger pines is very great often I think over 400 or 500 years. Told that in these old woods no traces of former fires. Thought however that remains of former forest growths. Increase of trees at first seems very rapid, rings of growth being from ⅓ to ½ inch. Afterwards very thin & fine almost like sheets of paper Seems question as to how far this very rapid growth can be accounted for on hypothesis of young trees springing up to replace others fallen by natural decay in old forests. Would be better explained by supposing that all came up together when not overshadowed by larger growth. Seems an interesting question whether trees ⟨must⟩ {may} not have sprung up on land recently ⟨evident⟩ elevated. Might the ages of trees at like elevations along the coast tally?

294. The Squamish Indians were concerned about letting another get hold of not only their hair but also their excrement, spittle, and nail parings. See Edward S. Curtis, *The North American Indian: Being a Series of Volumes Picturing and Describing the Indians of the United States, The Dominion of Canada, and Alaska,* vol. 9 (1913; reprint, New York: Johnson Reprint Corporation, 1971), 109.

295. Also called the *Union* or *Sudden Jerk,* the craft was a makeshift, scow-type side-wheeler built for Josias Charles Hughes of New Westminster. Powered by a threshing machine engine with a locomotive steam boiler, the vessel had no reverse gear and was extremely difficult to maneuvre. The *Jerk* was eventually destroyed by a fire on the North Arm of the Fraser River.

296. The "Douglas fir" was douglas-fir, *Pseudotsuga menziesii* (Mirb.) Franco; the "vine maple" was the vine maple, *Acer circinatum* Pursh.

Saw the tree selected originally to send to the exhibition As a spar, now cut up. Selected a tree for section & plank &c. & arranged with Cotterell,[297] the foreman for specimens of woods &c.

Back to the Mill in a canoe propelled by ourselves & a lazy Indian, arriving just in time to catch the ferry to Max's*. Travelled in to Westminster on wheels through slush & water.

Saw Fisher* Dr. Trew[298] &c.

Decr 4. Started at 7 A.m. in Steamer Enterprise for Victoria. Day fine throughout, though rather blustry & giving the old Steamer quite a tossing in rounding the point into the harbour. Arrived about 3 P.m.

The town in a ferment of excitement about the Memorandum of the Canadian Government virtually abandoning the Island Railway & offering $750,000 &c. in lieu.[299]

Got letters & papers. Washed up &c.

Decr 5. Cloudy & overcast, with raw cold wind rain commencing about 1 P.m. Saw Dr Carroll*. Reading & writing.

[On 5 December 1875, Dawson wrote a letter to his father but only a fragment of that letter remains.]

Decr 6. Engaged all day Calling on promised Contributors to exhibition, & writing notes to others. Wrote Fisher*, Robertson* (Quesnelle) Ewing (N.W.)[300] &c. Wrote to Selwyn* a short note promising particulars on Friday. Weather fine.

Decr 7. Rain all day. on business connected with exhibition all day. Evening finished reading Sproat's* scenes in Savage life.[301]

Decr 8. Cleared up for an hour or two before dark gadding about all day on business connected with Exhibition. Evening writing out list of exhibits & estimating space required.

---

297. John Austin Cottrell lived at Moodyville.

298. Dr. Charles Newland Trew (1837?–87), who resided in New Westminster, was surgeon to the New Westminster jail, the British Columbia Penitentiary, and the provincial Militia.

299. Dawson was referring to the order-in-council of 20 September 1875, issued by Alexander Mackenzie's Liberal government and drafted by Edward Blake, in which the dominion government argued that since the Esquimalt and Nanaimo Railway was a local work, taxation could not be raised to construct the line. Instead, the government offered an additional $750,000 as compensation for delays in the construction of the Canadian Pacific Railway. See Ormsby, *British Columbia*, 269.

300. Probably Alexander Ewen (1832–?) of New Westminster. In 1870 he was in partnership in the Alexander Logie & Co. fish canning company, but eventually bought out most of the partners. For a time it was called Ewen & Co.; at this time he was in a partnership as Ewen & Wise.

301. Gilbert Malcolm Sproat, *Scenes and Studies of Savage Life* (London: Smith, Elder and Co., 1868).

[Draft of a poem, probably written 8 December 1875]

> The Gilded age of life has gone
> Its [....] & its Strength have fled
> & left a pale thin ghost instead
> For my desire to feed upon.
> I know not what may lie before
> The past is graven on my mind
> & Still I turn & look behind
> with dimming eye on fading shore
> Loved Shore where I in childhood played
> By gurgling stream or on the strand
> we strayed {strolled} together hand in hand
> & thought the ocean Oh! So grand
> nor was afraid
> Adieu & time will blur the trace
> ⟨of joy or grief however deep⟩
> However strong of joy or grief
> oh added sting—
> Should in oblivion find relief

Decr. 9. Saw Dr Carroll* & as he leaves tomorrow for Ottawa got remaining money on Exhibition Acct. turned over (790 odd dollars) Got Macouns[302] plants looked up & taken to Muir heads[303] to be packed. Made several business Calls & wrote to Cotterell* & Hughes[304] about lumber specimens. Wrote descriptions of *P. ponderosa* & *Contorta* for

302. John Macoun had travelled across the province from east to west, leaving his botanical collections at various points. He asked Dawson to forward them on. Macoun to Dawson, 27 November 1875, Dawson Family Papers. Macoun (1831–1920) was born in Ireland, emigrated to Canada in 1850, and became a farmer. In 1868, he accepted a position as professor of natural history at Albert College in Belleville, Upper Canada. Later, Macoun accompanied Sandford Fleming on his expedition of 1872 and, in 1879, took a job as explorer for the Department of Interior. By 1881, he was promoted to botanist for the Geological Survey of Canada. Finally, in 1887 Macoun attained the position of assistant director and naturalist to the survey. See John Macoun, *Autobiography of John Macoun: Canadian Explorer and Naturalist 1831–1920*, 2d ed. (Ottawa: Ottawa Field-Naturalists' Club, 1979).

303. A reference to the firm of Muirhead & Mann, a Victoria contracting and carpentry business.

304. Josias Charles Hughes (1843–86), a native Upper Canadian, came to British Columbia in 1862 and settled in Moodyville when S. P. Moody bought the sawmill. After being in charge of clerical duties there, Hughes moved to New Westminster where he became provincial government agent. Before his premature death, Hughes also served in the British Columbia legislature and worked as a real estate broker and Indian agent at Metlakatla.

Barnard's Agents in upper country to procure me specimens by [blank]
Wrote Selwyn*. Prof T. Rupert Jones,[305] & a long letter to Father*.
Day cloudy & mild but without rain.

Decr 10. Got Macouns* plants packed, addressed, & sent off. Got
Consular certificate for them.

Saw Dr Carroll* off.

Afternoon Began examination of rocks of this neighbourhood at
Beacon Hill Park. Evening reading.

Decr 11. Morning. had agreed to meet Messrs Spence[306] & Nathan[307] to
make excursion to Dredger &c. in harbour. Weather however altogether
too boisterous. Call at Mechanics Inst. & pay $1.00 as Monthly subscrip-
tion to the library. Afternoon examining the shore N. of Clover Pt. till
dark. Evening reading. Day fine!

Decr 12 Reading Lords Naturalist in B.C.[308] All day. Day overcast &
showery.

Decr. 13. Got Fishers* packages sent over by Str. Enterprise, taken from
wharf up to Muir heads.[309] Also collected there various other exhibits for
packing. Visit from Dr Tolmie.[310] P.m. Examining the coast N.E. of

305. Thomas Rupert Jones (1819-1911) was a leading nineteenth century British geologist
and palaeontologist. Jones was an expert in many fields ranging from microzoa to
South African geology and wrote a voluminous number of articles during his working
career. See *Dictionary of National Biography, Twentieth Century, 1901-1911*, s.v.
"Jones, Thomas Rupert."

306. Thomas Spence (1826?-81) arrived in British Columbia in May 1858 and proceeded to
the Cariboo gold fields. After mining for several years, he won one of the contracts to
build the Cariboo Road from Boston Bar to Lytton. In 1865, he built a bridge across
the Thompson River at the location that now bears his name. In that same year Spence
was appointed the first civilian superintendent of public works for the colony of British
Columbia. When Dawson met him in 1875, Spence was directing the removal of Beaver
Rock from Victoria Harbour. See "Spence, Thomas," *Dictionary of Canadian
Biography*, 11: 844-45.

307. Henry Nathan (1842-1914) was a Victoria wholesale merchant, active in politics.
Nathan was elected to the British Columbia Legislature in 1870 as representative for
Victoria and to the Canadian House of Commons in 1871. Nathan served as a member
of Parliament until 1874, returned to Victoria for several years, then left for London in
1876.

308. John Keast Lord, *The Naturalist in Vancouver Island and British Columbia*, 2 vols.
(London: Richard Bentley, 1866).

309. Muirhead & Mann.

310. Dr. William Fraser Tolmie (1812-86) was one of the pioneer citizens of Victoria. Tolmie
joined the Hudson's Bay Company in 1832 and was assigned to Fort Vancouver on the
Columbia River, arriving in 1833. In 1859, he came to Victoria to manage the farms of
the Puget's Sound Agricultural Company. Tolmie was also a member of the Legislative
Assembly of Vancouver Island and later the representative for Victoria in the provincial
legislature. Upon his retirement in 1870, Tolmie spent much time on his own
eleven-hundred-acre Cloverdale farm. See "Tolmie, William Fraser," *Dictionary of*

Clover Pt. Day fine

Decr. 14. Met Mr Spence* & went with him to the Beaver Rock in the harbour. Descended in his shaft & saw the work P.m. Examining rocks near Foul Bay.[311] Evg. reading A fine clear & warm day.

Decr. 15. Calls connected with Exhibition P.m. At office plotting geological work &c.

Decr. 16. Morning got boxes from Fisher* N. Westminster, Boxes of specimens from Barnard &c. Took Exhibition goods to Muirheads. Geol. specimens to office. Afternoon tracing map of vicinity of Victoria. Letters from Selwyn*, Macoun*, & home this evening. Called on Jennings* & went with him & others to the Theatre.

Decr. 17. on business connected with exhibition & making enquiries. Packing fruit from Dr Trew* N. Westminster & Anderson* Saanich. Also other specimens. Evg. reading.

Decr 18. Packing boxes of specimens & addressing them Afternoon writing at office. Saw Capt. Holmes[312] of 'Maude' as to bringing flag-staff from Horse Shoe Bay.

Decr. 19. Sunday. Took a walk up to the Gorge, the day being fine but roads remarkably muddy. Great thickness of Shells & indian debris in some places on the shores of this arm. Afternoon & evening writing.

Decr 20 Morning writing & on ⟨....⟩ exhibition business Saw Mr Nelson* & the Capt. of the "Beaver" tug about Getting specimens across from Burrard Inlet &c. Afternoon writing at office. Posted letters to Selwyn*, Macoun*, Meredith[313] in answer to his communication as to cost of printing Boundary Commission report. Anna*, Father*, Mr Reid[314] Quesnelle &c. Evening writing & reading. Day overcast but with little rain.

Canadian Biography, 11: 885-88.

311. Gonzales Bay.

312. Captain Peter Holmes (1803-93), a native of Denmark, was one of the best-known mariners on the southern British Columbia coast. Holmes commanded J. S. Spratt's vessels the *Maude* and *Caribou Fly*.

313. Edmund Allen Meredith (1817-98) was born in Ireland and came to Canada in 1842. From 1847 to Confederation he was assistant provincial secretary of Upper Canada. In the new federal government, he served first as secretary of state for the provinces then, in 1873, became the first deputy minister of the new Department of the Interior. He retired from the public service in 1878, although he remained active on the Canadian Prison Board.

314. James Reid (1839-1904) was born in Wakefield, Lower Canada, and came to British Columbia in 1862. After mining in the Cariboo for several years, Reid opened a large store in Quesnel. Later, along with a variety of other business interests such as mines, steamers, and sawmills, Reid was a member of Parliament from 1881 to 1888 and senator from 1888 until his death.

G. M. Dawson to Anna Dawson*, 20 December 1875, Victoria

I have been writing So Many letters last night & today that I feel rather tired of it, but must not let the steamer Sail without Sending something home. Mails go twice a week by "the Sound"[315] & thence overland to Sacremento, but the steamer Saves several days in time.

Your letters acknowledging receipt of my first notes from Victoria since my return have only arrived a few days ago — So long does it take to question & answer from this desolate isle of the sea. I am sure I *meant* to say everything nice with regard to your engagement, So I am glad that you Kindly refrained from your first idea of scolding me. Joking apart you know I do not "gush" on paper, but I am really delighted, & if I Could only think of what to say & how to say it should write to Harrington* himself & tell him so, or rather congratulate him on his good fortune.

I have sent off by express to the Geol. Survey a number of boxes today, & in one of them have enclosed, addressed to Father*, a small thin parcel. It Contains two Photos. one of Victoria the great western Metropolis, the second of Yale on the Frazer R, where that stream leaves the Cascade Mts. Also a sketch of my own, the only one I have made this summer which I consider at all passable, please take the photos or the picture whichever you like best.[316] The Sketch is of Tatlayoco Lake where it runs up among the Cascade Mts. The proposed railway route passes along the bank to the left to the bottom of the lake, then crosses the head of the Homathco R which runs out of it, & follows its valley (behind the range of hills fringing the lake on the right) to the Sea. That is if the ry. is ever built it will go ⟨here⟩ thus, & I hope those fools at Ottawa are not going to throw away their last chance of consolidating the Dominion because there happens to be a commercial depression in the year of grace 1875.

The boxes will probably not arrive till about a week after this letter.

I fear this letter will be too late to wish you a merry Christmas, but if it does as it should, it ought at least to arrive Christmas week, & allow me to wish you & all at home a Merry New Year, which I hereby do with much earnestness.

I can hardly believe that it is so near Christmas as it is, the time seems to have slipped away So fast, & left nothing to show for it, & then to there is no proper winter to mark the time, only a prolonged & dismal Autumn, with the vine still clinging to the Mouldering wall & the rain & the wind are never weary. The grass is green & fresh looking, as it should be if

315. Mail received from across Puget Sound in Washington Territory. Mail would be brought there overland by train through the United States from eastern Canada.

316. None of these are traceable.

water will make it So, & hardy vegetables still Stand out in the fields; the thermometer only occasionally reaches the freezing point at night. The arbutus, an evergreen tree, is green in the woods, where the ground is also covered with mahonia bushes & Sal-lal plants — A species of *Gaultheria*. Now too the Moss which in summer is dried to a crisp & choked with dust, & looks altogether out of place; is washed Clean again & covers rocks branches & shingle roofs like so much wet sponge. The woods are uncommonly full of moss here, & not only underfoot, for it creeps up the tree trunks & settles in tufts & cushions even on the exposed branches. The Maple trees especially are generally Shaggy with moss of various colours, & now & then you may see a *polypodium* perched up aloft in it.[317] Now to stray seeds which in summer have become entangled in the Moss begin to sprout & you may see forests of little pines in some places growing up even on the trunks of the older ones. Where stalks of weeds have fallen, the Seeds are striking out even in the Maternal pod, under the influence of the damp.

I have an invitation to dine on Christmass with Dr Helmckin* (I hope that may chance to be the right spelling) It is very kind of the good man, & I hope I may appreciate it properly. He is a most excentric genius, & goes about with a great cloak of which the apperture Slews round in all directions but is never exactly in front. He has one grown up daughter, who — Shall I say it? — well she appears to squint, &, for your peace of mind be it added, is supposed to be engaged to a certain Mr N — after Such a description names Must be under the seal of — friendship.[318]

G. M. Dawson to John William Dawson*, 20 December 1875, Victoria

I have just finished my last letter for today, but must write a few lines still.

The thermometers, & your Dawn of Life,[319] arrived in perfect safety,

---

317. The "mahonia bushes" were either Oregon grape, *Berberis nervosa* Pursh, or tall mahonia, *Berberis aquifolium* Pursh; and "*Gaultheria*" salal, *Gaultheria shallon* Pursh. The "Maple trees" were either the bigleaf maple, *Acer macrophyllum* Pursh, or the Douglas maple, *Acer glabrum* Torr. var. *douglasii* (Hook.) Dipp.; "*polypodium*" was probably the common polypody or licorice fern, *Polypodium vulgare* L.

318. Dawson's reference is to Catherine Amelia Helmcken who was twenty at the time. "Mr N," perhaps Henry Nathan, did not become her husband; she married George Archibald McTavish on 4 December 1877.

319. J. W. Dawson, *The Dawn of Life; Being the History of the Oldest Known Fossil Remains, and Their Relation to Geological Time and to the Development of the Animal Kingdom* (Montreal: Dawson Brothers, 1875).

also by last mail a Sunday Magazine.[320] The Dawn appears to be very neatly got up & *looks interesting* I shall read it through at leasure. I must take an early chance of writing you Some description of the rocks in this neighbourhood, & of the traces of glaciation &c.

Your last enclosed Meredeth's* letter & Cameron's [321] on the cost of the report. I have answered the former as well as I can from memory, but should like to have my copies of correspondence & estimates Sent on sometime, in case further questions should occur. They are all in the black despatch Case.

In writing to Meredeth* I stated the circumstances under which the work was transferred to the Herald much as you did in your note to him. There are mistakes also in the account. A charge made for 46 pages "Maps & Plates" whereas there are only 18 plates & 3 maps, & the maps & one of the plates were lithos & only inserted by printers. The charge of $35.00 for "Tables & figure Matter" is also astray. This Kind of matter occurs *on* about 46 p. but by *measurement* there are only about 18 p. of such matter in the body of the report. Chapter headings & bulk of appendix not included, as there spacing out at least compensates for Smaller type employed. All this stated in letter to Meredeth*, & I should copy & send it to you but it is rather lengthy & I am tired.

The Commissioner wants to "raise Cain" at Ottawa because they tried to snub him there. There is much depression & anger here on Mackenzies* minute, which is taken by many to mean repudiation of the whole railway scheme. Property has fallen considerably in consequence. Brit. Columb. will refuse flatly to treat for any modification of Carnarvons terms.[322] If this shakes the ministery & a general election is brought on, B.C. & Manitoba will move heaven & earth to defeat them.

---

320. Probably *The Sunday Magazine for Family Reading*, published in London.

321. Donald Roderick Cameron (1834–1921), of the Royal Artillery, who had married Sir Charles Tupper's daughter in 1869, was British commissioner on the boundary commission. He was later commandant of the Royal Military College in Kingston from 1888 to 1896, before returning to his native Scotland where he died. See Parsons, *West on the Parallel*, 18–19; and Don W. Thomson, *Men and Meridians: The History of Surveying and Mapping in Canada*; volume 2: *1867 to 1917* (Ottawa: Information Canada, 1967), 164–76.

322. Dawson was referring to the order-in-council issued by the Mackenzie government which detailed the federal government's new railway policy. That statement was vehemently opposed by the British Columbia government as reneging on the terms earlier worked out by the governor general, Lord Carnarvon, and agreed to by both governments. For a discussion of the issues, see Ormsby, *British Columbia*, 261–78; for an analysis of Mackenzie's role, see G. F. Henderson, "Alexander Mackenzie and the Canadian Pacific Railway 1871–1878," (Master's thesis, Queen's University, 1964), 123–29.

Wishing you a Merry Christmas time & a happy new year

Decr 21. Called on Mr Charles Good[323] to get information on output of gold from Province for Mr Selwyn*.[324] Unpacking boxes of specimens at office & arranging them. Evening reading Vancouver's voyages.[325] Morning warm & overcast. About 1 P.m. heavy gale came on with much rain. Lasted nearly all night.

Decr. 22. At office Arranging statistics of Gold produce & labeling specimens. Walked out Fort St. Met Judge Crease,[326] Called at Duponts* but found all out. Evening reading. Day moderately fine, but raw Evening more rain. Shops & especially butcher's stalls now wear a Christmas aspect.

Decr 23. Day fine though cold & windy. Morning & afternoon Continuing examination on rocks along the coast from Ogden Pt inwards.

Decr 24. Morning making Calls & enquiries in connection with Exhibition. Afternoon labeling specimens & writing at office. Evening reading Vancouver's Voyages. Day cold & overcast with occasional showers of sleet.

Decr 25 Fine, & frosty for Christmas day, with a thin skim of frozen sleet or snow on the ground. Morning reading. Afternoon walked to Esquimault & back. Evening dined at Dr Helmckin's* with Marcus Smith*, Jennings* Gamsby,[327] & Mr Nathan*. Got home between 21 & 1.

Decr 26 Sunday Morning reading. Afternoon [finishing] some sketches, & for a Short walk. Evening reading & writing. Day Cold blustry & snowing slightly. Very unpleasant. Finished Vancouver.

Decr 27. Made various Calls in connection with Exhibition & question as to export of gold from Province. Afternoon tracing map in C.P.R.S. offices. Evening reading. Thawing & showery in the morning. Blowing a gale with heavy rain afternoon & evening.

Decr 28 At office all day labeling & arranging specimens & microscopic examination of some tripole earths &c. Steady down pour of rain. Evg.

323. Charles Good (1832-1910?) was both deputy minister of mines and deputy provincial secretary in the provincial government.

324. Selwyn requested "a statement from the most reliable returns and estimates of the total quality of gold that has been mined in British Columbia since its discovery" for the Philadelphia exhibition. Selwyn to G. M. Dawson, 29 November 1875, Dawson Family Papers, MUA.

325. George Vancouver, *A Voyage of Discovery to the North Pacific Ocean, and Round the World . . .*, 6 vols. (London: John Stockdale, 1801).

326. Sir Henry Pering Pellew Crease (1823-1905). See reference to Susan Crease, above, 3 November 1875.

327. C. H. Gamsby was also an engineer-in-charge with the CPRS.

reading & writing to William*.

Decr 29 Day fine, clear, & for the Season warm, but with a strong S.W. wind. Started about 10.30 for Foul Bay, & examined the Coast line to Oak Bay, returning at 5.45. Took lunch on the shore: A very heavy sea running in on Foul Point.[328] Evening reading.

Decr 30. At office morning & afternoon. Plotting work on map & writing up notes. Morning overcast, chilly & dark afternoon rain, Evening rain & heavy Storm of wind. Got great mail of papers, periodicals &c. & Xmas presents from home.

Decr 31. Spar arrived from ⟨Nanaimo⟩ Horse Shoe Bay Called on Mr Rhodes[329] as to shipping to San Francisco via Str Panama. He objects to taking the stick. Arrange to see Captain of steamer on Monday morning. Called on Capt Raymur* & Mr. Armstrong* as to getting spars out from England; Mr Selwyn* having thrown the matter back on our hands. Called on Mr Good* & Wells Fargo & Co[330] about Gold export of country. Paying other Calls connected with Exhibition & at work tracing a map in the C.P.R.S Offices. Evening reading.

Day miserable, torrents of rain varied by sleet & heavy wind. Letters from Home.

Jan 1. 1876. Morning packing Macouns* plants, Mr Jennings* having Kindly offered to take them with him to Canada. Tracing map. Afternoon Made a few Calls with Mr Jennings*.

Evening reading & writing. Day moderately fine throughout, & many callers in the streets.

Jan 2. Writing letters, reading, & for a Short walk. Day overcast but not raining.

Jan 3. Engaged all day on business connected with exhibition. Making calls & interviewing Various people. Messrs Cambie*, Jennings*, Harris[331] &c. leave by Steamer today. Evening reading. A few Showers but on the whole fine. Put cheques for salary amounting to $582 33/100 to Credit in Bank.

---

328. Harling Point.

329. Henry Rhodes of Henry Rhodes & Company, a Victoria merchant and commission agent firm.

330. The Wells, Fargo Express Company, the famous transportation firm of the American West, opened a Victoria office in July 1858. The company handled practically all mail to and from the United States, with the colonial government levelling a fee upon each item received. It was also responsible for most gold shipments to the United States.

331. Probably Dennis Reginald Harris (1851–1932), a qualified civil engineer who was employed by the CPRS.

G. M. Dawson to Margaret Dawson*, 3 January 1876, Victoria

The steamer for San Francisco leaves this morning & I had intended to have written somewhat fully yesterday, but found certain business letters I had to write took me so long, that at last I gave up & went to bed without writing anything for home at all. I will however take an opportunity of sending another note Sometime during the week by overland mail.

First I have to thank all members of the family for an unexpected shower of Christmas presents. All arrived Safely, & I must now in a general way thank each & every one without going into details. I am only Sorry that I have been unable to respond in a fitting way, but really there is nothing here, & if there was one could not get it across the Continent. The little mirror you Sent is very pretty & acceptable as that I had before was broken last summer.

I dined on Christmas day at Dr Helmckens*, as I told you I was to do. We had a very pleasant party Consisting of Mr Marcus Smith*, & Messrs Gamsby*, Jennings*, & Nathan* besides the hosts & myself. Dr H. Came out here years ago as physician to the H.B. Coys post, & married one of Sir James Douglas'. (the then governor & chief of the HB's) daughters, who died some time since.[332] Dr H aspired to various positions of trust, took a prominent part in bringing about Confederation, & having now retired from all public duties, nurses a Small practice in Victoria. As you may judge from his name, he is of german descent, & as from his name you might also divine he is one of the queerest & roughest looking specimens of humanity.

Please congratulate Eva* for me on having come so well through her examinations.

I enclose three Japanese stamps for Rankine*, which I hope will be new to him.

I cannot attempt to treat of any topics of importance in so Short a letter, so please excuse this time.

It seems I should have told you to plant the lillies in water with some clean pebbles in it. I am told that in earth they do not bloom nearly so well. Those I see about here are arranged somewhat thus, but are not in flower yet. [*Illus.*]

---

332. Sir James Douglas (1803-77) was governor of Vancouver Island, 1851-63, and of British Columbia, 1858-64. Born in British Guiana and educated in Scotland, he came to Canada in service with the North West Company, then with the Hudson's Bay Company. He founded, on the site of the present Victoria, the first Hudson's Bay Company post on Vancouver Island. He became governor of the island colony in 1851 and subsequently of the new colony of British Columbia. He was made a KCB in 1863. His daughter Cecilia, who had married Helmcken in 1852, died in 1865.

Jan 4. A fine & warm day. out from 10.20 till nearly 6 P.m. examining the coast from oak bay to Cadboro Bay. Evening visited Dr Walkem*.

Jan 5. At office morning & Afternoon arranging specimens, writing &c. Evening at library, & reading. Wrote to Ramsay,[333] Lesquereux,[334] & Belt.[335] Day Showery, evening blustry but fine.

Jan 6. unpacking specimens & writing letters. Evening reading, & writing home. Got letter from mother.

G. M. Dawson to Anna Dawson*, 6 January 1876, Victoria

I must thank you very much for your very acceptable present of a portable photo. album. Your photo. is very good, I think, fully as good as any you have had taken before. I have not shown it to the Creases*, nor did I dine there on Christmas day as you suppose in your last letter. The C's* are unfortunately in trouble just now. The second daughter while down at Esquimault paying a visit took Scarlet fever, & a day or two afterwards all those at home took measles, some of them very badly. I believe they have been unable to get servants & have had quite a time of it generally.

Now for All the other presents I have to thank the doners through you. Rankine* for his Capital diary, & Eva* for the peculiar cork pen-handle. There is nothing new here to report & things seem to have settled down pretty much into winter train. I am not working hard as you fear but taking life remarkably easy, & rusting slowly. Two or three years in this dead & alive place would cause anyone to loose all idea of the value of time, & quite spoil one for life anywhere else. Messrs Jennings*, Cambie*, & Harris*, three leaders of parties on the CP.R.S. left for Ottawa a day or

333. Sir Andrew Crombie Ramsay (1814–91) was then director-general of the British Geological Survey. One of the most distinguished nineteenth-century geologists, Ramsay had an enviable reputation as a field geologist and innovative theoretician. Like so many others, Dawson was heavily influenced by Ramsay's geological postulations and sought to apply his concepts to the British Columbia situation. See *Dictionary of National Biography*, s.v. "Ramsay, Sir Andrew Crombie."

334. Probably Leo Lesquereux (1806–89), who was an American authority on fossil plants and a respected specialist in mosses. A friend of Louis Agassiz, Lesquereux came to Boston from France in 1848 and was employed by Agassiz for some years classifying plants. He later developed an interest in mosses and published extensively in paleobotany. From 1867 to 1872, Lesquereux organized the fossils in Harvard University's Museum of Comparative Zoology. See *Dictionary of Scientific Biography*, s.v. "Lesquereux, Leo."

335. Thomas Belt (1832–78) was a well-known British naturalist. He did field work in Nova Scotia as well as in Nicaragua and Australia; while in the maritime colony he developed an interest in the glacial period and wrote extensively on the subject. See Anthony Belt's introduction to Thomas Belt, *The Naturalist in Nicaragua* (London: J. M. Dent & Sons; New York: E. P. Dutton & Co., 1911), vii-xxii, and especially xxii, where the works of Thomas Belt are listed.

two ago. Mr Marcus Smith*, & Gamsby* leave next boat, & then there will only be a few of the Subs. here. As for myself I dont think anything will induce me to spend another winter here, the most out-of-the-way Hudson's Bay post on the Continent would be preferable. The weather continues moist moister & moistest, though I must say we have had two fine days lately, & they were really very fine, & quite warm. Rightly concluding on both occasions that the weather looked Settled, I sallied forth to do a little Geology in the neighbourhood, took some lunch with me & worked all day along the shore, finding it almost hot in some places. One day there was a tremendous Surf rolling in & breaking against the rocks. I do not remember before to have seen such great waves Coming ashore, the spray flew high into the air, & went scudding across the grass. There are some beautiful spots along the sea shore here, at least they must be beautiful when the trees have leaves on them & the ground is not in the State of a quagmire. Sloping lawns naturally planted with scattered oaks & bushes, & splendid views of the Snow Covered olympian Mts. Mt Baker, the highest peak in Sight from here I have only seen once, & that in August last. On one occasion the smoke from burning woods cleared away enough to show it, but never since my return here have the Clouds forsaken it.

G. M. Dawson to John William Dawson*, 6 January 1876, Victoria

I have just been arranging the collection of fossil plants from Quesnel previous to packing it up for Montreal. I think there are Some things in it that will interest you. Part of the specimens I got while on the way up in August, & part Mr. S & self collected while on the way down in October. The impressions of leaves in white fire clay are from beds immediately in contact with the insect bed. There are a number of curious little things among them which I take to be the Seeds of some tree like the birch. [*Illus.*] Something like this magnified. There were also one or two seeds like this [*illus.*] which seemed to be those of some composite plant, but I am not quite Sure whether they have Succumbed to friction or not. Several of the leaves of one species of plant seem to have had some sort of fungus or gall growth on them somewhat thus. [*Illus.*] There are also some fruits preserved as casts in Sandstone. These appear to have been nuts & in many there is a Carbonaceous mass loose in the centre, still showing the general form (in a more or less imperfect way) of the shell. Most of these interior arrangements seem to have got lost or broken, but many seemed to resemble butternuts, hickories, or wallnuts. Some of which seem to have had a soft green rind which has left its impression in the stone. There are also a few plants from Blackwater. There was a maple Seed in very good preservation but I fear it may not be recognisable on arrival, also the seed of a coniferous tree of some sort. [*Illus.*] It will be interesting to know whether any leaves from Blackwater & Quesnel are the same. The formation is similar but may have been formed in different basins.

These specimens will go next Steamer but will not likely reach Montreal till a week or two after this.

By the way. What became of the part of the plant Collection which went to Hooker* for determination I remember seeing in a note you forwarded me from some one at Kew[336] that they were waiting orders. They should of course go to Cameron* with the rest.

With regard to the Boundary Commission of Alaska business, on the whole it would seem best not to make any application at present, but wait to see whether any expedition on a large Scale is to be started.

I enclose advertisement of two books I should be glad if you Could order & Send to me by post.

I have finished the perusal of the "Dawn" with much interest, & note the very favourable review in the *Saturday Rev*[337] which reached me from New York where I had no idea you were.

Jan 7. Examining minerals & ores with blowpipe,[338] at office. Evg. reading at home & at library.

A splendid clear & calm though rather frosty ⟨night⟩ day.
Jan 8. A fine day. Examining minerals with Blowpipe, & arranging section including ⟨lignite⟩ insect bed at Quesnel, for drawing. Evening at library & reading at home.
Jan 9 Sunday. Reading Prescotts Hist. of Conq. of Mexico[339] all day save during P.m. when for a walk. Hunting up a *fault* which I suppose to run

---

336. A reference to the Royal Botanic Gardens in Surrey, England, where Joseph Dalton Hooker was director at the time.

337. *Saturday Review of Politics, Literature, Science, and Art* 40 (1875): 653–54 contained a review of Sir William's *The Dawn of Life*.

338. "The blowpipe enables us in a moment, with no other fuel than that furnished by a common lamp or candle, to produce a most intense heat. In the blowpipe flame not only are most refractory bodies (platinum) melted or volatilized, but the most opposite chemical effects (oxidation and reduction) may be produced. Almost all mineral substances may be made to manifest some characteristic phenomena under its influence, either alone or in presence of certain other substances (reagents), and their nature may be thus surely and easily detected" (George J. Brush, *Manual of Determinative Mineralogy with an Introduction on Blow-Pipe Analysis*, 13th ed. [New York: John Wiley & Sons, 1893], 1).

339. William H. Prescott, *History of the Conquest of Mexico, with a Preliminary View of the Ancient Mexican Civilization, and the Life of the Conqueror, Hernando Cortes*, rev. ed., ed. John Foster Kirk, 3 vols. (Philadelphia: J. B. Lippincott & Co., 1874).

from oak Bay westward. Find gap on School ridge[340] in its course. Johnstone St Ravine nearly in a line with last & narrows of harbour at Hospital Pt.[341]

A very fine day.

Jan 10. Making Calls in connection with Exhibition. Afternoon at opening of the Local Legislature, & examining rocks on Promontory S of James Bay.[342] Evening reading. A fine day.

Jan 11. At Office Morning & afternoon, drawing Section of beds at Quesnel, & writing accompanying description. Evening at Concert in aid of Ref. Episc. Church.[343] A very fine day.

Jan 12. Engaged at office copying sketch of Nazco R terraces, & writing. Evening reading. Day overcast.

Jan 13. Arranging about landing of sections of trees from Burrard Inlet. Have come over in a scow, & from size Some difficulty as to getting onto any wharf. Mr Rhodes* agrees to let them lie in his store till ready for shipment. Got gold statement from Wells Fargo & Co. Photographs from Spencer[344] &c. P.m. made Several Calls & then attended for a Short time at the House. Wrote to Fisher* & Moody & Nelson*, Sending them cheques for their accts. Evg. reading.

Discovered *Ledas*[345] &c. in clay from well near head of James Bay.

Jan 14. Packing fossils &c. for Montreal. reducing sketch of Nazco R drift mounds. Evg reading.

Jan 15. Arranging & packing plants & fossils for Montreal & Macoun*. Drawing Blackwater R terraces. A fine & warm day but overcast. Evg. to

---

340. Probably Spring Ridge, on the edge of which stood a school reserve, now the site of Stelly Park.

341. Probably Songhees Point.

342. Finlayson Point.

343. The Reformed Episcopal Church of our Lord which had just been completed held the concert to help extinguish the debt on their new building. The *Colonist* noted that even though the concert was "rather too long" some 550 people were in attendance, including many local luminaries such as former Governor James Douglas (*Victoria Daily British Colonist*, 12 January 1876).

344. Stephen Allen Spencer (1892?–1911) came to Victoria in 1858 and was in business for some years as a "daguerreian artist" before disappearing from view for several years then re-emerging in Barkerville in 1871. Spencer subsequently returned to Victoria in 1872 where he operated a number of photographic establishments. Later in the 1880's, he entered into the cannery business at Alert Bay in partnership with West Huson and Thomas Earle. See his obituary in *Victoria Daily Colonist*, 16 August 1911; David Mattison, *The British Columbia Photographers Directory, 1858–1900* (Victoria: Camera Workers Press, 1985), S8–S9.

345. Fossilized bivalve molluscs of the Nuculanidae family.

opera which proved rather poor.[346] reading. Received by express dry-plates. By post Charts of Coast, & Nicholson's Zoology.[347]

Jan 16. Sunday. Wrote some letters, reading &c. Afternoon took walk on W side harbour. Evg. reading & investigating condition of dry plates received from Montreal. Box appears to have been opened, & Sawdust also damp.

Jan 17. Packing box at office. Called on Mr Rhodes*, Sproat[348] &c. on exhibition business, chiefly with regard to the flag-staff. Finished drawing of Blackwater Terraces. Evg. reading. A fine day.

Jan 18. Got boxes hooped up, addressed & taken to express office. Made arrangements for shipment of flag-staff, writing note to Prov. Secry. & getting him to write to H.M. Consul in San Francisco to get it attended to there. Found eventually When everything ready that Mr Rhodes* declines taking it this trip, having telegraphed to the Capt of the Panama now on the Sound. only reason that can be assigned that the steamer a little behind her time. Involves delay of at least another fortnight, & perhaps the loss of an opportunity at San Francisco.

Evening reading. & writing to Mr Selwyn* & home.

G. M. Dawson to Margaret Dawson*, 18 January 1876, Victoria

Late as it is I sit down to write a few words to send by tomorrows steamer. We have been enjoying a few fine days lately, & once last week it was quite warm. Tonight however I hear the wind howling & the rain coming down again. We have a little frost occasionally at night but have not had any snow on the ground for a long time.

About a week ago I went to a concert which was given in aid of the Reformed Episcopal Church here. It was fairly good on the whole. All the

346. Dawson is referring to the Marston-Bianchi Opera troupe from Portland, Oregon, who played the Royal Theatre for four nights. The performance Dawson saw included "selections from Verdi's emotional opera La Traviata and Donizetti's comic production, Don Pasquale, the interlude being devoted to ballads and instrumental music" (*Victoria Daily British Colonist*, 16 January 1876).

347. Henry Alleyne Nicholson, *Advanced Text-book of Zoology for the Use of Schools* (Edinburgh: W. Blackwood and Sons, 1870).

348. Gilbert Malcolm Sproat (1834–1913) was born in Scotland and came to Vancouver Island in 1860 under the employ of Anderson & Company, operators of a sawmill near Alberni. After returning to London, where he was agent-general for British Columbia, Sproat came back to British Columbia and was appointed joint commissioner on the Indian Land Commission in 1876. Upon resigning from that position in 1880, Sproat spent much time in the Kootenay region in various capacities such as gold commissioner and assistant commissioner of lands and works. See T. A. Rickard, "Gilbert Malcolm Sproat," *British Columbia Historical Quarterly* 1 (1937): 21–32.

performers Amateurs. The most amusing part of the affair was the Sudden extinction of the gas just as a lady had opened her mouth to Sing in response to an encore. After sitting in the dark a while, & Considerable investigation by those in charge it was found that there was no water in the metre. Last Saturday I went to See ⟨the⟩ an opera troupe which Came here with a great flourish of trumpets. It has turned out rather poorly & disappointed the people here very much. There was one person who sang pretty well, & that was all. You blame me for not referring in writing to various important topics, the truth being I suppose that in writing I think I must have previously discussed them. The Metis house looks well in plan, though of course everything depends on the situation, I suppose you will be planning to go down there next ⟨year⟩ summer. How is the new house in Montreal getting on? I hear from William* semi-occasionally & write to him at similar intervals I fear. You Seldom tell me anything about his movements in home letters. I hope he will get on well & find the Course of the *Ecolle*[349] to be useful & thorough. I dont particularly envy him in Paris, knowing what it is to be in London with plenty of studies to occupy all ones time. One might almost as well be in Timbuctoo —- or Victoria. The most unsatisfactory part of the whole is holiday time, I used to hate a holiday in London when they used to Shut up the Jermyn St library[350] & leave you to cudgel your brains to find out where to go & what to do.

Anna* I suppose is busy with preparations for the great event.[351] If it is really to take place in the course of the next few months — & I have hardly yet arrived at a clear realization of it — you must put me down for something useful in the present line, Say to the Amount of $400 or $500 dollars or any other sum you please. I must depend on you for Suggestions.

Please tell Rankine* I have got the Cartridges & note-books. All right, & Suitable. I enclose a few more Japanese stamps for him.

Jan 19. At office drawing map of route up the Chilcotin R.

Evening making up Centennial act & reading. Heavy fall of snow last night, & occasional showers during the day. Ground covered with slush. Lowering & overcast.

Jan 20. At office drawing map of Chilcotin R. Evg. reading, & wrote notes to Macoun*

---

349. Dawson's brother William Bell was studying engineering in Paris, at the Ecole des Ponts et Chaussées.

350. Dawson's reference is to his period of studies at the Royal School of Mines on London's Jermyn Street.

351. Anna's marriage to Bernard J. Harrington, which took place on 7 June 1876.

Post estimate of gold export to Mr Selwyn*.

A very fine day but cold & windy. Snow frozen on the ground

Jan 21. A fine clear frosty day. Morning called at bank with pass-book to have it made up & found that cheques put to Credit on Jan 3 could not be heard of & were not on Bank books. After enquiry it was found that they had been sent to Montreal, & were mentioned in the letterbook but had been otherwise forgotten. Made two or three calls on exhibition matters & wrote notes to [Barstow?][352] & Boscowitz.[353]

Afternoon drawing & listening to debate in the house on the railway resolutions.[354] Evening reading Bancrofts natives of Pacific States.[355]

Jan 22. At office drawing. Telegraphed to Selwyn* asking if spar shall be sent after delay it has experienced. Got letter from home Day fine & clear, Skating going on on ponds. Evg. reading.

Jan 23 Sunday Morning reading. Afternoon for a walk. Evg reading & writing. Day fine & clear with cold north wind. Noticed many robins & Finches (Junco hyemalis?)[356] here still though this most severe weather yet experienced this winter, & several inches snow on the ground. Finches generally grey or dun colour. Heads black. Male with reddish brown collar on back of neck & passing round over the front part of shoulders. Bill white.

Jan 24. At office drawing & plotting map. Went to here debate at house

---

352. Unidentifiable.

353. Joseph Boscowitz (1835?–1923), a pioneer fur trader and entrepeneur who came to Victoria in 1862. Boscowitz organized the Alaska Commercial Company with headquarters in San Francisco to exploit the north Pacific seal trade but soon disposed of the company. Forming his own new firm, Boscowitz proved a severe trial to the purchasers of the Alaska Commercial Company. Boscowitz also owned his own steamship line and, from 1896 to 1912, the old Victoria Theatre. See his obituary in *Victoria Daily Colonist*, 21 March 1923.

354. The resolutions were part of the controversy between the province and the dominion government over the failure to begin railway construction in British Columbia as provided in the 1871 Terms of Union. The issue here was Ottawa's failure to agree to Lord Carnarvon's settlement. See Ormsby, *British Columbia*, 266-69; British Columbia, *Legislative Journals*, 21 January 1876; and *Victoria Daily British Colonist*, 22 January 1876.

355. Hubert Howe Bancroft, *The Native Races of the Pacific States of North America*, 5 vols. (New York: D. Appleton and Company, 1874). Bancroft (1832-1918) was a prominent California publisher and historian interested in the history of the North American Pacific coast. In producing his many volumes, Bancroft employed a host of assistants who gathered voluminous notes and a large library of historical works. Even though the volumes issued by Bancroft's company appear under his name, much of the writing was done by others. See *Dictionary of American Biography*, s.v. "Bancroft, Hubert Howe."

356. The "robins" were American robins, *Turdus migratorius* L.; and the "Finches" were Oregon juncos, *Junco oreganus Townsend*.

for a little while. Evg. writing home & to Ward[357] (Keswick) reading. Day clear & fine, thawing in the Sun.

G. M. Dawson to John William Dawson*, 24 January 1876, Victoria

Nicholson's Zoology has arrived I am much obliged for it, as you suppose I have the Palontology. [358] I have also to thank you for Kindness in attending to various requests which Knowing how fully your time is occupied I hardly dared to make. The account of expenditure has come among other things. The Amount due for additional Commission expenses is so small that it hardly seems worth making any demand for it. The extra postages of reports, please Charge to me.

I mentioned in writing to Mr Selwyn* some days ago that I had found a few shells in clay from a well some few feet above high tide mark. They do not belong to the superficial layer of Shells & soil & old kitchen heaps which Surround the Coast, but some from the drift below & have an arctic appearance. There is a *Leda*, *Saxicava*, Small *noticea*, & a minute *Cardium*[359] I do not Know whether the species still inhabit the Coast they must be rather deep water forms at any rate. I cannot get them ready for mail this time, but will Send to Mr Selwyn* next post.

I have enclosed in a box shipped last steamer Some small pieces of woods, chiefly coniferous, of this country. The names given to them I am not in All Cases sure about, they are those I find in books on the Province — chiefly J.K. Lords book — & may have been since changed, or in some cases altogether wrong. Macoun* no doubt will be able to give a list from his collections. The red wood[360] included with the others is Calafornian. It is used somewhat here as being easier to work with than the Douglas fir.

357. James Clifton Ward (1843–80) was an eminent British geologist with whom Dawson had spent the summer of 1871 in field work. Ward graduated from the Royal School of Mines in 1861 and joined the British Geological Survey the next year. After a short stay in Yorkshire, he spent eight years surveying the Lake district around Keswick. Ward's excellent surveys and his several scholarly papers gave him a high place among field geologists. Shortly before his premature death, Ward quit geology, was ordained, and had just been appointed vicar of Rydal. See *Dictionary of National Biography*, s.v. "Ward, James Clifton."

358. Nicholson, *A Manual of Zoology*; Henry Alleyne Nicholson, *A Manual of Palaeontology For the Use of Students with a General Introduction on the Principles of Palaeontology* (Edinburgh: Blackwood & Sons, 1872).

359. "*Saxicava*" was a bivalve mollusc of the class Pelecypoda, Hiatellidae family; "*noticea*" a brachiopod of the Hemithyrididae family, *Notosaria* spp.; and the "*Cardium*" a bivalve mollusc of the family Cardiidae, subfamily Cardiinae.

360. Redwood, *Sequoia sempervirens* Endl.

I wrote to Macoun* about my collection of plants in answer to a letter of his asking me if they could be loaned for exhibition as a part of a General Canadian Collection at Philadelphia, Saying that I should have no objection to do so provided the ⟨refferences⟩ connection between the specimens & notes of dates & localities were not lost, & the specimens could be returned uninjured when all was over. Of these points I ⟨was⟩ {am} rather doubtful. The Manitoba Grasshopper Circulars are to hand & I will try to make some summary of them, though I am getting fearfully lasy, & it takes me about a week to do what I would formerly have done in a day.

When the extra copies of the Glacial Paper from the G. Society[361] arrive, if the list for distribution of reports has not been lost you might perhaps mail a few to ⟨those⟩ names of those ⟨which⟩ {whom} you think would be interested, & send a few to me here.

I find Bancrofts ponderous work {or such part of it as is completed} on the Native races of the Pacific slope in the Indian office here, & have just got through the perusal of the volume on the civilized races of Mexico.[362] Some parts of it are very interesting & others Very dry but it of course contains much information In fact I suppose all the authentic knowledge extant. The Mexicans have Some points of resemblance with the Indians of this northern coast, I think, which they do not posess with those of the North-East.

I dont know whether I told you that I got a Short vocabulary from the Chilcotin Indians last summer. I found the word *tinne* or *dinne* used for man as with so many tribes east of the Rocky Mts.[363]

Jan. 25. Morning at office drawing map. P.m. listening to debate in House on finance. Walkem* ministry defeated by 2 votes.[364] Evening reading & looking over Natures.

Jan 26. Drawing map Morning & afternoon Writing letters Evg. looking over grasshopper circulars & reading. A fine day thawing & mild.

Jan 27. At office drawing map. packed & sent off specimens of Conifers to

---

361. George M. Dawson, "On the Superficial Geology of the Central Region of North America," *Quarterly Journal of the Geological Society of London* 31 (1875): 603–23.

362. Volume five of Bancroft, *The Native Races*.

363. The Chilcotin Indian language belongs to the Athapaskan family which includes many groups east of the Rocky Mountains.

364. The Walkem ministry had embarked on a reckless public works programme, extending its credit and forcing it to seek funding from the federal government which it was otherwise at odds with. Walkem's supporters, "fearing that use might be made in Ottawa of his practice of borrowing large sums of money from the Dominion at the very time when his government was denouncing Canada as a defaulter on its railway obligations, had deserted him" (Ormsby, *British Columbia*, 270).

Englemann[365] & drift shells to Selwyn*. Wrote various letters & made Calls on exhibition business. Got letters from Selwyn* & Burgess[366]

Evening reading & going over grasshopper circulars.

Observed today curious crust or coating on Coals & back bricks of grate at office. examined it & have I think proved that volatilized zincic oxide, produced from some zinc compound which must be present in small quantaties in the coal.

Remember observing similar coating in Pictou caused by coal from New Glasgow mines, collected sample of flue-dust but did not examine it.

Jan 28. At Carpenters arranging about packing of specimens of woods &c. At office drawing. Enquiring about maps at C.P.R. offices. Evening grasshopper circulars & reading.

Min. Thermom this morning marked 12° but clouded over & temperature rose. Thawing most of day & now mild & wet.

Jan 29. At office working at map. Afternoon walk about Beacon Hill. Evening reading &c.

Day broken & showery with strong wind

Jan. 30. Morning reading. Afternoon for a walk & reading. Evening arranging grasshopper circulars & reading. Day cold overcast, & with showers of rain & soft snow. Mail steamer arrived this morning but mail not delivered.

Jan 31 At office mapping geology. Writing out Catalogue of exhibits. Writing letters &c. Letter from home.

Feb. 1. At Office writing & examining rocks &c. with microscope.

Evg. writing on Grasshopper. reading.

Day fine but windy.

Feb. 2. Morning at office writing Report.[367] Also at Custom House getting returns of various exports & imports for Exhibition Catalogue. Afternoon arranging about packing of boxes, & Shipment of flag-staff writing letters

---

365. George Engelmann (1809–84) was the ablest and best-known scientist in the Mississippi Valley for the fifty years of western American exploration and surveys. After receiving his M.D. from the University of Würzburg in 1831, Engelmann came to St. Louis the following year. Even though practising medicine, Engelmann continued his research interests in botany and wrote several monographs that remain essential references. He was also instrumental in founding the Missouri Botanical Garden which attained an international reputation in systematic botany. Engelmann greatly furthered American botanical research by maintaining close contact with many western explorers and acting as a clearinghouse for their work. See *Dictionary of Scientific Biography: Supplement I*, s.v. "Engelmann, George."

366. Thomas Joseph Workman Burgess (1849–1926) had been first medical officer to the British North American Boundary Commission. Trained at the University of Toronto, Burgess later became lecturer at McGill and medical superintendent at the Montreal Protestant Hospital for the Insane.

367. Eventually published as Dawson, "Report on Exploration."

for mail &c. Asked to give a lecture to the Mechanics Inst. Day fine
though rather dark.

G. M. Dawson to John William Dawson*, 2 February 1876, Victoria

With regard to the specimens of woods Sent some time back, I may
have forgotten to mention that the three small pieces of Juniper *numbered*, represent specimens Sent to Dr Englemann*. When I get the names
from him I will send them on.

I have received the no 8 French Objective,[368] & tried it with good result.
I do not hope however to get any micro. work done in unfavourable
Circumstances here this winter.

Powells Colorado report, which you mention I hardly think I need here,
at present at least. Is it published in Connection with the Clarence King, or
which Survey?[369]

I note what you say about Hind & the L of Woods rocks,[370] also
Venner & the Hastings Series.[371] Where has Hind* been writing about the
former?

Sun spot cycles Are {or should be} at present I believe just about a min-
imum of activity, but the times Seem to be out of joint somehow.

368. The objective of a microscope is the lens or combination of lenses which first receives
the rays from the object and forms the image viewed through the eyepiece. A "no 8
French" objective was probably one with a magnification of 80 X.

369. Dawson was referring to the work of John Wesley Powell (1834–1902), at that time in
charge of the United States Geographical and Geological Survey of the Rocky Mountain
Region, who carried out extensive surveys of the Colorado River region. The "report"
could be Powell's recently released third report, *Exploration of the Colorado River of
the West*. 43 Cong., 1 sess. House Misc. Doc. 300 (Washington, 1875). Clarence King
(1842–1901), who later became the first director of the United States Geological Survey,
also made surveys in the American southwest in the same period, as leader of the United
States Geological Exploration of the Fortieth Parallel. Although informally
co-operating, the two surveys were independent so that Powell's reports were not issued
under King's auspices. For a thorough discussion of these surveys, see Richard A.
Bartlett, *Great Surveys of the American West* (Norman, Oklahoma: University of
Oklahoma Press, 1962), 123–329.

370. Henry Youle Hind (1823–1908), while professor at the University of Toronto, was
employed by the Canadian government as geologist on the Red River expedition of 1857
and the Assiniboine and Saskatchewan expeditions of 1858. He published his
two-volume *Narrative of the Canadian Red River Expedition of 1857, and of the
Assiniboine and Saskatchewan Exploring Expedition of 1858* (London: Longman,
Green, Longman and Roberts) in 1860, but the publication referred to here is probably
a later one.

371. Henry George Vennor (1840–84), geologist and ornithologist, was a member of the
Geological Survey of Canada from 1866 to 1881. In his first three years with the survey
he did detailed work in Hastings County, Ontario. See "Vennor, Henry George,"
Dictionary of Canadian Biography, 11: 898–900.

I have got nearly ready a short note on the Grasshopper invasion of ⟨8⟩ 74,[372] with abstracts of information in circular, & will forward the whole soon, for publication in the Naturalist, where I suppose it will be accepted. I have also got under way a small circular for this season,[373] which I shall distribute only North of the forty ninth parallel. The Circulars will go back addressed to Montreal & will serve to give me a little employment next Autumn, if enough of them return.

I quite believe in the weekly budget plan but the mails here render it difficult to keep up to the system. There are two mails a week via Tacoma in Washington Territory & overland to Sacremento, but these are slow as compared with the direct steamer to San Francisco, which leaves *about* once a fortnight at very irregular dates. However I will try to do as well as I can.

I see my descriptive letter in the "witness,"[374] for which it was not intended, being rather too *plain*, however politics are running so high here now that probably no one will notice it. Prof Macoun* wrote in somewhat similar stream to Some paper in upper Canada last spring, & the "organs" here *went for* him for about a month to the extent of their vocabularies.[375]

Tell Mother there is no news this time so I could not manufacture a letter, but have posted some specimens of lichens, which about cover the oaks here; also a few joints of a Cactus from near here, which I was surprised to find the other day, & one or two small unknown bulbs I picked up in a field lately. The lichens will probably be squashed flat when they reach, but if moistened will expand.

Feb 3. Preparing letters for post. Called on Mr Rhodes* to try to get flag staff off, but again met with nothing but shuffling. Mr R. referred the

---

372. George M. Dawson, "Notes on the Locust Invasion of 1874, in Manitoba and the North-West Territories," *Canadian Naturalist and Quarterly Journal of Science*, n.s., 8 (1878): 119–34.

373. The results obtained by circulation of Dawson's questions are contained in his "Notes on the Locust in the North-West in 1876," *Canadian Naturalist and Quarterly Journal of Science*, n.s., 8 (1878): 411–17.

374. Probably "Things in British Columbia," *Montreal Daily Witness*, 7 January 1876, "From a Correspondent."

375. Actually there were two letters, one dated 17 May 1875, published in the *London Evening Advertiser*, 30 June 1875, and another dated 3 June 1875, published in the *London Evening Advertiser*, 5 July 1875. The reaction of the British Columbia papers was indeed swift and violent. An editorial in the *Colonist* bluntly advised "Prof. McCoun to desert the field of politics and stick closely to the pursuit of bugs and botanical curiosities" (*Victoria Daily British Colonist*, 18 July 1875).

matter to Capt Seybury[376] of the Panama, with at the same time a very apparent prejudice against the flag-staff. Capt S. after humming & hawing, — Mr R. meanwhile trying to prove that the flag-staff would be late, that it would be broken in taking on board &c. — finally Said he could not take it. Too heavy for hurricane deck, could not get on main deck because of Stantions &c. *This after through Mr R on a former occasion I had been told that there was no difficulty about taking the spar; & had not made any effort to get some sailing vessel from Nanaimo or elsewhere to take it on board, on that understanding.*

⟨Afternoon⟩ Very annoying & meet with persistent obstruction where there is every reason why all possible assistance should be given.

Afternoon at office writing.

Evening writing grasshopper notes.

Feb. 4. At office writing grasshopper notes. P.m. writing Report. Evg. reading.

Day fine, though blustry, & with rain about 5 P.m. Letter from Father*.

Feb 5. At office writing report. For a Short walk. Evening reading.

Feb 6. Reading & for a walk. Evening reading & writing home & to William*. Day fine.

G. M. Dawson to Rankine Dawson*, 6 February 1876, Victoria

Your letter written during the Christmas holidays arrived some time Since, & now you are no doubt grinding away again & looking forward with pleasure? to the Spring exams. You have never told me whether those express Stamps printed on the envelope (Wells Fargo & Co) sent last Summer from San Francisco were any use to you, that is to say whether they were legitimately inclusable (if I may coin a word) in your Collection. I can get both W.F. & Co's & Barnard's Express Stamps here if you want them.

There is quite a tempest in the political tea-pot here at present, & every body is electioneering & canvasing & standing in groups about the street Corners talking & button holing each other. The two rival newspapers[377]

---

376. Captain William B. Seabury (1840– ?) ran the route from San Francisco to Victoria from 1874. For four years from 1875 he commanded the steamship *City of Panama*, with occasional trips on the *Constitution* and the *Akaska*.

377. The *Victoria Daily British Colonist*, and Amor De Cosmos's new paper, the *Victoria Daily Standard*.

—like those of Eatansmill[378] — are going for each other in lively style, one comes out one day with a statement that the other is "the demented organ of a demoralized government" & the other next day incedentally mentions the first as "our low & Scurrilous Contemporary" & so on. The local government were defeated by a single vote lately, & now the new ministers are being reelected after accepting office. Altogether the system of government applied to this little place is Something like using the engines of the Great Eastern[379] to drive a churn, as a certain legislator is said to have remarked. The climate being So mild here, the ducks & geese do not all go south in winter. Many of them remain, & if by chance the ponds & lakes are frozen for a few days, betake themselves to the harbours & inlets. There are many ardent sportsmen who on Saturdays & Sundays make the whole neighbouring Country resound with Shooting, & if perchance they bring back one duck are greatly pleased. Grouse & quail[380] also frequent the Island, but all game birds are driven away for miles around Victoria by the efforts of the gentlemen aforementioned. Robins & the little black finches Sometimes Called Snow-birds, & also the chic-a-dees Seem to winter here, & I think I heard a Song sparrow Singing a few days ago.[381] The most revolting thing about Victoria is the Indian element. The gentle *Siwash* has a reserve just across the harbour, & also turns various unoccupied houses in the city into warrens. They are a most degraded lot, & are to be seen parading the streets in all their native ugliness & dirt at any time of day. It must give a stranger unaccustomed to the noble red man, a poor idea of a place to See an Indian dressed in a dirty white blanket with bare legs & feet, a head covered with shaggy hair never Combed since he was born, & a few bristly hairs sticking in his chin marching about at mid day.

[*Illus.*] Meant to represent Indian & Indianess but not altogether a Success.

378. Eatansmill was the scene of the corrupt election portrayed by Charles Dickens in *The Posthumous Papers of the Pickwick Club* (1836–37).

379. Britain's Great Eastern Railway.

380. The "Grouse" was probably the blue grouse, *Dendragapus obscurus* (Say); and "quail" possibly the mountain quail, *Oreortyx pictus* (Douglas), which was introduced very early to Vancouver Island.

381. The "black finches" were Oregon juncos, *J. oreganus*; "chic-a-dees" probably the chestnut-backed chickadee, *Parus rufescens* Townsend; and the "Song sparrow" the song sparrow, *Melospiza melodia morphna* Oberholser.

G. M. Dawson to John William Dawson*, 6 February 1876, Victoria

I have just written to William* addresing 86. Boulevard de Port Royal, which is I suppose still his address. There is nothing new to report here save a slight improvement in the weather, which is now warm & moderately fine, though the hills in the neighbourhood are still pretty well Covered with Snow. I am trying to get a short report of my Summer's work written, & when once fairly through I hope to be able to spend a little time on the rocks of the neighbourhood, which promise to be interesting, though they looked very hopeless at first. About Victoria nothing is seen but hard hopeless-looking highly crystalline diorites, standing up in lumps & knobs in all directions. At first these puzzled me a good deal, but I afterwards discovered that the Metamorphism & fracture was exceptionally great just here, & that at a little distance the arrangement is better shown. There are also bands of blackish clay-slates interbedded with hard felsites, greenstones[382] &c. sometimes Micaceous. As I wrote to Mr Selwyn* Some time since I am now convinced that the whole or nearly all the crystalline rocks are Contemporaneous volcanic productions, Some of them may have been lava flows, but others are distinctly ashes & breccias. The limestones previously described by Mr Richardson*[383] occur apparently generally among the greenstones, & are there. I have not seen much of them yet

I do not know if I told you before that I had been the means of loosing your pocket level last summer. I lent it to one of the C.P.R.S. Men who had broken his own, & he dropped it on a mountain & could not afterwards find it. I recovered the price, however from the Ry. Survey, So please order another for your own use, & charge it to my Account.

I dont' Know if you have paid any attention to the Indian question here. It has been attracting ⟨a good⟩ much ⟨attention⟩ {notice} for some time, but now seems finally settled on a pretty satisfactory basis.[384] The

---

382. "Clay-slates" was an old term for slates that is now sometimes used for argillaceous slate to distinguish this from slate developed in volcanic ash. "Felsites" were very fine-grained igneous rocks composed predominantly of quartz and feldspar; and "greenstones" was an old term for those varieties of dark, greenish igneous rocks which, on finer discrimination and in more modern terminology, would resolve into dolerites, diorites, and somewhat altered basalts.

383. James Richardson, "Report on the Coal Fields of the East Coast of Vancouver Island, with a Map of Their Distribution," in Geological Survey of Canada, *Report of Progress for 1871-72* (1872), 90-93.

384. Dawson was too optimistic about the issue being settled; the problem of Indian lands in British Columbia has continued unresolved until the present day. For careful analyses of the development of government Indian land policies in British Columbia, see Robin Fisher, *Contact and Conflict: Indian-European Relations in British Columbia,*

Dominion Govt wanted to Carry out in this Province a policy precisely Similar to that persued in Ontario &c. giving the Indians all ⟨large⟩ liberal reserves of Agricultural land & bringing them together & settling them in certain given localities. The Local Govt. would not alienate such large tracts as those required, & besides maintained that in proposing Such a plan the Dominion govt. did not understand the nature of the question, — which was true. Appropriatly large reserves to Indians so numerous as those here would practically block up many scattered areas of good land capable of settlement, & in some regions would take all the good land. Then along the Coast the Indians are fishermen, & might do well if encouraged in this industry, but would not farm, & might not like to be Carried from barren coast where they could Get good fishing to fertile land where they Could get none. Some of the Catholic Preasts showed considerable interest in the Indian reserve matter, no doubt intending eventually to get the land for themselves. The basis of settlement provides Small reserves for Indians requiring them, & provides that the reserve shall be increased or diminished to Suit the varying number of the tribe from time to time.

The Chinese New-year occurred lately & was the occasion of much Cleistial excitement. They visit each other, give & receive presents, & Keep open house, like any christians, but bunches indulge in fire-Crackers to Keep up their Spirits, or keep spirits away. For two days they Kept up a perpetual rattle almost day & night. The Chinamen are very useful here doing all manner of things which white men would not do. They preserve their Customs, & have lately got up a Joss house on a small scale. There are ⟨about⟩ {some} 1000 chinamen in this town making about one-fifth of the population. $32000 worth of opium paid duty last year for use in the province which would seem to imply that it takes something to ⟨console⟩ {reconcile} them to living here.

Feb. 7.

My usual luck! Having praised the good weather it has gone. Since early morning we have been experiencing a heavy storm of wind & soft wet snow, & now several inches of slush on the ground, & no sign of the mail steamer from the Sound, which I hoped might bring some letters, or which I might at least have acknowledged.

Feb. 7. Snowing & blowing heavily all day. At office writing report. Evening reading & writing. Got letters from Anna* & William*.

1774–1890 (Vancouver: University of British Columbia Press, 1977), 146–205; and Robert E. Cail, *Land, Man, and the Law: The Disposal of Crown Lands in British Columbia, 1871–1913* (Vancouver: University of British Columbia Press, 1974), 185–243.

Feb. 8. Fine overhead but extremely slushy & thawing. At office writing report. Evening sketching out lecture on glacial period & reading.

Feb. 9. Morning engaged making Calls & arrangements about exhibits. Afternoon writing report at office. Saw Mr Humphreys.[385] Evening writing & reading. paid Barnard express on Exhibition & Geol. surv. parcels.

Feb. 10. At office writing report morning & Afternoon. Evening copying out grasshopper paper, & reading. Day very windy with occasional showers.

Wrote letters to J.F. Allison.[386] Ewen* & Wise[387] &c.

Feb. 11. Writing memo of exhibits for Humphreys*. on outside exhibition business. P.m. going over specimens & Map with Tieddieman*. Evening Grass hopper Circulars.

Feb 12. Writing at office Am & Pm. Evening addressing grasshopper circulars.

Rain all day

Feb. 13. Reading &c. Evening dined at Walkems*. Wet all day.

Feb.14. Writing report At office. Calling on various people for Exhibition, & back at office writing. Evg reading & closing grasshopper paper. Showery but chiefly fair.

Steamer Panama arrived yesterday but ⟨no⟩ brought no mail even of newspapers. Letter from JWD by N. Pacific this P.m.

Feb. 16.[388] Went to gass works about specimen of coke. Sent express round for this & other articles. Writing report at office. Evening writing out Catalogue of exhibits.

Afternoon wet.

Feb 17. Making arrangements for shipment of specimens. Pm. Writing letters, & on other exhibition business.

Evening writing letters, finishing Catalogue &c.

---

385. Probably Thomas Basil Humphreys (1840–90), who at that time was finance minister in the British Columbia government. See "Humphreys, Thomas Basil," *Dictionary of Canadian Biography*, 11: 434–36.

386. John Fall Allison (1825–97) was born in Leeds, England and came to British Columbia from California in 1858. After a short sojourn in Victoria, Allison pre-empted 160 acres at Princeton on the Similkameen River. By the mid 1870's, Allison had expanded his holdings enormously and moved his family to Sunnyside on the west side of Okanagan Lake. For a discussion of Allison's life, see Margaret Ormsby's introduction to Allison, *Pioneer Gentlewoman*, xxiii-xl.

387. The salmon canning firm Ewen and Wise had a cannery located on the lower Fraser River. Dawson was seeking fish products for the Philadelphia exposition.

388. Dawson has missed an entry for 15 February 1876.

G. M. Dawson to John William Dawson*, 17 February 1876, Victoria

I had hoped to write long letters for this mail, but have been so busy all day, & evening as well getting arrangements made for shipping Certain exhibition articles, & the necessary papers & Correspondence Completed, that I shall only be able to make an excuse, & must write more fully by next Tuesday's mail.

I send addressed to you such account of the grasshopper raid of 1874 as I have been able to make out, in the form of a paper which I hope may be accepted for publication in the Naturalist. Two things are however against its general interest, viz. 1. that it is so long after date. 2. that much of the general information I have had to extract from my report. In case it should be too long, I have marked in pencil passages which may be omitted without much loss. If accepted, when in type please get 300 Copies struck off at my expense to satisfy promises of circulars. I have sent out circulars over Manitoba & the Northwest for last summer, with address envelopes to take them back to Montreal, where please Keep them for me, envelopes & all, as the post marks are often necessary in identification of places.

We are in a deplorable state here at present, the last steamer having failed, probably owing to Snow blocade on the railway, to bring any newspaper mail. Though letters come overland twice a week, we will have to wait till next steamer for the rest which will leave us a Month without Eastern news. We get a very small dose of telegraphic news daily *when the wires happen to be working*, but as they run goodness Knows how many Miles through uninhabited Country, & are half the time hung up on the trees instead of regular posts they are much more often out of order than otherwise. The Geol. Surv. of Cal.[389] has come on by express, Charges paid at the other end.

Thanks to Anna* for her last long letter of Jan 18. & love to all.

Feb 18. Engaged all morning seeing to shipment of specimens. Tender left with them & passengers for S.S. Panama at noon. Mailed all Grasshopper Circulars & letters. P.m. Writing report at office.

Evening reading. Day fine & warm.

Feb 19. Witing out fair copy of report all day & part of evening. Reading &c.

---

389. Dawson's reference is to the multi-volume set issued by the Geological Survey of California, all published in Philadelphia by Caxton Press of Sherman & Co.: J. B. Meek, *Paleontology*, vol. 1, *Carboniferous and Jurassic Fossils*; W. M. Gabb, *Triassic and Cretaceous Fossils*; W. M. Gabb, *Paleontology*, vol. 2, *Cretaceous and Tertiary Fossils*; and *Geology*, vol. 1, *Report of Progress and Synopsis of the Field-Work, from 1860 to 1864* (1865).

Feb 20 Sunday. Morning reading &c. Afternoon for a walk. Low tide & many pools in rocks bare. Observed what appear to be three or four different sponges. 1 bright yellow or green, thin encrusting with scattered raised oscula. 2. very similar but pale purple, sometimes faded to whitish, but never apparently yellow or green. Yet shape & habit So Similar that may be different Stage. 3. Yellowish compact & formless like ordinary Crumb of bread Sponge. 4 in very thin [curts?] in Sheltered spots bright scarlet. appertures[390] if any very Small.

Evening writing & reading.

Morning Scotch Mist. Afternoon fine but overcast & dull.

Feb 21. Going over report all day. Evening for a walk & reading.

Great excitement over the result of election & return of Elliot over Duck by great majority[391] Result Known about 6 p.m. & afterwards grand torchlight procession formed, band &c. & all the roughs of the town out. {Received Telegram from Perrault* sayin that exhibition articles should be sent. Wrote acknowledging}

Partly showery today

G. M. Dawson to Anna Dawson*, 21 February 1876, Victoria

When I last wrote to Father our condition here as to Mails was deplorable. It is even more so now there having been no relief. The last Canadian letters are now a Month old by their dates, & we cannot expect any newspapers for at least a week as they only come by the direct steamers once a fortnight, & the last steamer brought none. As for the letters I do not Know whether they are snowed up on the Union Pacific Ry, or somewhere north of Calafornia.

---

390. Given the relatively sparse data provided by Dawson, and the vast number of species present, it is virtually impossible to identify the specimens mentioned. For a systematic treatment of the region's sponges, see G. J. Bakus, "Marine Poelciloscleridan Sponges of the San Juan Archipelago, Washington," *Journal of Zoology* 149 (1966): 415–531.

391. Dawson's reference is to the provincial election in which the new premier, Andrew Charles Elliott, was re-elected in the Victoria constituency by the healthy margin of 445 to 282 over his opponent Simeon Duck. See the *Victoria Daily British Colonist*, 22 February 1876. Elliott (1829?–89) remained premier until 1878 when he lost his seat in the legislature. Born in Ireland, Elliott was admitted to the bar, Lincoln's Inn, in 1854. He arrived in Victoria in 1859 and was appointed judge of the district court in Yale and Hope. He also served as an assistant gold commissioner and stipendiary magistrate in Lillooet, high sheriff of British Columbia, and Victoria police magistrate before assuming the premier's position. After his defeat in 1878, Elliott travelled outside the province and was appointed a commissioner to investigate Indian disturbances at Metlakatla before his death after a lengthy illness. See "Elliott, Andrew Charles," *Dictionary of Canadian Biography*, 11: 299–301.

Here the weather is much the same as ever. Hardly a day without rain, but occasionally quite warm & Summer like, with birds singing & the willow Catkins beginning to come out. Then probably in a short time it will be blowing a gale with rain & perhaps sleet, & quite uncomfortably Cold.

The town today is in a great state of excitement over the election, the new Premier Elliot being declared head of the Pole after a pretty hard Contest. All the Elliotites are even now rushing about & congratulating each other, while the beaten party are doing the reverse whatever that may be, & both sides are indulging to the benefit of the Canadian revenue, in various exciseable articles.

I have Almost finished my Survey report, though unable to post it today. Tomorrow I hope to see it through, which will be a blessing, as I will then be able to get about again a little & do out door work in connection with the geology of this place. I hope Soon too to get the last of the Exhibition things away which will be another Cause of rejoicing. About the first of April from all I hear it may be possible to get out in the field in the Island or along the Mainland Coast without fear of being deluged or Snowed upon, & when this occurs it will be a third cause of delight, & infinitely preferable to living here in Victoria. If one can begin in April & go on till October it Should allow a pretty good Summer's work to be done, & that fairly over I shall be ready to return to Montreal for a Space.

This is a very unsatisfactory letter I feel, especially as it was intended as an answer to the long one you wrote me giving an account of your Visit to the Harrington Family. Still there seems to be no proper head of steam on. So having Netted wearily through the mental waters for some time without so much as Capturing a prawn, I think I must even give up for the present & go & post this, taking a walk at the same time among the free & independent electors of Eatansmill. Enclosed is a leaf of a Japanese [Punch?] for Eva* instead of a letter. If she can make out what it all means I shall be glad to know

Feb. 22. overhauling report Morning & afternoon Evening reading. A splendid day almost oppressively warm & bright & fine.
General reaction from election excitement in town.
Feb 23. Working on report &c. Wet all day
Writing out lecture
Feb 24. A fine day but Showery. Writing out lecture on Ice age for next Monday. {At work on diagrams for lecture}[392] Mailed Report, & three specimens of ⟨Wheat⟩ grain. Wrote Mr Selwyn*. Evening at Party At Judge Creas'* getting back at 1.40 A.m. Letters from home.

392. See 28 February 1876.

Feb. 25. Writing lecture. Seeing after Carpenter at work on Slab of Yellow cypress.[393] Evg. reading & writing. Day fine but chilly Last two nights frogs Croaking noisily. Wild gooseberry[394] beginning to be green. Willows Catkins budding out.

Feb 26. Finishing lecture. Looking after packing of things for exhibition. P.m. geologising. Completed survey of James Bay Point[395] & round by James' Bay & the Coast to Rhodes' wharf. Found a limestone bed at waters edge near the latter place Day Fine.

Feb. 27. Morning reading. Afternoon for a walk. Found shells like those already found near James Bay in one of the sea Cliffs of yellow Clay West of Beacon Hill. Same forms represented. Occur sparcely & irregularly in hard sandy clay with gravel, stones, & occasional large boulders, Seldom evidently glaciated. Deposit is that resting on the beautifuly glaciated rock surface & in Some places a hard yellowish clay without stones. In one spot this noticed to be full of holes like those of Saxicavas or pholads[396] but above the present high tide line. Some 6 inches deep, others worn away in bank till bottoms, which larger than apertures, exposed. Can only suppose that burrowing done before upper Clay beds formed. Evening reading & writing

Day Very fine.

Feb 28. Exhibition business. Looking over lecture. Reading. Evening delivered lecture[397] at 7.30 to a pretty good audience Say 100. Day fine.

Feb 29. Packing up objects for exhibition at Carpenters shop, getting lists of objects made &c. P.m. Continued Geological observations round Rock Bay to Esquimault bridge.

Weather Very blustry with E. wind

March. 1. Morning blustry. P.m. overcast & showery.

Writing out lists for boxes & Getting them numbered & Closed.

P.m. plotting geol. observations. Evening reading &c. Deposited cheque in bank for $266.66 being Salary to end January.

March 2. Examining rock exposures on all the Streets taking them system-

---

393. Yellow cedar, *Chamaecyparis nootkatensis* (D. Don) Spach.

394. Wild gooseberry, *Ribes divaricatum* Dougl.

395. Probably Laurel Point.

396. Stone-boring clams of the Lamellibranchiate family.

397. His lecture, entitled "Geology of the Glacier Period" was given under the auspices of the Young Mens' Christian Association. The manuscript is in the G. M. Dawson Papers, Bundle 64, McGill University, Rare Books and Special Collections, Montreal (RBSC).

atically. Morning & afternoon. Mr Janion[398] Called this evening to Say they would take the flag-staff! Now too late. probably moved to this action by outside pressure. Evening writing & reading. Day Very fine & warm — letters from home —.
March 3. Making arrangements for Shipment of specimens. writing letters to Selwyn*. Perrault* &c. Wet & stormy.
March 4. Closing & mailing letters. P.m. Geologising in neighbourhood of Victoria. Evg. at Mechan Inst. reading.[399]

G. M. Dawson to Margaret Dawson*, 4 March 1876, Victoria

I enclose William's* letter for return as requested, & much obliged for the use of it. I had intended to write home at Some length in answer to all letters received, but as usual find myself tired of writing now that [....] business letters are disposed of. I am sending off today a lot of packages for the exhibition which will nearly complete the business, & I hope soon to be happily relieved from it.

The weather begins to show signs of improvement. I saw a bank quite covered with daisies in flower a few days ago. — The common old country daisy which has run wild here. Gorse & broom have also become naturalized, & the former is already in flower.[400]

With regard to the $400 or $500 I quite meant it I assure you, & think the piano just the thing, & hope you will make the necessary arrangements as you See best.

I gave a short lecture here the other night to the Young Men Christians Associated! It went off well enough, but I felt rather ashamed of appearing in that connection, & will not be over persauaded to do so again, having not yet got to the point of looking with as great complacency on that, as I do on some other evils.

Williams* letter I hardly could understand as he Mentions all sorts of places & people I never heard of before, as though familiar from Childhood.

With love to all, & congratulations to Eva* on her exams.

---

398. Richard William Janion (1852?–89) was in business with Henry Rhodes as a commission merchant. The son of Richard Cheshyre Janion, who founded the partnership with Rhodes, Richard William was married to Rhodes's daughter. The younger Janion died at an early age in San Francisco.

399. The institute was located in the Philharmonic Hall on Fort Street. It was open until 10:00 p.m. daily.

400. The "old country daisy" was the common daisy, *Bellis perennis* L.; "Gorse" gorse, *Ulex europus* L.; and "broom" Scotch broom, *Cytisus scoparius* (L.) Link.

More on Tuesday.

March 5. Sunday. Reading, & for a walk in the afternoon. Strong Easterly Gale. Reading & writing.
March. 6. At work writing out observations, & plotting geol work. Wrote Hughes* & Ewen* & Wise. Enclosing cheque to latter. Posted letter to Leut Rowe*. Very windy day.
March 7. Morning at office getting table &c. Changed to room up stairs. Reading. P.m. geologising, but driven in by weather. Evening reading, about ⟨two⟩ {an} inch of slush on the ground this morning, & squally with sleet & snow in the afternoon
March 8. Morning at office. Dr Tolmie* Called &c. Looking over Anderson's* Map.[401] P.m. plotting geol. Work. Writing. Evening reading.

About two inches of snow last night. During day nearly all went. Evg. high wind & frost.
March 9. Writing & reading. Call at Creases*. Wrote P.W. &c. Evg reading Day fine but cold. freezing in the shade.

G. M. Dawson to John William Dawson, 9 March 1876, Victoria*

I have noted several queries [&c] in letters, to be answered, & must write before they are forgotten.

You ask if the Bulletins of the Hayden Surveys[402] Came. I got Several by last steamer (3) but did not think of looking to see where they Came from. It seems to me however that they had only U.S. Stamps. Dall has sent me copies of the Alaska Charts you mention. I wrote to him asking for a copy of his report on Mt St Elias,[403] & with this he Sent the charts &

401. Probably Alexander Caulfield Anderson, *Hand-book and Map to the Gold Region of Frazer's and Thompson's Rivers, with Table of Distances* (San Francisco: J. J. Le Count, 1858).

402. Like Powell and King, Ferdinand Vandiveer Hayden (1829–87) was a famous surveyor of the American west. Hayden's Geological and Geographical Survey of the Territories issued some fifty publications so it is impossible to tell which items Dawson was referring to. The publications of the Hayden, Powell, and King surveys have been indexed in Laurence F. Schmeckebier, *Catalogue and Index of the Hayden, King, Powell, and Wheeler Surveys*, United States Geological Survey Bulletin no. 222 (Washington, 1904).

403. See William H. Dall, "Report on Mount Saint Elias, Mount Fairweather and Some of the Adjacent Mountains," first printed in July 1875, as a separate in the United States Coast Survey, *Professional Papers*, series; and later as Appendix No. 10 to *Report of the Superintendent of the United States Coast Survey, Showing the Progress of the Survey during the Year 1875* (Washington: Government Printing Office, 1878), 157–188. William Healey Dall (1845–1927) was a renowned American naturalist and explorer. Dall studied zoology under Louis Agassiz before beginning explorations in Alaska in

other publications. The Indian Vase you Say Mr Selwyn* has given to the College, I remember, but we could not find out anything definite about its history, but that it was said to come from the Northern Coast. It is probably quite modern. The eagle or bird may be copied from the Russian or U.S. emblem, but may also just as well represent the Thunder bird of the Mythology of the Coast Indians. I believe Some of the Alaska tribes Make pottery, but will find out about it if I can.[404] The Californian Reports arrived Safely with nothing to pay at this end. I am disappointed in the *geology* which gives few general facts, & masses of details extracted from field books, printed in Sumptuous style as though results of great value. It will be of some use however. Before receiving your letter with note of Mr Whiteves[405] dictum on the fossils, I had come to the conclusion from the Palaeont. of Cal that they must be specimens of *Aucella Piochi* a shell characteristic of the *Shasta* or lowest group of the Calafornia Cretaceous,[406] & had stated so in a pencil note to my Report, Sent in to Mr Selwyn* Some time Since.

The Witness comes regularly, of late, I suppose you have Subscribed for it for me. It contains on the whole, more news than the Gazette.[407]

With regard to Dr Carpenter[408] & the new Shells. If it is decided that I shall explore the coast of the Island or mainland, I may be able to do some good dredging also, & as the Geol. Survey has no special place for Nat. Hist. collections I dont see why Dr C. should not have a share. I might be able to take a few spare days myself, at my own expense when the weather becomes finer. At present it is seldom fair & quiet for a whole day at once.

1865. From 1871 to 1884 he was associated with the United States Coast Survey, in charge of a scientific survey of the Aleutian Islands and adjacent coasts. Dall later transferred to the United States Geological Survey where he held the rank of palaeontologist. See *Dictionary of American Biography*, s.v. "Dall, William Healey."

404. No coastal tribes practised pottery making. The McCord Museum of McGill University cannot now identify this "vase" with anything in their collection.

405. Joseph Frederick Whiteaves (1835–1909) came to Canada in 1862 and was at this time curator of the museum operated by the Montreal Natural History Society. In 1876 he succeeded Elkanah Billings as palaeontologist to the Geological Survey of Canada.

406. The bivalve mollusc, *Buchia terebratuloides* (Lahusen), which indeed was a Lower Cretaceous fossil found in California.

407. The *Daily Witness* and the *Gazette* were both Montreal newspapers.

408. The Montrealer, Philip Pearsall Carpenter (1819–77), then one of the most learned authorities on molluscs, had an invaluable shell collection. Born in England and trained as a minister, Carpenter was primarily interested in the study of mollusca. He first came to North America in 1859 to arrange a number of shell collections, including some at the Smithsonian Institution. In 1865 he moved to Montreal where, despite having to teach because of adverse financial circumstances, he continued to collect and organize shells and arrange collections. See his obituary in *Montreal Gazette*, 25 May 1877.

I will See the Mr Middleton you speak of & find out what he has in the way of Collections.[409]

I have ⟨Mr⟩ Prof Hind's* letters enclosed by you. They are Certainly very flattering, almost too much So. What is causing him to take such a surprising interest in the N.W.?[410] In regard to the origen of the gold of the Saskatchewan &c. I have no doubt Prof H. is right in attributing it to the Laurentian region. I think Mr Selwyn* makes a similar statement in his report.[411] At the same time, I have had pointed out to me localities among the foot Hills of the Rocky Mountains, where the Northern & Eastern drift does not occur, but where "Colours" of gold are said to be frequent, by old miners whom I have no reason to doubt. It is also said by these men that gold in small quantities occurs in all the brooks flowing from the Rocky Mountains, near the 49th parallel at least.

With regard to extra Copies of the Report. It seems to me rather ⟨in of⟩ better not to ask for any more just now while the payment is still in question. Cameron* would no doubt be the proper person to Apply to. ⟨I⟩ I think everyone who has any claim to Copies must have ⟨had⟩ now been supplied, & if others really want the book they can always buy it.

I have made arrangements with Dr Tolmie* of this place, to get samples of the various Indian tribes, which are to be found in Victoria from almost all parts of the Coast. We are going to try to get vocabularies of some of the least known languages.[412] There is a very fair {subscription} public library here where some standard books are to be found, & also periodicals & newspapers. There is no parliamentary library, nor any chance of seeing scientific serials. There is no museum, but I have a room in the Govt. Buildings which is supposed to be about to be devoted to that purpose, when anything turns up to put in it. As yet I have only a few specimens of woods got while preparing those for the Centennial.

March 10 Day fine but cold in the shade & with still a little snow on the

---

409. Dawson's father had written of a Middleton, brother of a Quebec City businessman, who collected natural history specimens. J. W. Dawson to G. M. Dawson, 10 February 1876, Dawson Family Papers, MUA. The Victorian is presumably Robert Middleton, a typographical compositor.

410. Since serving on the Canadian expeditions to the northwest in 1857 and 1858, Hind had moved to the Maritimes, working on the geology of Nova Scotia and New Brunswick.

411. See Alfred R. C. Selwyn, "Observations in the North West Territory on a Journey Across the Plains from Fort Garry to Rocky Mountain House Returning by the Saskatchewan River & Lake Winnipeg," in Geological Survey of Canada, *Report of Progress for 1873-74* (1874), 58.

412. Later published as W. Fraser Tolmie and George M. Dawson, *Comparative Vocabularies of the Indian Tribes of British Columbia, with a Map Illustrating Distribution* (Montreal: Dawson Brothers, 1884).

ground. Writing & reading. Evg. occupied up Stairs parlour.

March 11 Dr Tolmie* according to engagement succeeded in mustering An indian & half breed with whom sat to work, & got 3 dialects of the Quaquielth language[413] of the N. end of the Island & adjacent mainland. Finished about 4.30 & pretty tired. Evg. raining. Day Cold, windy & overcast.

March 12. Reading. Afternoon for a wak with Mr Monteith.[414] Followed the coast line of the point between here & Esquimault.[415] Day unsettled, blustry. with some rain. Many Indian Shell heaps along this part of the coast.[416] Found in them a deer horn chisel, bone needle or awl, & barbed fish spear. Several nearly precipitous little points protected by earthwork like that of Beacon Hill point.[417] Also Saw where apparently Indian camp or village of some Kind had been. Low circular mounds, with depressed Centres.[418] Several of them near together, & from (say) 15 to 20 feet diameter. (Quqelly houses?)[419] [*Illus.*]

Mr A. Bowman[420] Called this evg.

413. The Kwakiutl are one of the two great divisions of the Wakashan linguistic stock, the other being the Nootka. The language, more properly termed Kwakwala, has several dialects and sub-dialects.

414. Probably William Monteith (1850?–1920) a Scot who came to Victoria in 1870 in the employ of Janion, Rhodes and Company.

415. In following the coast between Victoria and Esquimalt Dawson would have passed several points, the most prominent being McLoughlin, Macauley and Saxe points.

416. The many shell middens around the greater Victoria area are mainly associated with the recent shoreline. Judging from those that have been dated and from knowledge of sea level changes, most of these middens were developed within the last two thousand years.

417. The fortified earthworks like those at Beacon Hill Park (archaeological site DcRu 23) occur at several localities around Victoria and Esquimalt harbours. These were sites on small peninsulas with trenches dug across the landward end. A palisade of wooden stakes was placed around part or all of the peninsula. One such site, DcRu 123, was near the entrance to Victoria's inner harbour at Lime Bay, another above Flemmings Beach inside Macaulay Point (DcRu 21), and another on Dyke Point (DcRu 77) inside Esquimalt Harbour.

418. Probably a reference to sunken burial mounds or burial mounds dug out prior to Dawson's visit. Such burial cairns of earth, large stones, or combinations of these once occurred in several localities along the waterfront of Victoria and Esquimalt harbours. One, DcRu 52, was recently dated to approximately six hundred years old.

419. Ququelly houses were the semi-subterranean winter dwellings of northwest, especially interior, Indians. For a brief discussion and illustration, see Dawson, "Notes on the Shuswap People of British Columbia," *Proceedings and Transactions of the Royal Society of Canada* 9 (1891), sec. II, 7.

420. Amos Bowman (1839–94) began his career as a journalist before spending time with the California Geological Survey. (See below, Dawson to Margaret Dawson, 28 May 1876). After working with Dawson in 1876, Bowman surveyed and mapped the Cariboo gold fields under Geological Survey of Canada auspices. He later possessed considerable land

March 13. Called on Mr O'Reilley[421] & got from him as a loan a fine specimen of the Omineca Native Silver. At Office for a little while P.m. At office writing letters &c. Evg. reading. Wrote. Selwyn*. Perrault*. Posted. Bulkly.[422] Dunsmuir* & Diggle, & Bryden* asking Coal Specimens for Museum. Evg reading Darwin. Noting. Bancroft.*

March 14. At work with Dr Tolmie* getting Indian Vocabularies. Evening reading Day overcast & dull.

March 15. Geologising Morning & Afternoon Evening reading. Day very unpleasant squally with some snow. Partly clear

March 16. With Dr Tolmie* at office till 4.30 getting Indian Vocabularies. Evg. at library, & reading at home. Day Partly Clear, fine, but chilly.

March 17. Wrote Selwyn*. packed & sent by express specimens of gold & Silver. Could not find Col. Lane[423] to get his promised Specimens from Omineca, but have sent own from Mr O'Reilley*. Reading. Evening at Mr Fellows[424] to dinner, Dr Tolmie* being there also.

March 18. Morning posting letter & Attending to various matters of business, reading. Afternoon Examining coast about Indian Reserve. Evg. reading.

March 19. Morning reading Bancroft.* afternoon for a walk. Evening reading & writing. Day gloomy, chilly, & wet throughout. Said to have been a slight earthquake at a few minutes before eight this evening, but must have been *very* slight as few people felt it.

holdings in the upper Fraser Valley. For Bowman's Cariboo work, see his "Report on the Geology of the Mining District of Cariboo, British Columbia," in Geological Survey of Canada, *Annual Report 1887–88*, n.s., 3 (1889), pt. I, Report C, 1–49.

421. Peter O'Reilly (1828–1905) was an Anglo-Irishman who came to British Columbia in 1859. Shortly after, he was appointed stipendiary magistrate for Langley District, then for Fort Hope District. He later served as magistrate and gold commissioner in a variety of other mainland areas. In 1863 he was appointed a member of the British Columbia Legislative Council, serving until 1871. He became Indian reserve commissioner for British Columbia in 1881 after the resignation of Gilbert Malcolm Sproat. See Margaret A. Ormsby, "Some Irish Figures in Colonial Days," *British Columbia Historical Quarterly* 14 (1950): 61–78.

422. Thomas A. Bulkley, an English-trained civil engineer, owned and managed the Harewood Coal Mines, near Nanaimo. Bulkley later left British Columbia for India, where he was senior resident engineer in Bombay.

423. Charles C. Lane was co-owner of Lane & Kurtz Mining Company, which was very active in Omineca district mines during this period.

424. Either Arthur or Alfred Fellows who were partners in the hardware merchant firm of Fellows and Roscoe, in Victoria. Later in 1883 the brothers sold their interests to E. G. Prior and spent much time travelling between Victoria and England.

[Draft of a poem, 19 March 1876]

I am sitting here & thinking by the
Sunshine of today
of the problems men have pondered &
may ponder on for aye
of the long unsolved questions, of eternity, & time
That have lived in every nation {mortal}, every nation, every clime.
Are we nearer, any nearer to the
Knowledge we desire
As we mould the faith of ages to new
forms upon our fire.
We may see a little deeper, with more
microscopic Ken ⟨(gaze)⟩
In the building & the weaving of the earth-world
now than then
But when patiently, with Science, we undo
the tangled scene
on with doubting footsteps follow dim perceptions {conceptions}
through the brain
{or follow dim perceptions through the chambers of the brain}
Are we treading on an onward path
or do our footsteps tends
Though labyrinths of stuff & mind to bring us
in the end
To that dark verge where all we Know, ends
in the dim unknown
That view of a great starless void which these have
outlook on.
made their own
Who walking by less hidden paths
have dared to draw the veil of light
& trembling strain (turn) their useless
eyes {orbes} on the cold realm of night.

GMD
    March 19. 1876.

[Dawson wrote some notes dated 19 March 1876, in a separate small volume found with his personal diaries and entitled "Glaciation Indians &c. &c. West Coast 1876."]

Mr Peel[425] of New Westminster tells me of existence of stone circles at McNeils Point[426] near Victoria
  Graves on Macaulay's plains[427] opposite Mr Pooley's,[428] near Victoria. Square "fort" partly obliterated by agriculture near Clover Pt.[429]
  Says that near government buildings New Westminster a Sort of terrace above the river with many old indian shell heaps with mussels oysters &c. *which do not now inhabit the Frazer or its estuary.* Seems to indicate former change of level. *If* coast now sinking & indian remains of date prior to its rise, must be of very remote date.[430]

425. Probably Captain Adolphus Peele (1841?–1916), a pioneer resident of New Westminster who had reached British Columbia from England in 1862. Peele was a keen student of natural history and a staunch supporter of British traditions.

426. Dawson's reference was to the large, ringed stone burial cairns above the east side of McNeil (Shoal) Bay. The two still remaining, site DcRt 30, located on Anderson Hill, have not yet been systematically excavated. McNeils Point is probably a reference to an unnamed point of land at McNeil Bay.

427. This site, recorded in the 1970's as DcRu 22, was a burial cairn complex observed by several others around the beginning of the twentieth century. Unfortunately, the entire area was altered as a military defence site in the Second World War and no cairns or even photographs exist today.

428. Charles Edward Pooley (1845–1912) arrived in Victoria in 1862 and, after a few months in the Cariboo, secured a clerical position with the government, eventually becoming registrar of the British Columbia Supreme Court. He was admitted to the bar in 1877 and had a very lucrative partnership with A. E. B. Davie. Elected to the British Columbia legislature in 1882 as representative for Esquimalt, Pooley remained a member for twenty-two years. See E. O. S. Scholefield and F. W. Howay, *British Columbia from the Earliest Times to the Present*, 4 vols. (Vancouver: S. J. Clarke, 1914), 4: 90–91.

429. There is no other record of a "square fort" near Clover Point. A shallow midden site, DcRu 11, is recorded at the northwest extreme of the peninsula.

430. Dawson is describing glacial marine to early postglacial marine sediments overlain by Indian middens. He somewhat overemphasized sinking of the land in the last several hundred years but correctly hypothesized earlier more dramatic sea level changes. After the recession of the last glaciers from the southwestern coast of British Columbia, "sea levels were high between 13000 and 9000 B.P. In some areas a brief submergence occurred within this period. Sea levels were about 10 m lower than at present in some parts of the area between 9000 and 6000 B.P. During the last 5500 years sea levels have not fluctuated significantly from the present" (J. J. Clague, "Late Quaternary Sea Level Fluctuations, Pacific Coast of Canada and Adjacent Areas," in Geological Survey of Canada, *Paper 75-1C* [1975], 17). For Dawson's elaboration of his evidence, see his "Note on Some of the More Recent Changes in Level of the Coast of British Columbia and Adjacent Regions," *Canadian Naturalist and Quarterly Journal of Science* n.s. 8 (1878): 241–48. For a discussion of human habitation in the postglacial period see W. H. Mathews, "Late Quaternary Environmental History Affecting Human Habitation of the Pacific Northwest," *Canadian Journal of Archaeology*, no. 3 (1979): 150–52; and Grant Keddie, "Thoughts on the Status of Cultural Continuity and Change among Prehistoric Salish Populations," *Midden* 14, no. 4 (October 1982): 8–13. For a review of sea level changes on the northwest coast see John Clague et al., "Late Quaternary Sea Levels and Crustal Movements, Coastal British Columbia," *Canadian Journal of*

Also tells me of graves of peculiar Sort near Leech R. V.I.[431] Built up of flat stones, long coffin like boxes on surface. No remains but very fragmentary bones found. Indians of the coast afraid of the locality, & have a tradition of a race *without Joints in their Knees*, who formerly inhabited it. Told that Similar Story of Jointless legged indians told by Indians of coast at Nanaimo, of the interior.[432]

Told by Mr Hughes* that Squamish Indians of Burrard Inlet will not Kill wolves. Say it spoils a musket to Shoot a wolf with it. one indian Known to have shot a wolf afterwards Sold his gun.[433]

May Vancouvers account of fortified villages on the coast to the North Serve to account for works at Finlayson's Point & elsewhere? See especially Vol VI. p. 46. Though often mentioned elsewhere. Isolated flat topped rocks fitted with projecting platforms, on which breast work.[434] Think J.G. Swan also mentions pallisades round coast villages at Cape Flattery (Examine work in this regard)[435]

Oak Bay shell heaps from 6 to 8 to ten feet thick along the high water mark. Evidently indian throughout & from Subsidence of coast probably, are now being cut away at high tides. Their base below highest water mark.[436]

Earth Sciences 19 (1982): 597-618; and Mathews, Fyles, and Nasmith, "Postglacial Crustal Movements," 690-702.

431. No further information exists on these burials; a systematic survey of the area has not been done.

432. There are a number of stories told by various groups of natives about other natives with wild or strange qualities. The race without knee-joints is one of this class.

433. The Cheakamus people were said to have descended from wolves; this may have influenced the Squamish attitude toward the animal.

434. According to Vancouver, "these fortified places were well constructed with a strong platform of wood, laid on the most elevated part of the rock, and projecting so far from its sides as to overspread the declivity. The edge of the platform was surrounded by a barricade raised by logs of wood placed on each other" (Vancouver, *Voyage of Discovery*, 6: 46-47).

435. See James G. Swan, *The Indians of Cape Flattery, at the Entrance to the Strait of Fuca, Washington Territory*, Smithsonian Contributions to Knowledge vol. 16, no. 8 (Washington, 1870), 51, where he notes that most fortified villages had been abandoned by 1869; "the only one I know of at present, between the Columbia River and Cape Flattery, is at Kwilleyute. A precipitous rock, several hundred feet high, situated at the mouth of that river, is still fortified, and to all Indian attack is perfectly impregnable."

436. Dawson was right in assuming some submergence of the land. Recent investigations illustrate "there has been minor subsidence on the inner coast" (Clague, "Sea Levels and Crustal Movements," 613). See also Mathews, Fyles, and Nasmith, "Postglacial Crustal Movements," 696-97, and fig. 4.

March 19 1876. At Mr Dodds'[437] at the Gorge. Victoria. B.C. Saw Some interesting Indian remains. Skulls & implements supposed to belong to an "extinct race". The persons to whom the bones had belonged were evidently buried, Mr D. thinks probably covered up by Material of shell heaps — which here largely developed — being piled on them, mound like. The area of the "Mound" which, not very well defined, in which remains found, very Considerable say perhaps from description 20 feet. Remains about 6 feet below Surface, & skeletons originally of a good Many people,[438] some at least of whom had been buried {in} sitting posture. Mr D. also informs me that he found {remains with} skulls of the ordinary flat head type above these now more particularly referred to, & as though buried Subsequently. Also that over the remains trees some of them 18 feet in the Circumference had grown Since they were deposited. There appear to have been a number of individuals buried here all of whom have not yet been disinterred. Mr D' States that he noticed the difference between the flat head & these older skuls, which is also apparent from the fact, that while he reburied the flat head skulls he preserved the most perfect of the others. The skulls are of a very low type. The forhead. in profile retreats very rapidly, & viewen in front is very narrow, with the fore part of the head pinched upward into a ridge along the Suture. The back of the skulls (2 now remaining) have apparently been somewhat flattened & distorted, probably by the Cradle board though not perhaps intentionally. The ridges for muscular attachment about the occipital region are not specially prominent, & the skulls are not unusually thick. The profile of the face is markedly prognathous. There is no appearance of distortion of the skull unless it be at the back as above Stated, & if this part has not been modified by pressure the heads have been distinctly brachycephalic

The tools found with the bones, so far as I could learn were as follows.

---

437. Probably Martin D. Dodd, a hotel keeper, who lived on the Gorge.

438. There were several archaeological midden sites extending along the Gorge. The site of Mr. Dodd's was probably DcRu 7, which was extensively disturbed by early house building on the north side of the Gorge. Many observers noted the discovery of artifacts and human remains in this area. Most coastal shell middens in the Victoria region contain interred human remains; artificially deformed and undeformed skulls have been found in the same deposits. These remains are usually in a flexed position and some show evidence of burning. Further studies are necessary to determine when the practice of artificial cranial deformation began and to what extent it was practised within various populations. The practice was definitely prevalent on the southern tip of Vancouver Island in the last one thousand years and was carried on by the makers of the large stone burial cairns. The Songhees Salish stopped the practice in the late nineteenth century. For an illustration of cranial deformation, see Keddie, "Thoughts on the Status," 8–9, fig. 1.

Bone pin or awl, or instrument used in weaving mats? About 9 inches long, shaped thus. [*Illus.*]

Bone implement pointed, & hollow on one side [*Illus.*]

Small agate & hard black slate arrow-heads. Some So Small as to Seem only Suitable for shooting birds. Shaped thus. — [*Illus.*]

Long stone spear-head.

Broken Stone implement, or net sinker, shaped thus. [*Illus.*] perforated, & about 2″ diameter

Head of stone hammer of ordinary shape [*Illus.*]

A number of polished stone wedges, or skin-scrapers, Some of them made of greenish material like impure jade or Serpentine, like wedges seen from excavations near New Westminster. Most of those here found too short, & with too blunt edge to make good wedges, & nearly all more or less oblique. Shaped Somewhat thus. [*Illus.*] Well polished.[439]

The teeth are much worn down in one skull still retaining a few. The posterior molar of the lower jaw has two fangs almost grown together, that next anterior to it but a single fang.[440]

Glaciation. Normal direction of grooving at Finlayson Point. Beacon Hill S 5°E. The eastern side of the rocky point forms the western edge of a wide bay, where a great mass of ice must have been. This side shows grooving & deep hollows, semicircular in outline with abnormal direction of S 35°W, showing departure from normal of 40°. The lateral ice has pressed in beneath the normal, where the latter descends a step thus[441] [*Illus.*]

Boulder of coarse grey granite near Cedar Hill church measured about 17′ x ⟨6′ 5″⟩ 9′ 11″ x 7′ 1″ & partly imbedded in the ground.

---

439. Hilary Stewart, in *Artifacts of the Northwest Coast Indians* (Don Mills, Ontario: General Publishing Company, 1973), includes illustrations of the tools mentioned. The two bone implements were split bone awls, 126–27. The "black slate arrow-heads" and the "stone spear-head" were both probably ground slate projectile points, illustrated on 75. The "agate" arrow-head was a flaked projectile point, illustrated on 76. The "Broken Stone implement" was actually the proximal end of a stone seal club, 80. The "stone hammer" was a flat top hand maul as illustrated on 53, which could be used on both ends. The "stone wedges" were actually nephrite or serpentine adze blades. For illustrations of such adzes and a discussion of their importance in northwest coast Indian technology, see 46–49.

440. Most teeth of older adults exhibit extensive attrition. The "fangs" referred to are simply the less worn outer sides of the molars. See Jerome S. Cybulski, "Tooth Wear and Material Culture: Precontact Patterns in the Tsimshian Area, British Columbia," *Syesis* 7 (1974): 31–32.

441. For a recent study of this site, see Stephen R. Hicock, Aleksis Dreimanis, and Bruce E. Broster, "Submarine Flow Tills at Victoria, British Columbia," *Canadian Journal of Earth Sciences* 18 (1981): 71–80. The phenomenon described by Dawson is also being examined by B. Hallet at the Grimmell Glacier in Montana.

Glaciation visible at the top of Cedar Hill or Mt Douglas on the shore of Cordova bay. As near as the traces would allow of Measurement course S.S.E. Height according to Adimaralty Map 696 feet.[442]

Also ridges & tails of gravel & sand on lee side of Cedar hill.

Evidence seems to be that glacial or at least cool Post Pliocene conditions succeeded immediately by inhabitants.[443] Find in some places sea shells, perfect & with both valves, & sometimes closed & still empty, & especially the characteristic Cardium, near the Superficial layers of the yellowish clayey deposits. These pass uniformly though pretty Suddenly into the blackish Surface soil, & with this appear the lowest layers of the Indian shell heaps & burnt stones. The dark Surface material no doubt indicates ⟨that the soil⟩ the advent of land plants forming vegetable mould. Thus the land occupied by Indians as soon as raised above the sea. Has the land been occupied before reaching its present level? Inland shell heaps might show this.

Almost certain that it has Sunk a little since first occupation.

Interesting to Know how the Northern Indians (Haidahs &c.) learned to work metals &c. & if art practised before white occupation. *Memorandum on Range of Buffalo* from Archd. McKinlay[444] *per* Dr Tolmie*. Before the Gun replaced the bow & arrow buffalo were abundant on the Snake River (or Lewis R.) & its tributaries as far South as Powder R. Occasionally small herds roamed over the prairies of the Shahaptami? River, Nez Percée & Walla Walla. Probably between 1815 & 1825 a few buffaloes

---

442. See Clapp, *Geology of Victoria*, 119, for a description of Mount Douglas and its drift tail. Ice overtopping this locality could have been up to three thousand feet deep. See J. T. Wilson et al., *Glacial Map of Canada* (Toronto: Geological Association of Canada, 1958).

443. The question of human habitation and the glacial and early postglacial eras, here raised by Dawson, continues to provoke discussion among both geologists and archaeologists. In a survey of possible migration routes through British Columbia in the glacial period, the archaeologist Knut R. Fladmark argues for the possibility of a coastal route where sea-level refugia could provide adequate locales for human occupation. See his "Routes: Alternate Migration Corridors for Early Man in North America," *American Antiquity* 44 (1979): 55–69. The geologist W. H. Mathews is less optimistic about the feasibility of humans entering new environments during the period of maximum glacial extent but concurs that areas of coastal British Columbia might have had habitable pockets where people could have survived. See Mathews, "Environmental History," 145–56.

444. Archibald McKinlay (1810–91) came to British North America from Scotland in 1831 to work for the the Hudson's Bay Company. He served in the Red River area, in New Caledonia, as chief trader at Fort Walla Walla, and at Oregon City. McKinlay retired in 1851 because of failing eyesight, but he set out for the Cariboo gold fields when his health improved in the 1860's. In 1863 he settled at Lac La Hache and later served as provincial government representative on the Commission on Indian Land from 1876 to 1878. He later moved to Savona, B.C.

have been Killed in the Grande Coulée — once the channel of the Columbia River — & north of the Blue Mountains, a spur of the Cascade Mountains extending eastward. I have seen quantities of buffalo bones on Powder River in 1840, & about 1833 When Ft Hall, a trading post on Lewis R, was established buffalo were numerous in its immediate vicinity.

The Indians of eastern Oregon ascribe the early dearth of large game on their lands to the formation in Severe winters of "ice Crusts" on the Snow. This I think happens oftener in Oregon than in British Columbia, but there also it has in the memory of white Men Caused great loss of horses.

For further facts, see "Nat. Hist. Washington Territory" p. 138.[445]

Glaciation. Rocks on Sooke R though hard & compact diorites show signs of heavy glaciation. Only in one place *direction* accurately notes, & there corresponds closely with river valley & direction near Victoria. (see notes)[446] freshly uncovered are smooth, but do not Show good striation from their soft character. The hard drift or "Cement" of Leach R &c. though *closely resembling* the *softer Material* about Victoria may perhaps be a sort of *Moraine profonde* similar to the little hard masses sometimes found wedged into Crevices of rocks near Victoria.

At the head of Cadboro Bay about 100 feet above the sea road shows in Cutting strat. & false bedded sands & gravels.[447] Near Leach R the Slabs Where The false bedding very regular & indicating N & S. Currents like those of the tides still running up the ⟨Strait⟩ {Gulf} of Georgia. The Southward or ebb tide seems to have been the stronger & to have most frequently left traces.

Rocks of Victoria &c. Compare with those (of about Same age?) described by J.A. Phillips Geol. Soc. Feb 23.76. Nature March 9. p. 379.[448]

Change of level of Coast. See Nat. Hist. Washington Ter. p. 22. where J.G. Cooper writes. "on some of the tide-meadows about Shoalwater Bay, dead trees of this species, (*Th. gigantia*)[449] only are standing, Sometimes in groves, whose age must immense, though impossible to tell accurately.

---

445. J. G. Cooper and G. Suckley, *The Natural History of Washington Territory . . .* (New York: Bailliere Brothers, 1859), 138.

446. There are no notes in the Field Notebooks, RG 45, vol. 134, PAC, that correspond with this reference.

447. A late glacial delta or kame deposit.

448. J. Arthur Phillips, "On the So-Called 'Greenstones' of Western Cornwall," *Quarterly Journal of the Geological Society of London* 32 (1876): 155-79. The paper was noted in news from "Societies and Academies," in *Nature* 13 (1875-76): 379.

449. Western red cedar, *T. plicata.*

They evidently lived & grew when the surface was above high water level, groves of this & other species still flourishing down to the very edge of inundation. But a gradual, slow sinking of the land (which seems in places to be still progressing, & is perhaps caused by the undermining of quicksands) has caused the overflow of the tides, & this Killed the forests, of which the only remains now left are these Cedars. This wood is perfectly sound & so well seasoned as to be the very best of its Kind. Continued & careful examination of such trees may afford important information as to the changes of level in these shores. That these have been numerous & great is further shown by alternating beds of marine shells & of logs & stumps, often in their natural position, which form the cliffs about the bay to a height of 200 feet. But while these remains show that the changes took place in the latest periods of the Miocene tertiary epoch (?) there is no evidence in the gigantic forests still living on these cliffs, that any *Sudden* or *violent* change has occurred Since they began to grow — a period estimable rather by thousands than by hundreds of years.''

Change of level of Coast of V.I.

Indian legends concerning Cape Flattery &c. (Swan Indians of Cape Flattery. Smithsonian Contrib. 1869) pp. 2.57 Long ago but not at very remote period, waters made island of point of C. Flattery. Water Suddenly receded leaving Neah Bay perfectly dry. Four days reaching lowest ebb, then rose again without any waves or breakers till it had Submerged the Cape, & whole country except tops of Mts at Clyoquot. Water on rise because very warm. As it came up to houses people floated off in Canoes, with the current, which set strongly to the North. When waters went down portion of tribe found themselves beyond Nootka, where their descendants now reside, & are Known by the Same name as the Makahs in Classet or Kweuaitchechat. Many canoes came down in trees & were destroyed. Water four days regaining accustomed level.

Lake back of Clyoquot V.I. where many Indians say that quantities of old bones of Whales.

March 20 Writing & determining minerals with the blowpipe. Evening reading. Wet day Letters from home.

G. M. Dawson to John William Dawson*, 20 March 1876, Victoria

I have lately been dipping into Brancrofts* 5th Volume, & find that he gives a very good résumé of facts Known as to directions of colonization of America, & pre-Columbian discovery. He is not at all inclined to admit the connection between the Mexican &c. traditions of floods &c. & those mentioned in the Bible, & it is a great pity that the stupid spanish priests have distorted so many of the Stories that it is impossible to tell exactly what is original & what is not. Yet there seems to be enough Similarity to prove a common origen, or at least Communication of ideas from a similar source.[450] One of the most curious, which he does not mention, though in reading a former volume it struck me, is the number of Central American nations who attribute the ⟨origen⟩ {material} of Man to the earth or dust. This is an idea which {it} would hardly seem ⟨to⟩ possible to account for except on the hypothesis of an original tradition, or as a deduction from facts too philosophical for the Indians themselves to make. I see Bancroft states that there are forty-one instances of Japanese Junks drifting on the West Coast of America between 1782, & 1850; only twelve of which were deserted.[451] Also that several Japanese words occur in the Chinook language,[452] all of which would Seem to show that Behring's Straits aside, there Can be no particular Mystery as to the way in which this part of America may have been peopled. All this you probably Know before, but having nothing else to write about, I thought better to make a letter out of Something.

I had a letter from William* the other day dated Feb. 4th. The North Pacific is Just in, & I hope on going down to the post office to find some home letters

I note the mention of the *Harbour Bond*[453] in your last, which is of course quite satisfactory to me G.M.D.
March 21. Working with blowpipe. Afternoon Collecting shells in Clay near entrance of harbour. Evg. reading & writing out a ⟨copy of⟩ vocabulary for use with Indians tomorrow, the Smithsonian vocabulary[454] having

450. Flood legends are common on the northwest coast, but there is no demonstrable connection with those of Mexico or that of the Bible.

451. Bancroft, *The Native Races*, I: 52. Bancroft was quoting Charles Wolcott Brooks, the Japanese consul in San Francisco, who had prepared a manuscript on the relations between Asia and western North America. His papers dealing with Japanese shipwrecks on the Pacific coast and with the antiquity of American natives were read before the California Academy of Sciences in 1875 and 1876 and published in the Academy's 1876 *Proceedings*.

452. Ibid. v. The Chinook Jargon and not the Chinook Indian language is meant.

453. The harbour board of Montreal administered the city's port and was empowered to issue bonds for modernization projects, mostly associated with deepening the channel, adding rail facilities, or improving docking for ocean steamers. A harbour bond would have been a safe and normal investment for a Montrealer.

454. George Gibbs, *Instructions for Research Relative to the Ethnology and Philology of America Prepared for the Smithsonian Institution*, Smithsonian Institution, Smithsonian Miscellaneous Collections no. 160 (Washington, 1863).

been apparently lost in some way.

A fine & warm day.

The shells in clay or hard sandy clay are evidently for the most part undisturbed. The Cardiums? having both valves & being often still empty. Ledas in the Same state. Some of the pebbles yet show ⟨marks⟩ bases of attachment of the ⟨balanus⟩ Small Species of Balanus[455] which is not uncommon.

The matrix in Some places a very hard sandy clay with rusty & weather stained cracks traversing it in all directions.[456] Little trace of bedding, with occasional large stones or boulders, {Very like some sections of boulder clay on the plains} but these very Seldom Showing signs of glaciation, though sometimes distinctly. In other places the deposit more Sandy & gravelly & bedding (often inclined) quite distinct. The very fine homogenious yellowish-weathering blue clay seen lowest in the bank in some places, ⟨on⟩ evidently only a form of the same deposit. The beds in some places very irregular & almost as though stirred up. The granite fragments are often quite decomposed & Soft, & the shells have evidently been partly destroyed by the action of Carbonated waters, & are quite tender. This notwithstanding the hard matrix, & their position only a few feet above high tide mark, showing that they must have been last to emerge. The same action *continued a little longer would have removed all trace of marine life*, {as completely as seen in prairie drift, which must have been very long exposed in most places} & has probably already destroyed any foramaniferal remains[457] that may have been included. Large boulders are Scattered throughout, but are more abundant toward the top of the deposit, which is generally Capped by a layer of sand, gravel, & boulders much Coarser than the rest, & probably in part at least, due to rearrangement along a coast line. In Some places as in a ditch in Cook Street the characteristic *Cardium*? occurs almost immediately below the black Surface Soil, & in others, near the shore, the lowest layers of the Indian heaps of shells & burned stones Coincide with the lowest of the black earth. Showing apparently (as I have not yet found the shell heaps far

455. Crustaceans of the genus *Balanus*, which includes modern barnacles.

456. This deposit is a typical glaciomarine sediment with ice-rafted stones and boulders, weathered and iron-stained near the surface and blue at depth. For a full description, see Hicock, Dreimanis, and Broster, "Flow Tills at Victoria," 71–80. Some granite fragments, especially those with black mica, can be friable. See R. M. Bustin and W. H. Mathews, "Selective Weathering of Granitic Clasts," *Canadian Journal of Earth Sciences* 16 (1979): 215–23.

457. Unicellular protozoa which secrete a test or skelton, usually of lime. They are important as fossils, especially in the Tertiary, where they may be locally present in sufficient numbers to be major rock-building constituents.

from the Shore) that the last elevation pretty sudden to about the Modern level of the coast. That formation of black soil from vegetable mould *began*, & that at *same time* first Inhabitants took posession.

The drift deposits resting on the *perfectly* polished & striated rock Surfaces. (Surfaces striated in Such a way as to *necessitate* glacier action) & yet holding shells, would seem to imply the gradual retreat of a glacier foot which had pushed into the Sea, & that some species of molluscs followed it pretty close as it went. The ⟨....⟩ mounds forming Beacon Hill, & those heaped on the N.E. Side of Spring Ridge,[458] behind the town, & well exposed in an old gravel quarry there (see geol. notes)[459] are probably ⟨....⟩ referrable to the coarser re-arranged Surface layer already spoken of. They may be in part old terminal & lateral moraines ⟨when⟩ left at different stages of retreat, but are more likely the deposit of stranding ice, modified by Currents. The Materials are coarse sand & gravel with many large & small boulders. The largest boulders high up, but filled in between with smaller stuff, & often almost entirely covered up & concealed by it, as though, the submergence still continuing, the Supply of ice capable of transporting large blocks had failed.

(For Sect. of drift deposits resting directly on glaciated rocks See Geol. note Book.)[460]

There does not seem to be any very distinct line between the different characters of deposit, though in hollows tough blue clay seems nearly always to occur on the rock, or separated from it by a thin layer of "dirt" & gravel. The general tendancy seems to be to increase in coarseness upwards. Perhaps deepening water till near the last allowing ice of greater burthen to float over the country.

April 22.[461] At office getting Indian Vocabulary Afternoon examining rocks about ogden Point, & collecting marine animals &c. along the beach. Day fine & warm.

April 23. Heard that steamer had arrived from Burrard Inlet, & on going to wharf found that some but not all specimens had arrived. Found also letters from Glassey* & specimens of grain from Kamloops &c. Got all taken up to Carpenters shop. Wrote notes. Packed Silver specimens to send by post. Afternoon Collected willows & other plants. Willows now in

---

458. A conspicuous rise of land in the vicinity of present-day Fernwood and Chambers streets, which then was on the edge of the settlement of Victoria.

459. See G. M. Dawson, Field Notebooks, RG 45, vol. 134, no. 2791, 16v, PAC.

460. See G. M. Dawson, Field Notebooks, RG 45, vol. 134, no. 2791, 99, PAC.

461. Dawson has the wrong dates for entries from the 22d to the 26th. The month should be March, not April.

full bloom. Red flowering Current[462] beginning to come out. Caught a frog[463] & got various other specimens.

Made inventory of Glasseys* specimens & Sent with note to Selwyn*.

Evg. at Concert in aid of St. Andrews Church.[464]

April 24. Morning geologising. Afternoon plotting geological work, writing &c. Evening reading & writing.

Day fine.

April 25. Morning writing & observing eclipse of sun. Afternoon looked for fossils in rocks of Foul Bay — unsuccessfully. collected a few flowers. Evening reading. Day unpleasant, cold with snow flurries & high wind

Observed first dandylions[465] in flower today. Not yet very abundant here, & said to have been introduced about three years ago only.

Received telegram from Selwyn* asking if Local Govt. will defray cost of gold model.

April 26. Morning reading. Afternoon walked out to Cedar hill or Mt Douglass with Mr Keith,[466] ascended it, & returned by 5.50. Walk about ten miles. View Magnificent. Day fine though a few flakes of snow in the morning, & chilly & windy.

Found several species of flowering plants, all Strangers to me, & *all very small*. Seems to be characteristic of earliest flowers here, & very different from earliest in Canada in this respect.

27. Making up Centennial account & writing letters. Packing grain specimens &c. Occupied some time with Dr Tolmie* getting vocabulary from Chilcotin Indian. Day horribly wet & stormy. No Mail by North Pacific.

28 Day showery & overcast throughout preventing me from taking the field. Went about town attending to various business matters. Wrote Dr Engelmann* Prof Macoun*. Gavin Hamilton[467] &c. Afternoon writing out Geological notes. Evening visitors. Reading. Bought a rather

---

462. Red-flowering currant, *Ribes sanguineum* Pursh.

463. Either the red-legged frog, *Rana aurora aurora* Baird & Girard, or Pacific tree-toad, *Hyla regilla* Baird & Girard.

464. According to the *Colonist*, "the programme consisted of beautiful solos and choruses selected from the most renowned oratorio writers with here and there a sacred song from such able composers as Glover, Hatton, Reynolds and others" (*Victoria Daily British Colonist*, 24 March 1876).

465. Probably the introduced common dandelion, *Taraxacum officinale* Weber.

466. Probably J. C. Keith, a ledger keeper for the Bank of British Columbia.

467. Gavin Hamilton (1835–1909) was the Hudson's Bay Company factor at Fort St. James on Stuart Lake. Hamilton arrived in Victoria in 1853 and entered the service of the Hudson's Bay Company at Fort Langley. After briefly leaving the company in 1857, Hamilton returned until 1879 when he retired and erected a sawmill and grist mill on the Cariboo Road. See also Gavin Hamilton, Reminiscences, MG 29, vol. 7, PAC.

remarkable Indian mask of Egyptian Cast of features?

Saw an Indian woman going about the Streets today with a basket of fresh herring spawn for Sale. It was attached thickly like small shot (but transparent & colourless) to filaments of sea weed &c. Told by Dr Tolmie* that the Indians of some parts of the coast collect great quantities of the spawn at this season. This especially the case at Millbank Sound. The practise to lay Spruce branches in the bottom (weighted by stones?) & afterwards Collect them with spawn attached at low tide. The spawn then Carefully dried, & packed in boxes as an article of food. It comes in Some quantity to Victoria at the proper season. How does this habit of spawning agree with that of the eastern herring?

March 29. Day unsettled with occasional showers, some sleet. Morning out pacing & examining rocks on the Cedar Hill Road. Afternoon ⟨wet⟩ paced & examined rocks to Esquimault Mr Monteith* accompanying me. Got back after six. Evg. reading.

March 30. Attending to various business matters about town, making arrangements for packing last specimens &c.

Afternoon Pacing & examining rocks on Saanich Road. Came across country to the Cedar Hill road. Evg. rather tired reading &c.

Day fine but chilly.

G. M. Dawson to Anna Dawson*, 30 March 1876, Victoria

I have had your picture of Montreal from the Mountain, now for some time, & have been daily intending to thank you for it by letter. If the second copy is as you Say ⟨as go⟩ better than the first it must indeed be good, as the one I have gives the idea remarkably well — exactly as I remember it. I also have your long letter — I forget the date — but about March first — By the same mail I had another long letter from Ella — Mrs Kemp[468] — enclosing a Sort of Christmas Card, but beautifully painted by herself with rosebuds forget-me-nots, & dear Knows what besides. I must answer her soon.

No one has ever yet told me what like the photographs from Ottawa — Commission views — were, whether satisfactory or not, & how many. Dr Burgess* writes that he has just received his. He also informs me that he has an "heiress"[469] I daresay you remember he was married last winter. Quote the — what you are pleased to Call general — "honey moonish"

468. A Scottish relative, Mrs. William Kemp, of Leith.

469. In 1875, Dr. T. J. W. Burgess, lecturer at McGill and former colleague of Dawson's on the Boundary Commission, married Jessie MacPherson, second daughter of Lt. Col. Alex MacPherson of Whitby, Ontario.

aspect of the news in your letter Things seem to be taking a similar turn here, if one may judge by the general tenor of the conversation of the people. This may partly arise however from their having nothing else to talk about. I do not *particularly* object to your sermons as you seem to think I do, except in so far as they occupy space which might be devoted to other objects. Believing as you do, you cannot help feeling as you say, but I am sure you would be the last person in the world to ask anyone to *try* to make themselves believe in that which does not appear reasonable to them; for this would be mental dishonesty just as bad on one side, as if you, believing as *you* do were to try to force yourself to think something else. — But I tread on dangerous ground, for I feel what I write will be weighed, & if wrong impressions are conveyed they Cannot at once be rectified. I hope all you *think may be* true on *another* subject, is not, for I feel unable to take exactly the same view, & fear I never shall. — But here again I leave the solid ground & must flounder onto terra firma by assuring you of ⟨my⟩ {the} constant rememberance of your affectionate Brother

Evas* letter is received. please thank her for it & give her my love

March 31. Morning & afternoon writing up notes &c. day overcast & chilly with strong wind in morning. Measured (Paced) ⟨pase⟩ base line on Queen's avenue, connecting Cedar Hill & Saanich road work. [Parted?] some of work evening reading.

April. 1. Wrote lists for Cases & got Articles numbered & packed up. Met Dr Tolmie* at office & engaged getting indian Vocabularies Evening reading in house & at library.

April 2 Dr Tolmie* Called according to arrangement at 9.30 Engaged at his house all day with three Indians getting vocabulary. Back again about 9 P.m. A fine day but chilly.

April. 3. Got invoices for boxes & arranged for shipment. Wrote Selwyn* & Perrault*. P.m. Geologising on ridges near Dr Tolmies* & Swan Lake. Evening reading & writing A very fine day. roads dry for first time Since last autumn.

Mr Todd[470] told me yesterday that about four years ago, & at other times he has distinctly Seen flame issuing from Mt Baker at night. Also that about the date above given "a shoulder" of the Mt fell in. The flames &c. do not come from the top but some way down one Side.[471]

---

470. Probably James Hunter Tod (1818?–1904) who owned a prosperous farm in the Cedar Hill district. The son of John Tod, the Hudson's Bay Company pioneer in northern British Columbia, James Tod worked his farm for over fifty years.

471. This disturbance is poorly documented. S.D. Malone and David Frank mention one in 1872 but give no source. ("Increased Heat Emissions from Mount Baker, Washington," *Transactions of the American Geophysical Union* 56 [1975]: 680). No further evidence

April 4. Pacing roads & laying down rock exposures from 10 Am to nearly 6 P.m. Got round by Burnside Road & Dead mans River[472] Bridge. Evening reading. A fine day.

Saw this evening in passing through the Indian village[473] a large quantity of Herring spawn in process of drying. The Cedar & Spruce branches on which it has been deposited (See former note)[474] are hung up on poles like the herrings themselves.

April 5. Plotting work at office morning & afternoon. Evening labeling specimens &c. & reading day fine but overcast.

April 6. out all day measuring roads by pacing & examining exposures. Evening reading. Day fine but overcast, & windy in Afternoon.

Notice Indian burial Mounds or Cairns very frequently Formed of stones piled together into small mound generally of roughly rectangular form. Often some distance from the water, & generally on some rocky little hill, or near the base of such. Probably position chosen not for any other reason than abundance & proximity of suitable stone.[475]

Little shell heaps found scattered through the woods in all directions, about Victoria. Often far from the shore. Formed no doubt by parties of Indians hunting, hiding from enemies, or digging Kamass Root.[476] Do not follow Any definite lines as though marking former level of the sea, & are always so far as yet seen very small, implying only limited occupation. Do not begin to compare in size with the large & regular heaps near the present shore. Implements very rare in Shell heaps[477]

is provided in Harry M. Majors, ed., *Mount Baker: A Chronicle of Its Historic Eruptions and First Ascent* (Seattle: Northwest Press, 1978).

472. Craigflower Creek.

473. Songhees village.

474. See 28 March 1876.

475. Burial cairns could be round, oval, rectangular, or irregularly shaped. The known surface cairns were often on a hill slope behind or in proximity to a coastal shell midden, in some cases 0.5 kilometre from the water.

476. Bulbs of the blue camas, *Camassia quamash* (Pursh) Greene, and the great camas, *Camassia leichtlinii* (Baker) Wats., were a staple diet item of most northwest coast Indian groups. Among the Coast Salish in the Victoria region, "the camas beds were divided into individually owned plots, passed from generation to generation. Each season, these were cleared of stones, weeds, and brush, often by controlled burning. Harvesting continued over several days with entire families participating. The soil was systematically lifted out in small sections, the larger bulbs removed, and the sod replaced" (Nancy J. Turner, *Food Plants of British Columbia Indians* Part I: *Coastal Peoples*, British Columbia Provincial Museum Handbook no. 34 [Victoria, 1975], 81).

477. Small shell concentrations of from five to ten metres in diameter are occasionally found inland. No such sites have been systematically excavated, but they probably represent temporary camp sites used for the purposes indicated by Dawson.

Interviewed Mr Dodd* at the Gorge about the "humming fish" about which I had heard. He tells me it is a fact, that a humming drumming, or booming noise is made by the fish under water, heard plainly in a boat. He has caught the fish, & describes it as with a large head tapering rapidly to the tail, & with two Conspicuous fins behind the head. No scales, though head hard & body soft. Is sure of identity, as even when out of water if touched on the head emits sound. Hears the noise in Summer, & has noticed it only between the Gorge & Craig flower.[478]

April 7. out all day Geologising. Day overcast with a few showers in the afternoon, but mild & pleasant.

Evening reading &c.

Saw a humming bird[479] today.

April 8. At work at office all day writing up notes & arranging specimens. Morning overcast very windy & cold Afternoon partly fine.

The "Beaver Rock" in the middle of the harbour blown up at 4 P.m. in presence of a great crowd of spectators.[480]

Went with Mr Homfrey's[481] to see his collection of Shells, which very pretty but arranged soley for beauty in a couple of glass cases.

April 9. Sunday Morning reading. Afternoon walked to Esquimault. Evening reading & writing home & to Ella.

Vegetation now advancing rapidly. Red flowery current in full bloom everywhere. *Parshia*?? nearly past flowering. Earlier willows past flowering. Daisies in bloom everywhere (The common English daisy run wild, & not uncommon in patches in vicinity of Victoria & Esquimault.) Saxifrages on the rocks just about to flower. White adder's Tongues in bloom. Maples budding out strongly on the point of flowering. Wild gooseberries Just about to flower.[482]

---

478. The fish could have been the plainfin midshipman, *Porichthys notatus* Girard, also known as the "singing fish," which lacks scales but has one tiny and one long dorsal fin, not two conspicuous ones. Alternately, it could have been one of the two drums on Sciaendae known from British Columbia: the white croaker, *Genyonemus lineatus* (Ayres), or the white seabass, *Cynoscion nobilis* (Ayres). These have the large head tapering to the tail and two conspicuous dorsal fins, but they also have scales.

479. Rufous hummingbird, *S. rufus*.

480. See *Victoria Daily British Colonist*, 8, 9, 12 April 1876; and Dawson's more detailed description in his letter to his mother, 9 April 1876, below.

481. Robert Homfray (1824?–1902) was born in England and trained in engineering. After spending time in California, Homfray came to Vicoria where he was a civil engineer.

482. "Daisies" were the common daisy, *B. perennis*; "Saxifrages" saxifrages, *Saxifraga* spp.; and "White adder's Tongues" were probably leathery grape-ferns, *Botrychium multifidum* (Gmel.) Rupr.

G. M. Dawson to Margaret Dawson*, 9 April 1876, Victoria

I fear I have allowed rather a long period to slip past without writing home, but if so must plead the lack of landmarks or anything of particular interest.

I have Just been writing to Ella Kemp* to thank her for the beautiful illuminated Card she sent me in her letter received Some weeks since. I think I discribed it to Anna*.

I suppose I told you Some time ago of the departure of the steamer "Sir J. Douglas" with a party of engineers &c. on board, for Gardiner's Inlet, some miles north of here. They were to make the steamer a base for an expedition on snow shoes or otherwise, across the Cascade Mountains, & were Supposed to return in six weeks, having only a little more than two months' provisions. Ten weeks have now elapsed & they have not got back, & people are naturally a little anxious about them. The Steamer "Otter" has been sent off today to find out the cause of the delay & aid them if necessary, & I hope we may soon hear good news.[483] I felt half inclined to go up on the Otter myself, but did not know She was going till a few hours before She sailed this (Sunday) morning, & besides felt that at the best I could do little geological work, while here I can put in the time steadily for some time to come at regular work.

A great event took place yesterday. At four in the afternoon the the Beaver Rock, in the Middle of the harbour was blown up. Work has been going on on it for about a year. It lay below the water level, but by means of a Coffer dam a shaft was sunk on it, & tunnels were then excavated in three directions. The whole being ⟨filled⟩ charged ⟨up⟩ with 450 pounds of dynamite, & about the same weight of black powder, was Successfully exploded by electricity at the time stated. The water side was lined with people anxious to see the blast, which raised a considerable column of water sticks, smoke, spray &c. to a height of about sixty feet, making no more than a dull thud, & was then over. It is not yet Known how thoroughly the rock has been disposed of.

You ask for a sample of my routine here, which it is hard to give, as I have no invariable routine. While working at my Report &c. I spent most of the day over at an office with which I have been supplied in the local government buildings, varying the monotony of writing by Calling & recalling on people about things for the exhibition. Having now practically

---

483. A CPRS party directed by C. H. Gamsby left Victoria, 1 February 1876, on board the *Sir James Douglas* to explore interior railway routes at the head of Gardner Canal. After the ship failed to return at an appointed time, the *Otter* was sent out to investigate. The *Sir James Douglas* returned, however, on 17 April, having been delayed only by inclement weather on the north coast.

disposed of Exhibition & such work I am devoting Most of my time to a careful examination of the rocks within walking distance of this place, with the idea of eventually mapping them. Every now & then I find it necessary to take a day indoors to write out notes &c. The weather is now pretty fine, & I have in view a visit to Leach River, not far from here, & once producing Considerable quantities of gold; & another to Burrard Inlet. Not yet having received any definite instructions for my Summer's work I Cannot of course Know what my mode of procedure will be. Father* writes that at Ottawa he heard from Mr Fleming[484] that he wished to get me to examine country where his parties were to be working between Ft George & the sea. This region is for the most part densely wooded & much like that I travelled in last summer. Unless Something of more than usual interest should be found, one might do almost as much in Such a country by a few weeks run as a whole season's work. The southern Part of the Mainland area about Okanagan, Nicola, Kamloops &c. being *open* is a much more promising region for working up a good geological Section in a short time.

Many people here have asked me to "Come & see them anytime" &c. &c. but I have not availed myself much of these Kind offers, finding it much more pleasant to stay at home & read in the evenings. The truth is there are *very* few people here whom I care to know well, or about whom I would put myself to the slightest trouble to be more than acquainted with.

April 10.76.
Yours of March 17 Just received. Williams* enclosed now returned I also send a flower of the Adder's tongue now out, which I found in my rambles today. The flower is represented by a white species here.

April 10. out all day pacing & examining rocks on Cedar Hill Road. Evening interviewed a packer (R. Ridley)[485] on prospect of getting to

---

484. Sir Sandford Fleming (1827-1915) was one of Canada's greatest engineers. After arriving in British North America in 1845, Fleming was employed as chief engineer of the Intercolonial Railway. In 1871, as engineer-in-chief of the CPRS, Fleming faced the onerous task of surveying and locating possible routes and a western terminus for the transcontinental line. Especially in British Columbia, Fleming endured frustrating political wrangling over the various alternatives as well as constant friction with subordinates such as Marcus Smith. Nonetheless, Fleming thoroughly examined options and provided a wealth of engineering data for the Ottawa decision-makers. Fleming aided Dawson by supplying him with goods and allowing him to accompany the railway surveys parties. See Lawrence J. Burpee, *Sandford Fleming: Empire Builder* (London: Humphrey Milford, Oxford University Press, 1915), 106-39.

485. Robert Ridley is listed as a miner in Hibben, *Guide to B.C., 1877-78.* Dawson describes Ridley in his letter of 28 April, below.

Leach R at this season. Reading. Mailed letters to Mother* & Ella*. A fine day.

April. 11. Morning at Office writing up notes, making tracing, labeling specimens, & enquiring about map of Leach River. Afternoon Examining coast between Victoria & Esquimault, Dr Walkem* accompanying me. A very fine day. Evening reading & writing.

April 12. Started at 10 A.m. Walked to Esquimault examining part of old road on the way. All the afternoon in boat examining rocks of harbour Returned to Victoria by Stage at 5 P.m. Evening reading, labeling specimens &c.

day very fine

April 13 Walked to Esquimault, got boat, & all day examining rocks of harbour, which pretty nearly completed. Return by stage. Evening at library & reading &c. Letters from Home

overcast with some showers in the afternoon.

⟨Told on good authority (Mr Homfray* & another Gentleman independently) that the tooth of a Mammoth or Mastedon was found on or near Cedar Hill (Mt Douglas) on the surface, or a short distance below it at the time of the Gold excitement Some years since.⟩

Cultus![486] said to be only part of some fishes head!

April. 14. Good Friday. Morning reading changing paper on plants &c.

Afternoon examined rocks of ridge between Cedar Hill Rd, & Dr Tolmies* farm.

Day fine but blustry.

April. 15. Arranging various little matters. Met Dr Tolmie* & went out with him to his house to do some work on the Indian vocabularies. Afternoon at office looking out traps for expedition to Leach R. & Making other arrangements. Large mail of newspapers by Str City of Panama.

Evening reading news &c.

Day fine.

April 16. Day wet throughout. Reading & writing. Afternoon for a walk.

G. M. Dawson to John William Dawson*, 16 April 1876,[487] Victoria

The White Pine Must I think be *P. Monticola* not the Sugar pine. *Lambertiana.*[488]

---

486. Chinook Jargon, "no good."

487. The date reads 1875 but should be 1876; Dawson was not in British Columbia during April 1875.

488. Dawson was correct since only the western white pine, *Pinus monticola* Dougl., and not the sugar pine, *Pinus lambertiana* Dougl., is found in British Columbia.

The Hammock arrived yesterday all Safe, & may prove a very useful affair. The only difficulty which may occur will be in finding proper Supports for it. Please accept thanks. I have made out a list for the distribution of the Grasshopper Papers, when ready, & now enclose it. It is not complete as I should like to send also to people who took the trouble to reply to my first Circular from ⟨....⟩ parts of the U.S. Not considered in the article. These names may be found as Stated in note at end of present list. There is no hurry about the posting of the papers I thought perhaps Rankine* might find spare time enough to do it after his exams. are all over. I should like to have Say twenty copies here. Dr Tolmie* & I have now got ⟨about⟩ vocabularies more or less complete of about 15 languages & dialects of Indians of the Province. Dr T. will look over them during the summer & add notes of habitat of tribes &c. We were thinking of publishing them in the Can. Naturalist. but do not know whether they would be *too heavy* for it or not. They should be printed in parallel columns say 15 vocabularies of about 200 words each. Please let me Know what you think about it. They will not be ready till next autumn.[489]

I enclose a Memorandum of several books bearing on this country which I should like to have if you happen to see them at reasonable rates in any of the Second hand Catalogues.

On Tuesday I am thinking if the weather holds fine of starting on a Short expedition of a few days to Leach River, about twenty miles inland from here, & formerly Celebrated for gold though now abandoned. I will give you an account of the trip on my return.

The Steamer Sir J. Douglas has just come in safe & Sound to everybodies Satisfaction, the Otter having missed her on the way & still engaged in the search for her.

Mother asks for the Tent to take to Metis. Of Course I Am very glad that it Should be used. It needs a pole however which if made on the original model will be in two pieces Shaped thus. [*Illus.*] The Iron ferrule ⟨for⟩ or Socket for uniting the two pieces is wrapped up with the tent. However if only for comparatively permanent erection a Spruce stick will do as well, only letting them take care to make it at the top So as not to Cut through the Canvass I enclose Williams* last letter to Mother* — returned perused

April 17. Making arrangements for expedition to Leach R, & attending to other business about town. P.m. writing up Geol Notes.

Evening packing. writing & reading.

---

489. See above, G. M. Dawson to J. W. Dawson, 9 March 1876.

day fine but cool.

G. M. Dawson to Anna Dawson*, 17 April 1876, Victoria

Your letter of — no date I see but posted March 29th has just arrived. The mails begin to show Signs of greater regularity now. Many thanks for the photo of "Bernard" now to form part of the family group. I have received from time to time several Papers &c. from him for which I suppose I should have written to thank, but perhaps you will undertake the office for me.

Williams* last *via* Mother dealt with a gigantic oyster feed to which he was a Party. His account was wonderfully circumstantial, & lead up to the Culminating point with the greatest precision, not ⟨....⟩ even omitting that it was a fine night. How jolly his coming home will be. I have not heard from him very often this winter direct, but when he gets back & is relieved from his home Correspondence hope to have long letters. One thing in his letter Certainly struck me with surprise, — the monstrous imposition of Charging 9/6 for a lot of extra luggabe between London & Paris! Everything here is so dear & done in such a miserable unthrifty splashing way that you would be lucky to get anyone to move your luggage for 9/6, yet I can remember that when in England I thought 10/ a Sum quite worthy of consideration. You say some of my letters have a *blue* tone I think I may repay the complement if such it is, after reading your extremely Cynical remarks on the Natural History Society. You seem to consider it — in vulgar parlance — "too thin". But I shall not embrace the opportunity afforded by these remarks for a moralising Sermon

I am very Sorry to hear of Agnes Stuart's[490] death it must indeed be very Sad for Anna[491] coming so soon after her other troubles.

The daisy coincidence is certainly an odd one. Hyacinths & Tulips are now out & some of the trees have burst their buds & are showing a little green.

[Dawson fails to write journal entries for the period 18 April to 22 April, while on the Leech River expedition. He is returning from Leech River via Sooke when he recommences entries on 23 April.]

April 23 Left Sooke with Mr Switzer[492] about 9 A.m. driving to

---

490. A great aunt, Agnes Stewart, née Rankine.

491. Agnes Stewart's daughter, not Anna Dawson.

492. John Switzer had come to the area in 1871 and bought 546 acres on what later became James Dunsmuir's estate, Hatley Park. Switzer erected a tannery and shoe and boot factory on the location but sold the property in 1881.

"Lawrences"[493] at Junction of Happy Valley Rd. thence walking into Town, arriving at 3 P.m.

Found various letters & Telegram from Mr Selwyn* requiring me to remain in Victoria till amended instructions for Seasons work reach ⟨from by Montreal⟩ by mail. Reading &c.

April 24 Monday At office arranging specimens &c. W. Russell[494] Came up by Steamer this morning & occupied most of Afternoon. In "The House" for a little while. Evening reading.

April 25 Hard at work all day writing up notes & plotting work. Discovered an error in the tracing Supplied by Lands & Works Office, of Leach R which has been confusing me a good deal.

Evening reading, pressing plants &c.

April 26. At work on notes & account of Leach R.[495] Evening reading &c. Wrote to Mr Selwyn*.

Ap. 27. Morning on business about town. Saw Capt Spring[496] as to possibility of engaging Craft &c. &c. P.m. At & about Esquimalt with Russel* defining the edge of the Intrusive mass. Letter from Home. Evg. reading, pressing plants &c. Remitted to [Roach] S.F. $34.00

A very fine day, warm & summer like

April 28 Out all day geologising accompanied by W. Russel*. At Cedar Hill & Cordova Bay. Very fine day.

Evening reading, pressing plants, at library &c.

G. M. Dawson to Margaret Dawson*, 28 April 1876, Victoria

Since my return from Leach R I have been occupied with writing up notes & office work chiefly, but yesterday & today have been out again, trying to do what I can to the working up of this region before leaving it.

I left here for Leach R last Tuseday week, & returned last Sunday afternoon. Leach R is not much more than 20 Miles from here but rather diffi-

---

493. John Laurence was a farmer at Glen Lake.

494. Possibly Thomas Russell (1836–1912), who was born in Scotland and came to Victoria to work for the Hudson Bay Company's Craigflower farm. In 1870 he superintended the Queen Charlotte Coal Mining Company's Cowgitz mine. He later served as Victoria city treasurer.

495. Later published as George M. Dawson, "Report of a Reconnaissance of Leech River and Vicinity," in Geological Survey of Canada, *Report of Progress for 1876–77* (1878), 95–102.

496. Captain William Spring (1831–84) was a Victoria shipowner who had arrived in the settlement in 1853 and was active in the Hawaii trade.

cult to get at. I got a Packer,[497] Indian,[498] & horse, drove out to Goldstream, about ten miles, & Camped for the night at the end of the ⟨trail⟩ road. The weather had been quite fine & tempting for some days before, but on this particular day it showered at pretty frequent intervals, sometimes rain & sometimes Sleet. The next morning, getting up early, we found the ground covered with white frost, & a thin skim of ice on the water, we were also rather discouraged to learn that two miners who had wintered at Leach River had the day before tried to get in with a mule to Carry out their blankets tools &c., but had been unable to do So on account of snow! Having come So far however, I thought it must be pretty bad to make us turn back. From Goldstream to Leach R is an old pack trail, through deep heavy woods most of the way. In we went, & Sure enough, when the track had ascended to a considerable height among the mountains we began to find patches of snow, & the whole appearance of even the bare ground was such as to show that the snow had Just left it. The first snow was near a place Called the "Summit House", an old log shanty an Inn of other days, now with half the front stove in & the chimney tumbled down, but with a conspicuous notice requesting people not to damage the property. We had about three miles of ground covered with wet, but pretty hard snow, often over two feet deep. We trudged through it not without difficulty, & some danger to the horse in passing over bridges with broken planks concealed by ⟨the⟩ snow, & finally arrived at "Leach Town"[499] on Leach R about 3 P.m.

There were a number of shanties standing here till last Autumn, when a fire swept through, destroying all but two. Imagine a little flat at the Junction of two small but rapid rivers, & hemmed in by mountains, or at least good sized hills, shaggy with pines & spruces. The flat itself Surrounded by large tall firs, some living & others ⟨burned⟩ dead & blackened, & still covered with gigantic stumps, shrubbery & young timber Growing up on former small Clearings, here & there traces of mans former presence in the shape of broken tools & Crockery, but also, & more especially broken bottles, broken bottles & piles of broken bottles, Square & round everywhere. Imagine on the flat or what remains of it not

---

497. R. Ridley, see above, 10 April.

498. A man named Lewis. See Dawson's Field Notebooks, RG 45, vol. 134, no. 2793, 9, PAC.

499. Dawson later added: "Leech River was discovered to be aurifereous by Mr. R. Brown's Government exploring expedition, in the summer of 1868. It attracted much notice, and it is estimated that about $100,000 worth of gold was obtained from it in a comparatively short time. Houses and stores were erected, under the supposition that it would prove a permanent mining region, but it is now completely abandoned" (Dawson, "Reconnaissance of Leech River," 95).

washed away or turned into a ⟨stone⟩ boulder heap during the Search for gold, seeing three unfortunate people wandering about looking for a level place to pitch a tent; & imagining this you will have Leach R, & the expedition. After settling down I went off looking at the rocks &c. There seemed no sign of any inhabitants Still remaining, but just about dark, wandering about near the Camp, I noticed Something moving about among the stumps, or rather as it seemed to me gliding along in a Certain direction, something that looked like a man, but seemed to be preternaturally tall, & to be carrying some large dark object on its Shoulder. I never before saw anything So much like a spectre. I watched it Pass rapidly along towards one of the Cabins yet standing, but could hear no noise, when — thump, unmistakably the sound of someone throwing down a heavy log, & in about ten seconds — "Hallo! Who's here?" & enter into the light of the Camp fire the *recluse of Leach R*, or at least So I called him. A rough looking miner, bearded & ragged, clothes now pretty much all of a colour whatever they may originally have been, pants ending below in fringes the result of long wear, boots decidedly demoralized, & hat battered. "How de do" I said "I have come in here to have a look at the rocks & country generally & I daresay you Can give me Some information about it" "Well" he said "I've been in Australia Calafornia, Cape of good Hope, England, Canada, all over New Zealand, in Natal Mexico & other places & Ive seen an *awful* Sight of men — ahem, but touching this river now if that man Scott was here he might tell ye that he got good prospects here or there or praps on the peninsula of one of these here mountains, but then he's the most —- dead beat liar I ever see — ahem — well there's a man we Call "Doc" well we went for to prospect the upper part of this river — it was litnin — well we went — ahem — a — & on the first day we Met two bears Just crossing a crik — a — this gun I wager her agen any in the country, that is for throwin a ball she has the best of metal in her & is a condemned Prussian Muskit & what do you think I paid for her?— a —well jist *one* dollar, ye See She was the last of" &c. &c. Afterwards his name turned out to be Lewis, & he was of great use, as I got him for a Small Sum to show me about the country which he Knew well. His method of speech however as you will see was rather inconsequential, & I think he has become slightly cracked from living so much alone. Sometimes in going down a long hillside he would give a whoop, Swing his "Prussian Muskit" round his head, & go capering over the logs with his legs flying in all directions like a ballet dancer.

The packer I had was also a peculiar genius with the well Known Name of Bob Ridley. He had once been a sailor in H.M. Navy & has interminable yarns about Sanguinary battles in the old Chinese war, & with pirates in Borneo. He was also with Fremont[500] & some of the earlier explorers of California, ⟨but has ran & has⟩ before the discovery of gold, & had been up gold mining at Peace R. but has never "struck it rich" & on his way down from the latter place got turned over in a canoe, lost his "dust" & two of his companions. (My letter is already too long & I cannot give the rest of the Leach R. expedition at present.

G. M. Dawson to John William Dawson, 28 April 1876, Victoria*

I have a number of letters from you to acknowledge, the latest bearing date April 7. I had a letter from Mr Selwyn* Some time Since confirming the Arrangement by which I was to devote this season to the Structure of the Island, & mentioning the Sum of $2500 as the wherewithall. This is not large for this expensive country, but I think will do if not frittered away in Small expeditions as I find on enquiry I can probably run a sloop or small schooner for Somewhere about $200 a month. Since receipt of the letter, however, & on my return from Leach R, I got a telegram dated Ottawa Ap. 20 Stating that instructions for Summer's work then mailed, & saying to stay in Vict. till receipt. I do not of Course know what the change may mean, but must soon get off. I hope I may be able to devote at least a good portion of the Summer to the Island Coast.

I note what you say about the forest protection bill for Manitoba, but should *not* like to apply for any appointment under it.[501] I am sorry Cameron* troubles you by writing on the Report question. I can quite understand his grumbling about the cost however. How did the Ottawa Govt. Get hold of the balance of the copies? Laird[502] only wrote for 250, & I told the Herald people when these & those on the distribution list were supplied to turn over all remaining to Dawson Bros, who were to hold them on sale *for the Commission.*

500. John Charles Fremont (1813-90) was a well-known explorer of the American west in the 1840's. Fremont explored territory along the Oregon Trail to the mouth of the Columbia River, the Great Basin region, and California. He also played a role in the conquest of California in 1846. See *Dictionary of American Biography*, s.v. "Fremont, John Charles."

501. An amendment to the federal land act for planting trees in the North West Territories. When debated in the House of Commons on 1 April 1876, David Laird, the minister of the interior, quoted from Dawson's Boundary Commission report, adding that "to the suggestions of that gentleman were owing the leading provisions of this measure" (Canada, House of Commons, *Debates*, 3rd series, 1876, 1002).

502. Probably David Laird (1833-1914), who had been appointed federal minister of the interior and superintendent general of Indian affairs in November 1873. Laird retained that position until October 1876, when he was appointed lieutenant-governor of the North West Territories.

It will not be necessary to open the new grasshopper Papers to get names to which copies of the paper should be sent, now that you have received my list. It might be well to open them however in case of any additional enclosures Needing some sort of reply should have been Sent. It is best to Keep the envelopes however in Case the proper addresses are not given within as sometimes has occurred; the post marks then being useful

April 29. Out all day Geologising at Cadboro Bay &c. Day fine with one or two showers.

Evening reading writing up notes & marking specimens.

Vegetation much advanced during the last few days. Maples in *full* flower with leaves well out. Wild gooseberries almost Past flowering. Woods of deciduous trees general green tint. Tulips in full flower grass beginning to grow long in rich ground. Fruit trees in flower.

April 30 Sunday. Morning reading arranging room &c. afternoon for a walk.

Evening walk & reading.

A fine summer like day.

May. 1. out all day geologising. Made the circuit of Mt. Tolmie by the road. Evening reading & writing up notes. Large flights of Cranes[503] passing northward.

May. 2. out all day geologising on Saanich & Burnside Roads. Evening went down to Esquimalt on arrival of steamer. Saw Camby* &c.

Reading &c. a very fine day.

May. 3. Called on Camby* & got letter from Mr Selwyn* of which had previous telegraphic advice. Changing base of operations to Mainland in conformity to Mr Lairds* views. Promises further details from Montreal. To depend for transport & supplies on C.P.R.S.

Writing up notes, & making up accounts. At office & about town attending to various matters. Evening reading newspapers arrived by last nights mail.

Day fine but overcast & chilly.

May 4. Morning attending to various business matters. Saw Mr Cambie* about plans of cooperation during the summer Learnt movements of parties, & facilities for doing work in connexion with them.

Afternoon got boat & went with Russel* up the Arm[504] to examine rocks there.

---

503. Possibly sandhill cranes, *Grus canadensis tabida* (Peters), but more likely the much more common great blue heron, *Ardea herodias* L., which is often mistakenly called a "crane."

504. Probably through the Gorge to Portage Inlet.

Evening reading.

Day unsettled cloudy & showery.

May 5. At office Packing up & arranging matters. Making out accounts & Statement of expenditure to May 1. The "California" left this evening for the North, Stickeen & Cassiar, the "Otter" leaves tomorrow morning at 4 A.m. The two steamers probably Carrying over 400 miners & others bound for the mines.[505] W   W Russell* leaves by the otter. Curious scene on departure of California. Deck Crowded with men of all classes, but generally in different Stages of inebriation. Wharf black with "friends" & others seeing them off. Men on board Singing talking vociferously, shouting &c. & waving goodbye's, which in the unstable state of some a dangerous operation. Lower deck Packed tightly with mules & Cattle, & every inch of room long enough to lie down on "spotted" for a bed by some one, the plan being to tack up a playing Card with the owners name above the Place appropriated.

The steamer however shamefully overcrowded, & should not have been allowed to leave port in the condition in which she was. People all wise & prudent after the event as in the case of the Pacific.

Saturday May 6. Went with Dr Walkem* in search of Shells &c. to Shoal bay.[506]

Day very wet, & returned to town pretty well drenched at about 3 P.m. Coopers[507] at Shoal bay Kind enough to ask us to lunch.

Evening reading & making up accounts of expenditure for exhibition.

Sunday May 7 Morning Reading. attending to specimens procured yesterday. afternoon for a walk. Evening reading, extracting notes from Nat Hist of Washington Territory.

A very fine day.

Oaks now beginning to leaf out, hawthorns, & alders about half leafed, former however not yet in flower though buds Showing. Populus balsamifera? covered with young Small green leaves. Lilacs not yet in flower though buds coloured. The ground every where covered with a carpet of buttercups in full flower. Probably *R. acris* introduced, See specimens. also in many places great quantities of Sorrel (*R. acetocella*) (intro-

505. Dawson is referring to the rush of gold miners that began in 1872 to newly discovered gold fields in the Stikine-Cassiar area in the extreme northwest of British Columbia.

506. Tsehum Harbour on the Saanich Peninsula.

507. Captain James Cooper (1821–?) was an agent for the Department of Marine and Fisheries, inspector of lights, and inspector of steamboats for British Columbia. For more information see "Cooper, James," *Dictionary of Canadian Biography*, 10: 196–97.

duced?) in flower.[508] Flowers falling from maple

May 8. At work all day making Purchases & arrangements for departure. Clearing out office at Govt. Buildings &c.

Day fine & warm

May 9. Packing &c. Compared Barometer with Standard at CPRS offices. Wrote Selwyn* Father*. Sent Acct of expenditure to May 1. to Grant*. changed all Plant Papers. Read a little.

Day fine & warm.

G. M. Dawson to John William Dawson*, 9 May 1876, Victoria

I have to acknowledge a number of your letters, the last containing Scudder's* post-Card, & Mr. Laird's* letter. I will answer Scudder* before long. The list of woods you refer to is I suppose that Sent for the Small blocks for microscopic examination. There were two or three small pieces of Douglas fir, so that if the list says *"none"* it must have occurred through a slip of the pen.

I am all in confusion as I write, being in process of packing up to leave here. I intend taking advantage of a few days at Bute Inlet in the first instance, the Sir Jas. Douglas steamer going up there to land one of the survey parties. I start day after tomorrow, in the morning, & will be back next week, but wish to leave everything here so that I can pick it up & set out for the interior *via* the Frazer R. You will no doubt have heard that Mr Selwyn's* idea of a Survey of the Island this summer has been over ruled at Ottawa, & that I am again to go up into the interior region. It will probably on the whole be more pleasant, as I will be more or less frequently in communication with the C.P.R. Survey people, most of whom I Know, & will also relieve me from the trouble of attending to my own Commisariat & transport arrangements. The chances for good geological work will probably be not so good however, though one Cannot tell. My present idea is if the François lake region can be finished early enough in the season, satisfactoraly to take a loop line by Kamloops & Nicola on the way down again in the Autumn.

As far as I can Judge from the state of the Vegetation here, I think we are about a month ahead of the average time at Montreal, but everyone Says spring this year is at least a month late. When summer really comes,

---

508. "The "hawthorns" were the black hawthorn, *Crataegus douglasii* Lindl.; "alders" either the red alder, *Alnus rubra* Bong., or Sitka alder, *Alnus sinuata* (Reg.) Rydb.; "Populus balsamifera" was the black cottonwood, *P. trichocarpa*; and "Lilacs" lilac, *Syringa japonica* Decne. The "buttercups" or "*R. acris*" were probably the tall buttercup, *Ranunculus acris* L., which was introduced; and the "Sorrel (*R. acetocella*)" was the introduced species the red sorrel, *Rumex acetosella* L.

however, on your side you will no doubt soon become equal, for everything goes on very slowly here. I am tired tonight & sleepy from packing, & so must ask to be excused writing more at present.

[The entries for Dawson's Bute Inlet trip, 10 May to 18 May 1876, are written on sheets from a small pocket diary, now loose in Dawson's main 1875–76 personal journal.]

WEDNESDAY, 10. Finished packing & arrangements for departure. Saw A Bowman* who volunteers to go with me for the Summer. Arranged the matter conditionally on nothing happening during intervening time to necessitate Change of plan. Dined at Crease's*, got back at half past twelve Changed clothes, went on board Str. Douglas & turned in.
THURSDAY, 11. Steamer started about 8 A.m. but lay off mouth of harbour waiting for some missing men till about 9. Steamed all day, anchoring about Sunset in Departure Bay. Very fine weather. Got a few Casts of the tow-net, & caught a number of small Crustaceans &c.
May. FRIDAY, 12. 1876. Left Departure Bay 5 A.m. Setamed till 5 P.m. & anchored in bay on N.W. Shore Stuart Id,[509] entrance of Bute Inlet. Morning squally. P.m. fine. Strong tide races about entrance Bute Inlet, making the steamer steer wild. Islands from Sutil Channel all bare & very rocky. White granite. Canoe with Indians Came along side after anchor down.
SATURDAY, 13. off 5 a.m. Steamed up Bute Inlet, arriving at Waddington Harbour before noon. The mountains above about 3000 ft covered with a fresh fall of snow. Torrents & little Cateratcts falling from cliffs in all directions. Clouds covering higher peaks. All supplies Carried up to depôt 2 m. up Homathco, by boat & canoe before dark. Took trip up to Depôt & examined rocks near mouth of river.
SUNDAY, 14. off 5 A.m. but on getting S of Mary Id[510] met heavy head wind & sea. Turned & anchored in Drew's Har. P.m. went on shore with Capt Morrison.[511] Got some plants, & found a Crane's nest with 2 eggs. Indian entrenchment. Got some tunicates holothurians[512] &c. by dragging

509. Big Bay.

510. Marina Island.

511. Captain Daniel Morrison (c.1840–1901), born in Nova Scotia, was a steamboater on Puget Sound from 1862. He worked on the *Eliza Anderson, Isabel, Alida,* and *North Pacific* before he became a deep-water pilot in the Victoria area in the 1870's. See F. W. Wright, ed., *Lewis & Dryden's Marine History of the Pacific Northwest* (1895; reprint, New York: Antiquarian Press, 1961), 190.

512. The "tunicates" or sea squirts were urochordates of the Class Ascidiacea; and the "holothurians" sea cucumbers of the Class Holothuroidea.

a swab overboard on a lead while the ship swung

May. MONDAY, 15. 1876. Left Drews Har. early with strong fair wind. Near Ballinac Ids[513] met heavy sea, & half a gale from the S.E. Got haul of dredge a few miles S of Dodd's Narrows, & a second on coming to anchor in Ganges Har. First 35 f. Second about 8. Both mud with Ledas &c. Evening Calm & beautifully fine. Whales[514] heard blowing near the vessel

TUESDAY, 16. Left Ganges Har 7 am & arrived at Victoria 11 a.m. Saw Cambie*, read letters &c. & decided to start for Quesnelle on Friday. Tracing map & making preparations Evg. at Driard Ho. & had a chat with Cambie* & Jennings*.

WEDNESDAY, 17. Busy all day with preparations &c. tracing map. making business Calls. Telegraphed A. Bowman*. Got invoice of photo. plates expected June 5. Not hearing from Bowman* Cannot engage a man.

May. THURSDAY, 18. 1876. Packing & making final arrangements for departure. Drew $300 to pay outstanding bills, & current expenses of trip. Drew on Mr Selwyn* for $800.

Saw Mr Cambie* & arranged to meet him on June 17 near Salmon House.[515]

FRIDAY, 19. Left Victoria 7 am. Arrive New Westminster 8 P.m.

May 19th. 1876

[Dawson ends the loose sheets with a note, "Cont. at May 26th. 1876 in the Note Book of 1876." The intervening period is documented in his Field Notebook (RG 45, vol. 134, no. 3044, PAC). There, a small journal is appended to Dawson's Field Notebook covering the early part of the 1876 field season. Since this small journal is more similar to his personal journals than the Field Notebook, it is included in the present edition. The 26 May 1876 entry is the beginning of the volume entitled, "Diary and General Note Book, George M. Dawson, May 26, 1876." A telegram addressed to Dawson, a rough vocabulary of Lillooet Indian words, and a "possible story among the Cree," have been excluded.]

May 19. 1876. Left Victoria in Str. Enterprise, with A. Bowman* at 7 A.m. Arrived in New Westminster 3 P.m. Got luggage transferred to Str. Royal City. Saw various people. Dinner at Colonial. Paid visit to Mr

513. Ballenas Islands.

514. Pacific killer whale, *Grampus rectipinna* (Cope).

515. On the Dean River. See below, 18 May 1876.

Nierin.[516] Slept on Board Royal City.

vegetation much about same stage as at victoria. lilacs now just beginning to flower in both places. A few mosquitoes, said to be the first, now about. "Shad flies[517] abundant. The run of Salmon Said to be poor this year.

Shown a large boulder which found on the hill above New Westminster, bluish quartzite full of *Aucella piochii* exactly like Taltayoco L. rocks

People somewhat excited at reported discoveries of coal. Men having simultaneously brought specimens from Langley & Pitt R. Saw a specimen from between Pitt R & Port Moody which though probably a lignite, is a very good one, & would yield a coke. The bed said to be 16 inches thick. The second locality, perhaps a Continuation of the same Seam, a few miles back of Langley on the opposite side of the river from the former. Shown a specimen of Similar fuel, representing a bed about 2 inches thick on the Brunette R about 3 m. from New Westminster, also a specimen of a larger seam, Said to be an overlying one of true lignite. Told that a thick bed (17 ft) exists near Sumass Lake,[518] a farmer there Called York,[519] knowing about it.

A few days work in the district would I think enable one to Show on the map the areas probably occupied by this lignite formation, those of the projecting older rocks. The flat delta land of the Fraser Mouth may cover A region where the tertiary has been swept away, making it softer to show this "alluvial" than to continue the Tertiary across it.

Drift at N.W.[520]

Examined some drift sections about New Westminster, better than those before seen. Some thickness of stratified & rolled sands & gravels, irregularly bedded, & below this, apparently not separated by any very distinct line, what appears to represent a boulder clay. Where unweathered blue, & hard & full of large & small boulders & pebbles, mostly rounded, but some distinctly striated, & others angular. More or less sign of Stratification through the whole, & a general likeness to the ⟨rocks⟩ beds

---

516. Unidentifiable.

517. The common mayfly.

518. Or Sumas Lake, later reclaimed and used for farm land.

519. Thomas York was hired from Yorkshire to work in the Hudson's Bay Company's Nanaimo coal mines. After three years there and a year at the Whatcom mines, he went to Yale then Spuzzum before finally settling as a farmer on Sumas Prairie in 1865.

520. For a description of these deposits, see J. E. Armstrong, *Surficial Geology of New Westminster Map-area, British Columbia*, Geological Survey of Canada Paper no. 57-5 (Ottawa: Queen's Printer, 1957), 3-9; and J. E. Armstrong, *Surficial Geology West of Sixth Meridian British Columbia*, Geological Survey of Canada Map no. 1484A (Ottawa: Geological Survey of Canada, 1980).

as seen near Victoria. In some places pretty extensive beds included of blue Sandy clay with few stones. Similar formation to the upper (& probably also to the lower) of these deposits, seen in many places in low banks further up the Frazer.

Cherry Cr Silver locality.[521] Mr Van Bremmer?[522] gave me some authentic information about this place, where he was engaged one Summer prospecting. The vein occurrs in the bed of the Creek between two classes of rock, a Sandy slate, & a hard blackish Slate, the latter much shattered. The best ore was taken from a lenticular mass[523] marked A, from the surface. The wall of sandy Slate was vertical & polished, & on following the mass down it wedged out leaving a Smooth hollow 'like a pot hole'. A shaft Sunk 36 feet, & drift run in below the Mass showed no ore, or any sign of a vein, not even a streak of Clay. The black slate hereabouts, & elsewhere, is much shattered & full of little lenticular patches & small strings of quartz with ore, sometimes in great part composed of silver ore. None of these large enough to work, & do not show sign of uniting downwards. The Main vein is traceable on the surface some distance, & near B. is quite distinct, but filled only with hard & perfectly barren quartz. Heavy gold found in the Same Creek. [*Map.*]

G. M. Dawson to Margaret Dawson*, 19 May 1876, New Westminster

Here I am on my way up the Fraser River again for my Summer's work. On My return from voyage to Bute Inlet I found I had only two days & a half to Complete all arrangements, & between one thing & another did not manage to Get time to write. Now I only drop a note to Catch the Mail, & will give more detailed accounts from Some other point on the way. The Bute Inlet trip was very pleasant, though not offering much opportunity for geological work beyond getting a general idea of the

---

521. "The occurrence of exceptionally rich silver-ore at Cherry Creek, thirty-three miles east of the head of Okanagan Lake, has been known for a number of years, and several attempts have been made toward the development of the deposit, but difficulty has been experienced in following the vein. . . . Average specimens broken from a large mass of the richer ore, yielded on assay 658.43 ounces of silver to the ton. In addition to the vein here particularly referred to, several other silver-bearing veins have been found in the same neighbourhood" (George M. Dawson, "The Mineral Wealth of British Columbia. With an Annotated List of Localities of Minerals of Economic Value," in Geological Survey of Canada, *Annual Report, 1887–88*, n.s., 3 [1889], pt. II, Report R, 68).

522. Captain James Van Bremer (1830?–95) was an ambitious and versatile entrepeneur who came to British Columbia in 1860 after a sojourn in California. A partner of S. P. Moody in the Moodyville sawmill, Van Bremer established the first ferry service across Burrard Inlet to Moodyville. He also had an interest in the Hope Silver Mine and owned large amounts of real estate in the lower Fraser Valley.

523. A mass or bed of rock thinning out from the centre to a thin edge all around.

country. The scenery is magnificent on Bute Inlet, Something like the Saguenay but on a larger Scale, mountains from 5,000 to 8,000 feet high rising abruptly, sometimes precipitously, from the Margin, & holding glaciers (though small ones) & eternal snow.

On the way back I got three Casts of the dredge & a few interesting Shells.

I have Just been interrupted. Expect more from next Stopping place.

May 20. Started 7 A.m. for Yale. Tied up for night a few miles below Hope.

Fraser water 9 a.m. 49°

Sumass Landing. Mouth of Sumass R. A rocky Knoll Stands up which comprised of hard bluish fine grained material like quartzite. Somewhat resembles rocks of L.C.C. Series. Appears that a good deal of stratified rock on the Western flanks of the mountains about here.

Gl. distinct fluting on the rocky Knoll above mentioned, seems to point down from the Sumass Valley, touching the Frazer obliquely.

May 21. River water 6 A.m. at Hope = 47°

Start early & reach Yale about 10.30 A.m. Arranged about passage &c. Men of survey going off at once in two coaches. Afternoon took a short walk. Day fine, though clouds hanging about the mountains in the morning.

Vegetation here about equally advanced with Victoria, though perhaps a *trifle* later. *Acer Macrophilly* being yet in full flower. *A. Circinatum, Cornus Nuttallii,* & *elder,* also in bloom. *Aquilegia Canadensis* just coming in bloom.[524] *Lilacs* at Hope just out. *Rhodadendrons* from Skagit R, transplanted to Garden at Hope, beginning to flower.

on the Mountains much snow Still lying in ravines, & on the tops above a couple of thousand feet.

Terraces about Yale (see sketch)[525] Appearance of indistinct terraces with narrow treads, perhaps morainic "plastered up" against the mountain sides. The lower ones, not far from the river show many very large rounded, or more or less rounded boulders, & one or two Seem to run out into points partly across the valley Suggesting Moraines. B. ascended one of the higher, making it by barometer 800 feet above the river, says does not show rolled pebbles, but apparently entirely composed of angular

---

524. "*Acer Macrophilly*" was the bigleaf maple, *A. macrophyllum*; "*A. Circinatum*" vine maple, *A. circinatum*; "*Cornus Nuttallii*" western flowering dogwood, *Cornus nuttallii* Audubon; "*elder*" probably the red elderberry, *Sambucus racemosa* L.; and "*Aquilegia Canadensis*" western columbine, *Aquilegia formosa* Fisch.

525. No such sketch appears in his field notebooks nor among the drawings now held by the McCord Museum.

debris. The highest *perfectly distinct* terrace, seems to be about twice as high as the last mentioned, or say 1500 feet. From the 800 foot terrace brought down a fragment of dark mica schist with Kyanite & garnet crystals.[526]

Copper. Half or three quarters of a mile down the road to New Westminster traces of Copper appear in a dioritic gneiss, stains very distinct, Surrounding small patches of decomposed sulphurets.[527]

Indian Shell heaps. Saw at the door of an Indian wigwam a considerable pile of Mussel Shells, covered with barnacles, & which had evidently been recently used for food, & must have been brought up here from the sea, perhaps Burrard Inlet. Shows danger of Supposing former presence of Sea to account for inland localities of sea shell-heaps.

Hope Silver Mine[528] A. Watson[529] of Victoria gives me some valuable information about this mine, Says the rock containing the vein he calls a porphyry, also that at the very Summit of the Mountain in which the vein occurs, & in the upper part of the same rocks, he found well preserved fossils, "like cockles". Also that small quantities of mercury appear in conjunction with the Silver ore, & may be seen in *minute Globules* on the Surfaces in wet weather.

Cinnibar.[530] A Watson* also tells me that small pieces of this ore found at & near Boston Bar when cleaning up Gold sluices.

May 22. Left Yale 5 A.m. & reached Lytton about 6 P.m. Day fine & very

---

526. The "mica schist" was a strongly foliated crystalline rock, composed of the mineral mica, formed by dynamic metamorphism. "Kyanite" was an aluminum silicate found in metamorphic rocks, commonly as blue crystals; and "garnet" was a family of minerals, silicates of aluminum, iron, manganese, chromium, calcium, and magnesium which are red or green in colour and externally cubic in form.

527. "Dioritic gneiss" is fairly coarse-grained metamorphic rock made up of bands which differ in colour and composition, some bands being rich in feldspar and quartz, others rich in hornblende or mica. "Sulphurets" is a minering term, meaning metallic ores, usually sulfides. A preferable term is concentrates or sulfides.

528. "About 1871, veins of silver-ore were discovered in the Coast Mountain Range at Fort Hope [Hope] about six miles south of the town. The first vein discovered, named the 'Eureka,' crops out about 5000 feet above the river-level, is well defined, and from four to seven feet thick, and has been traced 3000 feet. A tunnel 210 feet long has been driven into this vein. . . . The ore is described as argentiferous grey copper, and contains from $20 to $1050 of silver to the ton. While this vein was being opened, another, about 300 feet distant, was discovered. This is much richer, and is called the 'Van Bremer'" (Dawson, "Mineral Wealth of B.C.," 72). See also Dawson, "General Note on the Mines and Minerals of Economic Value of British Columbia with a List of Localities," in Geological Survey of Canada, *Report of Progress for 1876-77*, 131-32.

529. Presumably Adam Watson (1824?–80) sometime miner and blacksmith.

530. Cinnibar is mercuric sulphide, the principal ore of mercury, occurring in red crystals or masses. Being very heavy, it would be caught in gold sluices.

warm. Roads in good order & country dry.

Vegetation at Lytton slightly in advance of Victoria, roses being in bloom in exposed situations. *spira* in full flower, yarrow in flower. Large *Sunflower* Same as that Collected at Drew's Harbour in full bloom, Chokecherry in full bloom.[531] & hawthorn (*Crataegus*)

Told that the Indians Take the roots of the Sunflower in question & eat them, also that in August they Collect the seed & make a Kind of "Soup" with them.[532]

A large *pentstemon* (P. Salsuqinesas?)[533] very abundant on dry banks from about the suspension bridge onwards. Now in full bloom.

The Jackass Mt Conglomerates seem to contain many rounded fragments of granitic & crystalline rocks clearly referrable to the Cascade Series,[534] & thus Showing the metamorphism of these rocks to have occurred before the formation of the Conglomerates.

Terraces[535] Besides the lower terraces everywhere visible along the river, in some places very high benches show in patches far up the Mountain sides. About 1.m. above the *Stoyama R*[536] of the Admiralty Map (s of Jackass Mt) some of these are probably as much as 2000 feet above the stream, or at the very least 1500. Near Lytton the terraces first become well defined, spreading out into wide flat benches. Due to opening out of valley

Indian Remains on the slope by which the new bridge across the Mouth of the Thompson is reached,[537] some curious hollows have been formed in the hard Sand of the bank, & afterwards filled with gravel &c. At first appeared like artificial excavations, for burial or other purpose, & seemed to show that the upper layers of the hard sand had been deposited by water after the holes were filled, implying a stage of water in the river

531. The "*spiraea*" was spirea, *Spiraea* spp.; and "yarrow" the common yarrow, *Achillea millefolium* L. The "*Sunflower*" balsamroot, *Balsamorhiza sagittata* (Pursh) Nutt., was closely related to the coastal species, *Balsamorhiza deltoidea* Nutt., which Dawson refers to. "Chokecherry" was the black choke cherry, *Prunus virginiana* var. *melanocarpa* (A. Nels.) Sarg.

532. Dawson's description of the use of balsamroot, *B. sagittata*, closely corresponds to that of modern ethnobotanists. See Turner, *Food Plants of Interior Peoples*, 115–19.

533. Possibly the coast penstemon, *Penstemon serrulatus* Menzies.

534. The Cascade series is now subdivided into early Cretaceous granitic rocks and surrounding early pre-Mesozoic metamorphic rocks.

535. The "lower terraces" fall into much the same category as those near Yale — outwash gravels incised by postglacial river cutting. The "high benches" are likely kame terraces, built along the ice margin or into marginal ice-dammed lakes.

536. Stoyama Creek.

537. The bridge had been completed only that year.

about 100 feet above the present. Found a small piece of bone carved like a human face, a mica bead, & small shapeless pieces of bone in the bottoms of these pockets, with abundant fragments of charcoal. Closer examination however showed that the pockets were not excavations, but ruts cut down the steep front of the bank by floods, & afterwards filled in with debris, which is distinctly stratified. There is therefore no clear proof of great age.

Elevation & Section Somewhat as below [*Illus.*]

Pinus ponderosa Mr Eberts[538] tells me that he saw large groves of this tree about 40 miles up the N. Thompson, which is further North than I have yet noted it

May 23. Left Lytton about 4 A.m. arriving at Clinton about 8 P.m. Day fine & very warm.

Height of grain Between Cache Creek & Clinton Several farms at a very high level. The highest by barometer, about 2800 feet. Assured that wheat will ripen, though not generally grown, barley being a Surer Crop & better paying. Probably about the extreme limit of grain for this region.

Section About ten miles S. of Cornwall's, nearly opposite "Oregon Jack's"[539] across the river, a good chance to measure a Section probably over 2000 or 3000 feet which appears to be Cache Creek beds.

Fossils. L.C.C. Gr. Behind the 89 m. Stable in fragments of a peculiar brownish limestone.

Stratum, which have come down from the hill, fossils are reasonably abundant & well preserved.

A day on the hillside would probably give good result.

Coal. Told of Coal cropping between Lillooet & Bridge R, not far from the former place. The stage-driver from Clinton to Lillooet promises to bring specimens to the former place.

Terraces.[540] Carefully examined, & looked out for terraces all day, &

---

538. Probably David MacEwen Eberts (1850–1924), born in Chatham, Upper Canada, who only recently had arrived in Victoria. Called to the British Columbia bar in 1880, he was elected to the provincial legislature in 1890 as member for Saanich. He served as attorney-general in three administrations and spent a term as speaker. Eberts later was appointed a judge of the British Columbia Court of Appeal.

539. Or John Dowling, who occupied 160 acres in the Ashcroft district from May 1862. He is not John Walsh, the Oregon Jack whom Justice Begbie labelled "a very notorious character."

540. The surficial deposits described by Dawson are examined in detail by J. M. Ryder in, *Terrain Inventory and Quaternary Geology Ashcroft, British Columbia (92–I NW)*, Geological Survey of Canada Paper no. 74-49 (Ottawa: Supply and Services Canada, 1976); and, *Terrain Inventory and Quaternary Geology, Lytton, British Columbia*, Geological Survey of Canada Paper no. 79-25 (Ottawa: Supply and Services Canada, 1981).

do not think any theory will account for them but a lake or extension of the sea to their level, & the Subsequent cutting down of the rivers through the deposits by change of elevation of land, or outflow of the stream, by erosion or otherwise When the Thompson Valley widens about Cornwall's the general appearance will not tally with the idea of the plastering up of terraces on the river banks while the stream cut down. They spread in some places quite widely, & show in Sections both parallel & transverse to the valley, nearly horizontal beds of clay & gravel, which generally dip at *low* angles toward its centre. Some the gravel beds about this part of the river may be traced in its banks for a great distance.

As might be expected, the lower terraces are nearly always the best preserved. The great horizontal spread of some of the terraces & nearly horizontal position of the gravels, with general contour of Country, the chief arguments for lake deposition of clays & gravels. From about the great slide or avalanch 6 ½ m. above Nicommen the gravel boulder & Sand terrace materials of the Frazer & mouth of the Thompson, change to clays & clayey gravels, & this ⟨Change⟩ continues at least to the S. Side of the "Green Timber" In some places several hundred feet of nearly horizontal clays exposed in great banks. These worthy of Careful examination in case of included remains. Fine clayey beds like these also show lake deposition. The whole appears Certainly to be later glacial, or post glacial.[541]

The places & heights by Barometer & estimate of the highest terraces observed, as follows. It must be remembered that in coming into the Country one ⟨leaves⟩ {has} an open valley to the sea always behind, & tracing the terraces from point to point, with little or no interruption, & higher step by step as the road goes to higher levels, & the higher valleys of the Streams are reached, & the more secluded nooks among the Mountains where denudation has been prevented, leaves a strong Case for marine access to the whole interior[542]

May 24 Started early & drove to Bates or the 15 m. house,[543] arriving between 9 & 10 A.m. having made a distance of 103 m. Day very warm, though cloudy in the afternoon

---

541. For these "clayey beds," see R. J. Fulton, "Silt Deposition in Late-Glacial Lakes of Southern British Columbia," *American Journal of Science* 263 (1965): 553-70.

542. Here again Dawson expounds the now discredited idea of a major marine inundation of the interior of British Columbia. The presence of the terraces obsessed and misled him. "The display of terraces or 'benches' on the Fraser and Thompson rivers and some of their tributary streams is probably as imposing as can be seen anywhere. . . . it would seem that some at least must owe their origin to the general inundation of the country, and its subsequent gradual drainage" (Dawson, "On the Superficial Geology," 111).

543. Dawson meant 150 Mile House.

Moraines of the Lake La Hache valley. See last years notes.[544] Seem undoubtedly heaps of this origen, though considerably modified by water. Must be older than the Surrounding terraces.

Lake La Hache, seems pretty evidently held in by drift deposits.

It need not necessarally be supposed that the valleys were ever, even during the greatest submergence, entirely filled with gravel &c. to the height of the highest benches. In any case ⟨....⟩ there must have been a considerable "sag" from the edges toward the centre of the valleys, & it may also be that they were originally filled with moraines, or that mounds formed by stranding drift ice &c. were cut ⟨down⟩ down by the water

Near Cornwall's the more or less regularly terraced slopes show frequently a tendency to break up into long boat shaped ridges, apparently showing a current of water up or down the valley when the water *much* higher than at present. In some cases, "tails" of drift Seem to Shelter behind projecting rocks, & are generally longest toward the south.[545]

Bunch grass when this grass much eaten down by Cattle. dies out, & is replaced by sage (*A. frigida*) This cattle eat & thrive on in winter, but do not eat in summer. ⟨When⟩ the bunch grass {also} wears out by too great feeding over, & near Cornwall's large areas near the road are almost ⟨bear sand⟩ bare sand, or show a stunted {& scattered} growth of *Echinospermum Lappula?*[546] scarcely over 3 inches high.

Dessication. Told by several people that a very marked change to greater drought — perceptable in the interior country. Lakes & ponds decreasing. This not only judged of by old water lines, but by known recession of water in Small lakes. No other Cause to which Can be attributed than the destruction of forest by fires &c.

Horse-fly Cr,[547] reached by a trail from the 150 m. house. Told that from 15 to 20 men now in at this place commencing work, very good prospects having been found. Pay dirt supposed to be deep, which reason given why this place not a success before.[548]

Vegetation on getting up on the Green Timber Plateau between Clinton & Bridge Cr a well marked change in advance of spring observed. Aspen

---

544. Dawson's field notebook containing his 1875 Lac La Hache notes is lost.

545. The terrain described by Dawson is now recognized as "drumlinoid topography," that is with drumlin forms and unspecified substratum (Ryder, *Inventory and Geology, Ashcroft*, 8).

546. Bristly stickweed, *Lappula squarrosa* (Retzius) Dumortier.

547. Horsefly River.

548. Dawson later concluded: "Good 'prospects' here, and in 1876 a considerable influx of miners, but without good returns" (Dawson, "Note on Mines and Minerals," 143).

poplars[549] instead of being well leafed out, are here just unfolding, though the trees distinctly green at a distance. Willows still in full flower, but few other plants in blossom.

Mt. Begby[550] a hill about 100 feet above the level of the plateau of the Green Timber, near its highest point. Climbed it & got a magnificent view showing an immense stretch of plateau running up the centre of the province, the deep valleys hardly noticeable, & the whole seemingly densely wooded. A part of the Selkirk range[551] visible to the S.E, & the snow clad summits of the Eastern part of the Cascades to the west. The hill itself a much jointed mass of hard dioritic? rock, apparently without doubt belonging to the Basaltic series, though rather different from most of the rocks. The hill is broken & rubbly to the south, while the top where unweathered they are smooth & rounded, & show the same character on the Northern steep slope. Little doubt that ice action indicated though direction uncertain, no striation being seen.

Cariboo Road Told that last stage got only as far as Van Winkle, with much difficulty, the road being blocked with snow, in some places Said to be 12 feet deep. Mail carried in by Indians. Snow fall this winter at Cariboo very heavy, though elsewhere in the interior not excessive. *The past winter* considered a fair average one. Stock wintered well, though the season rather longer than usual. Early fall & late spring. Told that snow has only left the plateau above Soda Cr &c. about 3 weeks.

May 25. Start at 3 A.m. & arrive at Soda Creek about 8 a.m. Empark on steamer & get off at 9 a.m. Toiling up the river all day. Tied up for the night about 24 miles below Quesnelle.

The River in heavy flood, from sudden melting of snow on the mountains during the last few days. Water now flowing over the lower benches & islands among the young leaves. Current turbid & strong, from bank to bank with no slackwater or eddy. Drift timber in great quantity coming down from the banks, & old drift piles. As much as the steamer can do to make way against it, sometimes Stationary on a riffle for several minutes together while every ounce of steam given to help her up. Drift continually getting entangled in the rudders & making it hard to steer.

At Soda Creek the basalts are seen in horizontal beds Capping the highest banks of the river,[552] below, in the immediate vicinity of the town

549. Trembling aspen, *P. tremuloides.*

550. Mt. Begby rises to a height of 1400 metres.

551. More likely the Monashee Mountains.

552. Dawson here describes a composite section, with late Miocene basalts on top and a southwest dipping succession of Eocene lavas and minor sediments beneath. There is no sign of a vent.

blackish quartzites & slates apparently of the L.C.C. Gr. come out.

A few miles above Soda Cr, on the West bank a section showing horizontal basalts, underlaid in a nearer slope by beds apparently basaltic with a clear westerly dip. These are evidently fragmental & seem to rest on softer beds, perhaps sand or gravel. below these hard reddish Massive basaltic? beds. May the deposits, & sloping position indicate part of an old vent?

Opposite Alexandria the highest part of the bluff show a capping of horizontal basalt, with whitish yellow beds evidently running under it. These may be Lignite formation, or drift or other sands & gravels. They form a nearly vertical front & are apparently much hardened.

May 26. River higher than yesterday & filled with drift timber.

Crawling up all day with frequent stoppages to Get sticks &c. out of the rudders. Arrived at Quesnel 6 P.m. Found the Sawmill & other buildings submerged, & told that the water now within a few inches of the flood mark of last June, which is the highest Known.

Men & Supplies sent ashore & Camp formed. Decided to sleep on board tonight.

High water Generally occurs on dissolution of snow on higher mountains about June 20. Last year a flood on April on breaking up of ice, & a second & higher at about the date above Mentioned.

River water 45°F

[Dawson here begins his main 1876 journal, entitled "Diary & General Note Book, George M. Dawson, May 26. 1876."]

May 26. 1876. Arrived at Quesnel Mouth by steamer from Soda Cr, about 6 P.m.

May 27. Slept last night on board steamer, went into camp this morning. Went over to Quesnel, looked over & selected what required for Summer's work &c. From Yesterday evening to this evening water has risen 5 ½ inches.

Gave Bowman* cheque for $170 being payment in advance on wages.

May 28. Sunday. Writing home for this afternoon's mail, changing plants into dry papers, & collecting those now in flower about here. Got a base measured with B. & estimated the velocity of the river, now I am assured higher than last June, which up to this time the highest water Known. Since last evening water has fallen 8 inches.

Base measured 544 feet. Time occupied by Sticks floating down centre of river 41 4/10 Seconds (average of 5 Close observations) This equals 8.93 miles per hour velocity of surface & centre of current.

Estimated width of river now 350 yds. Average depth 18 feet. Sectional area 29,700 or taking the full velocity for all parts of the stream outflow of about 23,522,400 cub. ft. per minute.

Vegetation. Many of the more peculiar western & dry Climate forms met with on the lower part of the waggon road, now lost, Indicating a greater rainfall northward. Grain grows without irrigation at Quesnel.

Plants now in bloom. (see specimens Collected) Strawberries still with many blossoms, wild cherry in full flower. Wild gooseberries & currents with young berries forming. *Cornus Canadensis* Just beginning to show white blossoms, *Viola Canadensis* in full flower. *Amalanchier Can.* in full flower. Willows past flowering. High-bush Cranberry? in flower.[553] *Sheperdia Canadensis* berries forming.

Mosquitoes beginning to appear

G. M. Dawson to Margaret Dawson*, 28 May 1876, Quesnel

I sent off from New Westminster, on the way up here a short note to someone at home, I really forget to whom. As I may not now have another chance to write for a long time, I must now try to give you some idea of my probable movements during the Summer &c. The region which I am directed to examine particularly lies east of the heads of Dean & Gardiner Inlets,[554] on the Coast, & between it & the upper Part of the Fraser R about Fort George. The C.P.R. Survey Parties will be operating in the same region, & I am to trust to them for transport & supplies, which will relieve me of much trouble. The parties referred to are as follows. *Jennings** working on the lower part of the Salmon R[555] running into Dean Channel. *McMillan*[556] working N. of the upper waters of the Blackwater R. *Hunter*,[557] running a line from the Salmon R. diagonally to

553. The "Strawberries" were the wild strawberry, *Fragaria virginiana* Duchesne; "wild cherry" probably the pin cherry, *Prunus pensylvanica* L., or the bitter cherry, *Prunus emarginata* (Dougl.) Walpers; "wild gooseberries" *Ribes* spp.; and "currents" also *Ribes* spp., "*Cornus Canadensis*" was the bunchberry, *Cornus canadensis* L.; "*Viola Canadensis*" probably the yellow wood violet, *Viola glabella* Nutt.; "*Amalanchier Can.*" the Saskatoon berry or serviceberry, *Amelanchier alnifolia* Nutt.; and "High-bush Cranberry" possibly the high-bush cranberry, *V. opulus* var. *americanum*.

554. Dean Channel and Gardner Canal.

555. Dean River.

556. D. McMillan, an engineer-in-charge with the CPRS.

557. Joseph Hunter (1842–1935) became one of the most recognized surveyors and engineers in British Columbia. Hunter had come to the Cariboo in 1864 as a miner and surveyor and was elected to the provincial legislature. In 1872, he joined the CPRS and conducted some of their most memorable explorations, including a pioneer trek through the Pine River Pass in 1877. In 1883, he was the chief engineer-in-charge of building the

Ft George. Mr Cambie* now in charge of the B.C. Surveys in place of Marcus Smith* will visit all these Camps, & explore other parts of the region as he may find opportunity. I hope to be able to travel with him a good deal, & take advantage of trails &c. which he may cut, which I could not manage alone. At the same time I am to have a Separate rig so that should it be desirable I can at any time break off & explore elsewhere. From here, my course in the first instance will be to the Salmon House, near the head of Canoe navigation on the Salmon R, where I expect to Meet Mr Cambie*, (who comes in from the coast) about the 20th of next month. Beyond that I have at present no plans.

Before leaving Victoria I was enquiring for a Cook & general assistant to take up with me, & thought of making up my party with such a man, a packer, & one or two Indians. ⟨I proposed⟩ I could not however find such a man to suit me, but a young fellow Called Bowman*, hearing accidentally that I was enquiring for someone to go with me offered to come. I had known him slightly in Victoria, & at first thought he might get tired of the job, but as he stuck to his offer after having had some time to consider, I finally accepted his services. He is a Canadian born, but has been some years in the U.S. & worked at one time on the Californian Geol. Survey. & is really a very good & enthusiastic geologist, & will be to Some extent a companion.

We Camped here yesterday, on the opposite Side of the river from the Town of Quesnel, & may have some time to wait till slow Pack trains arrive. McMillan* & his party are also here waiting, & a "deputy purveyor" who is going in to Meet Cambie* with supplies, & with whom I propose travelling for the present. It is just possible that I may start tomorrow, or the day after with McMillan* on a flying reconnaissance, & arrange to meet the Supply train at a given point in about a weeks time. This would enable me to see a new section of country, & do Something instead of waiting here, where I cannot even collect fossils, the beds being now covered up by the flooded river.

May 29. Making preparations for leaving on a reconnaissance trip to the Is-cul-Taes-li R,[558] & Country westward, with McMillan*. Leave Bowman* in charge of *material*, & hope that he & Ross[559] will get off next Saturday, & meet me on the Blackwater.

Esquimalt and Nanaimo Railway then general superintendent and vice-president of the line until retiring in 1918. See his obituary in *Victoria Daily Colonist*, 9 April 1935.

558. Euchiniko River.

559. Probably A. W. Ross of the CPRS.

May 30 Up early & off about 8 A.m. Reached Goose L[560] about half way to Blackwater Bridge by 3.30. Camped beside Mr Dewdeny[561] who had left yesterday morning, but only got this far. Day rather blust blustry with passing showers, but evening Calm & clearing.

Vegetation on the higher ground passed over today appreciably behind that at Quesnel, but not very far. The difference much more noticeable when elevations above 2000 ft reached *Arctostaphylos, Uva ursi*, a species of *Arnica?*, a *Nardosmia Fragaria, Viola Cucullata, Alnus* in full flower.[562] Leaves of *populus tremuloides.* still soft & brown.

Fires have passed extensively & often over the Surface of this part of the country removing the original thick growth of *A. douglasii* & *P. contorta* & even the windfall, almost completely over great areas. Small alders, aspens, & scattered scrub pines coming up, but grass in tufts, which appears pretty good feed, but said to be *wiry & sour*, & distasteful to horses & Cattle. Represents ultimate stage of plateau forests destroyed by fire. If better grass or other fodder could be induced to spring up, great areas might be burned off for stock runs.

A dandylion abundant in some places near Quesnel, & also here near the trail at this evening's Camp. Seems indistinguishable from T. deus-leonis, & if so is already a well established exotic. {probably a different species, abounds all way up the Blackwater}[563]

Terraces &c. May the highest level of good terraces in B.C., where they join the upper hilly drift, equal the period of water action represented by the Missouri Coteau?[564]

560. Herkyelthtie Lake.

561. Edgar Dewdney (1835–1916) was by that time a well-known surveyor and explorer who had covered much of British Columbia's interior. Later, he became politically prominent as lieutenant-governor of the North West Territories, minister of the interior in the federal government, and British Columbia's lieutenant-governor from 1892 to 1897. For a description of Dewdney's career see Sue Baptie, "Edgar Dewdney," *Alberta Historical Review* 16 (1968): 1–10.

562. "*Arctostaphylos, Uva ursi*" was kinnikinnick, *A. uva-ursi*; "*Arnica*" arnica, *Arnica* spp.; and "*Nardosmia Fragaria*" probably Arctic colt's foot, *Petasites frigidus* (L.) Fries. "*Viola Cucullata*" was a species found only in eastern Canada. Dawson was probably referring to the northern bog violet, *Viola nepherophylla* Greene. "*Alnus*" was either the Sitka alder, *A. sinuata* or thinleaf alder, *Alnus tenuifolia* Nutt.

563. Could have been the common dandelion, *T. officinale*, or another species such as *Taraxacum ceratophorum* (Ledeb.) DC., or *Taraxacum lyratum* (Ledeb.) DC.

564. Any comparisons between the Missouri Coteau and the interior of British Columbia probably should be downplayed. Even though both regions have been glaciated, the points of comparison that Dawson was thinking of are elusive.

Glacial events as follows?[565] Great glacier. Striation. Tsa Whuz Mt. Surface plateau Chilcotin &c. — great Submergence, modification of old great moraines, formation of hilly boulder clay. Rather sudden partial emergence, leaving upper level clays &c. little mod. from deposition from ice, rather gradual, perhaps spasmodic complete emergence, forming terraces. Small glaciers pushing out into sea in some places to near the close (see remarks on Country about Nazco. Tatla[566] &c.) Probably no glaciers on V.I. after great glacier, proximity to Sea water & greater warmth preventing except in higher mts. Traces about Victoria then of great glacier period, with deposits made at its foot during its retreat, afterwards modified by water, terraced &c. during emergence. In higher mts. of V.I. might find traces of small local glaciers, certainly would, for some still exist.

May 31 From Goose L. to Blackwater Bridge, about 25 miles, a long day. Pleased to find the bridge still in place, though had heard at Quesnel report that in danger of being Carried away by flood. Water had touched the stringers, but now about 4 feet below them.

Perhaps a little good land in the valley S of the Trail, but greater part of region almost or entirely useless. May not a great part of the higher plateau however by turned into summer grazing lands of fair quality by burning off all scrub &c. Perhaps might induce growth of some better fodder than the wirey grass now obtaining.

Missouri Coteau The upper hilly drift deposits of this country much resemble the Coteau in many respects, but the latter has been bare of trees, & consequent denudation has made hills more stoney, & filled up many valleys partly. May origen be the Same?

Ledum latifolium Saw Labrador tea[567] abundantly in swamps today for the first time.

565. Dawson's comments about glaciation are interesting in that they represent an early stage in the development of his thinking, when he was seeking to integrate observations made on the coast with evidence from the British Columbia interior. In spite of having the data from only one summer and a stay in Victoria to support his concepts, Dawson had already formulated in outline a systematic concept of British Columbia glaciation. The idea of a "great glacier," a submergence, and a second glaciation, integral aspects of his initial systematized glaciation theory, are all here. For Dawson's later published treatment of glaciation based on the 1875 and 1876 field work, see his "On the Superficial Geology."

566. See 9 September 1875.

567. Labrador tea, *Ledum groenlandicum* Oeder.

[verso]

Two mts of Mackenzie.[568]

McM. nearly lost

Is Cul taes li valley see Mackenzie[569]

Bridge building

Humming Bird.

⟨Ne cha Co corrupted from Many Beaver paw R.⟩

other name of Is Cul taes li.

Tracha L = Tsi-tza {Cha} or Big Stone L.[570]

Curlews[571] nest.

[end verso]

June 1. Travelled from Blackwater Br to crossing of Bella Coola Trail with a small river running S.W. into the Is-cul-taes-ly R. Indians call the Creek Na-tan-i-Koh, or "Leaf River.[572] Distance about 22 miles.

Staid behind with McMillan* near where the B.C. trail leaves the Blackwater to look for a Bench Mark. Got separated, & thinking him ahead rode on. Overtook packs, but find he had not come up. Waited an hour & a half by the trail, when he arrived, having been lost some time. Rode on & found the Packs stopped on bank of Na-tan-i-koh, which in flood & not fordable. Camped & looked about for means of Crossing. Chose a place & built bridge to pack supp over. Intending to Swim the animals. Took nearly all evening building bridge, the current being strong.

Found a humming birds nest attached to a sprig of spruce & overhanging the water, a few feet above it. Female sitting on the nest, very tame, allowed approach to within 4 feet. Brown back, whitish breast with a dark spot. Nest built of downy material, probably from anemonies. Covered with white lichen & black moss outside. One white egg.

June 2. Got supp packed over bridge & overflowed swampy flat to W.

---

568. According to Alexander Mackenzie, "at five we quitted our station, and proceeded across two mountains, covered with spruce, poplar, white birch, and other trees. We then descended into a level country, where we found a good road through woods of cypress" (Alexander Mackenzie, *First Man West: Alexander Mackenzie's Journal of His Voyage to the Pacific Coast of Canada in 1793*, ed. Walter Sheppe [Berkeley and Los Angeles: University of California Press, 1962], 194). Mackenzie was coming from his previous camp in the Euchiniko (Is Cul taes li) River valley and entering the valley of the West Road River.

569. Mackenzie only briefly commented of the Euchiniko River valley that "we came to an uneven, hilly, and swampy country, through which our way was impeded by a considerable number of fallen trees" (ibid.). Mackenzie's party spent the night of 6 July 1793 near the Euchiniko River.

570. Tsacha Lake.

571. Long-billed curlew, *Numenius americanus* Bechstein.

572. Nataniko Creek.

side. Swam animals, & got off rather late. Rode ahead with McM. & after striking the Is-cul-taes-li went off to follow the ⟨old⟩ Railway location line of Y. party last summers. intending to cut across the trail ahead & intercept the packs. Got involved in bad country, lakes & swamps, & eventually got out on the river west of the trail. Found an indian trapping who explained the country to us. Set out down the river to look for packs, & after going round Several swamps &c. found them camped. Had something to eat ⟨&⟩ got animals repacked, & went up the river to where had met the Indian, about three miles. Camped.

Tried to engage the Indian, or another old man to accompany us, but they seemed rather reluctant, & wanted high pay

Indian Called Indian Johnny & speaks English well. Tells me that the lake Called Thra-cha on the map, really Called *Tsi-cha* meaning big-stone, or mountain. *Ne-cha-coh* corrupted from name meaning beaver paw R. {(not correct)} He does not Know the Is-Cul-taes-li as such but as the U-tsan-i-Koh.

Saw a curlew's nest today, roughly built of fragments of sticks on the ground. scarcely at all concealed, on rather bare Sandy flat ⟨covered⟩ with scattered scrub pines. 4 eggs. Spotted with dark brown.

June 3 Feed being poor, animals had strayed away during night & Could not be found for some time. Got packed up at last, & off by 9 A.m. Followed for about 4 miles northward the Indian trail towards Stony Cr. Struck the Na-tan-i-koh & then turned west, continuing in that course, or very nearly the remainder of the day. Got from swamps to windfall & from windfall & brule back to swamps, & thickets almost enough to scrub one off the horse. Much chopping necessary in places. Got into a rather broken country with low hills & ridges chiefly composed of basalt boulders. Basalt in place at Camp.

Camp beside a pretty little brook with dark brown water, tried fishing unsuccessfully.

June 4. Sunday McM inclined to have a day of rest, but feed being poor decided to push on. Travelled about 5 miles cutting through some bad brush & windfall, & progressing slowly. Arrived before noon at an abrupt gorge like brook[573] flowing sward & joining the Is-Cul-tais li about a mile off. Fire had passed Several times over the country & left it bare, with some pretty good grass. Camped. P.m. ascended a ridge about half a mile off to get view & bearings. Heavy Showers at intervals with some thunder

Larch a single small tree of larch L. occidentalis?[574] growing on the

---

573. The brook remains ungazetted.

574. Most likely the tamarack, *Larix laricina* (Du Roi) K. Koch, since the western larch, *Larix occidentalis* Nutt., does not grow in that region.

burnt ground. About 4 feet high & apparently thrifty. leaves about half out.

Memo. Note vegetation springing up on burnt plateau (pine country) Grasses naturally growing apparently of little value. Can any hardy grass or other plant be introduced. In some places much vetch & pea vine[575] comes up also giving very good feed. Often considerable areas of bear-berry, & moss. (?species) Change of climate by burning off wood! Not disadvantageous, for the most valuable fodder (viz bunch grass & sage) grow on dryest ground. Bunch grass & sage country would extend.

Humming birds may seen almost everywhere over this country, which appears strange in a region so far north, & at elevations over 3000 feet.[576]
[verso]
   Ta-tlat.
   Kuy-a-Kuz
   Ta-tl-Kuz.
   Rain
   Great valley.
   Indians.
   Trees destroyed by parasites.
   Indian on trails, [decalluce?] since Indians died of small pox
[end verso]
June 5. Morning dark & showery, left Camp & travelled westward cutting way through windfall & thick young scrub pines & aspens, though occasionally getting a little open ⟨ground⟩ ground along the margin of a swamp. About 11 o'clock struck a deep ravine & brook, which followed a short distance brought us out on the prairie-like northern bank of the *Eu-tsin-i-Koh* or main branch of the *Is-cul-taes-li.* Found an Indian trail, & followed it up along the river till half past three. Heavy rain all day. The river valley averages about a mile wide, & the northern Slope is well covered with grass, with occasionally a little *Sage,* & in some places large patches of wild onions.[577] The river about 50′ wide & 5′ deep with clear brown water. Now in flood. Where the river first struck found a long lake Called by the Indians *Tas-un-tlat.*[578] It seems to be nearly divided in one place by a peninsula from the North bank, & has many small islands covered with trees. At evening Camp at upper end of another long lake called

575. The "pea vine" was peavine, *Lathyrus* spp., such as the Sierran peavine, *Lathyrus nevadensis* Wats., or cream-flowered peavine, *Lathyrus ochroleucus* Hook.

576. The Rufous hummingbird, *S. rufus,* breeds as far north as the Alaska coast and the southern Yukon.

577. Nodding onion, *Allium cernuum* Roth.

578. Batnuni Lake.

Klun-chat-is-tli. Of similar character to last, & about half a mile wide.

The Eu-tsin-i-koh valley Very pretty, & Capable of affording food for a large number of animals. Some fine flat hay meadows not far above the water level. The South side of the Valley mostly thickly wooded, being damp & not easily burnt off.

On camping got large fires going to dry clothes &c. Shortly after heard a shot not far off, fired as a sort of Salute by an Indian, who with his little boy soon appeared, coming down the river by the trail. Seemed much pleased to see us, & said that when first he heard the bell of the horse he thought Cluscus L. Indians had come over, & was very angry. Got a good deal of information about the country & trails from him, & much of his personal history into the bargain. He was on his way down to Quesnel Mouth with a large pack of skins to trade. Said his father had died when he was very little, & his mother & nearly all his other relatives during the Small pox epidemic about 13? years ago.[579] Told us how he buried all one after another but never took the disease himself, till at last "*connoway mamalouse, nika one stop!*" Hi-yu Sick tum-tum, hi-yu Cly."[580] &c. Seemed really fond of his little boy Who bright & intelligent looking. Told us that the Trails about which we were enquiring were now nearly all bad & filled with fallen timber. That before the small pox swept off most of the Indians, many & good trails in all directions, now few & faint, & in attempting to follow, sometimes see trail, Sometimes not. Tried to induce the Indian to Come along with us & act as guide, but he in a hurry to go to Quesnel. At last he promised to think about coming with us one day to show a Short way by a trail southward up one of the branches of the river. To give definite answer in the morning. The little boy furnished with a curious implement for procuring the Cambium layer of P. Contorta for food. A sharpened stick with wedge like end, tied at the upper end to a piece of bone with chisel shaped outer end, something like a shoe-horn. With the first a longitudinal incision made, & the bark peeled off. The sweet pulp then scraped off the wood & eaten by the second.[581] The whole carried through the belt. Also furnished with horn spoons of bone manufacture, & this shape. [*Illus.*]

---

579. The reference is to the epidemic of 1862 that began in Victoria then spread rapidly into the interior with serious effects on the Indian population. See Andrew H. Yarmie, "Smallpox and the British Columbia Indians: Epidemic of 1862," *British Columbia Library Quarterly* 31 (1968): 13–21.

580. Or "Konaway memaloose, nika one stop! Hiyu sick tumtum, hiyu kely," Chinook Jargon for "All dead, I one stop! Much grief, much lamenting."

581. According to Nancy Turner, the scrapers used by the Indians were "made of caribou antler, deer ulna, or black bear shoulder blade" (Turner, *Food Plants of Interior Peoples*, 59).

June 6. Find the Indian disposed to accompany us. Arrange terms. When he hoists all his goods & chattels up into a tree & leaves them, Intending to return tomorrow. Morning fine, but heavy rain & thunder in the afternoon, again wetting everything. Crossed the Eu-tsan-i-Koh without much difficulty, though the little Indian boy going over behind McM, fell backwards into the water while the horse rearing up the [further?] bank. Followed a large branch, probably forming about ⅓ of the main stream at the point of Junction, & Called *Tai-uk* to its source in *Choo-tan-li* L.[582] a sheet of water one or two miles long. Had some difficulty in crossing at the outlet of the lake, the water being ponded back by beavers. On getting over found the old Indian trail completely blocked by heavy & recent windfall, & occupied the remainder of the afternoon cutting through about a mile & a half of it, in heavy & incessant rain. Camped between two small lakes called *Kuy-na-bun-Kut*.[583] Got large fires going & began drying up. on one occasion during the morning one of the pack mules in attempting to jump over a log, fell, & rolled end over end some way down a steep bank till stopped by a lot of windfall logs. Not seriously hurt, though might well have been Killed.

Indian tells us that the water of *Kuy-a-Kuz* L. flows northward to the Nechaco. That that of Ta-tuk L, runs to the Chillacoh.[584]

June 7. Gave the Indian $2.00 instead of the $1.50 promised, but told him he must show us the beginning of the good trail southward which he had told us of. Immediately on leaving Camp got into heavy windfall which the Indian had not Known of, & engaged till 1 P.m. Cutting laboriously through it & round the worst part of a long swamp. Crossed the swamp safely, though it looked a very bad place & about ¼ m. wide. Deep moss & scattered Engelmanns spruce. along the margins. Found the trail, & dismissed the Indian. Had a little lunch & then proceeded southward over a broad & high ridge or gently sloping plateau. Country covered with dense growth of black spruce & scrub pine. Thin & tall. Ground clothed deeply with spongy, green moss, but hard & stony below. The whole saturated with water, & steady rain coming straight down between the tall trees making it very uncomfortable. Saw some patches of snow deep in the shady woods at an elevation of about 4000 feet. Descended the S. slope of the ridge, meeting with some heavy windfall, & about 6.30 P.m. Camped at Sus-cha L. Cold wet & tired. The horses & mules now very hungry, having had little to eat since leaving the Eu-tsin-i-koh valley. Made large fires & turned in. The place as dismal looking a one in wet weather as can

---

582. Chutanli Lake.

583. The lakes remain ungazetted.

584. Chilako River. Dawson's informant was correct about the drainage patterns.

well be imagined. The ground had been recently burnt over, leaving little but sand. Straggling tall spikes of scrub pine, (many of them dead) on the higher ground. Tall spirey black spruces, often really *black* & Shaggy with black moss, in the swamps.

June 8. on leaving Camp had some difficulty at first in finding the trail, but at last picked it up & followed it the remainder of the day, though often so faint that for a time lost. Crossed over several broad ridges, & valleys, cutting through some heavy windfall, & reached the Blackwater at 5.30 P.m. Found McM's Camp only about half a mile off, the party having come up last night.

Saw shortly before reaching the Blackwater a very large bear, grey above, & probably a grizzly.[585] It was climbing up the rocks about 1000 yards off, & turning round occasionally to have a look at us. The mule bell had evidently disturbed it

June 9. Mr McMillan* finding the country N of the river at this point not what he had expected, moved camp about 7 m. up the R to the head of Eu-chun-i-coh L of the map or as it is called by the Indians *Cush-ya*.[586] Nothing yet of the Pack train from Quesnel with Ross* & Bowman*, so decided to accompany him. He & I still sharing the same tent, & a second also being used by his men belonging to the Geol. Survey. New tents for party expected by the train. Most of day occupied getting camp moved & tents &c. arranged in new place.

G. M. Dawson to John William Dawson*, 9 June 1876, Euchiniko Lakes

I have just got back from the flying expedition I spoke of going on when I wrote from Quesnel. The weather was wet & unpleasant, & not much of Geological interest turned up. I am quite well but the tents are being pulled down for another move & I Cannot write more by this Chance, but take the opportunity to let you know where I am. In about seven day's I hope to meet Mr Cambee* on the Salmon R.

June 10. Writing up notes & plotting track survey. Pm visited the falls of the Blackwater about 1 m above here, called Cush-ya-nyne-ti by the natives. Fall of about 15′ over basalt, rudely columar. Very pretty with amber coloured water of the R. lit up by the sun.

Obsidian Indians tell me that not far up the Blackwater a high moun-

---

585. It probably was the grizzly, *U. arctos horribilis*.

586. One of the Euchiniko Lakes.

tain of (or yielding) this material.[587] As I understand it the mountain referred to is the first of the ⟨large⟩ three S of the R marked on the map W. of here. {no. = Anahim's peak.}

June 11. Sunday. About camp all day, part of time occupied with map, working out Barometer Heights with McMillan*.

spruce. In swampy ground at elevations between 3000′ & 4000′, on way S from Eu-chin-i-coh R, noticed a spruce different from any I know.[588] Growing rather sparingly in Groves of *A. Engelmanii*, but quite distinct from it in foliage. Cone not seen. Bark of young branches smooth like "balsom" & with little blobs of gum under the bark in the Same way. In the old trees (which in general appearance not unlike *A. Eng.*) the blobs turn into horizontal swellings, which mark the otherwise Smooth bark very regularly. See. specimen. {June 21. Noted a few more trees of this kind.}

June 12. Still no sign of pack-train or party. About camp. Made sketch of Cush-ya L. &c. Some Indians Camped near us now engaged in preparing the cambium layer of the Scrub-pine. (stick a muck-a-muck)[589] They scrape it off in long ribbands & putting these in two layers, one across the other, spread the sheets so formed, which resemble mats, on poles to dry. The taste is quite sweet, but slightly resinous & not otherwise agreeable.

June 13. McM's party move on about 3 ½ m to shore of *Ky-a-Kuz L.* Still no news of pack-train, Decide to accompany them. Harvey[590] who is staying down near the crossing with the horses, having instructions to come up for me immediately they arrive. They Cannot get over the river in less than half a day which will give me time to get down. walked on to new camp. Spent some time trying to engineer a trail round a long swamp running up from the lake. finally camped on S. side of swamp. Mosquitoes quite troublesome.

June 14. Charles Seymour[591] Came into camp about 3.30 with news that

587. Obsidian is a black, wholly glassy volcanic rock. Dawson later notes that the obsidian source is Anahim Peak (see 21 June 1876). For a discussion of this obsidian locality, see D. E. Nelson and George Will, "Obsidian Sources in the Anahim Peak Area," in Simon Fraser University, Department of Archaeology, *Current Research Reports* (Burnaby, B.C., 1976), 151–54.

588. Probably alpine fir, *Abies lasiocarpa* (Hook.) Nutt., since Dawson seems to group the spruces (*Picea*) and true firs (*Abies*) together. Alpine fir does have smooth, grey bark with prominent pitch blisters in young trees, and obvious horizontal markings of the bark in older trees.

589. Chinook Jargon meaning, roughly, "that one can eat the wood."

590. Frank Harvey, a Kamloops packer.

591. Seymour was a miner who had worked in the Omineca district and probably elsewhere in British Columbia. In 1880 he left for the South African diamond fields.

Pack-Train, Ross* & Bowman* had arrived at the lower crossing to Cluscus. Party expect to cross tomorrow wait till morning before setting out to join them, hoping to see McMillan* Who is out exploring up the lake. Received letters from Ross*, Barnard* (referring to specimens of coal) Telegram from W W Walkem* saying that two of my Centennial Cases detained at San Francisco, railway demanding freight in advance. Now too late to do anything, even if possible to communicate.

[Draft of a poem, written on back of telegram]

> Just as a wee maid when she stands
> with downcast eyes & folded hands
> to say her oft conn'd task
> So blushing on some mossy bank. Where days are
> long & woods are dark,
> or Crowded thick twixt lichened stones
> where some old glacier laid his bones;
> Those nodding bells are swung.
> Fairer than all, ⟨&⟩ {where} all are fair,
> within the flowery band
> & breathing out a perfume rare
> where the tall ranked pine trees stand
> In the lone distant northern land

June 15. Started at 7 am McM, not having returned, rode about 20 m down to Pack Train Camp at Mouth of Cluscus L. Creek. arriving at 1 P.M. in time for lunch. Found good raft made & rope stretched across, most of stuff already over. Animals & Cattle Swam over during the afternoon Safely.

Overhauled *ictus*[592] Found that gun had fallen over Some hill with a mule & ⟨been⟩ had the barrel bent quite out of shape. Took it to pieces, oiled it packed it in a gunny intending to send it to Reid* at Quesnel to wait my return: one of bottles with developing solutions broken, & labels off all the other bottles. Got them repacked. Mosquitoes & black-flies very bad today

Lignite C. Seymour* tells me of locality where combustion of lignite was in progress some years ago, perhaps yet going on. Place on Lightning

---

592. Or "iktas," a Chinook Jargon term with various meanings for "things" such as trade goods, merchandise, or almost any possession. Here it means "gear."

Creek Cariboo. From 2 to 4 miles above the Old "Dad Morland ranch.[593]
June 16. Started pretty late various Causes of delay arising. McMillan*
appeared about 8.30 on the N bank of the Blackwater, having got back
from his exploring expedition yesterday. Crossed & talked over ⟨line⟩
result of his trip. Finds valley opening W. of Choo-tan-li L & running
down to near head of Chit-il-Kuz L,[594] which N. of Kuy-a-Kuz & connected with it by a rapid stream.[595] Grade rising up the Valley from
Chit-il-Kuz he thinks will be 40 to 50 feet for 10 or 12 miles.

Travelled on the Eushya R[596] some distance W of Upper Cluscus L.
Fine grassy Slopes along N side of Cluscus L. Valley. Beyond Cluscus
Lakes, barren & stony. An indian House at upper end of first Cluscus L.
Saw Fannie & a few other indians there. At one time a H.B. Fort[597] here.

Wrote home, also note to Barnard*, & one to Reid* of Quesnel
advising him that broken gun sent to his charge & asking him to forward
another. Cluscus L Indian engaged to Carry mail out tomorrow & return
along trail westward with mail till he finds us.

Aphamisomenon from Ross'* pretty minute description it must be this
plant which makes the waters of Tsa-cha — (Thracia) Lake,[598] thick
during the Summer.

Cluscus L Valley seems to continue on Eastward parallel to Blackwater
east of the point where the stream breaks through to the River.

593. D. C. Morland was an American best known for his involvement in allegations of land
     improprieties (the Cottonwood Scandal of 1862) with Justice Matthew Baillie Begbie.
     See David R. Williams, *"The Man for a New Country": Sir Matthew Baillie Begbie*
     (Sidney, B.C.: Gray's, 1977), 190–97. By 1872, he had left British Columbia for
     California and Arizona.

594. Tatelkuz Lake.

595. Chedakuz Creek.

596. Kushya River.

597. The post, established about 1834, was intended to serve both the Carrier and Chilcotin
     and thus prevent them from disposing furs to free traders on the coast. By 1850 the post
     had been abandoned. Dawson further commented that "at the west end of the first lake
     an Indian house is situated, and this has for a long time been a rendez vous for the
     natives, the site of an old establishment of the Hudson Bay Company being visible near
     at hand" (George M. Dawson, "Report on Explorations in British Columbia chiefly in
     the Basins of the Blackwater, Salmon, and Nechaco Rivers, and on François Lake,"
     Geological Survey of Canada, *Report of Progress for 1876–77*, [1878], 24–25).

598. "The name meaning giant stone, or mountain, and referring to the rocky hill on its
     north bank, is changed to Thracha on some maps" (Dawson, "Report on
     Explorations," 25n).

G. M. Dawson to Margaret Dawson*, 16 June 1876, Kushya River

Again a chance occurs of Sending a mail back to Quesnel, but again small chance of making proper use of the opportunity. We have had a long day & a hot one, & I feel more inclined for sleep than prose composition. I am now fairly on my way toward the Salmon River, having connected with a C.P.R.S. train of about sixty pack mules, travelling thitherward. I hope to meet Mr Cambie* there next week, & do not yet Know quite in which direction I may go afterwards. My reconnaissance trip to the north with Mr McMillan*, from which I had just returned when I scrawled my last brief note, was not of much geological interest, though we discovered a fine river valley with lakes & good grass, & a fair Chance for a railway line; & made altogether about sixty miles of new geography. We had very wet weather for several days, & were frequently drenched, & also had to contend with much tangled windfall & thickly wooded country, very difficult to get animals through at all. Altogether we were not sorry when we struck down on McM's Camp on the Blackwater. The mosquitoes & black flies are now just beginning to be troublesome, but are not yet unbearable. Spring, or rather summer is very late this year, probably a month later than usual, the rivers are Still high, & the swamps wet & mirey.

I am longing to get a mail to hear of all going on at home. This I suppose will reach you at your new Metis house, you must let me Know how you like it.

Too hot all day, & now that the sun is down chilly, with perhaps even a frost during the night. Such is the climate of this plateau region, advantageous in one respect *viz* that it Keeps the mosquitoes quiet after dark letting one sleep well.

Sometime I hope to get a chance to write a long letter, meanwhile I suppose short notes are better than nothing, & I must make up for deficiency in other respects by adding much love to all at home.

June 17. Travelled from before 9 A.m. to about 4.30. Pm but made only about 11.5 miles trail being bad with swamps & windfall. Mules nearly all mired along the margin of Tsa-cha L just before camping. Lake having overflowed the trail. Day remarkably fine & very warm.

Flora of B.C. may be divided probably into 4 main classes Coast = V.I. & W of Cascades. Northern temperate & with pretty abundant rainfall. Plateaux & country generally N of a certain line. Desert & dry country River valleys &c. of the Southern region. extension of American desert &c. Alpine = Peaks of Cascades & Rocky Mts.

June 18. Travelled on to 3rd or upper Crossing of the Blackwater R. got into camp pretty late owing to difficulties with swamps &c. Find the river very high & rapid, & though evidently somewhat lower than formerly, again rising slightly. The water brown & *turbid* differing from the Clear brown water issuing below the large lakes.

Being no feed on this side of the R, the mules horses & Cattle swim over. The Current being rapid, a rather exciting operation, but all safely across.

Evg. wrote up track survey. Put some plates in the Camera backs, though sorry to find Some apparently spoiled by rubbing together. Mosquitoes very troublesome

The Douglas fir does not seem to occur in this region of Country. Probably not W. of the mouth of the Is-cul-taes-li. Have noted it before some way N. on the trail from Blackwater to Ft George, though I cannot remember whether at Ft George itself. Seymour* tells me it only goes a short way up the Quesnel R, not reaching into the Cariboo Country at All. Noticed it on the Nazco & all along Chilcotin to Tatlayoco L.

A. Engelmanii now just beginning to shed its pollen. Ledum latifolium in good exposures just on the point of flowering, though in most places not So far advanced.

June 19. Engaged all day getting Cargo rafted across the river, which quite rapid. All safely over about 4 P.m. Day cloudy & dropping rain about Noon. Evening fine.

Plants. J. 19. A. Grass frequent in tufts especially on higher plateaux country, often where otherwise very barren. Also in Blackwater Valley. — B. *Arnica*? abundant on all plateau country, growing where burnt & bare & also in deep mossy woods, though in latter locality generally without flowers.

C. abundant on plateaux & B.W. Valley.

D.   "   plateau & BW valley along edges pools & swamps. E Castillya Common along grassy Northern banks of BW & other valleys.

Obsidian Indians tell me that beyond Eliguch L[599] of map (as I understand them) & to the South of the Salmon R. a *Small* mountain where much of this material.

Names of Mts. The three masses of Snowy Mts S of trail marked on the map called as follows from E to W according to the Indians. 1. *It-chá* 2. *Il-ga-chuz* 3. *Tse-tsutl.*[600]

Names of lakes Lake E. of the Indian House passed yesterday names as

599. Eliguk Lake.

600. Rainbow Range.

per track survey. Next west running into last *Klootch-oot-a.*[601] Next west (Cultus Coole of map) *Tsil-be-Kuz.*[602] This the Indians tell me means runs directly into the Blackwater a few miles above this crossing.

The Blackwater Called here *Ul-ghā'-Koh*.

The lake called Eliguck on the map pronounced as near as I can spell it *Uhl-ghák*.

"Granite" according to Ross* begins going W about the Second fall on the Salmon R.

June 20. From Blackwater Crossing to Camp near Indian House Elikut L. Rain in the afternoon.

Find four Indian women & Some children living in house here. A Sort of shanty quite open in front, & with free ventilation in other directions including the roof. poles stretched across inside hung over with trout drying or dry, & many spruce bark bales backed full of dry fish.

Saw a nice rabbit skin blanket, & wished to buy it, but the Klootchman afraid of her husband, to whom it belongs, & who now absent. Saw the Indian women boiling up fish heads in pots about a foot square, made of wood about 3/8 inch, ingenously bent round.[603] The boiling accomplished by dropping heated stones into the pot, a pair of tongs composed of a couple of long sticks tied together, being used for lifting them. [*Illus.*] The dry fish have the back bones removed, & when crisp ⟨are⟩ the fins tail &c. are broken off & the whole pressed down by the hand so as to pack in a solid mass into the bale.

The trout at present Seem to be running *out* of Elikut L. down the stream, & are caught in a contrivence not before seen,[604] but as drawn on ⟨opposite⟩ {next} page. [*Illus.*]

Both plans represented for catching fish on way downstream, & differ from the general arrangement with converging wicker points to catch fish going up stream. Latter generally as follows, in part sectional view. [*Illus.*] Wood used to make the rods seems to be dry P. *Contorta*.

Indian dogs The dogs in possession of these Indians rather peculiar, nearly pure white, with rather long, but coarse hair, & prick ears. fox-like expression, but rather larger than Coyotes. Tails bushy & flattened horizontally. Said to be beaver dogs, used in hunting beaver, & following them

---

601. Cluchuta Lake.

602. Tsilbekuz Lake.

603. For an illustration and discussion of this method of cooking, see Stewart, *Artifacts of the Northwest*, 84.

604. Stewart in *Indian Fishing*, 112, states that the weir-trap arrangement described by Dawson could also be used to catch fish going upstream. For an illustration of the cylindrical trap mentioned, see ibid., 114.

into the water.

June 21. From Elicut L. to Gotcheo L.[605] Day cold & blustry with occasional Showers had a touch of diarrha & consequently found travelling
rather disagreeable.

Gotcheo L. a Celebrated resort of the Indians, a building of their's
existing here Known as the Culla-Culla House, or Bird House, a large
Crow Carved in wood, rather neatly, & painted black, adorning one gable.
The Indians tell me that the [abode?] made by Bella Coola Indians, the
natives here not understanding painting & decoration so well. A curious
instance of mingling of customs of two now friendly tribes. A door in each
end of this Shape [*Illus.*] that at the west end being surmounted at each
side by a painted Colossal figure resembling a bear, more than anything
else, the design as near as I can tell exactly resembling the peculiar Haidah
style of art. The inner side of the East end covered with a corresponding
picture, but this time of two gigantic birds touching their bills above the
door. Also in the same style. Both in red paint. Various other designs on
the inner walls, some evidently secondary & added fancifully by poor
artists. Among most conspicuous a red hand with claws. The Carved
figure of a blackbird already mentioned stands on the head of a long
snouted monster with a good row of teeth on each side, which the projecting end of the roof tree.[606]

Near the Culla Culla House two remarkable posts standing in the
ground, which I find on inquiry hold the mortal remains of as many
Indians.[607] They have been here a good many years, but not very long, as

---

605. Gatcho Lake.

606. In his published report, Dawson adds that the house was "the best built of any I have
seen in the interior. . . . Though repaired for a great *potlatch* this summer, it bore
marks of very considerable antiquity" (Dawson, "Report on Explorations," 25). He
thought it the house mentioned by Alexander Mackenzie in the 1801 edition of his
*Voyages from Montreal on the River St. Laurence, through the Continent of
North-America, to the Frozen and Pacific Oceans: In the Years 1789 and 1793 . . . .*
(London: T. Cadell and W. Davies, 1801), 307.
　　"Culla Culla" is Chinook Jargon for "bird." This coastal-style house was probably
built by the Ulgatcho Carrier between 1780 and 1790. "A probable reason for the selection of Gatcho Lake as the location for this longhouse was its strategic position on a
major crossroads between the coastal village of Bella Coola and other communities on
the Interior Plateau. Thus, the settlement could have functioned as a redistribution
centre or, more plausibly, allowed the Interior Indians easy access to the Coast people
whom they greatly admired and emulated, and often lived with" (Paul F. Donahue,
"Ulkatcho: An Archaeological Outline," *Syesis* 6 [1973]: 175).

607. Such disposal of the dead was a Carrier convention. The body was cremated and the
following day the father's phratry gathered the calcined bones in a box and handed
them for safekeeping to the phratry of the deceased, who then repaid them in a
potlatch. "About a year later, the father's phratry built a wooden grave-house over the
cremation site, and deposited the bones on top of a post carved with the crest of the

some men now here remember having seen them. Besides these a couple of interments of recent date, & in ordinary style, to be Seen. The posts referred to each about 10′ high, & from 18″ to 2′ wide at the top, narrowing slightly below, where they are inserted in the ground. A hollow has been made near the top of each, on the North side, & in these the *burnt* remains of the Indians placed. The opening to hollows Closed by boards, one of which fallen off, showing a bundle of birch bark, still in good preservation. This post also surmounted by a black bird Carved in wood, the other without this addition. Some designs in red have also been painted on them outside but are now quite indefinite. [*Illus.*]

Obsidian From Careful inquiry I find that the source of all the obsidian used by the Indians of former days, the Mountain Called Anahim's Peak, a remarkably abrupt hill S. of this place, & between it & the Bella Coola Trail. (See geol. notes)[608]

June 22. From Gotcheo L. to Camp on Salmon River

June 23 Made only about ten miles down Salmon R having to cut new trail round several swamps, where old track along river margin flooded by the high water. Camped by the border of the stream in a pretty little meadow surrounded by tall spruce & pines on three sides.

Day fine but with some slight showers, now, 9.30 P.m. raining heavily.

Country passed over almost entirely burnt, very extensive fires must have swept over it a few years ago. Tall standing black poles, & as yet, little windfall. Some fine meadows of limited extent along N side of Salmon R valley, & in many places among the burnt sticks luxuriant growth of grass & pea-vine springing up. If completely burnt off, good pasture.

Vegetation, probably owing to lower elevation, & influence of sea, now decidedly in advance of any seen lately. The perennial lupin, noticed for the first time, & in abundance. Many tall aspens growing Scattered among the coniferous woods. *Aquilegia Canadensis* in flower. *Cornus Canadensis* Common. J. 23. A. *Smelacina*. Species common from Quesnel to here generally in open grassy patches. J.23. B. *Arcto-staphylos* — common everywhere. J. 23. C. *Thalictrum* common along N banks of Blackwater Eu-chun-i-coh, & this river, growing mixed with grass.[609]

deceased's clan or phratry" (Diamond Jenness, *The Carrier Indians of the Bulkley River: Their Social and Religious Life*, Smithsonian Institution, Bureau of American Ethnology Bulletin no. 133, Anthropological Papers no. 25 [Washington: United States Government Printing Office, 1943], 534).

608. See G. M. Dawson, Field Notebooks, RG 45, vol. 134, no. 2793, 47v, PAC.

609. The "perennial lupin" was Nootka lupin, *Lupinus Nootkatensis* Donn; "*Smelacina*" the star-flowered Solomon's seal, *Smilacina stellata* (L.) Desf.; and "*Thalictrum*" was meadow rue, *Thalictrum* spp.

June 24. Made a very short trip owing to bad State of trail, & the fact that much of that made last season, now overflowed by the Salmon River. Camped a few hundred yards N of Camp 30 C.P.RS. near the border of an overflowed Swamp, & in a dense grove of Western Scrub Pine.[610]

Saw ⟨Small⟩ one or two Small patches of snow still remaining in dense shady & mossy woods.

Day though fine Cold & blustry.

J. 24. A. *Viola* (yellow flowered)[611] seems same as that collected on Sooke R. V.I. now in flower in these woods. Noticed for first time today, & in abundance. J. *24. B. Lycopodium*[612] this with the other species common in these woods, & not rare N of the Blackwater further East. See last years notes for observation on Ft George Trail.[613] Collected specimens of the spruce mentioned under June. 11. now pretty abundant.

June 25 Sunday Ross* & the men go ahead to cut out a trail to the branch of Salmon R, about 8 m. from here, where Hunter* is to begin his line, & where Camby* is likely to meet us. In Camp all day.

Find the beautiful little orchid which noticed at intervals since leaving Quesnel, & here very common in patches 4 to 6 feet in diameter, in cold dense mossy woods, to be *Calipso borealis.*[614] ⟨Collected specimens of⟩

About 9 Pm. Seymour* & Charlie Fortier[615] returned from their ⟨June 26.⟩ trip to the Salmon House, not having been able to get further down the river, or communicate with Cambie* or Hunter*, owing to the high state of the water in the stream entering the Salmon R, just below the House. The Indian bridge at Salmon Ho. has been carried away, & therefore impossible to cross & take the usual route down the N bank from that place.

June 26. All packed to move Camp about 5 miles ahead, as far as the trail cut out. Mules & horses however had gone astray, & not turning up by 3 P.m. decided not to move Camp even in event of their being found. Set out with B to visit fall on Salmon R about 3 miles below here, examined

610. Lodgepole pine, *P. contorta.*

611. Probably the evergreen violet, *Viola sempervirens* Greene.

612. Ground-cedar, *Lycopodium complanatum* L.

613. "There is continued evidence of approach to region with greater rainfall in passing from Blackwater to Fort George. Mosses and various species of *Lycopodium* begin to grow abundantly in the woods, and a few miles before reaching Fort George species of *Ledum latifolium* were seen for the first time" (Dawson, "Report on Explorations," 245).

614. Fairy slipper, *Calypso bulbosa* (L.) Oakes.

615. Charles E. Fortier worked for the Hudson's Bay Company in the 1860's around Kamloops before settling up the North Thompson River, near the mouth of the Clearwater River. He was later drowned when the rope broke on the ferry at Savona.

rocks on way & at fall.

Fall now full of water, & very grand, falling through a tortuous rocky channel a height of 80 or 90 feet in two or three leaps. Here the river ceases its smooth valley, & the plateau, & falls at once into a Canon. The water does not pause at the foot of the fall, but continues as a foaming rapid as far as it can be seen, & in fact to the sea itself

Mosquitoes & black flies very bad today.

Indian Food The black moss or lichen growing in abundance on the lower dead limbs of the trees in thick woods, in many places, is used by the Indians in seasons of dearth. They save it, packed in bales during the summer, & then I am told beat it up with water, mould it into Cakes, ⟨before the fire,⟩ & roast it before the fire. Indians also in times of famine, further south, roast & eat the leaves of the Cactus.[616]

on the Coast, where the elder berry abundant, it is gathered a hole made in the hot ground near the fire, lined with the leaves of the skunk Cabbage, the berries placed in the hollow & cooked to a sort of pulp.[617]

Legend. C Seymour* tells me a story of the Saanich Indians, to the effect that long ago an Indian tired from Swimming, lay down to sleep on the Shore. Some wolves came along, & taking posession of him Carried him to their cave, which contained plenty of all sorts of meat hung up. They were about to kill him, when a she wolf, very fine looking, took a fancy to the man. He was turned into a wolf & married the she wolf, & still lives with her. When the Cowichen Indians are on the way to Attack the Saanich Indians, this man-wolf warns the latter of the approach of their enemies by howling about their Camps.[618]

---

616. Dawson's description of the Indians' use of "black moss or lichen," *Alectoria fremontii* Tuck., corresponds closely with that of Nancy Turner. According to Turner, the cactus, prickly-pear, *Opuntia* spp., was more widely used than Dawson supposed. See Turner, *Food Plants of Interior Peoples*, 35–39, 131.

617. On the coast, the red elderberry, *S. racemosa*, was most often utilized by the Indians. Nancy Turner augments Dawson's description by noting that after the berries were pulpy, they "were ladled into cedar frames set over warmed skunk cabbage leaves from which the mid-veins had been cut, then dried on a rack over a small fire for about 24 hours. The resulting cakes were tied in bundles and stored in cedar boxes" (Turner, *Food of Coastal Peoples*, 125).

618. In his unpublished Saanich notes, Diamond Jenness records a story, presumably from Tom Paul of Brentwood Bay, which is an exact analogue of this. The hero's name is Xetalaq and, in this case, gives warning against invading Kwakiutl by means of wolf howls. See Jenness notes, Canadian Ethnological Service, Canadian Museum of Civilization, Ottawa. Charles Hill-Tout's "Story of Sematl," collected in Victoria, has a similar abduction by wolves. See Charles Hill-Tout, *The Salish People* vol. IV: *The Sechelt and the South-Eastern Tribes of Vancouver Island*, ed. Ralph Maud (Vancouver: Talonbooks, 1978), 153–55.

Mr Hunter* with three Coast Indians arrived this evening, having been obliged to come up by a new route through the Mountains N of the Salmon R, owing to the bridge At Salmon House having been carried away. Had a long & hard trip. Mr Cambie* & Mr H's party, only waiting to hear of our arrival, to start up.

June 27 Left Camp at 10 A.m. Walked ahead with Bowman*, making a paced survey of the trail, which nearly cuts across strike of rocks, collecting specimens & looking for dip. Waited about 3 m from Camp for train to Catch up. Reached Camp about 3 m up the Il-tas-you-co R[619] from its junction with the Salmon R, by 5 P.m. Day overcast with occasional slight showers. Flies very bad.

The Il-tas-you-co at present carries perhaps about ⅔ as much water as the main Salmon R. It is clear or very nearly so, & greenish in colour, differing markedly from the yellow muddy aspect of the other stream.

The descent from the general level of the Country to the stream very sudden, the valley under a dull sky looking shut in & very deep. Filled with large & very tall trees, & carpeted with deep soft moss. The muffled descent altogether much reminded ⟨one⟩ of one Doré's pictures.[620]

For some time back, Say at any rate since striking the Salmon R, the woods have been of a much more varied character, a circumstance better marked here than before. Pines, & spruces of the two varieties growing together, & often fair sized Aspens in some abundance standing among them. Trees also of larger growth than on the interior plateau.

The balsom spruce (a. grandis'.) before referred to, here very common, & some trees over 2′ diameter. Saw also in this valley for the first time, small hemlock trees, also a pine different from *Contorta*, though not very markedly till number of leaves in each bundle examined.[621]

[verso]

Indian name R.

Beaver work.

Upper C.C. Gr.[622]

[end verso]

619. Iltasyuko River.

620. Paul-Gustave Doré (1832–83) was the most popular French book illustrator of the mid-nineteenth century. His work is characterized by weird and fantastic scenes.

621. The "balsom spruce (a. grandis')" was not the grand fir, *Abies grandis* (Dougl.) Lindl., but, as noted earlier, the alpine fir, *A. lasiocarpa*. The "small hemlock" was the mountain hemlock, *Tsuga mertensiana* (Bong.) Carr; while the "pine different from *Contorta*" was the whitebark pine, *Pinus albicaulis* Engelm.

622. The Upper Cache Creek group, according to Selwyn, consists "of a great volume of bluish, dove-colored, and white limestones, often a good marble, intensified with brown dolomitic limestone, red and green shale, and epidotic and chloritic rocks" (Selwyn, "Journal and Report," 60).

The undergrowth in these woods consists generally of following plants. *Lonicera Involucrata*, & a second white flowered species (see sp.) *Shepherdia Canadensis* The evergreen pink star flowered Shrub. (Vaccinium?) A second true *Vaccinium. Mountain Ash* shrubby. *Linnea borealis* (here & everywhere) *Cornus Canadensis*, the small yellow Sunflower. *Arnica*? already referred to. Also noted today the red osier dog wood *C. Stolonifera*?[623]

June 28 Moving about Camp, writing &c. Afternoon walked Some way down the river through the woods, but soon found the rocks to Cease. ⟨Took⟩ In examining rocks just opposite Camp found fossils! Belemnites &c., not abundant, but fortunate that found at all, as should never have looked for organic remains in rocks of volcanic origin, & of the appearance of these.[624]

J. 28. A. Dense wood. C. Mountain Ash. (See when first obs.) D. Alder. probably same species Seen everywhere. E. Hemlock, first obs. about here.[625]

June 29. Occupied all day collecting fossils, & measuring a Section of the beds. flies very bad.

Indian mail carrier arrived from Quesnel, but with only two notes from Mr Reid, for me. Other mail matter having been sent to S. party. Brought also a gun, some alcohol, & Caps, written for to Mr Reid*.

Examined some beaver work near here. The animals have a well beaten trail running up about 100 yards into the woods to a grove of poplar (aspen)   these are cut down & lying in all directions, Some partly Cut into lengths for transport. The trail evidently a logging one. Bushes & branches interfering with it bitten off, & in one or two instances, small dry logs lying across it, have been notched out on the trail, to allow the logs to

623. The "white flowered species" was possibly the Utah honeysuckle, *Lonicera utahensis* Wats. The "pink star flowered Shrub" was probably a blueberry or huckleberry, *Vaccinium* spp.; the "true *Vaccinium*" possibly the black mountain huckleberry, *Vaccinium membranaceum* Dougl. ex Hook.; and "*Mountain Ash*" either the Sitka mountain-ash, *Sorbus sitchensis* Roemer, or western mountain-ash, *Sorbus scopulina* Greene. "*Linnea borealis*" was the twinflower, *Linnaea borealis* L.; the "small yellow Sunflower" possibly balsamroot, *B. sagittata*; and "red osier dog wood" the red-osier dogwood, *Cornus stolonifera* Michx.

624. "Belemnites" were Belemnoidea, fossilized cephalopod molluscs with internal chambered shells important palaeontologically because of their massive skeletal elements. Dawson was more informative about this in the notebook. "Found fossils! in the bluish felspathic rock opposite the Camp this evening. Belamnites &c   Appears to place in its general position the whole older volcanic series" (Field Notebooks, RG 45, vol. 134, no. 2793, 53, PAC).

625. The western hemlock, *Tsuga heterophylla (Raf.) Sarg.*

slide along. The trail ends below in a sort of ditch or Canal, probably partly natural, but evidently improved. Sticks &c. removed. By this the lengths of log are floated the rest of the way to the river.

Indians tell me the name of this river is — *Pun-chi-as-coh.*[626] That of the Salmon R — the *Ches-le-coh.*

Seems very likely the rocks of the Upper Cache Cr. Gr. of Selwyn & Richardson. may be somewhat mod. form of these here Seen; & may conformably underlie the Jackass Mt Conglomerates. (*Vide. specimens*)

June 30. Moved Camp about 2 ½ m. down Stream, with Mr Hunter* &c. Afternoon visited a large fall about a mile Still further down. The fall a very picturesque one, the water passing down over gently inclined beds of bluish felspaltic material, in the opposite direction to their dip. Two leaps, the first broad & making a descent of about 25'. The water then boils & foams in a wide rocky basin, before being jostled together again by the rocks on the two sides, into the throat of a narrow chasm. Here confined between vertical walls of rock it, & a mass of seathing foam, it makes a second descent about equal in height to the first.

Cedar Near the fall first observed *Cedar* in Some abundance, though not forming large trees. C Seymour* tells me that the *Douglas fir.* occurs first about the Salmon House, the *Cedar* also appearing.

July. 1. About Camp. Changed paper of plants, wrote up notes, reading &c.

July. 2. Sunday. Went with B, & an Indian to pack the camera, down the river to the fall. Took a view looking up stream from a short distance above the fall, & a second, of the fall itself.[627] Forgot to bring an axe & had some difficulty in removing small trees which obstructed the view. Sent the Indian back to Camp with the Camera, & went on down stream, to the junction with the Salmon R. Went a [Sort?] way up the latter, examining the rocks, & then returned to camp. No news of Cambie*, or the rest of Hunter's* Party. A short distance above the Junction of this river with the Salmon, the latter is narrowed in to a tortuous rocky gorge, ⟨for a⟩ through which the water rushes with great velocity. The rocks in broken rugged masses, very picturesque, & from them a fine view down the Salmon R, which runs pretty straight for about ¾ m. with a S.S.W. Course. The valley closed by a remarkably rugged & very high peak of the Cascade Range,[628] covered to a great extent with snow, which today hardly to be distinguished from the fleecy clouds which hang about it.

626. Another name for the Iltasyuko River.

627. For the second view, see "Photographs," 2 July 1876, GSC132–C1 (PA 51037).

628. The exact peak is indeterminate, but possibly Sea Lion Peak or Mount Bernhardt.

July 3.

Walked up the river to the Packer's Camp (6.m.) Got horses there & went on to the end of the trail at the large lake,[629] returned riding to Camp arriving about 6 P.m. No additional rock exposures on this side of the river. A fine view from one point on the trail of the third Snowy range & Mts to the west of it, including the remarkable peak seen from the Salmon R yesterday, which may be Called Castle Mt for want of a better name. Flies very bad on way up.

[verso]

Elder noticed in flower a short distance below the lake, also in a shady spot a few plants of the Devil's Walking stick *Panax Horridum*?[630]

[end verso]

July 4. About Camp sketching, writing &c. About 4 P.m. heard shouting across the river, which being answered by 3 shots, in a few minutes replied to by another shot. Shortly after Cambie* & the party appeared on the river brink, & before dark all ferried over, two by two, on a raft. Report the road very difficult, & had to make a considerable detour, & leave the bank of the Salmon R.

Letters from Home to May 8, also notes from Dr Tolmie*, & A.C. Anderson* of Saanich. Newspapers we have to later date from Quesnelle.

G. M. Dawson to John William Dawson, 4 July 1876, Iltasyuko River*

I date from the river as above, though you will not find the name on the maps. It is a north branch of the Salmon, or Deane River, & brings to the latter a great part of its water. The Mouth was seen last year on the Salmon R, Survey, & from its appearance there, & other facts it was considered likely that a good alternative line could be found eastward by following it up. Mr Hunter* is in consequence commissioned to run a trial line from here to Fort George, following a course about E.N.E. Where we are at present Camped is about two miles above the mouth of the river, which joins the Salmon about 9 miles above the Salmon House, & some 30 odd miles from the tide water at the head of Deane Channel. This is the point near which I hoped to Meet Mr Cambie* about June 17th, but owing to delays consequent on the non-arrival of Supplies at Quesnelle, & on the bad state of the trail, & flooded condition of the rivers, we did not reach this river till June 27th; & then found neither Cambie* or Hunter* here. C. Seymour* & a man Called Fortier*, had been Sent ahead to let Cambie* & Co know of our arrival, that they might Come up the Salmon

629. Sigutlat Lake.

630. Devil's-club, *Oplopanax horridum* (J.E. Smith) Miq.

R, on the Certainty of meeting the supplies, but returned after a few days, to say that the Indian bridge across the Salmon R. had been Swept away, & that they Could not get any further on the left bank, as a small glacier stream there was swolen to the dimensions of a river, over which they could neither raft, nor make a bridge. The Same evening Mr Hunter* arrived with three Coast Indians, having come up by a circuitous way through the mountains to the north. Seymour* was then again sent off to let Cambie*, & Hunter's* party Know of our arrival, & try to make his way down on the right bank, obviating the necessity of Crossing Salmon R. We now almost hourly expect to see the whole party, & will all be very glad when they arrive, for Mr Hunter* is fretting about loosing time for his long survey, & I have no doubt Mr Cambie* is doing the same, while I have about exhausted the locality geologically, & shall be glad to move off again, & get some more of the area of country I am expected to examine, gone over. When Mr C. arrives I fear his plan may be, in the first instance to strike back for Quesnelle, in which Case I shall probably have to separate from him at once, & try some line more novel, & leading eventually northward.

Though I am tired of this place, my time here has not been altogether misspent, as I found a good locality for fossils, & have got with Bowman's* aid quite a collection from it. The fossils are probably about the same horizon as those from Tallayoco L last year *viz* Shasta, or lowest California Cretaceous. They are much more varied here however, in species, & the fossiliferous rocks are distinctly associated with a Volcanic series of great thickness, proving the age of this peculiar series to be as I had suspected at Taltayoco L. There are therefore two quite distinct volcanic formations over this part of the Country, one, chiefly felspathic, & often porphyritic, attached to the base of the Cretaceous & perhaps going down towards Jurassic, the other, unconformable, & post-tertiary, represented Chiefly by basaltic & doleritic[631] flows. In some cases there is a little difficulty in distinguishing between the two classes of beds, but generally the distinction is easy. I hope before leaving this region to be able to ascertain the relation of the older volcanic Series to the Crystalline rocks of the Cascade or Coast range.

I have had no mail matter yet since leaving Victoria (May 19) & must take some Credit to myself for writing this into a Vacuum; however there will soon be a chance to mail this to Quesnelle, either by Cambie*, or a returning pack train, & I must not miss the opportunity. We have had one mail from Quesnelle with Victoria dates to June 15, but my part of it owing to a stupid mistake, miscarries & went off to S. Division

631. The adjectival form for dolerite, a medium-grained, basic igneous rock.

(McMillan's*) on the Eu-chin-i-coh, or somewhere thereabouts. When I may be able to Connect with them I do not yet know. Some letters may probably come up from the coast when the party arrives.

July 5. Since writing, Mr Camby* & party have arrived, coming in yesterday evening. I have your letter of May 8, also letters from Anna*, & Mother*, not quite so recent dates.

The Indian vocabularies include all the words you note, being uniformly based on the vocabulary given in the Smithsonian Instructions for ethnological observation, a copy of which you gave me. I will try & get them into shape on my return to Victoria.

I leave here tomorrow, going probably a days journey with Cambie*, & then dissolving partnership with him, as he is anxious to reach Quesnelle at once, & does not yet Know what his plans afterwards may be. We have a provisional arrangement to meet about the middle of August at Fraser Lake, near the E. end of Francois L. & on the telegraph trail.[632]

July 5. About camp all day, writing letters, packing, & arranging about supplies for departure. Wrote Home (R. P.)[633] Selwyn*, Tolmie*, Scudder*, Perrault*.

July 6. Started about 8 A.m. & travelled till about 3 P.m. reaching the point on the Salmon R where lunched June 23, & following the trail formerly traversed. Glad to be able to turn horses & mules out to good feed again, as they have had rather a hard time of late, & were last night tied up near the camp without anything to Eat. Have now *about* (though probably barely) a months provisions. Intend to leave Camby* tomorrow at the Salmon R Crossing, & go in the first place toward Salmon House. Camby* returning post haste to Quesnelle. Day threatening & now showery & overcast.

Four Indians appeared shortly after camp made, from Gotcheo (or Il-gatchio) Lake, on their way down to the Salmon House with the rest of their friends to the Annual fishery there. The "stick" Indians[634] having for long maintained the right to this salmon fishery station, though near the coast. A fact perhaps partly due to its inaccessibility from the sea. Indians tell us that last winter the stick Indians of this part of the country wintered at the salt water with the Bella-Hoolas.

632. The Collins Overland Telegraph was part of a Western Union project to connect North America to Europe via the Bering Strait. Work halted in 1866 after the successful laying of the Atlantic cable.

633. Presumably Rankine Dawson and Papa.

634. Carrier or Chilcotin Indians from the bush country of the British Columbia interior, originally so-called by the Indians on the Pacific coast.

July 7. Part of morning occupied getting horses shod & put in order. Set out about 10 a.m. Travelled on with Camby* & party to Crossing place of Salmon R. Found there a whole tribe of Indians on their way to Salmon House for the Annual fishery there. Men women children, dogs, & a few horses.[635] Got some Indians to work on the promise of a dollar each, to make a good raft for the Crossing & Got everything over before dark. Horses fording the river a short way further down without loosing bottom. Indians Crossed over afterwards, & so camped on the s bank in the midst of them.

Asked about the chief buried at Tsick L[636] of the maps. His name *Noos-'til.* Apparently much thought of by the Indians, & a man of more than ordinary character. Conceived the idea of making a broad fine trail from Quesnelle to the sea, & did the chopping which we have seen in some places further back. Trail 10 feet wide, & almost like a road near several Indian Houses, but soon degenerates again on leaving their vicinity. As far as I can make out Some great feast for the dead, in which all the Indians to present foot to the deceased, will come off in one or two years. Now dead about 3 years.

Amusing to see the Indians with all their goods crossing on the raft. The dogs gradually finding themselves left alone, set up most dismal howling, & finally after running up & down the bank, one by one plunged in & crossed.

Made arrangement with Seymour*, that if he reaches the Junction of the B.C. trail near Cultus Coolie L, before me, to leave a cache of provisions, from Jennings* Stores. Expects to reach there from 18 to 20 prox.
[verso]
Compared barometer with Camby's* Small one this morning, the result being

Camby's* 26.37
Dawson's 26.47. or +.10
[end verso]
Saw a very old Indian who remembers seeing the first white men who penetrated this part of the country. Says 4 white men, with one gun (then a novelty to the Indians) Came from the E walking, & got two Indians from near Il-gatcheo L to go on with them. The Indians returned but the white men went on to the Sea by the Bella Coola Trail. (Can they be iden-

---

635. There were fifty to sixty Indians, representing, Dawson thought, the entire native population "of a tract extending beyond Lake Tschich northward, and nearly to Cluscus Lakes eastward" (Dawson, "Report on Explorations," 29).

636. Tschick Lake.

tified as any of the first explorers).[637]

[verso]

8. See notes of flora. Indians on the march River bridges, bad trail range of salmon names of places. Trails of which told

Fine view

glaciation theories chief at Tsi sick L.

[end verso]

July 8.[638] Off by 8.30 & travelled to Tanyabunkut L.[639] of the map. Trail in places, bad, & had two bridges to repair. Mules Several times mired. Heavy rain in the afternoon.

Passed the Indians on the March, in several parties. Men women children & dogs packed. Goods in square wooden boxes, or where small packs in network bags hung over the back, with generelly a blanket slung over each. All seem in good humour, & as though going to annual holiday excursion. Some fine swampy meadows on today's route.

[verso]

Indians eat Heracleum lanatum?[640]

[end verso]

Glaciation   Proof of Movement at one time from Interior region towards & through the coast range, & generally Southward & Southwestward.[641] From striation of Peaks. Vancouver Isd Glaciation &c.[642]

Proof that at subsequent period transport of material from the Mts (& striation) Eastward. Proof of great submergence & ? where to fit in.

Perhaps thus. Continental glacier, gradual? retreat with partial submergence along Coast (V.I. beds &c.) Continued retreat, leaving the Interior

---

637. In 1793, Alexander Mackenzie, with his cousin Alexander Mackay and six Canadian voyageurs, were the first whites in the region.

638. Now, as Dawson noted elsewhere, "I parted from Mr. Cambie, who continued eastward on his way to Quesnel, my party consisting, besides myself, of A. Bowman, assistant, one Mexican packer, and one Lillooet Indian packer and cook" (Dawson, "Report on Explorations," 29).

639. Tanya Lakes.

640. The cow-parsnip, *Heracleum lanatum* Michx., was widely used as a green vegetable by numerous Indian groups. See Turner, *Food Plants of Interior Peoples*, 95–97.

641. Dawson noted that moraines near the upper end of his Tanyabunkut lake had rounded rocks that showed evident glacier motion southwestward and thus had an "important bearing on general glaciation theories" (Field Notebooks, RG 45, vol. 134, no. 2793, 61, PAC).

642. Dawson here was further refining his theories of British Columbia glaciation by building upon new data. For a formalized account of his earliest ideas about Cordilleran glaciation, see his "On the Superficial Geology." For an evaluation of Dawson's concepts, see Tipper, *Glacial Geomorphology*, 71–72.

plateau dammed up westward. Ice masses left for time on elevations of plateau (Sources Nazco &c. &c.) forming local glaciers. Large local glaciers from Cascades. Intervening ice burdened water to which sea perhaps did not gain access. Possible periods of increase & decrease. Final decrease as water able to flow westward by opening of ice stopped gaps in Cascades. Formation of terraces.

[verso]

A theory by which to arrange facts, independent of foreign theories, perhaps untenable; but provisional.

[end verso]

July 9. Made late start, ⟨owing to⟩ waiting to take photographs of hills &c. from a good point of view above Tany-a-bunkut L.[643] Two Indians appear to have attached themselves to us, the rest waiting to fish in Hatty L.[644] Camped about 3 Pm, having come About 10 m. part of way over ⟨very⟩ bad trail. Writing, changing photo plates, & pressing plants, till late.

Fine in morning, overcast & gloomy, ending in rain with thunder in the afternoon.

Got an Indian to go for a specimen of "fire stone" about which had formerly heard reports, by giving him $2.00. Brought back a very good sample of lignite, which may be important.

[verso]

Glacial theories

proof of movement from & toward Mts &c.

names of places—

[end verso]

{Jy. 8.} on dry partly burnt ground S. of Salmon R crossing noticed following plants. Much more advanced than in dark woods elsewhere. Lonicera involucrata fl. Pyrola rotundifolia showy colour. Fragaria virginiana in flower. Anemone (white see sp.) in flower. Rubus or dwarf raspberry (white & red see specimens. in flower) Red Castillya in flower. Yarrow beginning to flower. Linnea in bud. Ledum latifolium a few flowers in advanced situations. Sedum (see sp.) in flower.[645] Epilobium not yet in flower)

643. Of the four exposures Dawson took, only one remains. See "Photographs," 9 July 1876, GSC133–C1 (PA 37532).

644. Probably Rainbow Lake.

645. "Pyrola rotundifolia" was the large wintergreen or common pink pyrola, *Pyrola asarifolia* Michx.; "Fragaria virginiana" the wild strawberry, *F. virginiana*; "Anemone" wind flower, *Anemone multifida* Poir; "dwarf raspberry" probably dwarf raspberry, *Rubus acaulis* Michx.; "Red Castillya" Indian paintbrush, *Castilleja* spp.; and "Sedum" stonecrop, *Sedum* spp.; and "Epilobium" fireweed, *E. angustifolium*.

July 10. Moved on to place about 4 miles from Salmon House,[646] where best feed for animals, & above the bad hill. Lunched & taking riding Animals & a light pack started for Salmon Ho, reaching it about 4 P.m. The latter part of the trail rather bad, overgrown with bushes & a good deal of windfall. The hill descending to the Salmon House flat, about 500 feet very steep, the animals forming a close zig-zag on the side

The Indians who accompanied us rather disappointed to find the water still very high, & the salmon Just beginning to run in Small numbers. The Indians are about to reconstruct the bridge at the fall, which is necessary for their fishery, which is Carried on by suspending broad baskets below the brow of the fall, into which the fish jumping in their efforts to ascend, fall back. The bridge is now every winter carried away, though the Indians tell me that formerly it remained always.[647] It is made by placing sticks from the sides to a rock in the centre of the fall, now only uncovered at low water, formerly much higher. The Indians have a house on each side of the river, that on the S. side now pulled down & in a ruinous condition. The Indians lay the boards &c. aside each autumn, to prevent their destruction by weight of snow.

A remarkably fine Canon or chasm on the Tahyescoh about ⟨half⟩ a mile above its Junction with the Salmon R.

Noticed three Small heaps of stones near the trail not far from Salmon House resembling as much as Anything the old burial Cairns of V.I. on enquiry find the Indians have a superstition regarding them, that any man Passing without potlatching[648] a twig or stick to each, will soon die. In Consequence each cairn covered with small sticks. Indians Seem to believe that some people are buried here, but do not know who, some say perhaps the "tenas men" These last a Sort of mystical dwarf or gnome race who were formerly Supposed to steal Klooch-men &c. A circular hollow resembling the mark of a Kuquelly house, on the Salmon Ho flat, attributed by an Indian I asked, to the same agency. Long ago, he Said the little men slept there, making a fire in the centre.

646. Marcus Smith, in the narrative of his 1875 explorations, commented on the Salmon House: "here the river rushes through a narrow rocky gorge, the lower edge of rocks being about 20 feet above the level of the river, over which there is an Indian bridge or platform of round timbers. Immediately below this there is a fall of about 15 feet, over the face of which the Indians have constructed a screen of wythies, to which are hung pockets of network for catching salmon as they endeavour to leap the fall" (Marcus Smith, "Appendix I. Report on the Surveys in British Columbia during the Year 1875," in Fleming, *Report on Surveys 1877*, 167).

647. "A rock located in the middle of the stream and which helped support the bridge had so eroded that the structure now washed away every winter" (Dawson, "Report on Explorations," 31).

648. Or giving a gift.

Find that the Stick Indian name for money (Chinook Chicamen) is *Shoo-ni-a*, exactly that of the Chippeways of the East. Can it be an original similarity of language, or introduced by the old Hudson Bay traders.[649]

Another linguistic peculiarity. Beci or Beece the name for obsidian, & also for the mountain yielding it, is I believe the same as the Aztec Word for Knife. Supposing aztec affinities for the Tinneh people, can it be that the old aztec name of the Knife-yielding mountain has survived?[650] other names of places Show Similarity to aztec names, though if any meaning attached, now different. Ta-tla for instance given to 2 lakes in B.C. the same as an Aztec name meaning place of stones. *Tza-tza-te* A mountain on the Nazco[651] & probably meaning beaver Mt in Chilcotin the same as Tza-tsa-te-pec of the Mexicans, a name meaning "mountain of outcry" from a ceremony there performed.[652]

June 11.[653] Got photographs of Country about Salmon Ho from three different points,[654] & then hurried back to Mule camp. Packed up & off by 12.45. Camped at lower end of Tanyabunkut L of the map, finding our Indian friends all here before us, & likely to remain a few days till salmon plenty. our advent heralded by shouts & screams from all the juvenile portion of the Community, & pitching tents &c. seeming to afford an afternoons recreation to the Whole tribe, who squatted round watching the operetion, amusing themselves at odd moments by Catching vermin in each other heads, & killing it in the same way usual with monkeys.

Arranged yesterday for an Indian to go with us At the exhorbitant rate of $2.00 a day. Wanted him however even if at high price to show trail to the South, & indicate locality of the lignite region.

Indian food. Two additions to the dietary. one plant I believe the *Heracleum lanatum* of which the young growing stems eaten, after the skin peeled off. Not ill tasting. The second the pith of Growing shoots of fire weed (*Epilobium*) the stalks split up & flattened out & the juicy inner

649. The Carrier and Chepewyan are both Athabascan-speaking peoples, though this word may be introduced.

650. The Carrier and Chilcotin word for obsidian is "bes," but it has no affinity to the Aztec's word for obsidian or knife. See J. Richard Andrew, *Introduction to Classical Nahuatl* (Austin: University of Texas Press, 1975), 446.

651. Tzazati Mountain on the Nazko River.

652. Dawson's speculations seem to have been inspired by his recent reading of H. H. Bancroft.

653. The date should read July.

654. Only one of the three appears on the Geological Survey of Canada list (GSC135–C1) and it no longer remains.

portion scraped off & eaten.[655]

July 12 Started on foot with Bowman*, our Indian & a friend of his to visit the lignite locality. Found loose pieces on a brook or rather torrent, about 5 m. from Camp,[656] & by following up the brook a piece found the lignite in place. Section somewhat as below [*Illus.*]

Where cross hatched the granite remarkably decomposed & crumbling, suggesting that here a sample of the pre-lignite-era surface of the country, exposed Since by denudation, & which has not experienced the Glacial Scouring. Granite surfaces generally pretty hard & often glacier rounded.[657]

on return to camp had a long talk with the Indians about possibility of getting Southward & then Eastward to Ne-coont-loon Lake.[658] Find after much trouble & beating about the bush, that two trails going Southward toward the Bella Coola trail. one on low ground, the other following high ground, both considered bad, but the lower especially so. Find that my Indian only Knows the lower, & so obliged to pay him off & take on another who professes to Know the *Saghalie* trail.[659] Decide at least to attempt the passage thus to Ne-coont-loon & avoid returning by former route.

Obliged to give medicine to several sick natives, in the course of the evening. They come squatting round our camp at all hours & make themselves obnoxious by getting in the way of everybody.

[verso]

Visit Lignite

Talk with Indians.

Moneys Spent Acct.

Indian from Salmon Ho $2.00

Indian basket 2.00

" Blanket 5.00

To Indians building raft 4.00

Granite rotten where protected from drift.

[end verso]

July 13 After considerable hesitation as to best course, decided to start Southward, with an Indian as guide, notwithstanding the bad reports

655. For the Indians' use of the cow parsnip, *H. lanatum*, and the fireweed, *E. angustifolium*, see Turner, *Food Plants of Interior Peoples*, 95–97, 170–72.

656. Kohasganko Creek.

657. Dawson's analysis was probably correct.

658. Anahim Lake.

659. Chinook Jargon for "upper" trail.

Concerning the trail. If can get round by the Bella Coola to Necoontloon will not only save time, but visit a yet unknown region. Find the trail so far really bad, narrow & with a good many sticks, & also with very many & bad swamps & grassy meadows. Much of the country burnt over.

Had much difficulty with the mules, & after a hard day's work can show only a short distance traversed. one of the pack mules ruptured, either in jumping logs, or crossing some swamp, & died shortly after Camping. A great misfortune.

From a rocky knoll near Camp a magnificent view of the whole country far & wide, with the sun sinking westward over the glittering snow clad peaks or black bare summits. of the Coast range, & blue haze filling the bottoms of the valleys, a splendid picture.

[verso]

Kalmia[660] & other alpine forms.

[end verso]

Distinct glaciation, stri & general form, on same Knoll showing glacier or iceberg motion toward 310°W Magnetic. Here if anywhere traces of a great northern ice cap, to which this flank, at least, of the 3rd snowy range no real impediment.

July 14 Sketched the topography of the region embraced in the view spoken of yesterday,[661] while the packing up going on. Travelled southward till between 4 & 5 P.m. on a much better trail, though still from time getting Animals mired &c. Much good feed in little Alpine meadows scattered everywhere. These mostly swampy, though generally sloping, sometimes at a considerable angle. The whole ground saturated like a big sponge, & though the sod usually hard enough for animals to walk over without miring, many little holes & pools of all shapes let into it, here & there.

Soon after leaving camp got into green timber, which continued with occasional small burnt patches till within a mile or two of this place, where again everything burnt, & a forest of rampikes left behind. Woods generally pretty open.

A heavy thunder storm with drenching rain passed over during the afternoon, & several heavy showers during the evening.

Mosquitoes very bad.

Snow must be at least 3 feet deep in these woods in winter, from the great height of stumps chopped by Indians during that season.

July 15 Travelled Southward, following up a valley of one of the main branches of the Tahyesco, into a quite alpine region over 4000' above sea

---

660. Swamp laurel, *Kalmia polifolia* ssp. *microphylla* (Hook.) Calder & Taylor.

661. See G. M. Dawson, Field Notebooks, RG 45, vol. 134, no. 2793, 70-71, PAC.

level, & above the abundant growth of timber. A wide valley running southward along the eastern base of the first ridge of the coast range. The valley full of little rocky Knolls, & moraine material, wide grassy park like meadows, with scattered clumps of timber, though much destroyed by fire. Snow in great quantities every where, & water running from it.

The common trees P. Contorta, growing stunted though strong, & often forking upward. P *flexilis* not So common, though sometimes a fair Size.[662] *A grandis*, growing stout, with many low wide branches sweeping the ground, as often seen in this tree. Leafage appears closer, & more distributed round the branch than usual, & the bark to split up & become rough sooner. The whistling marmots making themselves heard among the rocks, & Cariboo[663] tracks abundant.

The Indian lead us over a short way to the Bella coola Side across the watershed, under the impression that I wanted to look down into the valley, but protested against mules going any further. Then found that to strike the trail to Ne-coont-loon Should have gone Eastward about 2 m. back. Also that no trail goes from this valley, but that not far to the east he expected to strike an old trail. The whole appeared so doubtful, that felt inclined to return the way we came, bud having come So far decided to devote the remainder of the day to proving the matter. Quite pleased to have done so, as on leaving the valley, & crossing a wooded ridge, found the whole country plateau-like & open. Made about 4 m. E. & then Camped among great patches of snow

July 16. Sunday. Travelled on Eastward under the Indians guidance & camped at 4.30 on the upper waters of the Cheddakulk[664] of Trutch's map,[665] finding a beautiful grassy meadow near the borders of the stream. Though about the Same elevation as last Night, little or no snow. (see remarks in other notebook)[666] Lost time this morning with the mule Frank, which in crossing a torrent missed its footing, & went down stream some way, getting Cut & bruised a little, but not badly hurt. The sugar, tea, rice, beans, oatmeal &c. forming one pack quite soaked. My plant

---

662. "P *flexilis*" the limber pine, *Pinus flexilis* James, is not found in the region. Dawson was referring to the whitebark pine, *P. albicaulis*, which is very similar.

663. The "whistling marmots" were hoary marmots, *M. caligata*; and "Cariboo" probably the mountain caribou, *Rangifer tarandus montanus* Seton.

664. Probably Young Creek.

665. J. W. Trutch, *Map of British Columbia to the 56th. Parallel, North Latitude* (London: Edward Stanford, 1871). Especially during the 1875–76 explorations, Dawson relied heavily on the map which was the best then available for north central British Columbia.

666. See G. M. Dawson, Field Notebooks, RG 45, vol. 134, no. 2793, 77, PAC.

Case & Camera, forming the other, thanks to a good manta,[667] & luck, (being on the upper side) escaped scot free, & nearly quite dry. Had Frank gone a few feet further he must have been carried away by the main stream & then nothing could have saved either him or his load, from going down over A series of rapids & waterfalls.

The Indian shot 2 whistlers[668] today, had one for supper & found the meat remarkably good, though not yet very fat.

July 17 Made about fourteen miles Eastward, most of the way through open Country like that before described, with many Swamps & lakes of small size. On descending gradually get into thicker timber P Contorta & A Engelmanni preponderating though still very scrubby. Ranges of remarkable bare peaks of volcanic rocks to the North, tinted on the slopes with red yellow &c. from oxidation & decay of rocks. Ruins of a great old volcano. Got a good outlook from one point seeing the valley of the upper part of Salmon R, & a lake which the Indian believes to be *Ne-coont-loon.*[669]

Camped by the bank of a large brook, or small river Called the *Too-cha-Koh,*[670] a tributary of the Salmon R.

No accidents to mules today.

Fine summer like day. Little snow seen today, though elevation little different from that of Camp where the surface Still to large extent covered. The local action of the mountains in Causing greater precipitation must explain it. It is important to Know that the great snowfall of the Coast range, decreases very rapidly eastward.

July 18. Travelled on Eastwards, making a good days journey, & reaching the bank of Salmon R at the lower end of Na-coont-loon L. Crossed the stream by which camped last night, the first thing in the morning, & during the greater part of the day followed near its S. bank. After a few miles struck the old Indian Trail, which led us to this place. Found it just in time on getting into the thicker timber, & saved much trouble & chopping. Had to make a small bridge at one place. Emerged eventually on a fine large grassy meadow bordering the lake, chose place for camping near the river bank, which is low & swampy. Soon after arrival saw two Indians at a distance on a raft, & before long they came into Camp. An old man with prominent wooden-like features, & a young one with little expression Save a Sort of astonishment. Both with faces varnished & blotted with

667. A blanket used on a horse or mule.

668. Hoary marmots, *M. caligata.*

669. Actually Abuntlet Lake.

670. Tusulko River.

blood from mosquito & black fly bights. Tell us that two other men & Several women at Ne-coont-Loon village, which we were rather surprised to hear, as had been formerly informed that all the Na-coont-loon Indians, had been moved down to the Chilcotin Country by orders of the priest. The Na-coont-loons a branch of the Chilcotins, & anciently at enmity with the Stick Indians to the north.[671] The Mountain Beece, or Anahim's peak,[672] the source of supply of obsidian for both regions, anciently, I am told, a scene of frequent fighting & much bloodshed. The Salmon R in this part of its course takes its name from the mountain Beece, being not *Islaho*, but *Beece-la-Coh* or Beece River.

July 19 Started early to go to Na-coont-loon Lake, which the Indians inform me is meerelya third expansion of the one we are now on.[673] About half a mile from Camp, came to grief in a deep creek with high banks, rode in & got off on the further bank & then attempted to lead out the horse. He however, after several vain attempts fell backward into the water, & was for a moment entirely submerged. Canteenes fell off during the operetion, but by great good luck recovered without much difficulty. Note-book slightly wet, map, compass & all else soaking. Returned to camp to get things dry, & the Indian report of the trail being discouraging, took back the horses. Bowman* went on on foot with an Indian of the place, & on returning reports the lower end of Na-Coont-loon L about 6 m S.S.E. Got all plants changed, & saw to building of raft for Crossing tomorrow

Black flies & mosquitoes horrible here, the day warm & still

---

671. A reference to "Nakünt'lun," which by 1892 was "almost deserted but originally the largest Ch. [Chilcotin] village" (Morice, "Carrier Sociology," pl. II). Recent archaeological research has revised the earlier assumption of a village structure among the pre-reserve Chilcotin, and scholars now favour the concept of a "dispersed community of single or a few multiple house locations around the lake" (Roscoe Wilmeth, *Anahim Lake Archaeology and the Early Historic Chilcotin Indians*, National Museum of Man, Mercury Series, Archaeological Survey of Canada Paper no. 82 [Ottawa: National Museums of Canada, 1978], 13). The "priest" was probably Father James Maria McGuckin from St. Joseph's, the Oblate mission near Williams Lake. For an account of his early work among the Chilcotins, see Margaret Whitehead, *The Cariboo Mission: A History of the Oblates* (Victoria: Sono Nis Press, 1981), 51–52. By the 1870's most of the Chilcotins had indeed moved east. A number of families remained in the area, leading a semi-nomadic life in the woods and mountains. On warfare among the Chilcotin and Carrier, see A. G. Morice, "The Western Denes—Their Manners and Customs," *Proceedings of the Canadian Institute*, ser. 3, 7 (1888–89): 141–42.

672. Anahim Peak.

673. From north to south the lakes are Abuntlet Lake and the two expansions of Anahim Lake proper.

[verso]

  Paid Indian $1.00 for help in building raft &c.

[end verso]

July. 20. Got stuff all rafted over the river, & set out North Eastward for Tse-tse lake[674] on the Blackwater Trail. Took along with us the old man who had turned up on our first camping here. He to show us the trail which rather dim, & now disused. Caching his beaver traps, & bringing 3 dried trout, greasy & dirty looking, on a string, which afterwards passed round the [waist?] helped to support his trousers. Hobbled along in front of us, & used his one eye to best advantage. Much trouble from swamps & windfall, though some parts of the way very good. Camped late, where poor feed for the animals, & myriads of mosquitoes. Could hardly find room to spread the tents among fallen & half fallen timber. Evening blowing up squally & appearance of rain.

[verso]

  Indian $1.00 for showing trail & chopping.

[end verso]

July 21 Some light showers early this morning but eventually cleared up. off by 8 A.m. & ascending the gentle slope of the flank of the 2nd range, soon reached an open broken plateau like that belonging to the 3rd range already mentioned.[675] Many small ponds & lakelets, brooks & streams & melting snow. ocre plants.[676] Could not Keep the old Indian trail there being nothing to mark it here. After camping our Indian guide "Jim" ⟨st⟩ off to Seek the trail ahead before we came to the head water of the northern slope. Returned after a couple of hours; having Succeeded. Saw 3 Cariboo today, & emptied my revolver at one without effect, at very long range.

  Camped in a pretty little nook, with fine feed, at elevation of 5500 feet, & near a big snow-bank. Mosquitoes voracious.

  A splendid view of the 1st snowy range, Blackwater valley &c from a hill near by. See what believe to be part of the Telegraph Range over 90 m.

---

674. Tsetzi Lake.

675. Dawson does not mention it here, but this is along the slope of his Il-ga-chuz Mountain where he observed the highest deposits of boulder clay, a significant fact in his evolving glacial hypothesis. In his notes, he recorded a high bench, with surface material evidently rolled and water-rounded, "like beach stuff. . . . This flat seems certainly to mark an old water-line (outline) probably, of the glacial submergence, & perhaps from its great height (Same as Camp about 5500′) shows limit of such submergence" (G. M. Dawson, Field Notebooks, RG 45, vol. 134, no. 2794, 8, PAC). For his interpretations, see Dawson, "On the Superficial Geology," 104, 107.

676. It is difficult to identify the plants to which Dawson was referring. A possibility is that one of the mountain saxifrages, *Saxifraga mertensiana* Bong., was once called *Ochraria* Small.

off. Also Cultus Coolie L of the map, near our destination, & part of Tra-Cha-Lake.[677]

July 22 Got a couple of photographs,[678] while camp packing in the morning, & then travelled northward All day, over a fairly good trail, though animals several times mired in bad swamps. Hoped to reach Tsi-tse L. but obliged to Camp about 5 P.m. Short of it, & on the bank of the Main stream of the Blackwater, which we very unexpectedly Came out on. It appears that the river runs from the East, & after doubling round Cultus Coolie L of the map, bends *Eastward*. Bad headache this afternoon.

Hot day.

Jy 23. Started again for Tsi-tse, & about 11 A.m. had the satisfaction of emerging on the main Salmon R & Quesnelle Trail. Found a Note from Seymour*, the promised Cache of supplies, & a mail! with all Sorts of Interesting news. Being Sunday, Camped at once to overhaul the find. Soon after Camping An Indian sent back to Quesnelle by Seymour*, appeared. Wrote answers to Some of letters by him (P. Selwyn*. Walkem*) Read papers, had a bath, Changed plant papers &c.

A fine & very hot day, with threatening of rain in the afternoon.

Jy 24 Travelled Westward about 18. m. to the old Camp at El-guk Lake. The intention now being to rejoin Hunters* party as soon as possible, learn Camby's* plans, & probably move northward to Frazer L. Day fine, rather chilly than warm, with fresh breeze.

Crossed the Blackwater easily by fording where formerly rafted. Paid off our Guide Indian Jim, & gave him A note to give to Mr Seymour* when he sees him at the Salmon House.

[verso]

Paid Indian Jim $22.00 for services as axeman & guide for 11 days.

[end verso]

July 25 Travelled Westward along the trail to Elgatcheo L, camping as before near the Culla Culla House.

[verso]

[Na cou mt.]

[end verso]

A pleasant though warm day. Hoped to get a photo. from the "Summit" but too hazy. Got a view this evening from above Camp show-

---

677. Dawson was tempted to stay a day and ascend the range to the west, but "our provisions being low, and not knowing exactly how far we might have to go to reach the Y. Division of the Railway Survey, thought it hardly safe to do so" (Dawson, "Report on Explorations," 37).

678. See "Photographs," 22 July 1876, GSC136–C1 (PA 37548). A second view does not remain.

ing part of 3rd range, & lake &c.[679]

Saw a few Sober, stupid, matronly-looking grouse, anxious for the safety of their young brood, now just beginning to fly.

The Culla Culla Ho the scene of the great "potlatch" spoken of some time ago. Now deserted by the Indians, who all at the Salmon Ho, or *Yel-tas*. Indians go to Salmon Ho from Eliguck, but not from *Tsi-tse*. The Potlatch in this case seems to have had Some significance, as a feast for the dead, as the two Graves only a few years old, seen here before, are now replaced by structures in shiny new wood, with fresh daubs of paint. The ground below also seems to have been disturbed, & the bodies have probably been reburied. From what I have heard it is probable that the potlatch in Such cases somewhat resembles a "bee" the Indians to getting presents &c. coming together to work at a new Grave for the honoured dead.[680] (see remarks on Indian Chief buried at Tschick Lake).[681]

The well marked line on the *2nd* snowy range (spoken of in other notebook & shown in Some of sketches[682] seems not only to be the end of vigorous timber growth, but to derive additional definitiveness from being the level of the drift plateau or old "Shore line" of July 22. It is remarkably level & distinct as seen from todays country.

Indian names of places.

	1st Snowy range		*It-cha*
	2nd " "		*Il-ga-chúz*
	3rd " "		*Tsi-tsutl*

Anahim's peak *Beece*.

Eliguck of map = *Uhl-ǵhak*

Eliguck stream *Uhl-ghak-Koh*

Lake Called Kultus Coolie on map = *Tsil-be-Kuz*

Hatty Lake of map = *Nats-i-tel-Kuz*.

July 26. All Packed & ready to set out for Hunter's* Party *via* the Iltas-you-coh, when an Indian who had been sent out from the party to Intercept McLeans* train, appeared. Had spent the night with Seymour's* train at Salmon R Crossing. Told us that latter would stay at Crossing all day, also of trail which would take us in near to Hunter's* party. Sent Casinto[683] down to Salmon R Crossing on Pinto, & travelled on by new

679. See "Photographs," 25 July 1876, GSC138–C1 (PA 52370).

680. Feast for the dead re-burial. See 21 June 1876.

681. See 7 July 1876.

682. See G. M. Dawson, Field Notebooks, RG 45, vol. 134, no. 2793, 47v, PAC, for Dawson's comments; and ibid., 80v for a sketch.

683. A Mexican packer with the CPRS.

trail about 8 ½ m. to Kwalcho L.[684] Camped. The lake a fine sheet of water, with a view of Snow Mts of the Coast range beyond its western end. Clean gravelly shore.

This lake Somewhat resembles Tatla in its narrow & long form, & position with regard to the mountains. Can these long lakes running out from the Mountains be explained by glacier action? Seems certain that Cascade Glaciers must have acted as far from the mountains as their Eastern ends stretch. May we suppose that in a somewhat irregular country, the Cascade glaciers were powerful enough by slight erosive action & the transport & rearrangement of Material, without actually hollowing out the lake basins, to *indicate* their position?[685]

Noticed one or two trees of Abies Grandis during today's march

July 27. Started round E end of Lake to find Hunter*. Before reaching it Saw the party moving up the lake on a raft.

Camped together at the E. end. No news from Camby*, or McMillan*, enabling me to decide on future movements.

Mail expected by McLeans* Train within 2 days at latest. Photo. plates also probably by Same train, according to Seymours* information. Mules & horses need a few days rest, backs being now very sore. Also need shoeing.

Found an Indian arrow head near Camp.

July 28. Attending to various repairs & Camp duties. Raining most of day.

Found Some interesting shells on the lake shore. A peculiar species of Linna, besides pretty typical L. Stagnelis. Also physas, an [Ariodon?]. Planorbis exacutus, & trivolvis?[686]

Found a small spongilla[687] growing attached to stones, almost always to the lower surface, & often near points of contact of the stone with those beneath, in such wise, that in lifting the upper stone attachments of the spongilla to the lower are destroyed, leaving it torn. Whole spongilla very

---

684. Qualcho Lake.

685. Dawson's surmise that glaciation would have at least indicated the position of lakes on the eastern side of the Coast Mountains was well-founded, for the movement of the glaciation was out from the mountains in a northeasterly direction. With their enormous erosive powers, the glaciers would have hollowed out basins which could later form lakes.

686. "Linnaea" were snails of the pond snail family Lymnaeidae; "L. Stagnelis" was the great pond snail, *Lymnaea stagnalis jugularis* (Say); "physas" snails of the tadpole snail family Physidae; "Ariodon" is impossible to identify; "Planorbis exacutus" the broad promenetus, *Promenetus exacuous megas* (Dall); and "trivolvis" either the larger prairie ramshorn, *Helisoma trivolvis subcrenatum* (Carpenter), or Binney's stout ramshorn, *Helisoma trivolvis binneyi* (Tryon).

687. A fresh water sponge of the family Spongillidae.

small, varying from the size of a split half pea, to the diameter of about ¾ inch. Many even of Small sized with ovules. Contour of well formed specimens flattened hemispherical, with one or two excellent orifices near the centre. Surface generally finely bristly. Colour pale greyish yellow. Some Specimens growing on more exposed surfaces of stones, have a laxer & more irregular form, seem more bristly in proportion, & are bright green. From what however seem to be transition forms, & the general resemblance, Inclined to think all one species. The difference of appearance being due to different exposure.

July 29 Moved Camp about 2 m. Eastward with Hunter's* party. Camping at a small lake about ¾ m long.[688]

Found spongillas very abundant in the lake, which rather stagnant, with brown, & rather warm water, evidently in Part due to beaver work. Spongillas here growing on Sticks & logs, & though probably all one species, & perhaps Also the same as that of the last lake, several forms represented. In one, generally in shady places the sponge irregularly, though on the whole radially, branching, branches flattened, & ending obtusely. In another, generally found where better light, the branches much longer, & generally acute, the branched portion often forming the elevated Centre of a rather broad flat base. Colour of the specimens bright green. Exhalent app. irregularly placed, not large. General Surface of the sponge rather bristly & irregular in form. [*Illus.*] Showery

July 30. Sunday Employed nearly all day trying to rig up a box to carry the dry plates after exposure & do away with necessity of Pacing them back in papers. Contrived a dark box with paper, Indian ink &c. & a plate box Sent with chemicals by Spencer*.

Threatening in the morning, but eventually a fine & warm day ⟨July⟩ {*July*} *31* Moved Camp about 5. m. Eastward. Walked ahead with Ross* exploring the country. Followed an Indian trail Eastward till struck the brook[689] from Ilgatcheo L. running northward, to the Nechaco. Found a fine grassy hillside where an Indian house, now burnt, had formerly been. Good feed. Hurried back to meet the Mule train & bring them on. Morning spitting rain in the afternoon raining more heavily.

No news yet of McLean* though we are hourly expecting him & his train, with news from Camby*, my new dry plates &c. We are now at the place he was directed to Camp the train at.

Find spongillas again in the brook at which Camped. Growing adherent to stones in the running water. Green, but where shaded yellowish. Generally nearly flat & thin, but when large 2 to 3 & 4 inches in diameter,

688. The lake remains ungazetted.

689. Entiako River.

becoming nearly half an inch thick in the middle, & throw up irregular flattened points exhalent app. rather large, but verry irregular in size & shape, Situated between the projections. General Surface rough, with projecting bundles of spicules.

Probably the same species as the last, though in a different river System.

Aug. 1. Still no word of McLean's* train. Changed plant papers &c. Changed plates in Camera.

Aug. 2. Visited a curious basaltic hill about 1 ½ m. down the Creek from Camp. Columnar basalt. tilted. Collected a number of plants. ⟨Change⟩ Packed all dry plant specimens.

Aug. 3. Went with Ross* to a prominent hill about 1 ½ m from Camp S.E ward, over which the trail to Gatcheo L. passes. A rather remarkable siliceous sinter deposit. Had Johnny pack the Camera up, & though a blustry day with showers took a view of Fawnies Mt[690] & the neighbouring country.[691] Took sketch of country to N. with bearings.

Messenger sent out to Gotcheo L. this morning returned about 2 Pm. with no news of the train. Something must surely have happened to it. Cannot well leave without hearing from Camby* both as to his own plans, & McMillans* position. on the latter depends the quantity of stuff necessary to take from here. Also now, rather short here of several articles of foot. McLean* is also to have my new supply of dry plates, & unless he has horse-shoes there are none for my animals, now nearly without.

Aug. 4. Waiting for news of the train. The ⟨line⟩ axemen Sent out toward Ilgatcheo L not returning, presume that may have met the train at the lake.

Cold windy weather, with wind from S.W. & occasional showers, still continues. Has been the same since we Came here. Cloudy generally stratus. Wind often gusty.

Aug. 5. Train arrived about noon. Having had to go to Quesnelle for some of supplies. Hence delay. No news directly from Camby*, or as to McMillans* Movements. Learn however that Harvey* with some Supplies sent to Fort Frazer. That Camby* gone to Victoria, intending to be at Blackwater on way north on the 12th. McM not yet left vicinity of Is-cul-taes-li. My photo. plates intercepted at Blackwater, & probably sent on with mail matter to Ft Frazer.

Shoes arriving, got horses shod. Made some other arrangements, & wrote letters.

---

690. Fawnie Dome.

691. See "Photographs," 3 August 1876, GSC139–C1 (PA 51038).

G. M. Dawson to Margaret Dawson*, 5 August 1876, Ilgatcheo River

I have been writing to William* & Anna*, & have I fear exhausted all the available news items of this out of the world place. However I enclose Annas* letter under cover to you as there are no secrets in it, & I do not Know what her address may may now be. When I get to Frazer Lake I hope to find a lot of letters to answer & to have a little time to do it in. Just here there is too much time & no inducement to write letters. I just chanced to remember today that I will need some clothes when I return to Civilization & thought if not too much trouble I would ask you to order them for me from Cathie of Edinburgh[692] Probably two tweed Suits with an extra pair of trousers for each would be about what is wanted. {(Trousers *not* lined)} One dark & rather heavy for winter, the other of coarse open textured tweed {light coloured}. Vests double-breasted & coats with a button at the Sleeve. I Suppose there will be time to get these out, & they may await my return to Montreal.

I want to know all about your Metis house, how it looks, & how you like it, & what sort of summer you are having. I dont Know what the weather may be further south & *lower down* but here we have had very little hot weather to complain of during the day & every now & then a skim of ice formed during the night at elevations of 3000′ to 4000′ at which we generally are.

The Mosquitoes black-flies &c. have been very bad at times, but for the present have quieted down a little. The cold nights are a blessing in one way, relieving one from their attacks for a time.

I see by your latest paper that France intends to preserve a "strict neutrality" — so that even if all the rest of Europe is thrown into turmoil by the Turkish trouble,[693] William* is likely to have a quiet time of it in Paris. When does he return, & how is he pleased with the result of his first years study?

Aug. 6. Sunday Got provisions for party for about 20 days Served out & final arrangements made, Mr Hunter* giving every facility. Will send two axemen[694] to accompany me, & 3 mules. one of the latter to be taken back by the axemen after ⟨leave⟩ reaching the Telegraph Trail. Finished writing

---

692. His regular tailor.

693. Dawson's reference is to the conflict developing between Russia and Turkey as a result of risings against the sultan in Bosnia and Herzegovina and the intervention by Serbia and Montenegro on behalf of the insurgents. France was averse to any direct engagement in the Eastern Question. Russia eventually declared war on the Turks on 24 April 1877, in support of the Balkan Slavs.

694. Anderson and McIver, noted at 4 September 1876.

letters &c.

Aug. 7. Monday Got off before 9 A.m. & travelled north eastward, following near the stream from Gatcheo L, which flows past Camp. Trail already Cut out for some miles. Caught up to our axemen about 11 a.m. & Continued on till 4 Pm. Camped on a low flat near Eu-ta-ti-ta-chuck L.[695] The lake an expansion gradually taking place on the stream, & opposite camp shallow with peaty bottom, & many Yellow Pond lillies (Nuphar polyseplum)[696] Travelled about 12 ½ miles

Aug 8. Heavy rain during the night & early morning. Drizzling till 7 a.m. At first in doubt whether to move Camp, but showing signs of Clearing, sent the axemen ahead, got packed & followed them at 9.45 Caught up after going about 2 ½ miles Much bad windfall, obliged most of time to travel along the flat border of the lake through willow & birch bushes. Crossed a large stream from the south near the lower end of the Lake.[697] This joins that we have formerly followed & forms quite a little *river*. Much time lost in looking for crossing of the large stream, & afterwards in getting round a long sleugh on its further bank. About 3 Pm. reached small pretty meadow near the river, which here bending westerly, caused us in a short time in following the high ground to get too far away from it. Found An old trail which perhaps 13 years ago had been cut out for horses. Followed it to the right for a short way, but finding it turning S of East, came back. Now imperative to get down to the river to Camp, so followed the old trail in the opposite direction till lost, & then a direction of W (mag) down to the bottom of the valley. Came out {At 5.30} on a fine wide grassy meadow, with clumps of willow bushes, & the river on the further side running under a tree clad bluff about 150′ above it. Flat topped, & evidently a well defined "bench"

Most of day occupied in driving mules & prospecting trail.

Aug 9. Axemen went ahead early in the morning. Followed with the mules at 9.45. For a few miles, good open country, & then some very bad windfall, which occupied all the rest of the day in cutting through. Got turned away from the lake by bad ground, & did not succeed in getting back to a camping place till 5.25. Next to no feed for the animals. A little thin "sour" grass in a mossy swamp constituting the pasture. Day overcast & showery throughout & in the evening settled rain. Made large fires & got things dry & comfortable as far as possible.

Aug 10. {Started 11: 45 A.m.} Heavy rain in the night, & morning still raining. Waited some time & at last, showing signs of clearing, sent the

695. Entiako Lake.

696. Yellow pond-lily, *Nuphar polysepalum* Engelm.

697. Probably Fawnie Creek.

axemen ahead, & shortly packed up & followed them. Moderately good country for a short way, then bad windfall, then an open Sandy bench along the lake shore, & only about 10′ above the water, let us along easily for a time. Then crowded out to the very edge of the lake by steep banks with heavy windfall, & followed along among & willows & alders, with a good deal of chopping, the rest of the day. Obliged to camp at 6.30 Cold, wet, & tired without finding feed for the animals, now suffering for want. Some of their backs also very sore from long hours in packing, Sores formed on the Na-coont-loon trip opened out afresh. Shower succeeding shower all day & raining heavily again in the evening, after showing some signs of clearing. Clouds above quite thin & light looking & the sun occasionally appearing through them, but rain still continuous.

Aug. 11. Sent men ahead to look for feed & cut trail. Reported swamp grass along edge of lake about ¾ of m off. As all packed, moved on & camped at feed. P.m. went prospecting for trail through a great swamp in which the lake ends. Found the lake shore could be followed for some way, the water being shallow, & bottom hard. In about half a mile however turned to Quaking morass. Men went out to look for way round the swamp & returned about 7 Pm. having found a route. Showers all day.

[verso]

Indian Names of places

Fawnies Mt of Ry maps = Toot-i-ĭ

Long lake opposite the centre of which, & on the south side, Fawnies Mt stands = *Eu-tsu*[698]

Detached Snowy Mt of Cascade Range[699] about 27 m N of *S′-gut-lat* L. (Shown on some sketches, bearing on from lake &c.) *Tsutl-tss-tle* meaning "Small Mt"[700] According to information from Indian "Charley" the N side of the mt descends abruptly to the shore of a long lake, which is very narrow, & called *Natl-took*[701] (meaning narrow) This runs, he does not know how far, into the snowy range, is the main source of the *Ne-cha-ko* & (probably with more or less interruption, as per map subsequently made by "charley" forms the western continuation of *Te-ta′-chuck* Lake.[702]

---

698. Euchu Lake or Natalkuz Lake.

699. Probably Eutsuk Peak, although the more distant, but higher, Wells Gray Peak may be meant.

700. Probably Key Mountain.

701. Natalkuz Lake.

702. This is more or less correct. Natalkuz Lake was fed by the Ootsa River from Ootsa Lake and Tahtsa and Whitesail lakes beyond. Euchu Lake was fed from Tetachuck Lakes, which received its waters from Eutsuk Lake. Natalkuz and Euchu lakes and the

S'-gut-lat = Stick Indian name for first large lake on the *Il-tas-you-co*, called by the coast Indians *Tsoots*?

Large lake according to Charley about 20 m. off {from Hunters* camp 10} & 10 m long running somewhere into S side of *Eu-tsu* Called *Eu-kwa-a-ti-ta-chuck*, or *Eu-ta-ti-ta-chuck*.[703] This must be the lake we are now (Aug 11) following.[704]

[end verso]

Aug. 12. Occupied till nearly 2 P.m. getting round the swamp & across two creeks which run through it to the lake. The second a rather large stream, now flooded by the rains, & full of logs & drift-piles. On getting across found ourselves tangled in a maze of beaver ponds & swamps with water running in all directions, Soft ground, & mud-holes. Mules nearly all down in Succession, & once or twice came near going under water entirely with loads. One Capsized completely & wedged in a small runnell with its feet in the air. P.m. struck good country along the edge of the river bank & followed along with little chopping till 5 P.m. Camped on the edge of the flat land & swamp of the river valley, where a little feed, & opposite the mouth of a Cañon down which the river seems to run.

Aug 13. Finding good grass, & animals & men in want of a rest, remained in camp all day. Wrote up notes, changed plant-papers. Got photograph from little hill behind camp[705] Ascended a hill about 300' high, on the opposite Side of the valley, getting a bearing on Fawnies Peak, & an Idea of the surrounding country. From the lake to this point, the river has followed a [devious?] course in a flat swampy valley, evidently formerly part of the lake. Here, while the wide valley runs on its course for a short distance at least, the water breaks off at right angles, entering a narrow & steep-sided rocky valley. Almost a cañon. Runs for about ¼ m S 80°W, & then turns off N 10°W.

Saw ripe raspberries today. Service berries beginning to Colour.[706] Strawberries pretty abundant in places yet.

Aug 14 left Camp with mules at 9.45 the axemen having gone ahead early. Got into difficulties at once. A mule rolling down a steep side hill. Much time lost in rectifying trail. Pm got into very thick small timber (young pines like oats in a field) & windfall. Got down into river valley & Camped

Nechako which flowed from them are now inundated by the reservoir formed by Kenny Dam.

703. Tetachuck Lake.

704. He seems rather to be on Natalkuz Lake.

705. See "Photographs," 13 August 1876, GSC140–C1 (PA 152387).

706. The "raspberries" were raspberries, *Rubus* spp.; and "Service berries" service berries, *A. alnifolia*.

at 520 beside the stream. Very little feed for animals.

Aug. 15. Up early, & axemen & Mr Bowman off immediately after break-fast. Horses & mules had strayed in search of feed, two of them eventually found across the river. Got away with train at 950. Travelled till 4 P.m. but only made 4.6 miles owing to the rough nature of the river valley, & having to cross the stream three times. Several of the mules down in the swampy edge, & the Cultus mule furnished by Alic McLean* capsized two or three times.

Aug. 16. Travelled on as usual, making about 6 ½ miles, passing the base of Fawnie, & camping on the right bank of the river at a height of 75' above it, in the midst of a tangled windfall. Much pretty fair going today however. River here flowing rapidly in the bottom of a cañon of ov.s. rocks 100' to 150' deep crooked & narrow. An unexpected development, & one which I fear will trouble Hunter* with his line. Men made a fire for their tent, which owing to dryness of timber &c. nearly set the whole windfall off.

Country so dry here that Can hardly have had the rain we experienced some days ago.

[verso]

Saw one or two trees of Abies grandis

[end verso]

Aug 17. {Got a photo of Canon}[707] Started early, & found that the axemen, with B., had got far ahead, having struck good going after burst-ing through the windfall at camp. Followed river for some distance, & then gradually diverged to the right over high gravelly benches & mounds, lightly clad with small poplar & pine. Soon Caught sight of Eu-chu Lake, from a little summit. our long desired point, & really a magnificent sheet of water. Struck down to lake Shore & drove the animals along the beach for about a mile, but found quicksand & mud below the gravel in so many places, that obliged to turn back to the woods, sloped gradually up & went along in partly open & lightly timbered country the rest of the day. Got an imperfect sight eastward from a hill, & bearing to bottom of bay of lake as I thought where good grass appeared. Struck off through the woods toward it, but found that I had seen one of Several small swampy lakes altogether S of the main one. Good feed however, so camped. The S. shore of the lake rises steeply to a height of 100 to 200 feet above the water. No streams enter the lake from the point where first struck to

707. See "Photographs," 17 August 1876, GSC141–C1 (PA 37547). This view was photo-lithographed and included in Dawson, "Report on Explorations," pl. VI, opp. 70.

Camp. Timber Scrub pine, poplar, & birch[708] in abundance, all small & thin.

About 0.3 m from Camp a remarkable rocky hill, about 300' above us. Ascended & got a magnificent view of the unknown country. The lake stretching westward in two long arms. River flowing eastward from lake.[709] Coast Mts in distance through a gap. Many little lakes swamps & green places in the dark woods close at hand. Sunset gradually growing redder. Occupied till last moment sketching & taking bearings, & then scrambled "home" through the brush & windfall in the dark.

Aug. 18. Got a photo. of Mt Fawnie &c.[710] Followed axemen at about 9.30. Struck a good country, & soon found the river flowing out of the great lake. A large magnificent stream more than 180' wide in many places, wide, deep, & clear with Clean bottom. Quite capable of carrying steamboats. No sign of life or present or former human visitors, even the Indians do not seem to frequent this region of country, as we see few marks of their presence & those many years old.

Travelled on over a wonderful moraine country bordering the river with pretty good going, though meeting unexpected swamps & lagoons which sometimes turn us back. Crossed a small river Coming from the south,[711] when B. & the men struck Eastward into the woods with the idea of cutting off a bend of the main stream. Got into bad windfall &c. & it being camping time, turned back & slanted down into valley of small river to where foot meadow. Camped with splendid feed for animals.

Bushes loaded with service-berries, now in many places ripe, & finer than I have ever seen, abound on many of the grassy hills. Pigeon berries[712] ripe in good exposures. *Viburnum opulus* beginning to colour. Bunch grass or grass resembling it common on southern Slopes today, also *Artemisia frigida.*

Aug. 19. on leaving camp had very good travelling, for a time ⟨of⟩ over lightly timbered Sandy flats & ridges. Then ran into a heavy mass of windfall, where a bend of the river forced us up to the steep South bank. Got about 1 ½ m during the afternoon. Camped on the bank of the river,

708. Western white birch, *Betula papyrifera* Marsh., or the water or black birch, *Betula occidentalis* Hook.

709. The "two long arms" were Natalkuz and Euchu lakes (now Intata and Euchu reaches of the much enlarged Natalkuz Lake reservoir. The river is the Nechacko.

710. See "Photographs," 18 August 1876, GSC142–C1 (PA 37546). This view was photo-lithographed and included in Dawson's, "Report on Explorations," pl. III, opp. 40.

711. Chedakuz Creek.

712. Bunchberry, *C. canadensis*.

late.

Aug 20. Horses had strayed in search of feed. Started rather later than usual, but striking in the main an open country, made a fair day's march. Camping only a few miles from the base of the step-like Mountain, seen from a distance, in the telegraph range.[713] The river here makes a great bend to the west & a large brook[714] joins it at the angle, from the East. Good feed for the animals for once.

Aug. 21. Off pretty early & travelled westward along the river over good ground for some distance. When river, however, began to turn northward to our course again, windfall appeared, & the valley continued rough & full of fallen timber. Camped at 6 P.m. cold, wet, & tired, on the bank of the river, here flowing in a Cañon 100′ below us. Blustry cold wind during the day, with showers of sleet & hail, & occasional rumbling of distant thunder. The river valley runs N. mag. for about 1 ¾ m from camp, then turns about N 30°W & at a distance of about 12 m. bears about N 20°W, & seems to turn abruptly to the East. It appears however to be too rough & full of windfall to follow further with any comfort. It will be best probably to strike Straight across the high-ground to presumed position of Chaka Lake.[715] We cannot be far from the Telegraph Trail though All Sorts of difficulties seem to intervene between us & it, which is very provoking when Mr Cambie* is probably before this at Fort Frazer, expecting me.

Aug 22 Horses & mules strayed away in search of feed. Got all packed up & ready. By 1 Pm all found but "Frank". Evident could not move today. Sent Casinto & Indian Johnny out again to look for Frank. Returned with him at 6 P.m. B. & the axemen out cutting trail. Changed plant-papers, wrote up notes, & got a photo. of the river Cañon.[716] Heavy fall of hail, covering the ground to the depth of half an inch at about 10 A.m. lay unmelted in the shade for rest of day.

Found a rude Indian arrow-head *beneath* the root of an overturned tree, in the soil attached to it. Tree not a large one, but arrow well buried in the surface Gravel & probably ancient.

Aug 23. Animals again strayed away but all recovered without much trouble. Started & travelled along trail cut yesterday. Got along well till one of horses (Dan) fell off the edge of a beaver-dam by which we were

---

713. Possibly Cutoff Butte. The Nechacko Range must be meant.

714. Big Bend Creek.

715. Tachick Lake.

716. See "Photographs," 27 August 1876, GSC143–C1 (PA 37545). This view was photo-lithographed and included in Dawson's, "Report on Explorations," pl. IV, opp. 44.

Crossing a swamp, into a bottomless Mud-hole. Thought at one time would have to abandon him, as all our efforts could not extricate him, & he appeared to be growing weak, & would not struggle even when beaten severely. At last got turned round by chance, & after wallowing through the mud some distance, got out on the grass. Did not get far on account of windfall, & dense thickets of small Pine. Camped in a small ravine, which apparently runs eastward to the Chellacoh.[717]

Aug 24. Got a pretty early start, & travelled till 5 P.m. but only made about 2 ½ miles on account of the extremely bad windfall incountered. Camped on border of Sluggish stream, with fair meadow grass for horses; about half a mile from a dome like hill of basalt with cliff & slide to the creek.

Very provoking to be so near our journeys end & not be able to get out on the telegraph trail.

Aug 25 Good going through open country along the bank of the Creek. Struck an Indian trail, which followed for some miles till it Crossed creek at Beaver dam.[718] Soon after lost the trail in a huge windfall. Got involved in fallen timber, & hard chopping all Pm. Lucky just before dark to strike on a pool with a little water & feed, in a hollow. ⟨Showery⟩ Tented in a tangled mass of fallen trees after cutting away logs enough to spread.

Aug 26 Rain during the night, & still raining in morning. Explored the neighbourhood, & found a way out of the windfall. Got into a belt of green timber & followed it, though a little off our course. Seemed to lead down to Supposed valley of Chaka L. got pretty good open sandy terrace country, & expecting every moment to see the lake, when suddenly surprised & staggered to find a great river instead. The Ne-cha-Ko again making another bend, our easting having been considerably overestimated. Camped late on the border of the stream. Showery till evening.

Aug 27 Would gladly have given men & animals a rest, both much in need of it, but now scarcely 5 or 6 days food left, & bacon practically done. Position much behind what had thought, & do not Know what sort of country may meet ahead. Travelled on through a pretty open country, though obliged to make a very tortuous course to keep it. Camped at 4.30 at *the* great bend, which had thought found last Sunday.

Saw a very old Indian trail today running down from the high benches to the river flat, also a blazed line, which ran in Same direction, a little further on, & terminated abruptly on the front of a clay bluff. Neither of them any use to us.

---

717. Chilako River. Dawson is now following Cutoff Creek.

718. Probably Cutoff Creek.

Showers during the day, & distant thunder.

Aug. 28. Followed round the bend of the river, & crossed a small stream running into it from the East. The river from here runs northward, gradually diverged from the immediate valley, edging up on the slopes of the mountain to the East, following open burnt ground, covered with low bushes, with much pea-vine, & thickets of raspberries loaded with fruit. Saw a black bear shambling away round the end of a hill, disturbed in his meal on the berries. Camped late, having some difficulty in finding feed & water without going down into river valley which very bad with windfall. Rain during part of afternoon & evening. Good Going most of day, & made a fair march.

Aug 29. Started pretty early though overcast & raining. Caught up to trailmakers after going about 2.5 miles. Found them standing round a fire drying themselves, & professing to be "played out". Much disappointed at this action as provisions now getting alarmingly short. Camped. P.m. cleared. B. & axemen went out exploring, got about 1 ½ m. of trail made, a route selected, & saw Chaka L. at an estimated distance of about 10.m. E.N.E. myself, from a prominent hill see country all flatting down northward, & a transverse E.W. valley at base of range of mts in which Frazer L. no doubt lies. Examined rocks, Repaired barometer &c.

Aug 30. Early start, & travelled on easily through pretty open country Eastward, gradually ascending on the flank of a mountain to the s, & finally gaining a good view of the lake & surrounding country. Then descended, & continued on, generally following open burnt Sandy ridges, & pushing to get out to the trail this evening. Got at last into rather worse ground, & finally penetrated a belt of standing dead timber, with some windfall, & came out on a Small lake or pond, which as first seen through the trees was taken for Chaka. Camped on the swampy edge of the lake which evidently dammed back by beavers, & surrounded by a belt of dead bushes & trees, Killed by the rise of the water. A fine day.

Aug. 31. After a little exploration & chopping extricated ourselves from the windfall, & got out again into a pretty open country, mostly burnt over. Got along quickly, though the lake almost seemed to recede from us as we advanced, & finally to our great joy came out on the long desired Telegraph Trail at 1.50 P.m Got a standing tree cut off at 4 feet from ground, squared, & marked as follows. (Pioneer Trail & blazed line to Ne-cha-ko R, Gatcheo L. & Salmon R. To Hunter's* Camp ⟨Aug. 7⟩ (6. miles N of Gatcheo L. (Aug.7.) 100 miles. G.M. Dawson A. Bowman*. Geological Survey of Canada. Aug 31. 1876). Got a small squared post also driven in on the edge of the trail, that the other (a few yards off) might not be missed by anyone searching for it. The point just at the S.E. corner of Chaka L About ½ m. from the water's edge.

Travelled on the Tel. Tr. for about 2 miles, when the bell horse, through shere stupidity & weakness fell off a bridge into a bad mud-hole. lost about an hour trying to get him out, & being then 4 Pm. Camped, Knowing that must have a good day's work out of the animals tomorrow.

Country fertile looking & chereful compared to any we have seen for some time, partly open, & with light groves of poplar, & fine meadows & slopes of grass & pea vine.

Plotted up work to date &c.

Sept. 1. Started early & travelled fast on the Tel. Tr. Came across a small patch of turnips which someone had sown beside the road, & made an assault on them just as they were. Not full grown yet. Passed Several parties of Indians Gathering service berries, which grow here to an extra-ordinary Size & in great profusion.[719] Met Packer Frank Harvey* on his way southward. Learn that Mr Cambie* has left for Francois lake & Country to S. about a week ago. Harvey* to wait for him on a point on the Ne-cha-ko R. Cambie* thinks from our being so late, either that something must have happened to us or that we have turned back.[720] No provisions belonging to CPRS now left here, & little or nothing at Ft Frazer.[721] Harvey* turns back with us to arrange matters, shoe our horses &c. Camp on the border of the river, & send an Indian to the Fort for our mail, which deposited there.

Sept. 2. Showery & lowering all day. Send axemen over to Ft to grind axes, & Mr B. to see about getting supplies for their return. Working myself at map & notes, & overhauling mail. On return B reports that he Can get nothing Mr Alexander,[722] the gentleman in charge has gone to Ft St James,[723] & not expected back till this evening. Mrs A. & a couple or subordinates will not take the responsibility of letting us have anything.

Fished a little while in the river this evening with poor luck. Only two salmon have yet come up, & the Indians expect the run will not be any, &

---

719. Saskatoon berries or "service-berries" *A. alnifolia*, were the most popular and widely used of all berries and fruits eaten by the interior British Columbia Indians. See Turner, *Food Plants of Interior Peoples*, 180–82.

720. Cambie had waited from 18 August to 25 August for Dawson but, running short of supplies and feeling that Dawson must have turned back, started alone. See Cambie to G. M. Dawson, 27 August 1876, Dawson Family Papers, MUA.

721. Originally a North West Company fort built by Simon Fraser in 1806, the post was taken over by the Hudson's Bay Company in 1821 and operated until 1900.

722. J. M. L. Alexander, who had been made a junior chief trader in 1875, was appointed a factor in 1879.

723. Originally known as Stuart Lake Fort or Fort Nakasley, it was built by John Stewart and Simon Fraser in 1806. Fort St. James eventually became the chief Hudson's Bay Company post in the New Caledonia District.

consequently a hard winter.

Sept 3. Harvey* must start tomorrow morning to make sure of Keeping his appointment with Mr Cambie*. Wish the axemen to go along with him, but have no food to send with them. Start about noon with a half-breed in Canoe for Ft Frazer. Wait a long time before the ⟨boy⟩ {young man} in charge could be found & finally hear that he will give us nothing Mr Alexander* not yet having returned. Explained matters to Mrs A. in bad french, & finally got 50 lbs of flour, & a piece of beef weighing perhaps 20 lbs. Got back to Camp in Canoe just before dark.

Ft Fraser consists of several tumbled down & dilapidated log houses, Standing in the middle of an open flat piece of ground not much elevated above the lake. To the south a range of hills & cliffs bounding the valley. A pile of drift Sand in the space in front of the buildings, old boots & moccasins, tin pans &c. strewn about. Groups of hungry, & dejected looking dogs wandering restlessly about in Search of food. (now on account of failure of salmon given only a little milk to live on) In the open poplar woods surrounding the fort cattle feeding, (a drove of perhaps 30 or 40 fine animals.

G. M. Dawson to John William Dawson*, 3 September 1876, Fort Fraser

I write this short note by a Chance which offers, but which may or may not carry it through to mail in reasonable time,— just to let you know of my continued welfare.

We had a very rough country between the place at which my last was dated, & this. A mass of windfall & thick timber & other abominations; & into the bargain bad weather. By sticking to it we made the trip in twenty-five days, arriving on the Telegraph Trail, just as our provisions were almost entirely out. Owing to the great time occupied, I find, that Mr Cambie* has now been about a week gone on his François Lake trip. He intends to leave the lake Somewhere, & go across the country to the south in Some direction he has heard of as being practicable, with a number of Indians to carry his Stuff. As soon as I can get the arrangements made, I propose starting to Circumnavigate François Lake on my own account. This *may* take ten days, after which I *may* Go down the Ne-cha-ko River to Fort George, sending the Pack Animals round there to meet me.

I do not write at length, feeling uncertain as to the promptitude with which this letter will reach Quesnel.

Sept. 4. Told men (Anderson & McIver)[724] that could give them the

---

724. James Anderson, axeman, and perhaps John McIvor, a sometime farmer on the North

provisions now Obtained to return to Mr Hunter's* camp. Could get nothing more to make up ration bill. That if they thought they could do on this they might start with Harvey*, we giving them the best mule we have got, & the fly belonging to my tent. The provisions *plenty*, but no bacon & will probably be reduced to bread before many days. Men decide to go. Furnish them besides beeff & flour mentioned yesterday with plenty tea, coffee, Sugar, & some apples. Also with fishing apparatus. B. finishes tracing of track Survey map. Write letter to Mr Hunter* to accompany it, also note to Mr Cambie*, note to Father*.

Get crossed over the river by Canoe, & Swim the animals before noon, pack, & camp within about 200 yards of Ft Frazer.

Evening Mr Alexander* arrives, but was unable to get Any bacon or other supply at Ft St James. Seems quite willing to do everything in his power for us. Arrange to see him again tomorrow morning.

Sept. 5. enquiring about Indians & Canoes & trying to get arrangements made for François Lake Trip.

Salmon. Mr Alexander* believes that a really good run of salmon only comes up here once in 5 years. Then very numerous, next year less, next still less, next almost none, & then a fine run again. This year the worst of the series. Formerly Salmon came up every year in quantity. Indians do not know what to make of the decline, & had for a long time an idea that the whites had put a complete iron grating across the river lower down, & that what few fish came, got through when this net lifted to take out the fish. used to importune HB people &c. to get this barrier taken away, if only for one day in the week &c. The salmon coming up here are a small variety about 2 feet long. They run up into Francois Lake, but not further S. on the Ne-cha-ko. Mr. A. has seen them also as far north as the upper waters of the Driftwood R. S of Bear Lake! (see Trutch's map) This must be about their farthest. A few large salmon also come up, but these proceed up the Ne-cha-ko, though probably not above the Cañon & rapids.[725]

Ft Connelly[726] of the map on ⟨Great⟩ Bear Lake, is still extant, & there is some sort of communication between it & a post lately established on

Thompson River.

725. The "small variety" of salmon was probably the sockeye salmon, *Oncorhynchus nerka* (Walbaum); and the "large Salmon" probably the chinook salmon, *Oncorhynchus tshawytscha* (Walbaum).

726. Or Fort Connelly, it was located at the north end of Bear Lake. The original fort was built in 1826 on an island in the lake.

the S branch of the Finlay R.[727] Also communication to latter place by McLeod Ft & Peace R. "McDonalds oil spring" of Trutch's map is a curious affair. Said to be a conical mound of stony material (probably travertin)[728] about 6′ high, with a basin like hollow in the centre, in which many bones, feathers &c. of birds & small animals such as squirrels. The Indians say birds flying along hover over the place a moment & then fall in dead. Mr. A. climbed on top & poked it up with a stick & says whether from imagination or not, began to feel giddy. (Probably issue of Carbonic Acid) No oil seen, only ferroginous skins on surrounding swamp water. Near Bear Lake, from description probably basaltic formation.

Ft Babine[729] Supplied chiefly by the Skeena R. Spring & Autumn the Coast Indians bring stuff up in Canoes, & then carry it across portage to head of Babine Lake. Could get Indians at Stewart L to head of lake. There get other Indians to Ft Babine on head of Lake, & if connection possible with Coast Indian canoes, very easily get down ⟨to⟩ Skeena R. Old Telegraph Trail as far as Skeena Crossing used in driving Cattle to Cassiare, & probably quite passable.

Formerly H.B. Co grew wheat, barley, &c. besides potatoes, turnips beets &c. The latter three still Cultivated & successful, though potatoe tops often killed by Summer frosts, in some localities. The place where H.B now raise potatoes however, has so far been free from frost. Mr. A. believes the Seasons are changing within the last 8 or 9 years. Formerly much rain in the winter & mild weather, last two winters Cold & severe throughout. Summer frosts formerly unknown, now common. Snow average on level about 2.½ to 3 feet at close of winter. Horses & those Cattle not specially cared about are allowed to winter out, & get through very well.

Sept. 6. Making arrangements for departure, with regard to stores, Indians &c. Mr Alexander supplies All he has flour, beef, potatoes, sugar, a little butter, coffee, matches &c. & about 15 lbs of bacon. Take plenty flour tea & sugar for trip, as much beef as will keep. Get loan of a net, & take tackle & ammunition, hoping when beef runs short to supply ourselves with fish or game. Mr. A. allows me privilege of returning any of these stores not used, & re supplying him with others from CPRS if afterwards [....]. What not returned in either way to be settled for on return. Walked

---

727. Dawson's reference is to Fort Grahame, the most northerly post in the Fort St. James region, located sixty-five miles north of the junction of the Parsnip and Peace rivers.

728. Or travertine, a kind of calc-tuff deposited by certain hot springs.

729. Fort Babine, at the north end of the west arm of Babine Lake, was built in 1872 to tap the trade from the coast to the recently opened Omineca gold fields. It superseded the older fort built on the lake in 1822.

over to Indian Village[730] at outlet of Fraser Lake, about 1 ¾ m. from fort. Bought Some berry cake to Supplement Supplies. Indians have a few fair log houses & a little Church much on the general plan of that at Ft George. Most of Indians now scattered about drying service-berries, which unusually Abundant this year. The process generally as follows— Berries boiled or parboiled in Kettles, or in a large bark cauldron heated by stones. Juice which runs from them carefully collected. Berries spread out on frames made of thin wood, Split up in pieces to about the Size of lattis & fixed with bark lashings to form a clue grating of parallel strips. These frames arranged horizontally on stages, below which fire kept Smouldering. Gradually dry, & when at right Stage, the juice again added & the whole flattened out into cakes about 2 feet long, 15 inches wide & ¾ inch thick. These dried on same stages over fire & in sun, & then Stored for use.

Canoe & men engaged not turning up till ten pm. began to be anxious, thinking they were about to back out. Had just sent messenger to their camp — 4 m. off, when they arrived.

Decide to Send Casinta down to Blackwater, with an Indian boy to help him, & orders to pack as much stuff up as he can on his well animals without overloading.

Wrote letters for dispatch. Home, McMillan*, Dr Tolmie*, & Mr C. Good* Enclosing in latter Cheque for freight charges paid by B.C. Govt. on delayed Centennial Goods.

[verso]

Sept. 2. Indian with Canoe to Ft Fraser $2.00
       3.   "   "   " 2.00
       4. Canoe Crossing supp over river 3.00
       6. Berry Cake (Indians) 2.00
[end verso]

G. M. Dawson to Margaret Dawson*, 6 September 1876, Fort Fraser

A few days ago I sent off a note to Father* by a rather Circuitous route, announcing my arrival in this part of the world, after having made the traverse from Salmon River —. A traverse occupying much more time & labour than I had anticipated. Having now a better chance of writing with some prospect of early delivery at Quesnel, I embrace it to scribble a few lines letting you know where I am, in case the first mentioned note should

730. Morices's "Natle" (Morice, "Carrier Sociology," pl. II), called "Naul-tey," by Dawson in his published report (Dawson, "Report on Explorations," 46).

misscarry.

If tomorrow morning is calm & fine, I hope to start for François Lake, & will not be back to this place again for ten, twelve, or fifteen days —as the case may be. All arrangements are made, & the Indians hired for Canoe have just turned up. The party will consist of Self, Mr. Bowman*, My Indian Cook &c. Johnny, & two Indians of this neighbourhood —names unknown. The packer & pack animals I am sending back to the CPRS Depôt at Blackwater for stores, having had to supply myself largely from the H. Bay fort here for the present.

Francois Lake disposed of I intend doing a few days work in this vicinity, then descending the Ne-cha-ko R to Ft George; & from there will be on the homeward track, with greater or less interruptions by the way.

We had a very rough trip through to here being 25 days on the way, & never meeting an Indian to give us any information, or coming across a trail going in our direction. Nothing but windfall & brule, & thick woods, with a country sometimes rugged in itself, & lots of bad weather making the landscape uncommonly dismal. Finally we broke out on the Telegraph Trail with just about two days flour & tea, & nearly everything else in the way of supplies finished.

I have Several unanswered letters from Anna*, William*, & Rankine*, responses to which I must still delay, & for the present send good wishes & love only.

The weather now seems settled & fine, & there is little or no appearance of Autumn yet. Frosts we have had at night from time to time all summer, but now though further north, we are lower down, & seem to have got into a more genial climate. The H.B. have a fine band of Cattle here, & a little farm, in which they raise potatoes, &c. Wheat & barly formerly grown are now neglected, & flour imported by the Telegraph Trail from the Southern part of the Country, & worth 20.c. a pound! Other prices in proportion. The H.B. Ft consists of a few dilapidated shanties. A new building is in course of preparation at some little distance. The gentleman in charge—a Mr Alexander*—is a well educated & *gentlemanly* man, is married to a rather good looking half breed & has a family of Small Children running about.

Sept. 7. After some delay, get all unnecessary Stuff packed in H.B. Store, canoe ready, & off by 9.15. Fine day with light breeze on lake. Indians about here very grasping. One came to camp this morning & had the cheek to ask $1.50 for three ducks he had shot. One of Canoe men complained that he had no blanket. Took no notice of the complaint, treating the matter as if entirely his affair. Finally, seeing he could get nothing, he got from an attendant friend — a blanket, before leaving, which had evidently been in reserve all the time. Men brought only 2 paddles in Canoe. The friend of course had another for Sale at a high price. Mr. A. Kindly found one more paddle for me, & eventually I bought "the Friends" too At a reduced rate. &c. &c.

Camped as I judge, about half way up the Stellaco R between F. Fraser & Francois or Ni-to-bun-Kut.

A neat looking Indian village[731] of 4 log houses, besides various outbuildings & shanties & a church, just within the mouth of the river on the S. side. Here saw a man who been with Mr Cambie* & returned when he left Francois Lake. Has been gone now from latter place 5 days. Paddles easily across Fraser Lake, & spent rest of afternoon poling up the rapid & tortuous Stellaco.

Douglas fir Again abundant round shores of Fraser Lake, though not observed in wanderings from lower Blackwater to this place.

Choke Cherry Noticed a few bushes of this plant near Ft Fraser
[verso]
Sept. 7. Paddle $1
[end verso]

Sept 8 Off early & at work all day, excepting time spent ashore at lunch, working slowly up the Stellaco. A fall of 5 feet half a mile above camp necessitating portage of all stuff, & many bad rapids, some requiring portage of less or more of stuff. Camped about half a mile along the N. shore of Francois Lake.

Saw many fine trout in river, shot a duck & grouse. Fine grassy hills on N bank of river near lake, with bunch grass, & in dry spots Sage.

Indians skilfull & worked well at poling. One great part of time in water, with nothing on but Shirt & breach cloth. Extraordinary mixture of languages in common use by the Indians obtained at Ft Fraser. Chinook, Canadian french, & their proper language indiscriminately mixed with fragments of English, the latter chiefly consisting of phrases new here perhaps but worn out elsewhere, such as *you bet*, & others of all sorts, picked up from whites. A fine warm & calm day.

Sept 9. Off early, & coasting all day along the N shore of Francois Lake. Clear sky & warm sun, with water as smooth almost as glass. Pretty little flats & points fringed with clean stony beach & alder, & covered with poplar, with undergrowth of pea-vine, epilobium &c. Steep banks in places beautifully coloured with first tints of Autumn affecting the shrubs

---

731. Morice's "Stella" (Morice, "Carrier Sociology," pl. II). Dawson comments about this and the other village nearer Fort Fraser (his Naul-tey) that they were "each inhabited by a few families, the remnants of a once more numerous tribe, who appear to live in comparative comfort and cultivate small garden patches, but are neither industrious nor cleanly" (Dawson, "Report on Explorations," 46).

& ⟨bushes⟩ herbs.

Keep track survey to locate observations, & examine rocks at all points, & frequently at intermediate places.

Get from my Indians (whose "country" is Stony Creek) the names of several constellations &c.

Great bear	called	*Yah-' ta* meaning *Old man.*
Corona borealis	"	*Eu-noo-tse-zil* meaning *Kequally House*

(Chippewas Call sweating boothe)

Group of 4 Small stars just East of the 3 prominent ones of *Aquilla* called *Ta-tsi* meaning The *ducks.*

Milky way called *Ya-ka-tsool-k* meaning The snow-shoe track (Chippeways Call the wavey's road)

Aurora Borealis Called *Ni-ha-pa-tun-ut* meaning as far as I can make out, — the fire or light Coming immediately before the snow.

Pleides Called *Sum-ni-tan-li* meaning Cariboo

[Draft of a poem, dated François Lake, 1876]

> I turned the page & slowly turned
> The yellow paper stained & old
> & marked what leaf was fairly writ
> & which was blotted & half told
> Of wearyness or grief or joy
> The hand had felt in its employ
> & where at length the pen was stayed
> & life's last entry weakly made.
> I read not words nor cared to know
> What thoughts had filled {thronged} the silent brain
> The story of a life was there
> ⟨The⟩ {An} echo of the old refrain.
> I knew I would not find enscribed
> The thoughts of night, the words of prayer
> The looks of love or hate & all
> That made ⟨makes⟩ {made} life {truly} dark or fair.
> All all had faded in the night
> Save what poor [outline?] here was spared

Sept. 10. Coasting along N. shore of Lake with fine weather & calm water. Beautiful views, changing rapidly as we round point after point. Surprise an Indian family in their camp at the border of the lake. Engaged in drying service berries, & present me with a small Sample of the fruit, which duly acknowledged by a Small return of tobacco. Seem fat & well fed between berries, fish, & bears. one of the latter must have been lately killed as paws hanging up still fresh. My Indians have all Sorts of news to exchange & at last can hardly tear them away. See growing on the shore a *Juniper*[732] which attains the dimensions of a small tree, having a trunk nearly 14 inches diameter, with ropy bark like the Cedar. Height not great, about 20′.

Camp on a low point with a beautiful outlook up & down the lake. Take a photo. looking down before sunset.[733]

Net set last night, this morning yielded 1 fine Salmon trout about 3 pounds,[734] & 5 large suckers.

Being Sunday the Indians seem to have extra devotions to perform, & in addition to the usual evening Prayer, have a sort of humming choral service morning & evening. When repeating prayers &c. kneel together on the beach or wherever convenient. The bishop has lately made the round of this part of the country,[735] & has no doubt stirred up much extra piety.

Where stopped for lunch, found an old canoe drawn up, & near it, tied to a piece of bark-string, & depending from a pole, a bundle of weeds, about 9 inches long, neatly folded together, & a piece of spruce bark, on the inner Side of which roughly drawn a figure something like that opposite. [*Illus.*] Could not quite understand the Indians explanation of these signs, but appears that the Indian owning the canoe left it here, & not having returned, or been seen for a long time, is supposed to be dead. These signs put up by some of his friends to make this known

Sept. 11. Following N. shore all day & Camped in the evening in the middle of the low ground at the head of the lake, on a low sandy beach. A fine day & the lake beautifully Calm with the exception of about one hour in the morning. Find that neither of our Indians have been further on the lake than *Noo-cho* Island (Big Island) & Consequently know nothing about it.

Caught a fine salmon trout, about 8 lbs, with the spoon; & this evening two ducks shot by one of the Indians. At this upper end of the lake, a stretch of marshy ground with many ducks, geese, cranes &c. frequenting it.

Saw a large bear this morning on a hillside rising from the water. The Indians instantly landed, & went after him, but he was too quick, & did

---

732. Rocky Mountain juniper, *J. scopulorum.*

733. See "Photographs," 10 September 1876, GSC147–C1 (PA 51051).

734. Lake trout, *Salvelinus namacycush* (Walbaum).

735. The Catholic bishop, Paul P. Durieu, who had been consecrated bishop of New Westminster only a year earlier, made a trip northward in the summer of 1876 to observe firsthand the mission work under his supervision.

not let himself be seen again.

Should much like to get on Na-din-a Mt beyond the W. end of the lake, but Indians do not Know whether any trail going towards it, or whether the little river[736] entering the lake is navigable. The mt probably 10.m. off & from 3000 to 4000 above the lake. Snow in patches still visible on it.

The elder of the two Indians Called *Je-sin* (probably the Indian equivalent of Jason!) drew up a map of Eu-chu & the country to the south, very correctly. Find that the Stream followed down to Eu chu is called the *Kes-le-Ko*, that below Eu-chu, on which Camped one night, the *Ched-il-kes*[737]

Sept. 12. Find my Indians do not Know anything about this part of the country, or whether the Nadinako R[738] is navigable or not, or if any Trails going westward toward Nadina Mt, from which a fine view might be obtained. Decide to try the river, & if possible ascend it to near the mountain. Get up about 5 miles, following an extremely tortuous course, & at last find the "river" which is deep & still in its lower part, turning into a mere brook with swift Current, & becoming too shallow for our Canoe. Return to Hunters* furthest, which marked by a post, about 3 m up the river, & after taking a photo.[739] descend again to the lake & begin return on its S. shore. Camp nearly opposite Noo-cho Island.

Now almost regret that did not start for Nadina even if two or three days occupied so. Taking enough food along, & blankets, cannot have been more than 12 or 13 miles from our furthest Rocks from appearance, & drift on base of Nadinako, no doubt older volcanic, but one might form a good idea of the country from this height.

A fine & warm day, with a little breeze from the eastward after noon, but now almost calm.

Sept. 13. Coasting along S. shore continuing examination, & measuring A base with micrometer[740] to fix certain points. When {nearly} opposite *Chez nun* Mt[741] stop for lunch, & then run across the lake to N. side, measuring back on base fixed before leaving, & securing points for triangulation to correct track survey. Camp at base of mt, intending to ascend it in the morning. Day fine & calm, & not oppressively warm Net

736. Nadina River.

737. Chedakuz Creek.

738. Nadina River.

739. See "Photographs," 12 September 1876, GSC148–C1 (PA 51050).

740. A Rochon micrometer is a telescope with internally mounted crosshairs by which intercepts could be measured on a rod held by an assistant at a distance. The distance could then be calculated.

741. Possibly Mount Colley.

yielded but one trout, & a few Suckers, last night.

Sept 14. Started immediately after breakfast with B. & the two Indians to ascend Chez-nun Mt, which found to be about 800′ high. Forced our way through dense thickets of poplar, with open patches & undergrowth of rank Epilobiums, Heracleums & tangled pea-vine; & then slowly clambered up the steep grassy front of the hill, where patches of Amelanchier & *Choke-cherry* abundant. When about ⅔ up Indians motion silence, having seen a bear at some distance below. Je-son rushes down the mountain again with a gun, & we wait above to see what success. Bear however not again seen. Must be very abundant here, as this same place where we saw a large one on way up the lake, & Indians saw & fired at another early in the morning. From Summit a very fine view, the long river like lake running almost to the horizon in both directions. Much fine flat fertile & partly open land on both sides of lake. Occupied all morning sketching & taking bearings. After lunch crossed the lake & continued along S. shore till 5.30 Day rather threatening & barometer falling, but continued calm & fair.

Caught with spoon, just before Camping, a fine salmon trout of 10 lbs & a large ordinary trout of about 4 ½ or 5 lbs. both in excellent condition.

Indians tell me with regard to my Island No. 2. (for name see track Survey)[742] that a story firmly believed — that a monster in the shape of a gigantic fish of some kind inhabits its vicinity, which is in the habit of swallowing any too daring explorer, — as I understand it — Canoe & all![743]

Poplars (aspens) beginning to show yellow tints in some exposed situations.

Sept. 15. Morning rather windy, & with low & falling barometer, afraid that travelling today might be interfered with. No weather however to stop us, & now nearly calm. Measured a new base, connected as well as could with points of old, & continued survey & examination of ⟨point⟩ S. side of lake

Surf of this mornings formation still beating in on beach with dull Sound.

Sept 16. Continued along S. shore of lake, Carrying on old points, & fixing a new base. Wind rather much at times, but only once in a squall obliged to make time for shore, with Some water in the canoe. Lost about half an hour on this occasion. Several slight showers during P.m. Trolling spoon-bait hooked a very large Salmon Trout, about 15 or 20 lbs. Drew

---

742. See G. M. Dawson, Field Notebooks, RG 45, vol. 134, no. 2795, 25v, PAC, where it is named "Tatl-gaz-noo Id."

743. See below, 16 September.

him cautiously in toward canoe, & Saw his grey-green back & large fins through the water for an Instant, then Charly making an effort to stab him with the knife, he made a great struggle & went off spoon bait & all to our great regret, as we had nothing for dinner. Camped early & got the net set out.

Foliage of poplars now beginning Sensibly to become yellow in many places. Foliage generally about this lake much more varied than usual. Spruce (, probably Engelmannii) abundant also A. Douglasii, especially on mountains. Spruce with large upright purple cone — rare. P. contorta sparingly. Juniper. White & black birch, aspen, balsom, Alders & willows attaining a tree like growth on low points. Amelanchier in Some places 12 feet high. Choke-Cherries &c. &c. in undergrowth. Notice also a small leaved bushy maple, & large thickets of Viburnum[744] heavy with berries.

Level of water & state of lake at various seasons. Highest water mark on rocks 4 feet above present stage. Various other lines below this. Water last spring must have been nearly or quite up to highest mark by beach marks shown me by Indian Charley, showing water level when he was here fishing, "after the leaves were out". Confirmed also by very abundant deposit of pollen of conifers with sticks &c. nearly 4 feet above present line (June?) Indians now with me, & others formerly, tell & have told me that this lake exceptional in its winter behaviour. The lake remains unfrozen long after the snow covers the surrounding country, & (as I understand it) in Some mild winters does not freeze at all, generally however ice forms, which may remain only a short time late in the winter & then "wake si-a warm — illihie"[745] goes away. In Severe winters remains 4 moons, but even then goes away early. The only other lake behaving in the same way, Known to these Indians — Na-to-bun-Kut or Babine Lake. On Fraser L. Chaka L. &c. ice always remains 5 months. Water high in the early Summer.

[verso]

Na-to-bun-Kut = long, or far away, lake

[end verso]

Learn some additional particulars with regard to the *monster* inhabiting this lake. Called *Klug-us-cho* or the big snake, & said to have a head a yard or more across. Lives in the mud at the bottom of the lake, or down in the earth below it, I cannot tell which, & occasionally comes forth in

---

744. The "Spruce with large upright purple cone" was probably the black spruce, *P. mariana*; the "White birch" the western white birch, *B. papyrifera*; "black birch" the black or water birch, *B*; "balsom" the balsam poplar, *Populus balsamifera* L. ssp. *balsamifera*; the "bushy maple" Douglas maple, *A. glabrum* var. *douglasii*; and "Viburnum" the American bush cranberry, *V. opulus*.

745. Or "wake siah warm — illahee," Chinook Jargon for "not far warm — country."

search of food. Generally pursues fish, & when its belly full retires below & sleeps. Indians may pass too & fro in Canoes often while it is in this state, & never see it. If however it is hungry & hears Indians passing, it rushes out, & making a great commotion in the water appears. The Indians may land & rush away into the woods, but by a sort of fascination are impelled back again. They may run away thus several times, but always return & are finally caught in the gaping mouth of the monster, who then throws them up in the air several times & finally Catching them as they descend head-first, swallows them.

A somewhat similar monster Called *Pe-cho* or the great Salmon Trout, is said to live in Chestalta L.[746] of the map, to live on fish, varied in the same way by an occasional Indian, but having the additional peculiarity of from time to time breaking up the ice on the lake in winter, by his violent movements. This breaking up of the ice Je-son assures me he has seen.

How water fire & daylight obtained by Ancient men. Very long ago men lived in the woods without daylight, water, or fire; or if they had any water it was a very little caught in birch bark spread out when it rained. All the water belonged to a grizzly bear" (Grizzly bear I think) who kept it beside him ⟨in a little Kettle⟩. Men wanted water very much, & at last one bolder than the rest, though still very much afraid, undertook to steal it while the bear slept. Creeping up, he Secured the prize & rushing away with it, here a little spilt out & there a little till at last the Kettle was empty, but where the water had fallen lakes & rivers remained. Still men wanted fire, & at last catching a Silver fox they split up Some wood very fine & attached it to his tail, & then induced him to go in search of fire for them. Fire, with water & daylight, were all the property of the said great bear. The fox crept up & running through the bears fire carried away a flame on the wood tied to his tail. Yet daylight was wanting, & again the Fox was the messenger. This time he seems to have been unable to steal the desired object placing himself not far from the bear he seems to have continued importuning the bear, till at last he, becoming angry, Said "here take it" & threw the daylight (or sun) at him, giving light to the earth for the first time.

[verso]

This story more Authentic probably as a part of the Adventures of the hero Us-tas[747] Told thus — Us-tas it was who undertook to Get the water.

---

746. Cheslatta Lake.

747. Franz Boas records some of the many versions of Raven's adventures in obtaining water, daylight, and fire. See Boas, "Tsimshian Mythology," Bureau of American Ethnology, *Thirty-first Annual Report, 1909–1910* (Washington, 1916), 641–63.
   Us-tas, or "Astas," as it appears in A. G. Morice's renderings of this story, is the Carrier name for the Hero-Trickster. In presenting the Haida creation myth, Dawson

The grizzly bear had a daughter, & Us-tas proceeded in this way. Turning himself into a leaf like that of a pine or spruce he threw himself into the coveted water. Soon the grizzly bears daughter came to drink & as she drank the little leaf floated up to her mouth. She pushed it away & drank again, but always the little leaf returned, & at last she swallowed it. Very soon she conceived & shortly after bore a male child, who grew up very fast. This boy — in reality Us-tas — constantly cried for the water, till at last the old bear said "let him have it to play with & perhaps that will Keep him quiet" As soon as he got it he ran off with the result stated opposite — the grizzly bear pursuing him.

{Can this story of the grizzly bear's daughter have anything to do with the Indian custom by which girls till of a marriagable age (or married?) have to drink always through a hollow bone, & on no account drink direct from a dish, or the lake?}

The method of obtaining fire also told differently & probably better, as follows. Fire the property of the same bear, & all the animals wanted to get it. The old grizzly Sat guarding it, & first one animal & then another rushed through the fire & Attempted to carry some off on its tail. All failed {the bear extinguishing it} till at last the young Cariboo — the most active & quick animal in the country — tried & succeeded. Off he ran hotly persued by the bear who was almost on the point of Catching him when he reached the edge of a lake, where a musk rat was swimming. Then the rat said "here my brother, give me the fire" so he gave it & the rat swam away with it, but the bear took to the water. The rat dived & coming up on the other bank took the fire under his arm & applied it to the woods & timber till all was in a blaze. Then the Indians got fire & have never lost it since. [end verso]

The Indians then proceeded to relate *"Leprates"* stories,[748] which they fully believe of course, & seem to think must be at least equally interesting to me as that above given. The deluge & the Creation & fall of man, followed in succession. Filtered through the priest & then the Indian mind, & finally told in Chinook Jargon, these Sounded equally improbable & absurd with the others. Charley got quite excited over the Creation, going through the form of moulding clay into the shape of man, & then blowing on it to signify giving the breath of life, then relating the creation of

recorded his surprise at finding it to be "substantially the same" as the Carrier (George M. Dawson, "On the Haida Indians of the Queen Charlotte Islands," Geological Survey of Canada, *Report of Progress for 1878-79* [Ottawa, 1880], 151).

748. This is a genre of stories that includes Biblical stories as well as those that make fun of priests. The word itself is an Indianization of the French word for priest. See Jarold Ramsey, "The Bible in Western Indian Mythology," *Journal of American Folklore* 90 (October-December 1977): 442-45.

woman, & the happy condition of the primaeval pair on a "skookum ranch" (=Eden) with plenty potatoes, turnips, carrots &c. &c.! Finally one tree with *olallies*[749] which was forbidden &c. Adding to the bible story the fact that the one Adam tried to eat stuck in his throat, forming the lump (Adam's apple) still clearly to be seen there!

Meteor, very bright, seen this evening about 8.20 P.m. First saw broad bright bluish reflection on the lake like that Cast by the moon, but Knowing the moon should not rise so early, caught myself wondering how it was, when the meteor appeared below branches of tree in front. Bright bluey-white light about equal, as I judge to twice that of Venus at present. Tail or train of no great length following behind, & general appearance as of a large star from signal rocket. Disappeared below horizon about [blank] falling at an angle of about 55° from horizontal, from the [blank].

Sept. 17. Sunday. Had planned to take photos. looking up & down the lake this morning, then examine the few miles remaining to the end, & camp for remainder of day, ascending some prominent hill if opportunity offered. Morning however dropping rain, dull & threatening, with appearance of wind. Wind soon began to blow hard from the East, raising a heavy sea, & continued so all day. About 5.30 pm. rain commenced & the wind moderated. occupied writing up notes & reading. For some time very uncomfortable from wind & smoke & sparks from fire, got brush screen put up however, & put a stop to the trouble.

Sept. 18. Heavy storm of wind from the westward, during the night & early morning. Calmed down Somewhat after breakfast, & able to get off. Continue along s. shore, but find it hard work in increasing wind to weather Point (E.2.) Run into great East bay,[750] & round it, but unable owing to increasing sea & wind to work up on the other side to mouth of river.[751] Pm Canoe ashore & wait patiently for amendment. Storm Slightly abated by 2.30. Indians propose to run the canoe & baggage down to the river themselves, while we walk across overland. assent to arrangement, & get all stuff put on sticks in middle of Canoe & covered with tarpaulin &c. Reach the river mouth after a rather fatiguing scramble of 50 minutes through tall epilobiums, grass, peavine &c. clothing burnt ground. Find the Canoe before us. Take angles to two last fixed points, closing Survey of lake, & run down river to first portage.

Evening try fishing but unsuccessfully, though many fish nibbling will not take. one duck shot by Je-son with bread &c. constitutes our supper.

---

749. Chinook Jargon for "berries."

750. The eastern end of François Lake.

751. Endako River.

Very remarkable low barometer during storm yesterday. In addition tc usual observations took half hourly readings as below, but not Sure that actual lowest stage observed.

1.30 P.m. = 27.34	2 Pm = 27.34.	2.30 = 27.33	3 P.m. = 27.31
3.30 = 27.28	4.10 Pm = 27.275	4.30 = 27.275	
5Pm = 27.27	5.30 Pm = 27.25.	6.10 P.m = 27.25.	
6.40Pm = 27.25	7.30 Pm = 27.26.	8 P.m. = 27.24	
8.30Pm = 27.23	9 P.m. = 27.24	9.30 P.m. = 27.225.	

[verso]

Notes on bar obs. 6.10 Pm rain beginning, wind falling

6.40	rain
7.30	rain, calm
8.00	" "
8.30	" "
9.10	rain, ceased, calm
9.30	" " "

[end verso]

Sept. 19. Got put across river in Canoe, & then walked down on the south bank with B. The Indians bringing the Canoe down the rapids, light. Country much open & with poplar groves, very beautiful with Autumnal tints. Arrived at Indian village before Canoe, very much astonishing the natives by our unexpected appearance. Could not communicate with them, as none could speak either Chinook, french, or English. Sat on the bank waiting Canoe the centre of an admiring crowd, part evidently of the "great unwashed." One rather pretty little Girl among the Children, all the rest decidedly plain. Many little patches of potatoes turnips &c. near the village, & one man owns 3 Cows! The gardens do not show much sign of Cultivation or Care, & the turnips Show tendency to become thick necks, though some of them of good average size. Got off in Canoe at 11.30 Stopped soon after for lunch, & camped early in a pretty little retired bay on the N. Shore of Fraser L, fringed with rushes & water lillies.[752] Rain & squalls during Pm. Evening fine & Calm, & apparently clearing.

Sept. 20. Night calm & fine, soon after starting however showers of rain with squalls of wind began to blow up, making it very cold & uncomfortable, made what progress we could, landing once during morning to get dry & warm at a fire. Not Satisfactory Keeping track survey on Pulpy Paper & trying to examine rocks in this weather. Lunched in a dry little nook in a volcanic conglomerate rock at the foot of a cliff.

---

752. The "rushes" were rushes, *Juncus* spp.; and "water lillies" probably yellow pond-lilies, *N. polysepalum.*

Indians point out several places along the shore of the lake to which Indian names attach. Two localities where designs have been made on the rocks by the *Aukulty Siwashes*.[753] Neither of them at all clear, nor apparently of any Significance, but Cultus *Mamook*[754] merely. One faintly shows as opposite, [*illus.*] red pigment on a whitish stain on the rock.[755]

Another place shows two very distinct Cracks in the cliff — parallel Joints — which receives a jawbreaking name, meaning something; I really could not exactly find out what.

The most remarkable place however is a flat Glaciated rock, sloping gradually up from the water, somewhat like a pavement. This they Call *Te-tinne-a-na-nes-tis*, & have a story that very long ago an Indian passing by along the shore, saw a large man lying asleep on the rock, who when disturbed jumped up & plunged under the waters of the lake, & was seen no more.

On arriving at Ft Fraser find that my Packer is waiting down at the river, having arrived two days ago. Nothing Known of Mr Cambie*, McMillan* & party to N.W. of Telegraph Trail according to letter received from Hanswam.[756] Find mail, with home letters &c. & Announcement from Father* that he is working me as a candidate for the Palæontology dept. of Survey vacated by Billing's* death.[757]

Glaciation clearly observed today for the first time in either of these two great lake basins (See notes for description)[758] The marks evidently those of a glacier moving down the basin of Fraser L under very considerable pressure, & forcing out through gaps at the sides in search of low country. Evidence however by still lumpy shapes of the rocks, smoothed & furrowed only on exposed surfaces & retaining much of pre-glacial form (Due to weathering along jointage planes in several directions) & also by hollows in pavement, rounded on one side & Smooth on the other like that Seen in Lake of the Woods; that ice though perhaps intense in action *did not last long here.* Perhaps the limit of the Cascade Mt. Glaciers when at

---

753. Or "Ahn-kut-te Siwashes," a Chinook Jargon term meaning, "Indians a long time ago."

754. Or mamook cultus, a Chinook Jargon expression meaning "to make bad or no good."

755. There are still two recognized pictograph sites on the north side of Fraser Lake. See John Corner, *Pictographs (Indian Rock Paintings) in the Interior of British Columbia* (Vernon, B.C.: Wayside Press, 1968): 442–45, sites 103 and 104.

756. Unidentifiable.

757. Elkanah Billings, the palaeontologist to the Geological Survey of Canada since 1856, died on 14 June 1876. In spite of J. W. Dawson's efforts on behalf of his son, Joseph Frederick Whiteaves was promoted to the position.

758. See G. M. Dawson, Field Notebooks, RG 45, vol. 134, no. 2795, 43, PAC.

their greatest extension (?) though hardly believable that they could have stretched so far.

No local cause seems capable of explaining formation of so Considerable a glacier, unless indeed descended from the hills about 600' above the lake, & overlooking it on S. Side.[759]

one feature with regard to Francois & Fraser Lakes deserves attention. viz. that both of them have granitic or duritic rocks at their lower ends, whereas the greater part of their basins are excavated in volcanic rocks of the older or newer series on hypothesis of glacial erosion might be maintained that these more resistent materials caused the formation of the basins. Further, it is remarkable that both lakes while thus with hard rocks at their lower ends also have comparitively low level country in the same position, while much of their length between high hills.

[verso]

Sept. 20. Paid "Indian Charley" $21.00 (see receipt)

    ″   Paid Je-son $10.00 being payment in part

Sept. 21. Paid Indian $1.00 for use of Canoe crossing stuff over river.

[end verso]

Sept. 21. Sent Je-son & Mr Bowman* down to Telegraph Crossing of Ne-cha-ko to see about getting packer & animals across, thinking it better to bring the whole to this place, where can store what not required in the fort, & eventually leave any surplus Stores as part payment for that got from H.B. Packs arrived about 1 Pm. Rough Squally day.

Evening held a very lengthy conversation with Je-son & his brother *Benita* who propose being my Canoe-men in future. B. vice. Charley resigned, the distressed state of his disconsolate *Kootch-man* preying on his mind. Mr Alexander* kind enough to help me in the conference by statements to him being translated into French Jargon to his servant, & by him turned into Indian. Answers returned through the same devious channel. Hardly Any wonder that much talking required to arrive at understanding. Indians Squatted round the open hearth in the ante-room of the HB establishment, rough & dirty.

---

759. Dawson was accurate in assuming a movement of the glaciers in an easterly direction: subsequent research indicates that the glacial advance which covered central British Columbia originated in the Coast Mountains and flowed eastward down the valleys. See Armstrong and Tipper, "Glaciation in North Central," 306. Here, in 1876, he was timid in his speculations, since ice covered all of the interior to a depth probably greater than five thousand feet. Dawson was also hesitant to ascribe glacial features to a massive glaciation covering the central region of the province. Nonetheless, he later abandoned the notion of localized glaciation in favour of the "hypothesis that a great glacier mass resembling the inland ice of Greenland has filled the region which may be called the Interior Plateau" (George M. Dawson, "Additional Observations on the Superficial Geology of British Columbia and Adjacent Regions," *Quarterly Journal of the Geological Society of London* 37 [1881]: 283).

Mr A. told me today several stories related by the Indians, mostly however in a rather fragmentary state, as he has not payed special attention to them.

Story of a fish woman of some Sort. Stuart L. Indians say that very long ago an Indian crossing the lake on the ice saw a very beautiful woman sitting upright on it, near a hole, arranging her hair, which was green. The Indian by a quick manuver got between the woman & the hole & would not let her to it, though she begged & prayed to be allowed to descend again into the lake. The Indian caught her & took her home, marrying her, but always being obliged to keep her tied up. After some time he had a child by her. The next Summer the Indians had a Cache of dried berries & grease, the contents of which seemed mysteriously to disappear. Theft was suspected, & one day seeing Something suspicious, the woman of the lake was watched, & seen on a point, throwing the cakes of berries into the water, & the boxes of greese, & finally, strapping her baby to her back, Jumped in herself & was no more seen.[760]

[verso]

A Cree story

[end verso]

Mr. A. Says there is a long story about the Summer & winter which he can hardly remember[761] — The winter animals at first had it all their own way, & winter was perpetual, the summer being bundled up in a package of moss, & carefully retained by the winter animals. It was intrusted to the Guardianship of a winter hawk, or eagle of some Kind, who Sat upon it, on the top of a pole Set in the middle of a lake. The Summer animals, Suffering it is to be presumed from the perpetual Winter, laid plans to obtain the summer. The Marten tried first in Some way but failed. Then the beaver tried, by swimming out under the water, & gnawing away the pole below Caused it to fall, but the eagle was flying about at a Short distance at the time, & carried the bundle sontaining the summer with it, so that the beavers plan proved a failure. Next the Otter tried, & by standing erect in the water looked so like a post that the eagle rested on him, when at once he Snatched the precious ball & diving with it, Carried it away to the summer birds. Next in Some way however, the fisher — which seems

760. Mermaid stories are surprisingly rare in British Columbia Indian mythology. The theme here is the same as that of the "Swan-maiden" stories, where a man holds the feathers of a goose-swan while she bathes and will not give them back until she marries him. They and their children eventually fly away. Jenness records a successful domestic life with a water nymph in his "Myths of the Carrier Indians," *Journal of American Folklore* 47 (1934): 255.

761. Compare "Determination of the Seasons," in Stith Thompson, *Tales of the North American Indians* (1929; reprint, Bloomington: Indiana University Press, 1966), 288.

to count as a winter animal — got the summer again & pursued by the summer Animals ran up a tree. The Summer animals were again non-plussed, but the frog Came to the front, & with a bow & arrows began shooting at the fisher till at last he was struck, when he dropped the Summer & sprang up into the sky where he yet remains, forming the constellation of the great bear —

Stories of Monsters in lakes Seem to abound.[762] Stuarts Lake & Babine Lake both have localities which the Indians are afraid to pass at night, saying that monsters, usually described as Snake like — live there. These are pretty modern stories about these Monsters too. Many years ago, perhaps about 1826 when Stuart[763] himself was at the lake Called after him, An Indian declared he had Seen, & fired at one of the monsters with his gun, & was afraid any more to go on the lake. Not long afterward A Sort of frothy Grease appeared along the flat southern shore of the lake, & of this the Indians collected many boxes full. Three men, half-breeds & Indians, of the company's Service, Some years ago positively declare that while crossing Stuart L, they were chased by a monster, which at first resembled a log lying on the water, & was rough & hairy. Its head was like a snake, & after they had got safely to an island, it Swam too & fro several times looking at them, or for them. They stayed on the island all night & next day pursued their journey.

Indian Names.[764] The Indians are said often to have Several names by which they are Known, & which they got at feasts given from time to time. They are seldom Called by their own names, however, but Generally Known as So & So's father or mother, giving the name of one of their children. If no children, very often their favourite dog chosen, & called the father of such & such a dog. Neither do they mention dead people by their names, but speak of them as the father of such a one &c.

The Indians of this part of the country all belong to the Carrier or Porteur division of the Tinneh.[765] They may be said to be bounded to the

762. Such was the case. Many lakes in British Columbia have an associated legendary creature. Jenness's "Myths of the Carrier Indians," 257, records for François Lake: "Long ago, too, there were other monsters here that destroyed the Indians, a big fish, a huge snake, and a great giant."

763. Dawson's reference is to John Stewart (Stuart) who established Fort St. James in 1806, travelled down the Fraser River with Simon Fraser in 1808, and supervised the North West Company's New Caledonia District from 1809. Dawson has the date wrong; Stewart wintered in northern British Columbia in 1806–7 but left the area in 1824.

764. For more detailed information, see A. G. Morice, "Carrier Onomatology," *American Anthropologist*, n.s., 35 (1933): 632–58.

765. Carrier is merely a translation of the French *Porteur*, itself a rendering of a Sekani word which was probably an allusion to the custom of widows carrying the cremated remains of their husbands on their backs. See Margaret L. Tobey, "Carrier," in *Subarctic*, ed.

south by the Chilcotins, & to extend to Alexandria & Quesnelle. Northward to N End of Fraser L, & even as far as Bear Lake, on a tributary of the Skeena. Also at the forks of the Skeena. North & East of these limits they pass into the Tacullies & Beavers.[766] The coast tribes seem to be increasing more rapidly in proportion, & encroaching on these inland tribes, to the north. A few years ago there were not many Coast Indians at Bear Lake, now it is almost in their posession, though they do not go East of the river at its mouth. The carriers Call these, & all foreign tribes *At-nas*. These now in question are a branch of the Chinsayans of Skena River.[767]

The carriers are all divided up into Totems or great families.[768] Here (Fraser Lake & all surrounding country) the great totems are the *Partridge* & the *Frog*. All of one Totem Call themselves related, & a man must not marry in his own totem. The frogs & partridges live together in the same villages, but in different families. A frog man & partridge woman being married, Continue each of their own totem, but the Children follow the mother, & are partridges. About the Forks of Skeena the Beaver is the great totem. When a frog (e.g.) dies the frogs of the community have to give a feast, & potlatch, Generally of torn pieces of blanket &c. when no return is expected. If however Shirts or whole Clothes given, they are kept strict remembrance of & supposed to be repaid by another present at the next feast given by the other totem. About a year after the death a second feast & potlatch is made, & a tomb erected over the body. The next death may perhaps occur among the partridges, when they will have the feast to

June Helm, *Handbook of North American Indians*, 6: 430. Tinne is a variant of Dene, a synonym for Athapaskan. See Beryl C. Gillespie, "Territorial Groups Before 1821," ibid., 168.

766. Compare Carrier distribution as described in Tobey, "Carrier," 413–15, 430, where "Tacullie," a word deriving from the Carrier name for themselves, is noted as being synonomous with Carrier.

767. Under pressure from the Beaver and Cree to the east, the Sekani had expanded westward in the late eighteenth and early nineteenth centuries and occupied the country around Bear Lake. The establishment of Forts McLeod (1805) and Connelly (1826) checked their expansion. Fort Connelly on Bear Lake became the rendezvous of the Sekani and Carrier as well as the Gitksan Tsimshian from the upper Skeena. The Sekani and Carrier were generally on friendly terms, but with the Gitksan, the Sekani waged intermittent hostilities and at last began to retreat eastward and northward. See Diamond Jenness, *The Sekani Indians of British Columbia*, National Museum of Canada Bulletin no. 84, Anthropological Series no. 20 (Ottawa, 1937), 11–12, 18. "Atna" is actually the Russian name for the Copper River Athabaskan group now called Ahtna. It may have been picked up by the Carrier. See Frederica De Laguna and Catharine McClellan, "Ahtna," in *Subarctic*, 661.

768. For a discussion of the Carrier organization into exogamous phratries, clans, and houses, see Diamond Jenness, *The Indians of Canada*, 3d ed., National Museum of Canada Bulletin no. 65, Anthropological Series no. 15 (Ottawa, 1955), 365–67.

make &c. All these old Customs however now rapidly going, the priest having forbidden feasts &c. &c. Still however they seldom or never marry one of their own totem. Once or twice however, even before the advent of the priest Such marriages were known, & the Indians were much Shocked, & would have nothing to do with the iniquitous couple, considering them, as they said, all the same as dogs.

It seems I did not get quite the correct version of the story about the glacier pavement a mile or two back on N Shore of lake. Asked an old man about it, who however not able to speak Chinook or French, but who afterwards told the Story to one of the HB men, who gave me the following. — This particular tale only part of a long series which attach to a certain ancient Indian chief, medicine man & hero generally, Called *Us-tas*.

— one of the Indians of Fraser Lake (Na-tle) had a swan cap, or head piece resembling a swan by which he used to conceal himself & wading deep in the water approach the swans & catch them by their feet below water, tying & securing them. Us-tas Coming along saw the arrangement, but said "that is nothing, Can you catch only one swan, let me try" Accordingly he arranged himself in the swan cap, & tying a rope round his middle entered the water, & soon caught five Swans, tying them all to his girdle. Then he threw off the swan Cap, & behold, the swans frightened flew up in the Air carrying Us-tas off with them & travelling away to the Sea (Ya-too-bun-kut) Next spring, when the swans came back Us-tas returned too, the Swans carrying him as before; & just as he passed over the end of Fraser Lake he bethought him of his knife, & cut the strings by which the birds Carried him. Down he fell on the rock before referred too, which was then however only soft mud, deep below the surface of which he sank. one of his friends, however, it seems, rubbed the surface of the mud (which appears to have hardened in some way) with ⟨greese,⟩ {beaver Castorum of which the Lynx very fond.} & going away, the lynx came along, & finding the grease, scraped away the mud — marking & Smoothing it in the peculiar way it now shows — till the face & eyes of Us-tas appeared. Then Came along a crow, & Seeing his opportunity, picked out the eyes & Carried them off. Soon after Us-tas got up, & taking some gum from a tree, began walking away, Knocking first against this, then against that, for he could not see. Then all the Indians laughed & said [....] Us-tas is blind at last, but Us-tas Said "wait, I know what I am about;" {I am not blind but looking for something} & Soon as he went along he heard some men {(preter natural beings of some Sort?)} Singing & making a great noise in the night, being in a large house. Us-tas said to himself what is this, & went up & into the house, & asked ⟨the men⟩ {An old woman whom he saw} what they were making so much noise about. They said we are glad, for we have got a mans eyes. Then Us-tas said "Let me look at one, & they gave one to him {but he said this is only one} ⟨then⟩ he held out his hand again & said let me look at the other. Then having them both he pushed them quickly into their places, & ran away as hard as he could, having his Sight perfectly again.[769]

Knowing well enough, while the old man was trying to relate this story to me, that he considered it a vintage of the most remote antiquity. I still asked him if he had ever seen Us-tass. He seemed quite shocked by my ignorance, & vehemently exclaimed A-ta! A-ta!! A-ta!!! (Long ago.) (*A-ta-tun-ne* the long ago or ancient people)

Sept. 22. Decide to Send B, with Lillooet Johnny & two Indians of the place up the Ne-cha-ko to examine the lower part of the river, & communicate with Mr McMillan* about Supplies, & money to pay men for trip to Ft George. Also to send him my map of the Ne-cha-Ko, & all the information I can about it. Myself to go with Casinta & the Indian boy he has had some time with him, across by trail to Stuart Lake, connecting with Mr Selwyns* line of last summer, & perhaps observing junction of some rocks seen here with the Cache Creek formation. Occupied making arrangements accordingly writing to McM. Cambie*, & a note home. Observing with M.T.[770] for index error & taking it to pieces to oil &c. &c. B. detained Somewhat by strong wind, but got off at last at 3 P.m. Got all packed & stuff not required put in HB. Store.

Nearly bothered to death by Indians coming begging shot, powder, every-thing & anything, & even though they did not Get it hanging round my fire & watching operations in the tent.

Day cold, with very heavy squalls of wind & a little rain & sleet. Night very windy.

Hear that Mr Cambies* Indians have just returned, that Mr C. has been to See Hunter*, & McMillan* (?) & is now off again to Quesnelle.

Sept 23 Up early, but horses having strayed far, not off till after 9 am. Take two pack mules & 3 riding animals. After a little trouble find a place to cross the Fraser L. river,[771] & march on till nearly 4 Pm. on what compared to most of trails, a very good one. Ascend gradually but continuously till attain a considerable elevation, when pass through the Crest of the mountain by a narrow & rather remarkable valley called the Porte d'enfer,[772] & camp not far beyond it.

---

769. For a close analogue of this story of Us-tas, the Trickster, and his substituted eyes, see Jenness, "Myths of the Carrier Indians," 208.

770. Micrometer telescope or theodolite.

771. Nechako River.

772. Dawson noted of this ungazetted feature: "A remarkable notch or gap in the crest of this ridge, called the Porte d'Enfer, conducts the trail across it, at an elevation of 3,790

Day blustry & very cold, overcast most of time, & during afternoon flurries of snow, leaving the ground this evening quite white, & the fir trees of wintry appearance. Now — 8 Pm — Calm & Clear.

Sept. 24. Up before sunrise & off early, a {thin} crisp coating of snow still on the ground, & ice quarter of an inch thick on little pools. Mule mired crossing a swamp shortly after leaving camp, & caused some delay. Travelled on till 1.20 when stopped at a lake[773] surrounded by extensive flat ground, partly swampy, & with excellent feed. Lunched & gave animals a chance to eat, they having been tied up all last night to prevent their return. On the march again at 3 P.m. & Camped at 6 Pm on the shore of Stewart Lake,[774] where the trail comes out, at the mouth of a small stream.[775] Some Indian houses, & one family living here, the head where off soon payed us a visit, & when asked his name said he was "watchman tyee"[776] A title & office given him by the priest. Clouding up gradually all day & now beginning to rain.

The bare white limestone mountains across the lake very remarkable in appearance & different from anything seen this summer, reminding in general aspect of some peaks of Rocky's.

[verso]

May ice have remained in lake valleys or if towards here cleared them out.

General glacier?

Great & long submergence sandy drift &c. with icebergs

Emergence & advance of glaciers among rounded drift

Complete emergence & final retreat of glaciers. by continuance of changes bringing on warm period[777]

[end verso]

Sept. 25. Raining all night, & morning still continues with very dark sky &

feet" (Dawson, "Report on Explorations," 51).

773. Either Marie Lake or Nanna Lake. Dawson calls it Chuz-kan Lake in his Field Notebook, RG 45, vol. 134, no. 2795, 46, PAC.

774. Stuart Lake.

775. Sowchea Creek.

776. "Being a grown-up child, the native must be constantly watched, often reproved, and his persevering powers at times tested. Hence the establishment of the watchmen, who are the eyes of the village chief" (A. G. Morice, *History of the Catholic Church in Western Canada from Lake Superior to the Pacific (1659-1895)*, 2 vols. [Toronto: Musson Book Company, 1910], 2: 290).

777. Dawson was still much influenced by the notion of glaciation followed by a general subsidence, inundation, and floating ice. Consequently, in his early published treatment, Dawson wholeheartedly accepted the water-borne ice concept. See Dawson, "On the Superficial Geology," 119-21.

cold wind. Decide not to start for Ft St James as cannot either examine rocks & take bearings with any comfort

Noon Showed signs of clearing & during p.m. only occasional showers. Reading, sketching hills round lake &c.

[verso]

Wages paid by CPRS.

Carjadores[778] $80 per month

White packers not Carjadores $60

Indian packers & assistant packers $60

Axemen & Indians not packers $45

Paying Indian packers $60 seems absurd as they do not Get such wages elsewhere. $40 I believe given by private packers on the Waggon Road

Wages at Kamloops

Carpenters & [....] at Camloops $4 to 5 per day.

ordinary white farm assistants $40 to 50 per month

Chinamen ordinary labourers, cooks &c. $35 to 50

Indians $35 to 40

Keep always included in engagement.

Board {& lodging} of labouring men (good fare) $20.00 per month. [end verso]

Sept 26. Started pretty early with the Indian found living here, & my Indian lad, in canoe for Ft St James, across the lake. Calm at first, but afterwards pretty rough, though not rough enough to be unpleasant even in our cockly dug-out, which not only open to general objections of Such craft, but unusually cranky, & quite lop-sided in every particular. Distance by time a little over 6 miles. Introduced myself to Mr G. Hamilton*, who welcomed me very kindly, though one of his children at present dangerously ill. Had a little second breakfast, & talk, & then under guidance of a Mr Hall[779] (clerk) for part of the way, went back to the Knoll behind the fort where limestone outcrop visible, & as I am told near the place where Mr Selwyn* last year got some interesting fossils. Made sketch[780] with bearings of view from hill, the most Surprising feature of which the amount of nearly flat low country southward & eastward, with appearance of fertile soil, being though generally wooded, more than half poplar, now turned bright yellow among the dark green conifers. Altogether a very lovely & extensive view. Spent several hours collecting, & finally sweated back to Fort about 4 P.m. loaded with specimens, having struck a pretty

---

778. Cargadores, teamsters.

779. Robert H. Hall was a Hudson's Bay Company clerk at Fort Simpson. He had previously served at Stuart Lake.

780. See G. M. Dawson, Field Notebooks, RG 45, vol. 134, no. 2795, 47–48, 50–51, PAC.

good "silicified" ⟨vein⟩ strick of the limestone, full of broken Crinoid remains, & in places charged with *Fusulinas* proving the Carboniferous age of the Cache Creek Rocks![781]

Wind rather boisterous on the lake & Mr Hamilton* Kindly pressing me to stay all night, allowed myself to be readily persuaded. Dined on delicious roast — beaver, & spent evening in conversation with Mr H, his brother,[782] & Hall*, & a young gentleman — Webster[783] — now here from Bear or Connoly Lake.[784] Got many interesting & important items, & with their help sketched out a route by which in future year may Cover an immense block of country to the north, easily & cheaply, using for most part regular lines of travel, & H.B. conveyances.

From accounts, seems that northern part of Trutch's map quite wrong with regard to Mountains. First the omineca Mts are said to be further N & perhaps also further E, in relation to the forks of the river, than represented; they also apper to unite more or less completely westward with other ranges, which practically Seem to block up the Northern end of the low country which the great lakes &c. are in.[785] Bear or Connoly's L. instead of being in a comparatively low Country as the map would indicate, lies in a deep narrow valley in the midst of *Snow clad* Mountains, not free of snow all Summer. The range running Northward along W. side of Tacla L also becomes snow-clad near the North end of the lake. The trail between Babine & Skeena Forks runs between high mountain ranges, in a narrow valley. The Skeena itself, for at least a part of its Course is confined to a narrow gorge between mountains comparable with that of the Fraser. Supposing the continuity of the Coast Range Southward, the depressed area about the Great Lakes, & N of Ft George &c. Communicates freely — without crossing many contour lines — only eastward through the Peace R. gap. A fact of great importance with regard to drift phenomena, & possibly also with reference to Cretaceous & Tertiary formations.

---

781. "Crinoid" refers to remains of Crinoidea, fixed or free-living marine Echinodermata such as sea-urchins; "*Fusulinas*" are single-celled, marine invertebrate fossils of the family Fusulinidae.

782. Probably Thomas H. Hamilton, who was a clerk with the Hudson's Bay Company.

783. Probably H. B. Webster, a Hudson's Bay Company clerk.

784. Bear Lake.

785. Dawson's assertions about the inaccuracy of Trutch's map were quite correct. On the map (see Trutch, *Map of British Columbia*), the Omineca Mountains, for example, are located much too southerly and are not connected to the Skeena Mountains, to the west, into which they merge.

The portage between the head waters of the Driftwood R (running to the Fraser) & those of Bear L. (Skeena) only separated by about 4000 yards of portage, not high ground.

A post on the N. branch of the Finlay[786] has been established this summer by Mr Hamilton*, to trade with the Siccanie[787] Inds. He is told by the Indians that only about 1 foot of snow falls in the winter, & that it goes off very early.

Got Some further facts about the encroachment of the Atanahs (Coast Inds. Chinsayans) on the Porteurs & Siccanies. The Movement began only about 3 years ago, & is caused by the fact that the Coast Indians are more numerous, & have exhausted more or less completely all their own hunting grounds. Their eastern boundary may now be stated as running from the Forks of Skeena to Tacla L, Bear or Connolly lake, & thence northward & westward probably nearly following the Sources of the N Skeena branches. Both the Intruders & sufferers know that the movement is unjust to the latter, but the former too strong to Care, & the latter too weak to resist, though should it come to actual war the Stick Indians, in the woods, are more than a match for much greater numbers of Coast Indians. Trouble between the tribes, seems to be anticipated by those knowing most about the matter.[788]

Canvas Canoe Young Mr. Hamilton has a small Canvas canoe, & advises me to get a good large one (say 3 fathom) made if visiting the northern part of the country, would be Very useful even in a packing trip to be able to navigate lakes or rivers met with. The Canoe simply made of *stout* canvas sewed together in the ordinary way, with a "casing" at the bow & stern for a small hand bent stick, which may remain permanently in place if desired. The seams are painted with boiled oil, & the rest of the Canoe may also be so if found necessary. The framing is made in about an hour when required. Bows of stick (more or less neatly made according to use for which designed at time) bent in transversely; & below them thin flat split pieces shoved in. The whole just as in a bark Canoe. Forget whether side poles (thwarts) go in casings or not. Recommended that should get light iron Socket pieces made for bow & stern. as opposite [*Illus.*]

---

786. Dawson must be referring to Fort Grahame which he earlier located on the "S branch" of the Finlay River. See 5 September 1876.

787. Sekani.

788. Having been forced westward by the Beaver and the Cree during the late eighteenth century and early nineteenth century, the Sekani Indians settled in the area around Bear Lake. With the 1826 establishment of Fort Connelly, built to accommodate both groups, conflict arose between the Sekani and the Gitksan (a division of the Tsimshian) over hunting rights around the fort. The result was the retreat of the Sekani to the north and east. See Jenness, *Sekani Indians*, 11–12, 18.

The Monster[789] Said to Inhabit this lake, heard something more about here. The grease said to have been picked up after the Indian fired at one of these creatures (see former account) confirmed. Said that Indians brought canoe loads to Fort of *rancid fat* Such as might have come off an [....], & that bought by women to make soap.

Two miners here on way down from Omineca, where notwithstanding removal of govt. official {(Page)}[790] times moderately prosperous, with a small number of men at work. No remarkable new discoveries.[791] Much in want of a School at Stewart L. though as yet unable to get one.[792] With Mr H's children, those of half-breeds &c. 20 or 30 could be got together. Also Seem to need a magistrate in this part of the country, which the centre for a large district, but much isolated, especially in winter

Sept 27 Meant to make quite an early start, but many little things in way. Breakfast *early* at 7 A.m. Indian to whom canoe belong off at devotions at the mission &c. Take a look at Garden at Ft in which Mr H. takes some pride. Cabbage, cauliflowers, turnips, beets, carrots, onions &c. grow easily & well. Cabbages & Cauliflower not forced in spring but sometimes attain very great size. Cucumbers grown in frame. Barley & potatoes grown in some quantity for use at fort. In Garden notwithstanding frosts (pretty severe one last night) Mallow, mignonnette, mesembryanthemum, Portulacca & sweet pea[793] in good condition.

Reach Camp at noon, lunch & off by 1.30 P.m. travel fast, & Camp on

---

789. See 21 September 1876.

790. F. Page had been provincial government agent in the district. Because of the decline of profitable mining, his office was closed.

791. Dawson further noted of the Omenica district that it was "first entered about 1864, but scarcely developed till 1867. . . . The area within which the greater part of the mining has taken place is scarcely more than fifty miles in greatest diameter, and includes the upper portions of Germansen, Omenica and Mansen rivers and their tributaries. This area is described as being hilly rather than mountainous, and is nearly everywhere covered by the dense northern forest. A very high opinion was at first formed by miners of the Omenica district, but when the Cassiar discoveries occurred, it was nearly abandoned. . . . This district is practically the most remote and inaccessible in the Province, the cost of supplies has always been excessive, and the difficulties in the way of enterprise in the form of exploration thus very great" (Dawson, "Mineral Wealth of British Columbia," 41).

792. A school opened in August of the next year but ran only two years. See Alexander C. Murray memoirs, PABC.

793. "Mallow" was mallow, *Malva* spp.; "mignonnette," mignonette, *Reseda* spp.; "mesembryanthemum" one of the carpet-weeds belonging to the genus *Mesembryanthemum*; "Portulacca," purslane, *Portulaca* spp; and "sweet pea" sweet pea, *Lathyrus adoratus* L.

Whool-tan Lake.[794]
[verso]
Sp. 27. Paid Indian for trip to Ft St James & back to Camp $3.00
[end verso]

Fort St James probably about as good a sample of a H.B. post as now extant, & the most important post in B. Columbia. The buildings rather old & dilapidated, arranged in square, inclosing a quadrangle, open behind, at a little distance the Indian village. Office, with a couple of desks & a table in one building, quarters for men &c. In main building, store, Mr H's residence, kitchen & common room or dining hall. The whole with rather dirty neglected air. In the dining hall Indians, half-breeds &c. constantly lounging about, coming in through the open door & going out at discretion. Opening off this room a Kitchen, with A lame old french-Canadian who says he has been here 33 years, as cook. on account of pleasant warmth of fire these cold mornings, Kitchen seems to be the common lounging place of inmates of fort.

Sept 28. Up at grey dawn, knowing we had a long way to go — but unable to get fairly off till 8 o'c as "Frank" had taken it into his head to go back on the trail toward Stewart L, having missed the other animals. Travelled on without stop till 5.30 P.m. when reached Ft Fraser. The day fine, but rather warm about noon. Find no traces of Mr. B. & party yet, though had expected them to arrive a day or two before us. Feel tired & have a headache from travelling so far in the Sun, so retire early.

Sept 29. Wrote up track survey. Took two photographs of lake,[795] & sketch of mountains with bearings from S. end of base line. About 3 P.m. Jason arrived with packet of letters & a bundle of papers from S. division. News that B, having heard of a lignite formation some way up the river had gone to see it, sending back Jeson & Benita in the Canoe, but Keeping Johnny. Proposes to meet pack train at Stony Cr. Canoe brings down a quantity of supplies from Ross*, who with Mr Hunter* is now nearly joined with McMillans* line. These supposed to offset against supplies drawn by me from H.B. Co. Evening devouring news & getting a number of stories about the Indian hero *Mus-tas*[796] from half-breed through Mr Alexanders* interpretation.

A fine cloudless & nearly calm day. Quite warm during P.m.

794. Marie Lake.

795. See "Photographs," 28 September 1876, GSC145–C1 (PA 51053) and GSC146–C1 (PA 51052). In his Field Notebook, Dawson records the photographs being taken on 28 September.

796. Us-tas the Trickster.

Mr. A. tells me nearly all the Indian storys here seem to centre about Us-tass, there are a few other legends however about localities &c. All over the country Us tass is localized & fitted to each place.

Story of two great beavers.[797] The Indians here relate that formerly, — very long ago of course — the Ne-cha-ko R was dammed up some way below thus by two enormous beavers. They point out a place where a ridge runs Across as the locality — At last the Indians Killed these gigantic animals & the water ran out, which had formerly flooded the whole country hereabouts.

Am told that there is a very great similarity between the stories of the Indians here & the Crees across the mountains — as an instance the story of Us-tas & the wild fowl is told there[798] — Mr A heard it at the Little Touchwood Hills[799] — Almost exactly as here. There however said to be a *manitou*[800] who was getting old & unable to hunt, invited all the fowls to a feast. The fowls to dance round A great Kettle with their eyes shut. This going on, the Manitou caught first one & then another & threw them into the Kettle. The bird making the discovery was a little duck like the buffle-head. On the alarm being given all the birds scrambled out as best they could, but this poor little fellow got the Kick, which is the reason that he always sits in the water with his tail straight upright!

Sept. 30. Hard at work getting supp in store weighed & stores apportioned out & Ictus Generally packed. Visited a rocky hill about a mile & a half west of the Fort. Evening had a long talk with my Indians through Mr Alexanders mediation & that of his man. They wanted this that & the other thing, higher pay to go to Ft George &c. Partly rendered discontented by rumours of the extraordinary liberality of the "line-men" & partly no doubt the result of their natural troublesome nature. The only excuse they have for asking more for the Ft. George trip is the fact that the H.B. Co give them $20 (in goods) for the trip there & back. Thus they argue that if they go there they must come back & should get at least that Sum! Finally arranged on basis that I shall pay $1.50 a day as before $1.00 for Canoe, & pay them at same rate — but nothing for canoe — & provision them for 6 extra days that they may return in. Seems pretty hard however that these lazy & dirty savages should stickle for Such high Pay, when so many white men, in other Parts of the world would be glad to do the work for so much less.

797. This is an example of common local etiological legends.

798. This is a story on the "Hoodwinked Dancers" motif. See Thompson, *Tales of the North American Indians*, 295.

799. On the Canadian prairies, at lat. 51°17′N and long. 104°15′W.

800. A spirit or deity.

[verso]

Sept 30. Indian stone axes	$0.50
Advanced "John"	$5.00
" "	$15.00

Advanced Jeson for self & canoe $30.00
Leaving just $20 due to this evening Counting.

Paid Mr Alexander*	$11.00 Cash
" " "	$42.92 by cheque
	$53.92 being Amt of his Acct for supplies.

{Oct. 1. Jeson gave back $18 in part payment for flour received (5 Sacks)

Leaving his acct thus. Cash payments	$22.00
Payment in flour	$30.00
	$52.00

Memo. with regard to flour & stores at Fort Fraser

Flour obtained from Mr Alexander*, (in all), & afterwards returned 300 lbs

Flour received from Mr Ross* by Canoe	600 lbs.
Bacon " " " " " "	197 lbs.

Bacon remaining from that brought up from Blackwater 28 lbs.

Took for trip	80 lbs bacon
Returned Mr. A.	15 lbs bacon

Leaving 130 lbs, of which all but 28 lbs "Haywoods bacon"

paid Charley $2.00 in bacon for trip to Stony Creek reducing the quantity in store to lbs. 22

Total flour in store 937 lbs.

Took for trip 237 lbs.

Returned to Mr Alexander* 300 lbs.

Leaving 400 lbs flour.

Gave "Jason" in payment for services ⟨5 300⟩ 250 lbs at rate of $12 per 100

Gave Benita 100 lbs at same rate

Gave "Johnny" 50 lbs "   "   "

leaving no spare flour in store

[end verso]

disposed of all the extra flour to the Indians at the rate of $12.00 per 100 lbs, giving it to them in part payment for wages. When they found they could not get it for less they no longer concealed their pleasure in getting it for so little, the H.B. Co selling at rate of $20.00 per ⟨Cwt.⟩ 100 lbs.

The Indians I am told have a story about the beaver & porcupine accounting for the fact that the beaver only has fat on its belly.[801] They say the Porcupine, by tales of some beautiful place, with plenty of food, induced the beaver to go with him on a long journey, which ended on the crest of a steep mountain. The beaver did not Know how to follow the Porcupine down, but at last turned over, & slid down on his back. The beaver then played the porcupine some trick in retaliation, which Mr A. Cannot remember.

This resembles the Swampy Cree, or Chippeway story by which they explain the absence of fat from all parts of the rabbit, but a little spot between the shoulders. (also from Mr A.) They say a manitou (or the manitou?) once filled a large pot with grease, & calling all the animals together told them they were to run in a race, & that the first to reach the pot & Jump in would always be fat. On the word being given, it was found that the rabbit had Secreted himself half way to the Pot, & so ran & jumped in before all the rest. It made the Manitou so angry to see such a poor little animal get the prize, that he lifted it out & holding it by the head, rubbed off with the other hand all the grease, but a little spot which escaped between the shoulders.[802]

Oct. 1. Indians not on hand very early, having to attend to devotions at the *Church-house.* When they arrived considerable excitement Caused by the absence of the Canoe, which had drifted away during the night, thanks to their devotion to talk. It was found soon however at no great distance. Horses also far away. off at last however, & get stuff horses &c. across the Ne-cha-ko & camp together on its East bank near the Junction of the Frazer L. Stream.

Write to B. & a note home in case any chance should occur of forwarding it from Stony Creek.

G. M. Dawson to Margaret Dawson*, 1 October 1876, Camp near Ft. Fraser

I have made it a practise this summer to send of a little note on chance whenever occasion offered, & though all may not reach you, Some at least probably do. This is one of these chances. I am now back here, (where my last was dated from) having completed my trip round Francois Lake, & since made a short trip over to Stewart Lake to connect with Mr Selwyns* work of last summer. I got a few rather interesting fossils there, having found a bed of the limestone full of silicified *Fusulinas*, proving the

---

801. Variations of this common story of a pair of tricksters coaxing each other onto their own favourable territory are dealt with in Boas, *Tsimshian Mythology*, 724.

802. This story resembles that given in Thompson, *Tales of the North American Indians*, 56.

Carboniferous age of the So-called Lower Cache Creek Formation — this for Father*.

I am now on the point of starting, tomorrow morning, to make the descent of the Ne-cha-ko River to Fort George, by Canoe. Mr Bowman* meanwhile going round by the trail with the Pack-train & meeting me there. My Crew consists of three Indians of the place, two of whom are very well acquainted with the river, & one of them having been on the Francois Lake trip also — A peculiar old character Called Je-sen which is so like Jason that I call him so. The Indians about here are a great bother, however, being inveterate beggars, though I believe in the main honest. If they were only Clean one might forgive them a good deal, but that they are *Not*.

I hope to be down at Quesnel about the fifteenth of this month, or rather before. The weather is now beautifully fine, warm during the day & cold at night, with the poplars in a blaze of yellow & in Some places already beginning to loose their leaves. We have seen a few flakes of snow already however, & before long may see more, warning one to be on the move southward.

With regard to the Palaeontology affair I suppose it is all Settled by this time, & I See an item in one of the Victoria papers stating that it was reported that Mr Whiteves* had been appointed, which I presume is probably correct. If so I am not in the least disappointed, as if I had been at home I Should probably never have entered the lists at all, & though there Are some things to be said in favour of the place there are many against it, especially the fact that for a long time to come I would not feel at all at home in it, or master of the Position.

I am ashamed of these little notes with next to nothing in them, but not Knowing whether I may not reach Quesnel before this does, I dont feel much inducement to write a long letter.

Oct. 2. Start with three Indians (Je-sen — Johnny, & Be-ni-ta or Peter) for Ft George. Casinta to start for Stony Cr & arrive there same night, but did not get off So soon as we did owing to straying of horses, & his natural lazyness, which Induced him to send Charley (whom I had engaged to go with him to Stony Cr) out after them, instead of Going himself. Made one portage of the stuff today & ran many little rapids & riffles. Jeson & Benita seeming however to Know the river perfectly well. Camped at 5 P.m. a fine day, but not too warm.

Oct. 3. Make a good early start & travel till 5 Pm, making a good day though meet with sever interruptions, besides the lunch stop. Soon after leaving camp, a shout announced that the H.B. Annual boat, now some days overdue at Fraser L, in sight. Poling up along the bank slowly &

laboriously. We soon shot down to them & then my Indians of course began an animated conversation with their "tillicums".[803] Pipes smoked & a stop of about 10 minutes indulged in. The boat in charge of a half-breed named Sutherland who spoke English well, as indeed his name should guarantee. A couple of miles further on Came to an abandoned house & some inhabited Indian Shanties, marking the Crossing place of the trail to Stewart Lake, a place of importance in the days of Omineca excitement. Here the Indians must have another little "wa-wa" & Johnny, who has been discontented with the dollar a day pay which he was receiving finally conceded to leave. Not much loss for though moderately Smart, inarguably lazy.

Musk rats[804] seem pretty abundant on this river, Saw several today ⟨coiled⟩ some of them coiled up asleep on dead branches projecting from the bank near the water level.

No rapids worthy of the name today, & much quiet deep water.

[verso]

Oct. 3.

Gave Je-sen $10.00 At Crossing of Ne Cha Ko & Stewart L. Tr

    Peter $5.00 "   "   "   " "   " "   "   "   "

[end verso]

Oct 4. Continue on down the Ne-Cha-ko R. Portage part of stuff at Rapid aux Isles a Pierre,[805] the Indians running in the Canoe with the rest. There is an old wagon road on the North bank of the river, made by "Guss Wright"[806] when he took his little steamer up by here to Stewart Lake.

Heavy gale from the west during Part of morning, with trees falling occasionally in the woods. Evening nearly calm, & fine.

Oct. 5. Delayed a little in the morning by heavy fog on the river, but after getting off, made good time, the stream being quite rapid. one bad rapid ⟨at⟩ "White Mud" the Indians ran. Took photo of gravel & Sand bank

---

803. Chinook Jargon for "the people, any people."

804. Muskrat, *Ondatra zibethica spatulata* (Osgood).

805. Located twelve miles in a direct course above the mouth of the Nechako River, the rapids later proved an obstacle to sternwheelers on the river.

806. Gustavus Blin Wright (1830–98) arrived in British Columbia in 1858 and was an industrious businessman involved in a multitude of construction and transportation projects in the area. The particular enterprise Dawson refers to was Wright's use of his boat the *Enterprise* to supply goods to the Omineca gold fields from a base at Quesnel. Wright's road-building activities ranged from building the Lillooet to Alexandria Wagon Road in 1861–62 to construction of the Eagle Pass Wagon Road in 1883. Later, Wright turned his energy to mining through participation in the Number 1 Mine at Ainsworth on Kootenay Lake.

from lunch point.[807] Arrived at Ft George at 3.30 P.m. passing one of the H.B. boats for Stewart L a few miles above it. Find, as had expected, that party not yet here. See Mr Ogden[808] who Kindly invites me to stay at the H.B. fort till they come. Pay off Indians, not without Some difficulty in making them understand the accounts, provision them as agreed upon & start them off on return trip.

A magnificent Indian summer day.

[verso]

Settled finally with Peter (Be-ne-ta) & Je-son. as follows.

Jeson. Total Cash payments $51.50
     Payments in flour at $12.00   <u>$30.00</u>
                                 $81.50

being total Amt due for services to date, & payment for Canoe at $1.00 per diem. Also payment for self for six days to take him back to Fraser L.

Be-ne-ta. Total cash payments $13.50
     Payments in flour   <u>$18.00</u>
                                 $31.50

being total due for services to date, & payment back to Fraser L. as above.

[end verso]

Oct. 6. No news of the Pack train. Slept late in conformity with the custom of the place. Took a photo. of the Fort & Indian Village from other side of river, then a view looking up the river from the fort.[809] Visited the Indian Church,[810] & got one of the chief men to introduce us to the Interior of it. Filled up with narrow boards for seats, a wooden alter covered with white Calico, a small cross of wood covered with red flannel, a few prints & pictures on the wall. In one corner a wooden & Calico erection for a confessional, with a grating contrived out of a board rather irregularly perforated by large Auger holes. on one side of the Alter the whip (a pretty formidable looking one) which is used to punish delinquents, is hung up. Saw also the Pictoriel pilgrims progress or road to heaven & hell[811] used by the "Poreo Oblats" in instructing the Indians.

807. See "Photographs," 5 October 1876, GSC149–C1 (PA 51049).

808. Charles Ogden, a clerk with the Hudson's Bay Company at Fort George.

809. See "Photographs," 6 October 1876, GSC150–C1 (PA 38066 and PA 51048) and GSC151–C1 (PA 51047).

810. For illustrations of churches such as the one described by Dawson, see John Veillette and Gary White, *Early Indian Village Churches: Wooden Frontier Architecture in British Columbia* (Vancouver: University of British Columbia Press, 1977).

811. The so-called "Catholic Ladder" was a simplified chart illustrating the major scriptural events and important developments in the Catholic Church. It was initially devised in the Oregon Territory by Francis Norbet Blanchet. For an illustration of a Catholic Ladder based on Blanchet's prototype see Morice, *Catholic Church*, 2: 290.

The copy belonging to this community carefully posed on a roll of Calico & in good condition. Our ciceroné vouchsafed to explain the thing to us. Pretty well drawn & hand painted in bright colours, & no doubt serving to Keep in remembrance the points of biblical history. (The publisher Ch. Letaille 15 Rue Garanciere Paris.

A very fine day.

Oct. 7. Still no news of the Packs though on the qui vive for them all day & repeatedly deceived by a cow bell tinkling through the woods. Took a ride with Mr Ogden* through some of the trails & round to where his men making hay.

Another very fine Indian Summer day.

Oct. 8. Waiting for train.

[verso]

Indian Converts. The only two missionaries at present in this part of the country reside at Stewart L, & make periodical visits to other districts generally annual or biennial. Missionaries Peres Le Jacque & Blanchet,[812] Frenchmen, the former described as a bigoted & meddlesome man, the latter as an ignorant & low-class priest. Both represented as not Setting at all a good example to the Indians in so far as cleanliness concerned. Their district embraces besides Stewart L & vicinity, Fraser L, Ft George, Babine, & Bear or Connoly Lakes. They travel to their outposts either by priviledge in the Company's boats, or with the Indians in Canoes. The Indians not receiving anything but blessings for their Kind offices, & being also depended on to furnish food. — In this connection a story of P. Le Jacque* & the Bishop (who made the rounds of the missions up here this Summer) occurs. The priest goes dead against the system of "advances" pursued by the H.B. Co with the Indians. Now while the priest & bishop were at Fraser L the Indians had nothing to feed them on but small Inferior fish caught from the river, the salmon not having arrived. One after another they came to Mr Alexander* asking advances of Flour, tea, sugar &c. which he Knew were intended for the reverent visitors, but thinking to pay them in their own coin refused, at last however giving way in some small particulars. The Bishop it seems could not well stomach such perpetual lenten fare, & got quite Iill, & lectured the Indians on the impropriety of feeding P Le J. on such food, telling them they should Keep some flour &c. by them for his visits. Subsequently Mr A. slyly

812. Father Jean-Marie Le Jacq (1837?–99) came to British Columbia in 1962 and worked for some years at St. Joseph's Mission near Williams Lake. In 1873, Le Jacq, in company with his fellow priest, Georges Blanchet, went to Fort St. James to establish a permanent mission station in the more northerly region. That mission, Our Lady of Good Hope, was the centre from which the two priests reached out into the other districts of north central British Columbia.

remarked to the Priest, that he was afraid he was rather glad that he had this time Given the Indians some advances.

The Indians though in the main amenable to the priests teachings are not Always & altogether under subjection, & I am told that the Forks of Skeena or Rocher de Bouler Indians laugh at those of Fraser & Stewarts Lakes for their extreme devotion, & while professed Catholics themselves, contrast the state of "Mr Duncans Indians"[813] with theirs. The priest they say has taught us prayers &c. & now we know them all but learn nothing else, while Mr Duncans* Indians learn to read, & have always plenty of money & plenty to eat! The whole of the Indians hereabouts are nominal Catholics, & are at present very devout from the stimulus of the Bishops recent visit. They are Kept up to the mark by a system of watchmen, chiefs, soldiers &c. appointed by the priest,[814] who has succeeded in doing away with their own old feasts & dances, which is as far as I can learn was all the religion they had. For offences they are flogged by the appointed officers & with the consent of the tribe, or perhaps disgraced by being forbidden the church. It is only about 8 years since these priests arrived, & it is extraordinary what a hold they have got on the Indians. Before their arrival Some traveling eccliastics passed through the country, & without leaving any very permanent impression taught the natives a few prayers &c. The only effect however being to inaugurate an improved form of medicine man, in some places. These hum-bugs[815] pretended to fall into trances, as of old, but now added for effect supposed interviews with the

813. William Duncan (1832–1918) was a prominent Anglican lay missionary who established the Christian Indian village of Metlakatla in 1862, near the mouth of the Skeena River. Duncan did indeed take special care to encourage a variety of industries that would further the Indians' economic circumstances. Unfortunately, Duncan's efforts were later marred by bitter strife and, in 1887, he led a band of followers to Alaska to set up a new village. See Jean Usher, *William Duncan of Metlakatla: A Victorian Missionary in British Columbia*, National Museum of Man Publications in History no. 5 (Ottawa: National Museums of Canada, 1974) and Peter Murray, *The Devil and Mr. Duncan: A History of the Two Metlakatlas* (Victoria: Sono Nis Press, 1985).

814. The system of discipline noted by Dawson was the so-called "Durieu System" instituted in Catholic Indian missions by the new bishop, Paul Durieu. For a brief description of this sometimes controversial method, see Morice, *Catholic Church*, 2: 350–52.

815. Dawson was referring to prophet cults in which "some concepts of Christianity preceded the missionaries into most areas of the Province, carried by 'prophets' who foretold the arrival of white men and the marvels they would bring. These mystics are said to have gained their knowledge through visions or by dying and returning to life after an instructive visit to heaven. They travelled among the tribes and harangued them instructing their followers, for example, to make the sign of the cross, observe the Sabbath, worship a supreme being, and publicly confess their sins" (Wilson Duff, *The Indian History of British Columbia* vol. 1, *The Impact of the White Man*, Anthropology in British Columbia Memoir no. 5 [Victoria: British Columbia Provincial Museum, 1969], 88).

priests God, & garbled storys of the creation flood &c. They had nevertheless influence with the people, & I am even told that on one occasion, one of them on awakening from a trance prophesied a great flood by which all would be drowned unless they followed his advice, which was that everyone was to go into the woods, find the largest Cottonwood[816] he Could & make a big Canoe. This being done, he continued to have pretended interviews with the almighty, but at last said that if they would give him the best & largest of All the Canoes he would speak for them — try to persuade the deity to spare them. He accordingly picked out the best Canoe, & postponed the deluge!

When the present priests came they are said to have carried the Indians over to their side in a wonderfully short time, whole Communities repenting & being baptized in a manner much resembling that told of the early spread of Christianity in Europe. Some bold individuals held out for a time, but public opinion at last forced them in also. The Babine L. Indians, a peculiarly troublesome lot, were rather obstreperous, but a remarkable (miraculous) incedent brought them over too. One of them being sick, the old medicine man insisted on performing his cure for him. Many of the tribe, being under the Influence of the priest Said not to do it, that the priest had said it was wrong &c. &c. But do it he would & so to the scandel of the Converts he went on with his ceremony, & after all sorts of mummeries he fell into a sort of trance, ⟨falling⟩ {stooping} on the Ground, & putting his head into a great pan of water, into which he was supposed to blow the evil influence. He remained so long in this position that the by-standers said he would drown, but his wife said oh no, let him alone he always does this, & would not allow him to be disturbed. At last they said he will certainly drown & notwithstanding the remonstrations of the wife, lifted him up & found him really dead. The widow however would not believe it, but said he was always thus, put the body in bed & sat by it all night, & only when decay set in was persuaded that he was really dead. This incident brought round all the recalcitrant Babine L. Indians to the priest. Told that there is little doubt that a protestant missionary coming would be able by teaching the Indians something more useful than the priests doctrines, would soon carry off all his converts. This Pere Le J. was turned out of Lillooet by Mr Good some years ago just in this way.[817] The Indians finally forcing him to give up the church

---

816. Probably the black cottonwood, *P. trichocarpa*.

817. The Reverend John Booth Good (1833–1916) was born in Lancashire and came to Victoria in 1861. He served at Nanaimo and Comox before taking on St. Paul's Mission at Lytton. He moved back to Nanaimo as rector of St. Paul's church in 1882, retiring from the position in 1910. See also F. A. Peake, "John Booth Good in British Columbia: The Trials and Tribulations of the Church, 1861-99," *Pacific Northwest*

they had built under his teaching, & which when they turned from him, he claimed to have the right to lock up & Keep from them. There is no doubt however that it would be up hill work to teach most of these Indians cleanliness or industry, though those of Ft George are much better in both respects than those of Fraser or Stewarts Lakes.

Indian Superstition. Told that the Indians are {(or were)} particularly Careful not to let the head of a beaver fall to the dogs. The bones are carefully burnt to prevent this. Neither were the women allowed to eat this part of the animal. I believe the restriction & precaution also applied to the bones of the eyes & feet. The Indians Say if infringed the hunter will have no more luck in beavers.

Also say that dangerous to speak lightly or disrespectfully of bears, & have various anecdotes to prove that people doing so have Shortly afterwards been torn to pieces by the Animals. The universal practice of hoisting the skull of a slain bear on a pole, I have never been able to get a good reason for, except that their fathers having done so, So they also do. It may be connected with the above however, or be a precaution to Put it out of the way of the hungry Indian dogs.

[end verso]

Oct. 9. Train arrived at 3.30 having left most of baggage & Mr Bowman* in charge at the Chellakoh R. crossing. No time to return tonight, So got them camped in the field near the fort. Hear that Millar[818] (packer) Crossed the river about six miles below the Fort at Bell's Crossing today, en route with some provisions & animals to help to bring Bell* out. In the evening got Old "Prince"[819] from Stewart Lake to relate the story, (or a part of the Interminable Story of *Us-tass*. Some anecdotes different from those before heard, others very nearly the same. Evidently ⟨differ⟩ slightly different versions in different parts of the Country. As sometimes told each

---

Quarterly 75 (1984): 70–78. A. G. Morice, the Catholic historian and missionary, says of this incident: "the Thompson Indians had shown themselves exceptionally slow in accepting the yoke of Christ in exchange for their heathenish rites. On the other hand, an Anglican minister had made their country his special field of labour, who did not scruple to represent the religion of the priest as unnecessarily hard and severe. . . . So it came to pass that this catering to the passions, joined to the usual liberalities, finally had the desired results, and a majority of the Thompson tribe embraced the schism of Henry VIII" (Morice, *Catholic Church*, 2: 353).

818. James Millar, in the service of the CPRS.

819. Chief Simio of the Stuart Lake Carrier was given the name "Le Prince" by French-Canadian traders in the area. He became chief in 1840 after the death of his father Chief Kwah. See J. D. Smedley, "Early Days at the Fort," *Cariboo and Northern British Columbia Digest* 4, no. 1 (Spring 1948): 10; and A. G. Morice, *The History of the Northern Interior of British Columbia—Formerly New Caledonia*, 2d. ed. (Toronto: William Briggs, 1904), 195, 280.

of the Adventures seems to mark the Creation of Some particular object. Unless Some such interpretation as this Can be fixed on the tale, most of it is utterly Meaningless. one Authority for instance says that when the Whisky Jack[820] told him he was eating himself (often he had Cooked a Certain portion of his body on hot stones, for misconduct) that he threw the piece away, & that sticking up in a tree it formed the birch fungus or Punk.

[The following are loose pages in the journal, labelled (in a different hand) "Tales Fr. S."]

[*Bourgois*?] invites all animals to a dance. All animals covered themselves with pitch, some {on} tails &c. Muskrats near door danced. At last one caught piece of fire & ran off (disappeared) before the B. could catch him. Then all the animals rushed out of the great Camp. The B. ascended a great hill & looked out, but it was too late. All the animals had fire.

The same B. had light, or commanded it. Only the red fox Could speak to him, & he Sat teasing him Calling light, light light. The daylight would sometimes almost come, but the B. would not let it & tried to Kill the fox, but he was too Smart for him. At last tired of teasing, Said let it be light, & it was. Water also Kept by the B. His daughter only would Get a drink now & then when the father allowed. The "Monde" only drank when the could get a little from dew shaken from plants into bark dishes. They all said we must have water & tried to Get it. The house locked, & only opened now & then to let the daughter out & in. Then *Ustass* Came on the scene (Prince does not Know from where supposed to Come) Asked the people why discontented looking. Said we have fire & light but want water & cannot get it. Said Ustass I will try, & then the people all glad. Said will try tomorrow. Bright & early looked for him but he was gone. The daughter Said she was thirsty. Got water. In the Cup a pine leaf thrown away, always another. At last drunk. Found with child. The B. then loved her ten times more. The B. attended to the daughter, the child born, a boy. In about a month the child began to Creep about. Before a year old walking all over. Always ran to the water, try & lift it, but not strong enough The B. said not to touch it & sent him to his mother, but then he cried & at last always ran back to the Keg. Tried to go out of the house, when he was Able to list the Keg, but the door always Shut. Used to cry & cry So that at last B gave some water to drink. Then wanted always more & more. At last induced to open door. Then always trying to take the keg out. The B. preventing. Said play inside as much as you like but dont take it out. At

820. Gray jay, *Perisoreus canadensis pacificus* Gmelin.

last the old B. tired. Ustass slipped the keg out, Suddenly grew up to be a man, & ran off full speed. Broke the Keg & sprinkling out water here & there said let there be a river a lake & so on. Stewart Francois Tatla & Babine lakes where he tripped & made extra sized lakes. The sea where the whole remnant was thrown out.

The B. higher than *Ustass* both eternal. ⟨& the B.⟩

People could not see *Us-tass* though present.

Now had water, fire, light but wanting something to eat, got hooks & fished. go far at last in a lake some fish took all the baits (bears fat) & broke the lines. At last made a great hook & line, & great bait. Threw in & at once caught, what really *Us-tass*. All pulled & when nearly out of water, Spoke, Said my jaw Come out, & it Came. The Indians pulled it out they said we have killed a man, & following the usual Custom when a man Killed, put the jaw in the Centre & began to dance round it. Then *Us-tass* Came out & ⟨said he⟩ wanted his jaw again, made a false jaw out of pine bark. Came round & heard dancing & singing. Saw 2 old blind women in a Camp. Asked what the matter. Told about the jaw. Continued talking to them. Said when you young said what hurt you most. They said the thistles. *Us-tass* went out & made water, & at once thistles grew up, which he plucked & returning into the lodge struck one of the old women, who at once died. Skinned the old woman & put her skin on. The remaining old woman, not Knowing ⟨that⟩ what had taken place wished to go nearer to ⟨see the dan⟩ hear the songs & Sent for her daughters to pack them there. They came, two pretty girls, & carried them over— Set *Ustass* in his disguise down near the jaw, & while they danced he took the jaw up & examined it, & said how is it put in. ⟨put⟩ turned it one way & another. Watched, & when nobody looking. stuck it in, suddenly became a man & bolted. They said oh this is *Ustass* ⟨ask⟩ {Catch} him Catch him. but just as taking hold of him turned into an old stump. They brought stone axes & tried to Cut it down, but all broken. Then got lots of wood & tried to burn him. All the wood & Gum burned but not the stump. Gave it up — Said Us-tass we cannot Kill him. As soon As gone resumed his shape & ran off.

Always in the woods. At last came to a Cariboo road or track. Said must try to kill Cariboo. How Kill. Said at last take strongest thing he had (penis) & make Snare. Made snare & Sat there. Soon a Cariboo Came along & caught. Then made a bolt & Carried him away. [pulled?] against trees. At last said wont do. Spoke to p. Said untie yourself. At once done, but the Cariboo got away.

Came to R. Salmon Coming up. Did not Know how to catch. Tried to make spear out of bone. Went out to void. Turned round to extrement, threw bone which he had been trying to make to it & said here, make me a spear. Came back & found two fine spears. Took them & said I was only fooling when I Said this. Then the spear at once broke up & the excrement sprang up & returned into him. Then all old excrements came calling like squirrels & seeking him. He tried to dodge but all entered in, & he heard them Calling inside. Then sorry that spears lost for river full of salmon. Could always hear the sound inside but did not Know how to get the spears made. At last took a sharp stick & thrust up his anus, but only saw blood on pulling it out. Smelt a little however, so threw them on the ground & Said make me spears if you please, & went away. returning found them made, but not so well as at first. Then began salmon spearing & caught very many, curing them. Got enough as he thought for the winter. Said go & make medicine, for he was a medicine man. got lots of stumps & set round in his lodge, Set them All singing while he danced in the middle & now & again passed the Grease round. A Salmon bone above Caught in his hair. Getting angry threw it out. Then all the [belis/beles?] went out, & nearly pulled him into the water when he tried to stop them.

Then the snow Came, snowed & snowed, while he was thinking of loss of Salmon. Covered his whole house. ⟨Said⟩ did not Know what to do. Said must try to get out. Took paddle & dug & dug. At last ⟨said⟩ Saw daylight, jumped out. Saw leaves flowers &c. & all Summer. His house looked like a little mountain, the snow only lying on it. (This the hill at the mouth of the Chillacoh) Went about in the woods, heard women singing. looks carefully about, Saw 2 fine girls singing. Saw them clothed in dentalium shells. He naked. Said how get near them. took leaves & made cloathes of. Said why wear clothes like these in hot weather. I have left mine off & wear this. Then they took off their clothes. Us-tass Snatched ran off, & put them on. Travelled on, saw a girl across a river. Did not Know how to reach her. Got p. threw it across the river. The girl did not see. All at once felt sick. They said *Us-tass* — followed it up, found a stump Tried all the Indian doctors to Get it out but could not. Father of girl had to build a house over her, where she remained fixed, & sick. By & by a musk rat sitting near the door said I can do what is needed. I can get it out. Indians told the father who said if he does I will give him lots of goods & Went & got broad leaved grass, & when applied, Could Cut the p— which nothing else Could do. Said now sing. Then all sang. The rat said my little daughter must Sing too, & she sang. Then went up & applied the blade of grass which instantly cut the p. The part cut off went into the girl, the rest returned to Us-tass. Still the girl remained sick The father however now returned to his old house. *Us-tass* now in a bad fix. Kept sneaking about. Came up to old woman. Said what are they making so much singing & dancing about. She said the Chief's daughter very sick & dying. Can no one cure her. All are trying but none of medicine men able.

⟨Told⟩ The woman told the Chief who Sent for *Us-tass* {disguised & painted}. Turned out All to make his ceremonies. Got lots of the siffleur robes piled on her. Again went for the Girl & recovered the lost part of his p. The Whisky Jack sitting above Called out Ustass is all right again. Then Ustass rushed out. The girl well. Followed again turned to stump. Then all Said this is Us-tass.

The Swan story with some Variations. The lynx smells Us-tass below the stone. Ustass sees daylight, when licked away. Then took one of his hairs & pushed it out of the hole, then Another, then throw out eyes, then the crow picked up. Meanwhile Us-tass Cut off his hands legs &c. threw All out. At last got out, put all together but could not find eyes. (Then went in search as before related, but this time two women had the eyes).

[The bound-journal entries resume]

Oct. 10. Up early & off with Mr Ogden* (who is going to Fraser & Stewart Lakes) Leave the Fort at 8.45 & riding pretty fast reach the Mouth of the Chillakoh at 1.15 The trail not very good, being a great part of the way through heavy old woods with bad windfall. The heavy growth, met with after ascending a steep slope, from the flatter ground near the river & the Fort, Consists of Douglas fir often over 2 feet, tall & straight, black spruce, Cottonwood, balsom (a. grandis) {some birch} &c. Thickets of Alders, elders, red dog wood, Maple! rubus Nootkatunis & devils-Club[821] in abundance. For the latter half of the way the country is partly burnt & open, Partly Clad with small P contorta & poplar, but all appears Good soil.

on reaching camp looked over & arranged specimens & goods ready for Start in morning.

Seasons at Ft George &c. Mr Ogden* tells me that winter may be said to set in about the first of November, though steady cold weather may not continue from that time. In December or January often a few days thaw. In March Thawing every day & freezing at Night. In April Snow all gone save small Patches in hollows. About April 20 Can begin working the ground. Here as elsewhere (Fraser & Stewart Lakes) *Summer frosts* Are said to have begun in late years only (Mr O. Says perhaps about 7 years) They usually happen in June & may occur for only one night or two, or three. In many cases At Stewart & Fraser cut down & retard potatoes. Here apparently not so Severe, though also touching potatoes. —

---

821. The "red dog wood" was the red-osier dogwood, *C. stolonifera*; "rubus Nootkatunis" the thimbleberry, *Rubus parviflorus* Nutt.; and "devils-Club" devil's-club, *O. horridum*.

(Potatoes now in field Killed down all but lowest leaves which still green. Roots well matured, (See specimens grown without any special care in ground worked for 6 or 7 years without manure!) The snow last winter excessive & said to be about 4 feet on the level. Appearance of vegetation would seem to indicate greater rainfall about here than at Fraser or Stewart Lakes.

Oct. 11. Did not get off till 9.30 A.m. having packs to arrange &c. Took Bell's* Trail down the Chillako R. Found some sticks to Cut from windfall since last season. Lost about an hour At one place looking for trail, which finally found to cross the river. The ford appears to have been Scoured out deeper since last year as it took the animals half way up the Aparejoes wetting some of the Cargo a little. Immediately after crossing struck McMillan's* trail of this year. He appears to have followed Bell's* Trail north this far, & then to have followed up the W. bank of the river. Got along better after Striking this new trail, as more easily followed. The trail rough however, being miry, & with steep slippery little hills. Obliged to travel till 6 P.m. & quite dark before finding grass & getting down to the river side. Camped without pitching tents.

The valley of the river after leaving the vicinity of its mouth, is wide & flat bottomed (probably from a mile to ½m wide) & bordered by abrupt hills at the sides, with occasional bare bluffs of white arenaceous-clay Some parts of the bottom land heavily timbered with Douglas fir, Engelmans spruce & Abies grandis; the two former often reaching a diameter of 3 feet. Tall & straight. A good many extensive patches of open grassy land, elevated from 5 to 10 feet above the river, & covered with heavy growth of hay-grass, mixed with *heracleum* & other rank weeds. Grass often 4 to 5 feet high. These flats seem to be more or less subject to flood, but the soil must be very fertile. At occasional intervals fine groves of Cottonwood are found. The trees often of great size & height One measured 4 feet from ground found to be 5′ in diameter, & apparently sound. — The river pursuing an extremely tortuous Course in the flat valley bottom, with many ⟨old⟩ slews & portions of old river valleys to the right & left.

Washed two pans of gravel at the mouth of the Chellako this morning, & got colours in both. In the second, the dirt for which was carefully Selected — found 8 or 10 small colours.

Oct. 12. Very heavy frost last night, thermometer falling to 22.5° F. Ice along the margin of the river. Off at 9.15 & travelled to 4.30 though with many misschances. The mules appear to be overloaded, & one of them has about a mile before reaching camping Place, finally given out. The trail like that found Yesterday, very trying to animals. Valley preserves similar characteristics, though now Somewhat narrower (averaging perhaps ½ mile) Trail goes along edge of plateau above in many places. The plateau apparently fertile soil, with a good growth of timber, but generally burnt on the W. bank. Flat, & based on disintegrated Surface, of the "*white clays*"[822] which form bluff in many places, overlooking the river valley.

The river valley looked at from above is very beautiful, stretching away with point after point formed by projecting edges of the plateau The river meandering among the mixed evergreen woods & poplar, with patches of prairie. The poplars here now lost nearly all their leaves in most localities. The grass russet brown except in some swamps which are yet green. Today & yesterday a peculiar blue Indian-Summer-like haze over the landscape, & no fog in the mornings.

Camp on the edge of the plateau overlooking the valley at a Small Swamp, with plenty of pea-vine in neighbouring burnt woods. Afraid to go further in case we should get into the night, as formerly. Spread blankets without pitching tents.

Oct. 13. Continue on up the Chillako River. Valley changes its character Somewhat. See other note book.[823]

Fine clear day & cold night. The frost remaining on little pools & Surface of ground all day in the Shade.

Oct. 14. Follow on up valley, & turn off to West by McMillan's* trail. Camp on the north bank of the West Branch of the Chillako or Mud River.[824] Clouds apparently coming up from the South & west gathering all day; now beginning to rain with temperature much higher.

Oct. 15. Immediately on Starting find ourselves upon the Telegraph Trail, our Camp having been only about ⅓ m. from it. Cross the river, & continue on arriving at Blackwater Depot (now abandoned) at 4 P.m. Find all Shut up. Nicholson[825] having left with Hunter's* party on the 8.th. Bell's* party not yet gone south. our old Indian friend of the *Eu-chin-a-Ko* making use of the house, en *route* with his little boy from Quesnel homeward to Tas-un-tlat with two pack horses.

Oct 16. Stayed all day at Blackwater Depot to rest & recruit animals. Making a sunday. Took three photo's of the terraces here so finely

---

822. "The silts or 'white silts' as they were [also] called by G.M. Dawson are the most conspicuous of the glacial-lake deposits, although they are not as widespread as a casual examination would indicate. They are mainly cream white to buff and in a few places grey and brown. These silts which are composed mainly of feldspathic rock flour, are finely stratified in parallel laminations a fraction of an inch to several inches, less commonly a foot or more in thickness. They grade laterally and vertically into sand and clay" (Armstrong and Tipper, "Glaciation in North Central B.C.," 301).

823. See G. M. Dawson, Field Notebooks, RG 45, vol. 134, no. 2795, 81, PAC.

824. Chilako River.

825. A. N. Nicholson of the CPRS.

developed.[826] Rearranged boxes &c. & prepared for Quesnel. Left one bag flour which we have too much, & which the mules now scarcely able to carry. Packer called Hutchins[827] with a large train passed bound for Quesnel this evening. Took a load up for HB Co, intended for McLeod Lake, but cold weather coming on he left it at Stewart Lake, fearing to risk his animals further.

Find in the Depot the box of broken photo plates removed from package by Cambie*. opened it & find several still good though all more or less damaged.

Oct. 17. Started about 8.30 & travelled to 3.30. Rexamined rocks near Blackwater Bridge. Got sketch of country to north & bearings on mountains from brow of valley.

Rain in the night a fine morning & rather blustry afternoon & evening.

Oct 18. Off by 8.45 & travelled till 3.30 reaching the Beaver Meadow about 8 m. from Quesnel. Snow on Some distant summits across Fraser South eastward.

Some rain & much wind in the night Day blustry & chilly. Evening moderate.

[verso]

Elko, Carlin, & Pancake Mt[828] Nevada. Coaly Shales sometimes used for Fuel in rocks probably Dev. or Carb. (compare with Coaly Shales of Blackwater) *AB*.

See also description of similar fuel in Arizona in Pacif. Ry. Rep.[829]

For heights of terraces see Bar obs. on way out. The highest seem chiefly terraced "boulder clay" of the usual character & with many glaciated stones — thus differing from the lower typical terraces.

[end verso]

Oct. 19. Part of horses & mules strayed during night, & prevented our getting off till 9 A.m. Started at that hour ⟨after the⟩ before the train & arrived opposite Quesnel at about 11 A.m. Got crossed over after Some difficulty in finding the ferry-man, & secured mail. Train arrived during afternoon & Crossed over below junction of Quesnel River to field with good feed for horses. Had fortunately told the ferryman to bring stuff up here. The animals landed on a bar struck direct for shore across a deep slough, having to swim some distance & completely wetting Provisions, aparejoes & blankets. Put up at the occidental Hotel. Brown & Gillis.

826. See "Photographs," 16 October 1876, GSC152–C1 (PA 51046); GSC153–C1 (PA 51045); and GSC154–C1 (PA 801278).

827. Probably Frank Hutchins (d. 1891), a teamster.

828. Pancake Summit between Eureka and Ely, Nevada.

829. The reference is untraceable.

Oct. 20. Getting stuff overhauled sorted & packed. Specimens repacked &c. Visit the red bluff below Quesnel River, but find the blocks of stone with fossil fruits have apparently been washed away. Telegrap line out of order since arrival till this evening, at 7.30 Pm Telegraphed to Father*, & to Mr Robson* Victoria asking latter to send mail matter to Clinton. Hear report that parties stopped on the way down to Survey a line on the Fraser R.

Seasons at Quesnel. Grain is put in from April 20 to the first of May. Potatoes somewhat later. Grain harvested about middle of August. Barley oats & wheat grown & succeed well. Barley & oats most profitable as can be sold for feed at Cariboo. ⟨Wheat⟩ No flouring mill nearer than Soda Creek to convert wheat to Salable form. *Night frosts* occur here occasionally in June & July. Usually not enough to do serious damage to potatoes though sometimes checking them a little. One year potatoes so frozen down as to prove a failure. (From what I can learn seems that climate here much about same as at Ft George, but if anything a trifle better than at Fraser & Stewart Lakes)

G. M. Dawson to John William Dawson*, 21 October, Quesnel

On my arrival here day before yesterday I found letters with home news to Sept. 6, the later dates having probably been detained in Victoria to await my arrival there. The line was not working till yesterday evening when I telegraphed letting you Know of my safe return to Civilization & also in answer to your telegram of Oct. 6 asking if I will Compete for a Chemistry Professorship at Ottawa.

I am truly sorry you have been at so much trouble about the Palaeontological affair, & the Sooner it blows over the better. Had I been appointed it would only have meant desperately hard work of a kind I dont' know whether I could stand, though of course I should have done my best. The thing having been decided there remains nothing but to forget it, & whatever I may do eventually if Chance offers to better myself by leaving the survey, it is evident that both my own Credit & duty require that I should finish the indoor work connected with my two last Seasons field work.

The weather is still quite fine & mild here, & I am about to utilize it by making a trip of a few days to the Cariboo region where they are just at present trying to open Some quartz veins &c.

I have made arrangements for the rest of my letters to be sent up from Victoria to meet me on the Waggon Road, & hope to be down at Victoria myself in about two weeks unless extremely fine weather should tempt me to make a Circuit through Kamloops Country with the idea of finding out enough about it to include it in a preliminary map.

This autumn has been remarkably fine & the latter portion of our journey very pleasant. I Came down the Nechaco or Stewart River from Fraser L. to Ft George in a canoe with two Indians, & then had to wait Several days at Ft George for the Pack train, & as there was nothing to do there this was rather tedious, however I was hospitably entertained by Mr Ogden* of the H.B. Co & regaled on dried beaver meat & other Articles of the Country.

I have not heard from Mr Selwyn* about returning to Montreal this winter, but have always understood that that was the arrangement. I shall Certainly do so if I possibly Can as I made up my mind last winter I would not spend another in Victoria If I could avoid it.

I have been hard at work all day getting things put in order here & as it is now getting late I must ask to be excused — till next time which will not be long now I have got back to regular Postal Communication.

[For the period 21 October 1876 until his departure from Victoria, Dawson does not keep a personal journal. While entries for these days are made in his Field Notebook (RG 45, vol. 134, no. 3044) the material is overwhelmingly technical in nature. His few non-geological comments are extremely brief, not descriptive, and thus are not included in the present edition. During this period, Dawson made a short visit to the Cariboo with Bowman. He examined the mines and collected specimens at Lightning Creek, Barkerville, Richfield, and Williams Creek, returning to Quesnel on 28 October. At Cache Creek he received a letter from John Glassey, the CPRS purveyor at Kamloops, offering him horses for a trip through the Nicola country. Leaving Bowman to travel alone to Victoria, Dawson took the stage to Kamloops, where he picked up supplies, mounts, and a packer named John Frank for a hurried excursion down the valley to the Coldwater River. While there he looked at coal deposits which he would examine more closely in 1877. Arriving at Lytton on 7 November, he took stage and steamer for Victoria.]

G. M. Dawson to John William Dawson*, 11 November 1876, on steamer Enterprise, *near Victoria*

I am now within a few hours of Victoria, on my way down, & learning that the regular mail steamer sails for San Francisco today, take the opportunity of writing a short note in case I do not get time after landing to write at greater length.

I have not had any news now for Some time, & may find letters from Selwyn* in Victoria when I get there. If I do not, in the absence of other instructions, & following what I understood to be the plan when I came out here first, & the general method of procedure I shall make my preparations & leave for Montreal as soon as possible. It will of course be impossible to get off by todays Steamer, & as it would be a waste of time to wait two weeks for the next, I may probably arrange to go overland to Sacremento by rail & stage. This trip If I make it will also be an interesting one, giving me a chance to see another region of the West Coast.

Since writing from Quesnel Mouth I have been for a few days at Cariboo looking at some quartz veins they have begun to work on &c. When on the way down again on the stage, I heard from Mr Glassey* of the C.P.R.S. that I Could have horses & a man to go through the Kamloops & Nicola Valleys, & so took the opportunity to go & learn something about the Nicola Coals,[830] which may be an important consideration in event of the railway coming down the Frazer, which from the results of surveys just completed seems not impossible. The Coals seem to belong to the lignite formation, but have been altered by pressure, & perhaps heat from a vast mass of volcanic rocks which overlie them.

So far the Autumn here has been very pleasant & open, though about five inches of Snow fell while I was at Cariboo, & there was a slight covering {(about ½ inch)} on the ground in the Kamloops Nicola Country, & hard frost every night. About New Westminster they have hardly had any frost yet, & the leaves, though yellow, are still hanging on the poplars & willows.

There is so much motion on this steamer owing to a little Chopping sea & rough working engines that I Cannot make anything but a scrawl of this letter.

[After arriving in Victoria on 11 November 1876, Dawson took a room at the Driad. He prepared his luggage for departure, closed accounts, and visited acquaintances before leaving on 20 November aboard the steamer *Dakota* for San Francisco, where he caught the train eastward. He arrived in Montreal on 4 December 1876.]

830. The coal localities visited by Dawson were on the Coldwater River near its junction with the Nicola River. For a more detailed discussion of the Nicola deposits, see R. W. Ells, "Nicola Coal-Basin, B.C.," in Geological Survey of Canada, *Summary Report of the Geological Survey Department of Canada for the Calendar Year 1904* (1905), 42-65. The coal beds have only been worked sporadically in the years since Dawson saw them.